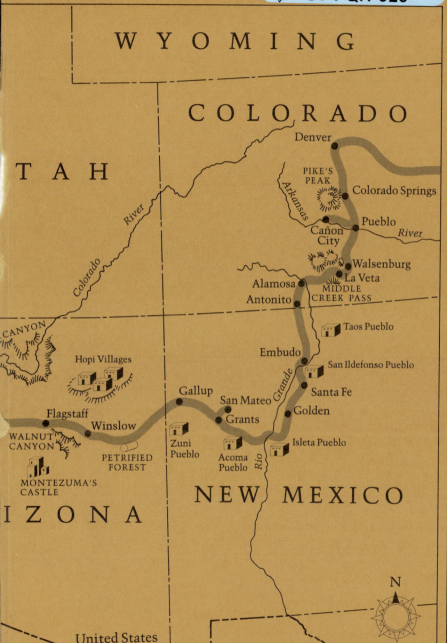

LETTERS
from the
SOUTHWEST

SEPT. 1884

Woodwar
Chillic

as. F. Pummis

CHARLES LUMMIS

LETTERS
from the
SOUTHWEST

SEPTEMBER 20, 1884, TO
MARCH 14, 1885

EDITED BY JAMES W. BYRKIT

THE UNIVERSITY OF ARIZONA PRESS
TUCSON

THE UNIVERSITY OF ARIZONA PRESS
Copyright 1989
The Arizona Board of Regents
All Rights Reserved

This book was set in 10/13 Linotron 202 Trump.
∞ This book is printed on acid-free, archival-quality paper.
Manufactured in the United States of America.

93 92 91 90 89   5 4 3 2 1

Library of Congress Cataloging-in-Publication Data

Lummis, Charles Fletcher, 1859-1928.
Letters from the Southwest, September 20, 1884 to March 14, 1885.

Bibliography: p.
1. Southwest, New—Description and travel.
2. United States—Description and travel—1865-1900.
3. Lummis, Charles Fletcher, 1859-1928—Journeys—Southwest, New.
4. Lummis, Charles Fletcher, 1859-1928—Correspondence.
I. Byrkit, James W.   II. Title.
F786.L934   1989   979'.02   88-27793
ISBN 0-8165-1093-3 (alk. paper)

British Library Cataloguing in Publication data are available.

Frontis: Charles Lummis, Chillicothe, Ohio, September, 1884.
Courtesy of Southwest Museum: negative no. 24,581.

CONTENTS

ILLUSTRATIONS

ACKNOWLEDGMENTS

I WOULD LIKE to express my thanks to Patrick Houlihan and Daniela Moneta of the Southwest Museum for their cooperation in helping me to obtain access to most of the letters Lummis wrote to *The Chillicothe Leader* during his walk from Cincinnati to Los Angeles. Jean Boulger and John Grabb of the Ross County (Ohio) Historical Society in Chillicothe and Nancy C. Erdey of Case Western Reserve University in Cleveland found those issues of the *Leader* which completed the set. They also provided other items of interest about Lummis. Flagstaff Public Library's John Irwin went well beyond all expectations, as usual, to help in the research of this book, while Evelyn Wong and Richard Foust of Northern Arizona University's Bilby Research Center were equally helpful in transcribing the letters.

INTRODUCTION

I N THE FALL of 1884, a bright, high-spirited, twenty-five-year-old man, Charles Lummis, began an odyssey that would, in time, be remembered as a pilgrimage. Starting from Cincinnati, Ohio, on September 12, 1884, Lummis "tramped," as he put it, for 143 days on a meandering and indirect route to Los Angeles, California, arriving there on February 1, 1885, to take a job as a city editor of the *Los Angeles Times* newspaper. While he was curious about, even fascinated by, the early part of the trip—to Denver, Colorado, where he arrived on October 23—it was not until he reached southern Colorado and northern New Mexico that he was "captured by the natives" and went through what amounted to a spiritual and aesthetic conversion to become a passionate, lifelong southwesterner.

Col. Harrison Gray Otis, publisher of the *Times*, paid Lummis to send ahead periodically by mail detailed reports of his trek, which were published in installments by the newspaper. These articles were so lively and informative that when he arrived in Los Angeles Lummis was welcomed as a celebrity.

During the next forty years, white, Anglo-Saxon, Protestant, and New England born-and-bred Charles Lummis became the most active exponent of Southwest culture who has ever lived.

Subsidized by the Santa Fe railroad, the *Times,* and other southern California commercial and industrial interests, Lummis
became a promoter, a patron, a publisher, a patriarch, and a
prophet. He encouraged and supported Southwest artist May-
nard Dixon, writer Mary Austin, and ethnologist Adolph Bandelier. He praised and buoyed poet Sharlot Hall, artist Thomas
Moran, and photographer William Henry Jackson. He led efforts
to reform United States Indian policy, to rebuild the California
missions, and to collect historical and anthropological documents and artifacts. He took and processed thousands of photographs of the people and landscapes of the Southwest, and he
campaigned to preserve the natural wonders of the region. In
general, he has been the most active force ever to identify,
describe, and record all of the many aspects of Southwest life.
Lummis died on November 28, 1928, widely recognized by his
contemporaries as an unparalleled leader in Southwest cultural
affairs.

The twenty-four letters published in this book constitute a
second set of letters Lummis wrote as he walked across the
country. They were written to and published by a Chillicothe,
Ohio, newspaper, the *Leader.* These letters contain the same
basic narratives found in the letters to the *Los Angeles Times,*
upon which Lummis' own book about the walk, *A Tramp
Across the Continent,* is based. But the Ohio letters manifest,
incomparably more than do the Los Angeles versions, Lummis'
brilliance, wit, candor, and ingenuousness, as well as his complex personality and character. In the reports to Chillicothe,
Lummis acknowledged that he did oftentimes wait a week or
more to craft his Los Angeles letters, taking much of his material from the Chillicothe versions and elaborating on some of
the more sensational episodes, as well as deleting less formal
and more gut-level passages. Upon comparing the two drafts, it
is easy to discern that Lummis spent considerable effort and
time striking out freely spoken and spontaneous details found
in the Ohio letters in favor of a more commercial, self-promot-

ing, and politic reporting for the California paper. Compared with the Chillicothe letters, the *Times* stories exaggerate Lummis' adventures as well as his level of conventional "maturity." (Intellectually, for his day, Lummis was *very* mature.)

In his book, *A Tramp Across the Continent*, originally published by Charles Scribner's Sons in 1892, Lummis wrote a still more refined account of his famous walk. Since the book drew much of its basic material from Lummis' letters to the *Los Angeles Times*, it stands as a third-generation adaptation which is even more highly selective and hyperbolic than were the *Times'* versions. As a result, the book was far more polished, more discreet, more simplistic, and even more self-promoting than were the letters to Los Angeles.

The book also appears to be much less honest than the Chillicothe letters. Two examples well illustrate this lack of fidelity to the traveler's first reports printed in the Ohio newspaper. In *A Tramp Across the Continent*, Lummis spends four pages (166–69) telling in considerable detail about a side trip he made during the week following Christmas of 1884. In the book he claims that he hiked fifteen miles southward from Cubero, New Mexico, to the Indian pueblo Acoma, which was, in his words, "the most wonderful aboriginal city on earth." The routes to the "Sky City," it is true, do go south from this part of Lummis' itinerary, but the details of his letter written to Ohio from San Mateo, New Mexico, on January 1, 1885, make no mention of Acoma. He states that in rough weather he walked from El Rito section house—near today's Mesita, New Mexico—to Cubero on Friday, December 26, a distance of about fifteen miles. Then, he told the *Leader*, on December 27 he walked from Cubero to Grants, a distance of approximately twenty-eight miles. These two days offered the only time in which he could have made the side trip to Acoma, and his walk from El Rito to Grants would not have allowed him the time necessary to make the additional thirty-mile side trip to Acoma and back. In his letter from San Mateo he gives no indication that he had ever even heard of Acoma. But in his book he writes that he spent a couple of days in San Mateo "packing my Acoma relics . . . and other curios."

A similar contradiction surrounds his experiences in northern Arizona. His 1892 book states that "Eight miles east of Flagstaff . . . I found my first ruins of the so-called cliff-dwellers," an obvious reference to the Sinagua Indian ruins at Walnut Canyon, Arizona. "I dug," he wrote on page 240, "from under the dust of centuries, dried and shrunken corn-cobs, bits of pottery, an ancient basket of woven yucca fibre . . . and a few arrow-heads and other stone implements. . . . [I]t well repays as long a visit as one can give it." But in the letter written from Peach Springs, Arizona, on January 20, 1885, he states, concerning his trip from Winslow to Flagstaff:

There are some relics of the strange cliff-dwellers near Cosnino, lying back in the mountains. I wanted the worst way to see them, but the snow was 2 feet thick through the pathless woods, and that settled it. I can't afford to catch cold just now. So I reluctantly turned my back on these interesting and unique homes of a forgotten race, and plodded on through the snow to funny [?] Flagstaff.

Lummis makes no other mention of Indian ruins near Flagstaff in either the Ohio letters or in his book.

In the years after he arrived in Los Angeles, people no doubt queried Lummis as to whether he had visited Acoma and Walnut Canyon on his tramp, and this gap in his experience embarrassed him. He probably felt that his authoritative credentials as a knowledgeable southwesterner demanded a claim that he had gone to such places. So he simply began to say that he had indeed visited them. And thus his lies appear in his book that way.

Years later, in 1926, Lummis inscribed in the visitor's register at El Morro (Inscription Rock), New Mexico, that he had visited this great Southwest crossroads in 1885, but a detailed study of Lummis' activities in 1885, whether on his tramp or at a later time, reveals no visit to El Morro or, other than his "tramp," no visit to New Mexico of any kind that year.

One story, which appeared in *A Tramp Across the Continent*, has provoked a well-known controversy among people who are familiar with the book, and for some it has thrown a heavy blanket of doubt over Lummis' credibility. During his hike through southern Colorado Lummis adopted a greyhound dog which he named "Shadow." The two became deeply attached to each other, and in the Ohio letters Lummis refers to their comradeship frequently as they traveled through southern Colorado, northern New Mexico, and northern Arizona. On January 23, near Yucca, Arizona, Shadow showed irregular behavior, which Lummis described in some detail in his book:

And on a sudden, as I strode carelessly along, there came a snarl so unearthly, so savage, so unlike any other sound I ever heard, that it froze my blood; and there within six inches of my throat was a wide, frothy mouth with sunlit fangs more fearful than a rattlesnake's! *Shadow was mad!* If I had never 'wasted' time in learning to box and wrestle there would have been an end of me. But the trained muscles awaited no conscious telegram from the brain, but acted on their own motion as swiftly and as rightly as the eye protects itself against a sudden blow. Ducking back my head, I threw the whole force and weight of legs, arms, and body into a tremendous kick and a simultaneous wild thrust upon the leading-strap. My foot caught Shadow glancingly on the chest and he went rolling down the thirty foot embankment. But he was upon his feet again in an instant and sprang wolfishly toward me. I snatched at the heavy six-shooter, but it had worked around to the middle of my back, and was hampered by the heavy-pocketed, long duck coat. Before it was even loosened in its scabbard, the dog was within six feet. I sprang to the edge of the bank and threw all my force into a kick for life. It caught him squarely under the chin, and rolled him again violently to the bottom. Up and back he came, like the rebound of a rubber ball, and just as he was within four feet I wrested the colt loose, 'threw it down' with the swift instinctive aim of long practice, and pulled the trigger even as the muzzle fell. The wild tongue of flame burnt his very face, and he dropped. But in an instant he was up again and fled shrieking across the barren plain. The heavy ball had creased his skull and buried itself in his flank. I knew the horrors of a gunshot wound; my poor chum should never go to die by inches the hideous death of the desert. A great wave of love swept

through me and drowned my horror. I had tried to kill him to save
myself, now I must kill him to save him from the most inconceivable
of agonies. My trembling nerves froze to steel; I must not miss! I would
not! I dropped on one knee, caught his course, calculated his speed, and
the spiteful crack of the six-shooter smote again upon the torpid air. He
was a full hundred and fifty yards away, flying like the wind, when the
merciful lead outstripped and caught him and threw him in a wild
somersault of his own momentum. He never kicked or moved, but lay
there in a limp, black tangle, motionless forever.

The self-glorifying purple prose speaks for itself, and anyone
with even a modicum of knowledge of the capabilities of mid-
nineteenth century small-arms weaponry would find such a
claim of pistol accuracy at one hundred and fifty yards to be
ridiculous. Lummis told a much less histrionic story in his
letter from the Mohave Desert, written on January 28, 1885:

But suddenly, as we were hurrying along, side by side, he [Shadow] gave
a savage snarl and sprang up at my face. More by instinct than anything
else, I gave him a fling, with the strap and my foot, down the embankment; but he was upon his feet again in a second, and dashed at me
with a growl that froze my blood. I saw his white teeth shining, while
from his jaws dripped a thick froth, and as I looked I felt a dumb terror
run through my whole body. *The dog was mad,* and there was I, . . . half
helpless, my revolver carelessly swung far behind my back for convenience in walking, and those fangs, infinitely more terrible than a rattlesnake's, within six feet of me.

I have been in some tight places, and seen some tough experiences
and close calls, but I would go through them again all in a lump, rather
than feel as I did for a second or two there. My first reach, of course, was
for the revolver, but it was slow work—too slow. I jumped to the edge of
the embankment, caught the dog under the chin with my toe as he
came up, and sent him rolling down again. Again he rallied and started
for me, but this had given me time, and as he came up the bank within
four feet of my hand, I threw down the heavy Colt and let her go. I
flatter myself I am getting tolerably clever with that gun, but my hand
wasn't very steady then. I was excited, and it had come to me that I was
driving a bullet into a dear and faithful friend. Poor dog! He rolled over,
and then started like a bird for the brush. That steadied my nerve in a
minute. My poor chum shouldn't go off to die by inches in the wilder-

ness—and I caught him on the wing. And then I sat down and dropped a little salt beside the track, for I had lost such a friend as one don't find every day.

His propensity for hyperbole—prevarication, even—and for melodramatic self-heroics undoubtedly helps to explain why Lummis has never enjoyed an enduring reputation as a serious writer. And yet, he stands today as the single most seminal and significant source of popular Southwest cultural impressions. In *both* the Ohio letters and the book Lummis distills and dramatizes the now classic romance of the Southwest. During this tramp Lummis became the first person to articulate clearly the region's seductive cultural and natural attractions, particularly those Southwest features which have seized the imagination and inspired the love and awe of people worldwide. No one before Lummis had so clearly identified and described the grandeur and the charm, the possible adventures and the "quaintness" of the region. Smitten by what he perceived to be the vitality of the American Southwest in contrast with the blasé and jaded East, Lummis laid the cornerstone for a monumental edifice of Southwest romantic imagery, a collection of great and enduring escapist fantasies that has lasted to the present day.

Prior to 1884, among writers and readers alike, the nation and the world understood this region to be a vast physical and cultural desert, repulsive and dangerous and totally without attraction other than its storied mineral wealth. In one year's time this negative image changed diametrically. The newly available, fast and easy transportation to the region made possible by the completion of both the Atlantic & Pacific (1883) and the Southern Pacific (1881) railroads played a role in this rapid metamorphosis, as did the 1884 publication of Helen Hunt Jackson's classic novel, *Ramona*. But the long-range impact of Charles Lummis' tramp observations contributed much more. Within sixteen years, a reputed Southwest regional Zeitgeist of adventure and enchantment became broadly public, and a "Southwest genre" had been established which has continued down to the present day. Southwest books of all kinds—history, anthropology, fiction, natural science, poetry, adventure, and discovery—soon flourished and were full of praise. In retrospect, Lummis' role in this particular conceptual development appears dramatically dominant. Between 1884 and 1900 Lummis did more, by far, than anyone else in identifying and publishing this romantic Southwest genre.

CHARLES FLETCHER LUMMIS, THE MUGWUMP

As early as 1880, numerous old-line New England Anglo-Saxon Protestants displayed a despondency born out of frustration due to what appeared to them to be the failure of American idealism. These same people, historian Richard Hofstadter has noted, comprised the Mugwumps ("Independents," they called themselves) who were unhappy with the selection of James G. Blaine, the "Grandee of Graft," as the 1884 Republican presidential nominee.* They considered Blaine to be darkly tarnished by the era's economic and political corruption. The Mugwumps bolted the Republican party at the June 1884 presidential nominating convention in Chicago and gave their support to Grover Cleveland and the Democratic ticket. Led by George W. Curtis, publisher of *Harper's Weekly,* and Edwin L. Godkin of *The Nation,* the Mugwumps directed their political energies toward revisions of the "abominable" tariff, the hard money policy, and the U.S. civil service "spoils system," as well as other reforms. In particular they deplored the corrupt politics of the Gilded Age's "Robber Barons," whom they felt manipulated the whole American political, economic, and social system all the way from the local precinct to the national presidency.

*The word "Mugwump" first appeared in 1872 in the Indianapolis *Sentinel.* The term's origin is hazy; some claim it was an Algonquin Indian word meaning "Big Chief." So in March 1884, the New York *Sun* used the term to ridicule the snooty, self-appointed brahmin intellectuals of the Republican party's liberal wing. Certain tongue-in-cheek historians say the Mugwump is a mythical bird who straddles the political and ideological fence with his "mug" on one side and his "wump" on the other.

Hofstadter described the Mugwump as a person or a descendant of a family of "moderate means," who up until 1870 "could command much deference and exert much influence." "Down to 1850, and even later," Henry Adams remembered, "New England society [and, therefore, by implication, American society] was still directed by the professions." In the post–Civil War period, all of this leadership changed hands. The growth of big cities and great industrial plants, the expansion of railroads, and the emergence of corporate America eclipsed the old society and the old order. As the older order deteriorated, the traditional "statesmen" and other leaders, both men and women of old families, college-educated with deep ancestral roots in their professions, businesses, and communities, and with a tradition of patrician *noblesse oblige*, increasingly found themselves excluded from the decision making of American society. During this time the parvenu—the Jay Goulds, the John D. Rockefellers, the Vanderbilts, Harrimans, Carnegies, and Morgans, viewed as vulgar and corrupt and obnoxiously materialistic by the old-line families—replaced the Mugwump preeminence in American life.

Helpless, impotent, bitter, the Mugwumps lamented their loss of stewardship and reform; but, most of all, they lamented the disappearance of the deference that previously had been accorded to them in their roles as political, social, and intellectual brahmins. In dozens of Eastern cities and towns, Hofstadter points out, the old gentry found itself "overshadowed and edged aside in the making of basic political and economic decisions." By 1880 the Mugwumps "were less important, and they knew it."

The Mugwumps flourished most conspicuously around Boston, and, Hofstadter noted, one sensed "among them the prominence of the cultural ideas and traditions of New England, and behind those, of old England. . . . They tended to look to New England's history for literary, cultural and political models and for examples of moral idealism." The novelists among them— William Dean Howells, Henry Blake Fuller, Robert Herrick—

portrayed the industrial barons as nouveau riche boors who were "devoid of refinement or any sense of noblesse." Basically conservative and believers in Social Darwinism as well as laissez-faire economics, the Mugwumps increasingly found their beliefs and their status at cross-purposes.

So what were they to do?

For a long time these proper Bostonians had known about the opportunities found in reactionary regional romanticism for an escape from unbridled capitalistic plutocracy. Despite their traditional purported distaste for unchecked consanguine aristocratic society and their avowed abhorrence of slavery, the old-line northerners (and southerners, too) had discovered and delighted in the misty, feudalistic Sir Walter Scott–Lost Cause mythology of the antebellum South, which they ingested as an antidote to the dyspepsia of nineteenth-century runaway American cultural and moral deterioration. They savored the visions of magnolias and colonnades, cotton fields and courtly plantation balls, gentle womanhood, and a chivalric code, and they devoured the baronial genre spawned by northerner John Pendleton Kennedy in his novel *Swallow Barn*, published in 1832. "It was obvious from the beginning," said William R. Taylor in his classic study, *Cavalier and Yankee*, "that *Swallow Barn* was a city man's somewhat patronizing argument for the parochialism of the country."

Swallow Barn and its Lost Cause literary descendants gave the northern city people, long before the Civil War and the great industrial onslaught, a fanciful escape from the growing frenetic whirlwind of buying and selling and the bitter perplexities of business. This antebellum mystique of earthiness and gracious baronial society characterized the popular conception of the South past the Civil War and well into the twentieth century. *Gone With the Wind* may have been its apotheosis. However, as early as 1880 the Boston Mugwumps needed and were searching for some other unspoiled American region where they could act out, if only vicariously, their genteel, feudalistic dreams.

Even more than they had done for much of the nineteenth century, the post-1884 Mugwumps, with Charles Lummis among them, wrote off the East as a loss and sought a reaffirmation of Rousseau's and Thoreau's contention that humankind strongly needed a closeness to "wildness" and "nature" and "open space" in order to achieve social stability, cultural "balance," and personal tranquility. (Today, the L. L. Bean catalog is based on the same tastes and values.) It was out of this escapist tradition, within this late nineteenth-century context and toward this Arcadian idyll that the Mugwumps derived their motives and objectives for reestablishing the American identity as a wild, bucolic, exotic, vital, enchanting, and innocent pastorale. They looked southwestward for an unspoiled American region where they could satisfy their desire for a reactionary agrarian alternative to growing American urban-industrial capitalism. And, they thought, it was a place, absent of plutocrats, in which they could regain their deserved deference.

What were the Mugwump-created Southwest images? Certainly not the topography and the climate. These Southwest traits defy and preclude any kind of romantic hyperbole. In what form, then, *did* the popular Southwest fantasies appear, and in what ways did Lummis influence or change them?

Specifically, the visions were societal ones. During the eighteenth and early nineteenth centuries, many European and American intellectuals, liberals and conservatives alike, tended to see "primitivism" as a virtue. This notion held that societies simpler than those found in Western Civilization are more fulfilling, more virtuous, and happier than "sophisticated" ones. "Such a state of existence," P. Richard Metcalf has written, "was held to be a desirable alternative to the discontents and debilitations of contemporary . . . society."

The white men who pioneered the nation's frontier, however, developed a much different impression of "primitive" cultures. Up until the 1880s, the pioneers saw the American Indian, for example, as a "vicious and blood-thirsty" savage. Nonetheless, among the Boston Mugwump literati a continued sympathy for primitivism inspired Henry Wadsworth Longfellow's *Hiawatha* (1855), just as it supported the earlier Indian heroics found in James Fenimore Cooper's *Leatherstocking Tales*. As a young man, Charles Lummis had read Mayne Reid's adventure stories set in the far Southwest, *The Scalp Hunters* (1851) and *The White Chief* (1860), two books which not only portrayed Indian savagery, but depicted cowardice, treachery, and viciousness among Southwest Hispanics, too. Despite his familiarity with Reid's point of view, Lummis thought more like Cooper, Thoreau, and Longfellow. Moreover, by 1884, virtually no solid vestige of frontier Indian barbarism remained, and Charles Lummis, as he worked his way southwestward, felt no need to become combative or alarmed or even wary. Sometimes, as his letters show, he became too *un*suspecting. Instead, he was, as he put it, "charmed" by all the "primitive" peoples he encountered in the Southwest. They included three main groups:

1. *The American Indian.* Lummis was among the first writers to perceive the Southwest Indian as a "noble" rather than a "blood-thirsty" savage. Lummis' Noble Savages were dignified and mystical as well as generous, gracious, trusting, moderate, brave, disciplined, graceful in movement and manners, contemplative, and wise. Lummis and Helen Hunt Jackson and other Mugwump writers and artists depicted Indians as being nonmaterialistic, highly moral, and transcendent. Like the classical versions, Mugwump Noble Savages were primitive but civil, and even though betrayed and abused, they remained fair, stoic, loyal, loving, and forgiving. To the Mugwumps, "civility" and "civilization" were antonyms.

2. *The Cowboy.* Despite being warned about the dirty and violent cowboys, Lummis immediately saw them as mythical "centaur figures," hard, lean, tall, and laconic. Cowboys "live lightly," each his "own man." They observe an inflexible chivalric code and usually are affiliated with a large, baronial cattle spread—or are drifting between jobs. Actually, the romanticist's cowboys appear seldomly to work; they are nomadic loners, always "moving on," and they represent honor, justice, rugged individualism, and unconscious antiurban-industrialism. Like the Noble Savages, Cowboys reject materialism and are symbols of cosmic goodness and courage. While Mugwump

Owen Wister enjoys the reputation of having created the first heroic Cowboy of this kind in his novel, *The Virginian* (1902), Lummis' letters anticipated Wister's work by eighteen years.

3. *The Hispanic.* In *Ramona* (1884), Helen Hunt Jackson laid down the archetype Southwest aristocratic Spanish ideal. However, Lummis, independent of Mrs. Jackson's influence, in the same year began to portray Hispanics as people who enjoy a relaxed, indolent, and gracious life in an ambience of Old World gentility, fountains and courtyards, mission bells and quaint adobe houses, halcyon days and starry nights. Both the patrician *hacendados* and childlike *pueblerinos* have close extended family ties and live in places *old* and *quaint,* be it mission or village or hacienda. Populated with kindly friars, dashing caballeros, jolly peasant families, and charming, beautiful señoritas, all with a heroic past of conquistadores and Castillian aristocracy, the Hispanic Southwest served as a welcome alternative to the cold, "success-oriented" Yankee Puritan tradition, as well as being a refined alternative to the boorish Gilded Age.

One can easily recognize the legacy of the southern Lost Cause mythology in Southwest imagery. Indians toil happily in the fields for Padre Agustín or Don José, rather than blacks for Ol' Massa; caballero is just another name for cavalier; sprawling ranchos and ranches replace the colonnaded mansions; and in either place no one *ever* is crass enough to talk about money, particularly *profits.* In both mythologies, greedy, ambitious Yankees destroy a cultivated and satisfying tradition. Both the Lost Cause and Southwest mythologies included what the Mugwumps felt was an essential recognition of the *loftier* aspects of Western Civilization: traditions, leisure, refined literary tastes, sartorial formality, and all the well-bred social graces, including courtliness. They wanted to advertise that they had made a knowledgeable choice, and that in opting for a southwestern setting they did not have to reject entirely the traditional trappings of decorous cultivation. So as a form of cultural defensiveness, Helen Hunt Jackson, Charles Lummis, and the later Mugwumps honored and publicized, in particular, the Hispanic patricians so as to reassure genteel newcomers and the rest of discriminating America that an ancient and refined European heritage could be found in this reputedly rustic region. (To emphasize that point, would-be cultivated Anglo-American immigrants brought with them to the frontier—around the Horn, across Nicaragua or Panama, in prairie schooners and sooty railroad cars—china, pianos, silverware, etiquette books, linen, crystal, and all the accoutrements of bourgeois respectability.)

While other regions of the Western Hemisphere had known the Hispanic, the Cowboy, and the Noble Savage, it was the Southwest's splendid setting together with the region's peculiar demographic mix that appealed to Charles Lummis and others like him. More than anywhere else, they found in the American Southwest all those characteristics that offered the most substantial escape from their unhappiness. Other regions may have possessed some of the attractive ingredients of the Mugwump mythology, but in the Southwest, land, sky, and people combined alchemically to create an hallucinogenic "Land of Enchantment." In this regional and simple cloudland the Mugwumps found—or, rather, created—an ideal at once feudalistic and innocent, simple and civil, polished and homespun.

Lummis, who embodied almost all of the Mugwump traits (financial well-being he did not enjoy), became the bellwether as well as the herdsman for the Mugwump flock that sought new pastures.

Unquestionably, the Mugwumps deplored the decline in their status. But their concern was not totally selfish. They believed, very strongly and moralistically, that America was in decay, and, therefore, they searched for new places to find the dignity and innocence and élan that they felt northeastern America had lost. "The future—the bright, far-ahead, vague Western Future—is to make up for all," wrote Caroline Kirkland in 1842. As compensation for some uncertain yet deeply felt loss, the American West—for people everywhere—has for almost two centuries represented the primeval goodness of a noble American lost dream, and has offered itself as a great open arena for the acting out, if only in fantasy, of that dream. The West, generally, and the Southwest, specifically, have represented a reaffirmation of idealistic, simple, honest, free, and primitive individualism in conflict with the all-too-real profit making and technological promise/threat of Eastern urban-industrialism.

Thus the region, mythically, became an effete and puerile gentleman's sandbox and a blue-stocking's Disneyland, and today is a quaint and safe fairy story for doctors' wives and other Junior Leaguers. The Cowboy Artists of America, El Santuario de Chimayó, Louis L'Amour, Tubac, Taos, Scottsdale, Santa Fe's Canyon Road and La Fonda, Durango, Colorado, Sedona's Red Rock Crossing, Old Tucson, several museums concerned with the romantic imagery of Southwest culture, and all of the other Southwest popular culture clichés serve as modern manifestations of this simplistic—and patronizing—mentality.

As a consequence of the Mugwump effort, all kinds of people everywhere have come to see the "Southwest heritage," even today, as possessing a fresh, expansive, and untouched quality that is still a mixture of Jeffersonian decentralized agrarian/pastoral self-sufficiency and the splendid if paradoxically decadent aristocratic baronialism of the ranch and hacienda. All of this popular imagery is free of Wall Street, labor unions, factories, federal bureaucracy, congested streets, acid rain, and all the other ills that seem to be such an oppressive and repugnant part of the industrial-urban way of life that characterizes the rest of the nation. (Just read the real-estate classified ad sections of the Sunday Arizona and New Mexico newspapers if you are not sure what this invitation to escape means today.)

The Mugwump image-makers gave us fantasies so powerful that they distract us and therefore obscure from view the Southwest's urban sprawl, pollution, land fraud, political intrigue, unemployment, penal atrocities, and general normal human folly.

Despite an avowed, and often patent, social conscience, Charles Lummis, more than any other one person, served as the dream-spinner for these colossal—and sometimes quite cruel—world-famous visions of the American Southwest.

By comparing Lummis' 1884–85 letters to Chillicothe with his 1892 book we are able to understand the way in which Lummis' imagination fed on his real experiences and guided him toward the rapid establishment of and a continuing hyperbolic reinforcement of the "mythical" Southwest. Not only did the letters to Ohio chronicle his metamorphosis from a New England Yankee into a passionate Southwesterner, they also reflect, to an observable degree, the swift evaporation of his last "objectivity" about the region. Never again was he so candidly political, so uncompromisingly graphic. And never again in writing (except in his *very* revealing diaries) was he so open, natural, and intimate.

Like his book *A Tramp Across the Continent*, virtually all of Lummis' writings about the Southwest subsequent to the Chillicothe letters reflect a Pollyanna and commercialistic perspective. That was what the literary marketplace wanted. People preferred it a certain way. And Lummis needed the income. This is not to suggest that Lummis was totally mercenary about the Southwest for the rest of his life. He truly loved the place, and, *when it was safe for him to do so*, he lambasted United States Indian policy and championed the effort to create national parks and monuments. But for the most part, his romanticism simply complemented the mood of the nation . . . and of the world.

The letters to Ohio also reflect an acute political awareness of and sharp sensitivity to late nineteenth-century American wit. Lummis displays an easy familiarity with a wide range of subjects, for he possessed tremendous powers of observation and a memory for details that enabled him to compose these long, casual essays for weekly publication in the *Leader*.

Particularly in the areas of politics and big business, Lummis' letters to Chillicothe show none of the great restraint so obvious in both the Los Angeles letters and his book about the trip. They are, in contrast, spontaneous, even rollicking in style.

Lummis knew his Chillicothe readers well, so he knew what he could and could not get away with. Moreover, he was *leaving* Chillicothe, so he felt little anxiety about antagonizing anyone or hurting his credibility in that city. He had total freedom to write to the people whose tastes, sense of humor, political attitudes, and curiosity he well understood.

For the first time since 1885, these letters are herewith presented to the public.

CHARLES F. LUMMIS: A BIOGRAPHICAL SKETCH

Charles Fletcher Lummis was born in Lynn, Massachusetts, on March 1, 1859, to Henry Lummis and Harriet Fowler Lummis. His mother died of tuberculosis when he was two years old. She was only twenty-two. Overwhelmed by grief and the responsibility of single parenthood, Lummis' father, a Methodist minister and scholar-educator, sent the boy to live with his maternal grandparents in Bristol, New Hampshire. There his grandfather, a rugged but well-educated saddlemaker and village judge, introduced the young boy to fishing, hiking, running, camping, jumping, as a result of which he developed a lifelong respect for physical strength and endurance. Lummis' father enrolled him in school at age six, but, according to legend, the independently minded and precocious boy lasted only one day. His father, a student of the classics, began to tutor the young Lummis at home in Latin, Greek, Hebrew, and classical history. Throughout his life Lummis displayed profound language skills. His grandparents and father indulged him, and Lummis grew up to be aggressive, even contentious.

At age eighteen he entered Harvard University, where, during the first weeks of school, upper classmen warned him that if he did not cut his hair shorter, they would. Charlie Lummis, the well-conditioned athlete, replied that they were quite welcome to try. A Harvard sophomore, Theodore Roosevelt, congratulated Lummis for his courage and spunk. The two remained lifelong friends.

Blessed with brains but not a bankroll, Lummis worked during the summer for a New Hampshire White Mountains resort, the Profile House, as a printer who produced the hotel's menus, announcements, handbills, and posters. During the summer of 1878, a by-product of this experience, *Birch Bark Poems*, tiny and meticulously produced books of his own poetry printed on peeled birchbark, brought him more much-needed income. Another by-product of this summer experience was a baby daughter, the consequence of a liaison with a young New Hampshire girl, Emma Nourse; Lummis did not learn about the child until twenty-five years later.

Lummis' scholarly interests at Harvard appear uneven, to say the least. He loved the natural sciences and discovered a passion for archaeology, and he enhanced his already substantial knowledge of classical history and languages. Chemistry, physics, and mathematics were another matter. And his scholarly intensity, to be generous, lacked resolve. On April 16, 1880, during Lummis' third year at Harvard, he married Dorothea Roads, a Boston University medical student. He left Harvard only a few weeks before he was to graduate; he had failed his trigonometry and analytical geometry examinations. Probably eligible to retake the tests, Lummis thumbed his nose at Harvard and walked away, a decision that he regretted the rest of his life.

In the spring of 1881, Lummis went to Chillicothe, Ohio, to manage a farm owned by Dorothea's father, Josiah ("Pater") Roads. Soon tiring of this dreary task, Lummis moved into town to become editor of a four-page weekly newspaper, the *Scioto Gazette*. Later he remembered that he served on this paper as "the local staff, the editorial staff, the library editor, the family-column man, the proof reader and whatever else came to hand." Here, no doubt, he sharpened his observational and reportorial skills. While at the *Gazette*, too, he met the many Chillicotheans who were to make up his readership during the tramp.

By the time Dorothea completed her doctor of medicine degree (in June 1884) and joined him in Chillicothe, Lummis was ready to move on. The climate, he claimed, boiled him in the summer, froze him in the winter, and created the conditions which ultimately caused him to suffer from malaria. He found his editor's job somewhat unsatisfying. Temperamentally restless, Lummis craved adventure. In his spare time he enjoyed looking for prehistoric human bones and artifacts at a site two miles northeast of Chillicothe, today known as the Mound City Group National Monument. The archaeological digs whetted his appetite for more archaeological knowledge. Moreover, Lummis' relationship with Dorothea began to deteriorate soon after she arrived in Chillicothe.

The American Southwest had intrigued Charlie Lummis for many years. As a boy, Mayne Reid's Southwest adventure fiction had fascinated him. The Southwest, he learned, housed North America's greatest archaeological treasure. It provided for Lummis an irresistible magnet. During the summer of 1884, he initiated a correspondence with Colonel Otis, the new owner of the *Los Angeles Times*. Otis offered Lummis a job as the newspaper's city editor and said he would buy him a railway ticket to Southern California. Lummis accepted the job. But he decided not to ride; instead, he said he would follow the railroad tracks westward . . . on foot. The two struck a deal, and Lummis began his preparations for his "tramp."

In 1883, workers had completed the Atlantic and Pacific Railroad, the last link of the route connecting the Southwest with the East. So during the summer of 1884 Lummis built a file or "routebook" of former Chillicotheans who had moved westward, and whom he could visit on his "tramp," particularly those who now lived in towns by or near the railroads he planned to track. He found these ex-Ohioans living as far west as Santa Fe, New Mexico.

After taking the train from Chillicothe to Cincinnati, Lummis started walking toward Los Angeles on September 13. Using his imagination and Yankee practicality, he had put together a set of functional hiking clothes: a snug pair of knickers or pantaloons to avoid the annoyance caused by, as he put it, "two feet of flapping trousers below the knee"; a white flannel shirt, tied at the neck with a blue ribbon; knee-length stockings; and a pair of Curtis & Wheeler low-cut buttonshoes. Several people in Chillicothe remarked that this outfit made him look like a baseball player of the time. A sturdy hunting knife hung from his waist, and in a money belt, next to his skin, he carried $300 in $2.50 gold coins. In addition, Lummis had with him a multipocketed duck coat and a broad-brimmed felt hat. As an experienced hiker, Lummis "traveled light" and carried only writing materials, fishing tackle, matches, tobacco, and a large revolver. He expected to stay in hotels until he reached the frontier, so he sent his rifle and camping gear ahead to Kansas. In December, in Golden, New Mexico, Lummis eschewed the knickers for a warmer and more Southwestern costume of white buckskin leggins with leather fringes two feet long. The shoes lasted all the way to Daggett, California.

Throughout his tramp, on side trips and digressions, Lummis wore a pedometer. When he arrived in Los Angeles on February 1, 1885, he calculated that he had walked 3507 miles in the 143 days since leaving Cincinnati.

In addition to his remarkable physical fitness, Lummis possessed other traits that would serve him well on his tramp: an unrestrained (and, at times, troublemaking) zeal, a buoyant good humor, a natural gregariousness, and a well-stocked raconteur's repertoire. His aggressive self-confidence many people construed as cockiness. Lummis seemed never to be intimidated by new places and settings or by strangers or even by the weather, which caused him much discomfort but drew few complaints.

Many of Lummis' letters to Ohio contain comments on the 1884 United States' presidential election. In the East he had considered himself to be a good conservative Republican, and early in his tramp he alluded to his Republican loyalties. In Seymour, Indiana, he said, "Politics in Seymour are hot. The Republicans have a huge wigwam and are booming things." "Even the Democrats," he declared, "will vote for Blaine." The Ohio and Missouri railroad, he protested, "is the crookedest thing I ever ran across, except, perhaps, Grover Cleveland's private record."

After crossing Indiana, he felt

a lively faith that the Republicans will carry the Hoosier state this fall. I talked along the way with everyone accessible: Republicans, Democrats, Green backers, Butler [Benjamin Franklin Butler, the Anti-Monopoly and Greenback parties' 1884 nominee for president] men, and disciples of St. John [John Pierce St. John, former Kansas governor and 1884 Prohibitionist candidate for president]: farmers, railroaders, section-hands, merchants, mechanics and editors, and nearly all the straws are blowing in a way to please me.

"Illinois," Lummis observed, "is solid Republican all the way through, and a Democrat is as hard to find as a good cigar."

West of St. Louis, other experiences distracted Lummis from political concerns. He didn't bring up the subject again until, in Kansas, he remarked that the former governor of Kansas and the Prohibitionist's candidate for the Presidency, John P. St. John, "is the most unpopular man in the state. . . . He is regarded as a fifth-rate lawyer, not strictly reliable, and a sad incubus upon the States." But this was Lummis' last political observation until after he left Denver. For the time, antelope hunting, rattlesnake-skinning, and other activities commanded his attention.

South of Denver, Lummis examined the great Northern Colorado Irrigation Company system and then observed:

This big monopoly, the Platte Canal Co., has acquired possession of great tracts of land along its [the canal's] course, and holds the thousands of acres at a ruinously high figure. It has also raised the price of all contiguous land to a point which shuts out the stockman and now bids fair to swamp the farmers. I have talked with 79* farmers—not to mention numerous outsiders—and all are as blue as Ohio Democrats. They are bankrupt and despondent, almost without hope. They have spent their last dollar, many of them, and do not know where the next is coming from.

---

*An example of Lummis' hyperbole!(?)

This was Lummis' first hint of any liberal-populist sympathy. A few days later he wrote, "I wouldn't swap my athletic stomach and my empty pocket for [William] Vanderbilt's dyspepsia and his bank account. In fact, I don't envy the red-faced, red-whiskered, unread billionaire—who looks like a hog and talks like a hostler [a horse's groom]—in any respect." But Lummis still lamented Democrat Grover Cleveland's successful bid for president. Of Cleveland's victory, Lummis said, "Well, if the people of these United States have . . . chosen the Buffalo Bull as their highest representative, I shall for the first time blush that I am an American."

Actually, in the weeks that followed, the letters show that as a consequence of the new experiences encountered on the tramp his own views were, indeed, changing rapidly. Lummis began to develop new economic and political sensibilities. He started to detect and resent the late nineteenth century monopolistic abuses of the west by such "Robber Barons" as John D. Rockefeller, J. P. Morgan, and Andrew Carnegie. He praised Colorado's sourdough prospectors as the true heroes of the West. Of Colorado capitalism, he said, "The East has her monopolies, and they are big and dangerous . . . but out here . . . monopoly has [Colorado] by the throat."

In this regard he developed independently the same political posture as his fellow New England Mugwumps, who bolted the party in protest against the Republican 1884 presidential nominee, James G. Blaine.

Lummis' liberal inclinations continued to grow. By the time he had spent several days in the mining town of Golden, New Mexico, he wrote, "You have always known me as a solid Republican, and I am one still, but our late defeat doesn't gall me as it did before I understood the situation out here." He conceded that Cleveland's election was a boon to the common man. "The political overturn this fall means life to New Mexico," he wrote on December 10, 1884. Successful western entrepreneurs such as Horace Tabor he pictured as evil claims-jumpers and heartless employers, and he displayed sympathy for the working man and all ethnic minorities. These were not late nine-teenth-century Republican sentiments.

But nothing so politically and economically "radical" ap-peared in his other publications written about the trip. And his subsequent letters to Chillicothe made little mention of poli-tics again.

Only the letters to the *Leader* reveal much about Lummis' religious attitudes. Always the preacher's irreverent kid, he coyly revealed his impious attitudes with flippant and extrava-gant metaphors: "When the Almighty had baked the rest of the earth's crust into biscuits, doughnuts and loaves of various form, He evidently took down his big rolling pin from the shelf of the celestial pantry, and took the still unbaked dough of Illinois to roll out pie-crust." Lummis went on, "For that mat-ter, I don't believe He even put it in the oven at all, . . . if you could see some of the mud I struck between Noble and Odin."

His attempts to euphemize profanity show equal imagina-tion as well as the vernacular of the time: "Dodgasted," "gee-whizzly gold-dusted to Jude," "bigodest," "damphools," "mill-dam outfit," many "blanketty-blanks" and much "———."

Other semi-vices he reveals only in the *Leader*, too. A hope-lessly self-indulgent nicotinist, Lummis describes "sucking so-lace" on a nine-inch cigar (a life-long practice); admits that back East he averaged eighty-seven cigarettes a day; avers that while tramping through New Mexico he smoked daily thirty hand-rolled cigarettes and says he puffed on "an impatient pipe" while hurrying along the Arizona railroad tracks. He was no friend of temperance, either. From Kansas he wrote:

I have been investigating this Prohibition question assiduously. . . . Well, no intelligent man can go through this State—so widely paraded as the scene of successful prohibition—and fail to see that prohibition is a sorry farce. . . . It is against my principles, as well as my tastes, to touch stimulants when on an outdoor trip of any sort, where perfect training is indispensable to perfect enjoyment; but along here I have been somewhat sacrificing myself in the interests of science and truth. . . . Well, then you can 'get what you want' almost anywhere. . . .

I had not been in [Lawrence, Kansas] two hours before I had half a dozen invitations to liquor up. . . . I have been content with a few drops and the truth, but could have drunk myself blind in a hundred places. That is the way prohibition prohibits in Kansas.

Later, as the years went by, Lummis developed his own struggle with John Barleycorn.

In his book and in his letters to Los Angeles, Lummis omits almost all these insights into his unconventional and somewhat disreputable attitudes and behavior.

In many ways, Lummis reflected the essence of late nineteenth-century American bourgeois thought. Approving of reason and science, he still admitted to being a romantic. Ordinarily positive, even cheery, he rages at sloth, deceit, greed, and ignorance. He decries Easterners, but in many ways Lummis is an archetypal Bostonian. Increasingly sensitive to reform and the problems of the proletariat, he remained awed by and deeply respectful of aristocratic refinements. He enjoyed a visit to a 15,000-acre cattle ranch in Kansas owned by a young Boston and Harvard man. Fitted out with "a stone mansion which would not look out of place in the finest dwelling street in any city," the ranch appealed to Lummis' sense of "noblesse," and the size, wealth, retinue, gentility, and comfort of this baronial estate entranced him. A six-day visit to the rancho of *hidalgo* Don Manuel Chaves in San Mateo, New Mexico, north of Grants, was the high point of his trip. His stay at the patrician Chaves home brought to a climax the spiritual, moral, and artistic conversion that ordained Lummis a true Southwesterner. Most of the rest of his life he wanted to be called "Don Carlos."

Lummis did not reject the East out-of-hand. He favorably compared Colorado Springs to "a bright New England town." But more often he referred to "the sleepy, fallow East." His strongest statements about the effete East he saved for describing Eastern tourists. About them he said:

I don't know why it is that folks who have good horse sense back at home in Boston, New York, or Cincinnati, can't get out here without turning into doddering imbeciles—but it seems that they can't. Such exhibitions of ill taste, bad manners, ignorance, and gullibility are to be met nowhere else. I trust . . . these frank folks out here . . . have a contemptuous pity for Eastern tourists who have become a synonym for all that is ridiculous and disagreeable. Now when a Westerner sees anything novel and surprising, he takes it all in without moving a muscle. . . . But an Eastern tourist will throw up his hands and open his mouth and slop over until the very dogs have run around to the drugstore for something to steady their stomachs. Right on the streets of Santa Fe intelligent and refined looking ladies have been seen to stop in front of a half-dressed Indian buck, gape at him, talk about him, and even pinch him to see if he was honest flesh. . . . There is absolutely no story so ridiculous that you cannot ram these tourists full of it, and of course the natives take malicious pleasure in filling them with guff. I am sorry it is so, for I like the East and its people; but if I stay out here much longer and see many more of its transient representatives, I shall have to lock up my respect or it will get lost.

After a few days in Los Angeles, he wrote, "I wouldn't be found dead back East, even if you'd whack up on the coffin."

Lummis first fell in love with the landscape of the American Southwest at Platte Cañon, Colorado, only a two-day walk south from Denver. Two weeks later, south of industrial and smoky Pueblo, Colorado, as he approached the Cucharas River, Lummis could see to the south the distant twin Spanish Peaks. He had now reached the northernmost border of an American *cultural* region which would make a profound and permanent impression on him. "The day [Saturday, November 15, 1884] was full of interest to me," he wrote, "for on it, I stepped across the line from an alleged American civilization into the boundaries of one strangely diverse."

Lummis admitted he had uncomfortable feelings about the Hispanics of the Southwest. "On the willowy banks of Cucharas Creek," he wrote, "I ran across a big plaza of Mexicans—'Greasers,' as they were called out here. A Westerner," he went on, "would no more think of calling a Mexican a 'Greaser,' than a Kentucky colonel would [think] of calling a Negro anything but a 'nigger'." In this plaza, he went on, "in lousy laziness, exist 200 Greasers of all sexes, ages and sizes, but all equally dirty." The Mexicans, said Lummis, "are a snide-looking set, twice as dark as an Indian" with "a general expression of ineffable laziness. . . . Not even a coyote will touch a dead Greaser, the flesh is so seasoned with the red pepper they ram into their food in howling profusion."

A few days later, however, he said, "I find the 'Greasers' to be not half bad people. In fact, they rather discount the whites, who are all on the make. There is only one sociable thing about the white folks all along the D. & R. G. [Denver and Rio Grande Railroad]—they will share your last dollar with you. A Mexican, on the other hand, will 'divvy' his only tortilla and his one blanket with any stranger, and never take a cent." By the time Lummis reached the upper Española Valley he was calling the Mexican plazas "quaint." And after asking a Mexican family for a tortilla, he received a red carpet welcome which included a custom-rolled cigarette, coffee with brandy ("aguardiente"), a platter of mutton chunks and three big tortillas. "I can stand it as long as they can," he concluded. By then, he wrote, he had "sworn in a posse of about twenty [Spanish] words, and handle them with the easy grace of a cow shinning up an apple tree tail first."

The first Spanish word he used in his correspondence to Chillicothe was *adios*, when he signed off his letter of November 18, 1884, from Alamosa, Colorado. It was an appropriate symbol of "goodbye" to the East.

Lummis also found Santa Fe to be "quaint," and this word along with "charming" leads the adjective parade still used broadly today to describe the towns, villages, and multi-ethnic culture of the upper Río Grande valley ("enchanting," a synonym for charming, and "romantic" are close behind).

In Santa Fe, his respect for the Hispanic culture swelled to admiration when he met Señor Amado Chaves, son of Don Manuel Chaves of San Mateo, New Mexico, "a young and polished gentleman from one of the most noted New Mexican families." This family would have a great impact on Lummis for the rest of his life. Later, thirteen miles east of Albuquerque at Carnuel, he "lost no time in getting inside a little . . . Mexican store . . . and struck it rich." When he asked ("in a wholesale assassination of Spanish") for food and a place to sleep, the proprietor, Ramón Arrera, took him in, filled him with wine and "a good supper of carne, chile colorado, cafe, y tortillas." "This was my first venture on chili colorado," he wrote, "and will be my last." But as time went on Lummis grew to love the hot and spicy Mexican food.

By the time he reached Albuquerque, Lummis felt qualified to spend several column inches giving the "Spanish scholars back in Chillicothe" a linguistic lesson *en Español*.

His love affair with the people and the culture of the Southwest was now flourishing. After enjoying such genuine and unconditional Hispanic hospitality, he felt ashamed of his earlier prejudices. (In his 1892 book, *A Tramp Across the Continent*, Lummis refers to the use of the word "greaser" only with contempt for the word and its users. With righteous indignation, Lummis wrote that " 'greasers' . . . [was] a nomenclature which it is not wise to practice as one proceeds south [from Cucharas Creek, Colorado] and which anyway is born of an unbred boorishness of which no Mexican could ever be guilty. They . . . are better taught than our own average in all the social virtues—in hospitality, courtesy and respect for age.")

During the nineteenth and early twentieth centuries, many literate bourgeois Americans found humor in word-play based on an expression from Alexander Pope's 1734 *Essay On Man*. Pope wrote:

> Lo, the Poor Indian! whose untutored mind
> Sees God in clouds, or hears him in the wind.

Pope's poetic intention and syntactical use of the interjection "Lo" (for "look" or "behold") invited ethnic condescension, and "Lo," as a proper name, became a parlor joke. It is true that on occasion during his tramp, Lummis wrote of "Lo" and referred to "Lo's poor kids" as "dusky pupils" and "young bucks." But, essentially, he had an open, even compassionate, mind about the nation's "Indian problem," and he wasted no time before introducing himself to the Indian culture of the Southwest.

His first encounter with western Indians took place at a government school for Indians near Lawrence, Kansas. The students, who ranged in age from eight to twenty-three years, were of both sexes. Many of them, he observed, were "stolid and dull-looking but there are plenty of bright faces." He described their English translation names—Fred Eagle, Frank Buffalo, Joseph Fireshaker—as "ridiculous." "The funniest was Moses Bears-ears," he noted. Assimilation through education seemed the way to solve the "vexing 'Indian Question,' " Lummis opined. "The Indian is generally accredited with endless laziness and stupidity in matters of school education, but after this visit I find it hard to believe the slander," he wrote.

His next substantial experience with Indians occurred in Española, New Mexico, where he showed a more typical patronizing tourist reaction: "Bucks, with bottles of whisky or plugs of tobacco in their hands, squaws with their big papooses slung across their backs, and youngsters of all sizes were crowding the [stores] and keeping up an incessant jabber." He continued that day (November 24, 1885) on down to San Ildefonso pueblo. There he met Alonzo, "who must be a sort of High Muck-a-Muck," and who took Lummis into his home and "was as courteous as anyone could have been." After a hot supper of mutton, tortillas, coffee, and "matchless" cheese ("never any other half so delicious") together with a sound sleep on a "luxurious bed" and a breakfast of venison, frijoles, coffee, tortillas, and a pudding called "panacha," Lummis found himself, as with the Hispanics, totally charmed. For the rest of his life Lummis saw Pueblo Indians as a superior class of the human race.

Even Pueblo Indians, though, had a developmental hierarchy, in Lummis' eyes. The Indians of Tesuque, he wrote, are "incomparably inferior to the Indians of San Ildefonso" who "are well built and sturdy . . . [and] have light, copper complexions, and good features."

Non-Pueblo Indians were another matter altogether. "A strange people are these Navajos," he stated. "Living among the Pueblos, they are as different from them as night is from day." He praised the blankets and jewelry he saw the Navajos making, but still he described these Indians as dirty, thievish, treacherous, ugly, and revoltingly licentious people when compared with the Pueblo Indians. Northwest Arizona's Hualapai tribe, he observed, constituted

the nastiest human beings I ever saw. Ugly in form and feature, slovenly in dress and intolerably filthy in person—I should hate to have any of my friends left where they had to look at such disgusting creatures. . . . Any sober, steady-going cow, of family intentions, would look at just one of those Hualapais and have a miscarriage forthwith. These Indians are as worthless as a pair of last year's linen pants . . . and their only industry seems to be prostitution.

Lummis' appreciation of cultural relativism still had some way to go. The more an Indian looked like a white man, the better Lummis liked him.

Of the United States Government Indian policy, Lummis reported that the average Indian agent's "highest use for the Indian is to skin him alive."

Friends back East had warned him about the "ferocious cowboys" out West, but after traveling several days with one in Kansas, who called himself "Antelope Bill," Lummis wrote that cowboys respected muscle and grit and energy and knew a real man when they saw one. He even referred to "the Centaur figure of a cowboy," thus elevating this western character to mythic status. In doing so, he anticipated by eighteen years the romantic attitude toward cowboys made popular by Owen Wister in his classic cowboy novel, *The Virginian*.

Lummis' rhetoric in the letters to Ohio shows much less polish than do the other printed versions of his "tramp." But the vitality of his details, impressions, and figures of speech in the Chillicothe letters cannot be found in the other two. And candor, intelligence, and informal style make the Ohio version incomparably more attractive. The color of Lummis' language blossoms as he moves westward. Never known for his temperamental stability, Lummis shows a vacillating roller-coaster ride of passion, joy, anxiety, anger, excitement, arrogance, gusto, incredulity, rapture, self-styled heroism, and unconscionable hyperbole.

Lummis understood his Chillicothe readership well enough to be quite natural and open. Expressing his reluctance to leave charming Santa Fe, he wrote: "It was as hard as breaking away from your best girl at 11:45 P.M., when she puts her soft arms around your neck and says: 'Oh, George, it is *real* early yet. Please don't go.' I presume you know how hard that is—if you don't, the sooner you find out the better."

For a man only twenty-five years old, Lummis displayed a broadly diverse and overwhelming knowledge of history, archaeology, linguistics, geology, law, poetry, classics, corporate organization, human folly, and politics. His vocabulary was extensive, yet throughout the letters his style was familiar. Effortless (he rarely did redrafts) and straightforward, Lummis' language exhibits both his academic and journalistic education; above all, he was a communicator. His energy, at times, outraces his eloquence, and his long paragraphs, Latinates, flamboyance, puns, syntax, and occasional sloppy spelling and grammar can be distracting. But overall, his choice of precise nouns and active verbs together with his basic honesty—hold the reader riveted to what amounts to outstanding storytelling.

Like most bright, young writers, Lummis loved to play with words. He called "Fort Wingate," "Fort Losegate." When he remarked that he had not seen a dam on either the Río Puerco or Little Colorado rivers, it was "doubtless because those measly little streams aren't worth a dam." His metaphors fairly bludgeon the reader; and he anthropomorphizes a lot. A hotel room in Missouri had mosquitoes "that sang arias from Wagner." A cook serves Lummis butter so rancid that it needs "no testimonial from me, being old enough to speak for itself, but not yet bald;" railroad tracks in Indiana are so crooked, they are like a "big black-snake with the jim-jams"; and another twisting rail-road, he feels, has no more need "to stagger around that way than there is for me to shave the soles of my feet." About the Atlantic and Pacific Railroad, he wrote: "If the 35th parallel is to be held responsible for the crazy wanderings of that track, it ought to be put at once in an asylum for inebriates."

Lummis cannot resist puns either. He says his pedestrian "pilgrim's progress was not troubled by a single Bunyan"; he looks for an "Italian summer" when he gets to Arizona but decides "it is summer else." On the prairie "silence not only reigns, it fairly pours." He, himself, groans over such painful expressions, and begs the reader's forgiveness. Lamy, New Mexico, he assures us, "is no relation to our old friend, 'Now I Lamy.'"

He is addicted to slang. His language skills and "show-off" personality naturally encouraged this. No doubt his four years at Harvard supplied him with a sizable lexicon of collegiate patois vocabulary. "Sand" is the Lummis vernacular for "true grit." People get "mashed" a lot; not inebriated, but excited or enthusiastic. The word "clever" he uses as an all-purpose positive adjective; at different times it means "likeable," "charming," "witty," "knowledgeable," "hospitable," "adventurous," and "wise."

Lummis waxed wise, himself, at times. "Real pleasure never bunked in the same house with heavy cares, and never will," he wrote. "If we never were young," he observed, "we'd never be fools, but we'd miss a heap of fun." Of his considerable hardships on his tramp he said, "There can be no such thing as enjoyment unless we are able to contrast it with pain."

Lummis had a sharp ear for dialect. He mocked the Missouri version of "prairie" with "purayra." And he quoted the concern an Irish woman in Colorado expressed about his spare frame: "Faith, the owld carpenter shud 'ave put a pane o'glass [magnifying glass] in front of yees, to show where the lot is." One night near Pueblo, Colorado, Lummis was turned out into the cold by inhospitable potential hosts, but a young, "frank-faced" Italian

track-gang laborer told him: "Me no hav-a but three-a blanket—
me give-a you two." Stunned and appreciative, Lummis, in his
own vernacular, responded: "I'll be gee-whizzly gold-dusted to
jude if he didn't do it, too." After he broke his arm, another
maternal Irishwoman, Mrs. Kelley, in Hualapai, Arizona, took
pity on him. Noticing his bandaged hand, she exclaimed: "Och,
the poor lad! The poor, brave lad! Out in this wicked country
wid a broken arrum. Poor lad!"

Some of his awareness of dialect took its inspiration from
C. F. Browne, a popular writer of the time who published under
the pseudonym of Artemus Ward. Lummis acknowledged Ward
as the source of such expressions as "amoosin," "immejit,"
"sez," and "yallar dorg." On February 1, 1885, Lummis arrived
in Los Angeles and, in Ward's words, into "the buzzum of the
family."

No doubt, too, Lummis derived some of his ear for dialect
and other stylistic forms from Mark Twain, who, in 1884, published *The Adventures of Huckleberry Finn*. Lummis' account
of a toper with the jim-jams in Antonito, Colorado, sounds
much like the drunken ravings of Pap, Huck's father. (Ironically,
Huckleberry Finn was banned the following year in the library
of Concord, Massachussetts, that near-by Boston community
and hotbed of liberal thought, as "trash and suitable only for the
slums.")

Throughout the tramp, Lummis, a craftsman and purveyor of
classic New England wit, treats serious subjects humorously
and humorous subjects seriously. For example, coming out of
Cerrillos, New Mexico, headed for Golden, a number of people
assure him, as he proceeds, that he's on the right road, but each
sequential person gives him a higher figure of the mileage yet to
go. When he finally gets to Golden, he not only observes that the
miles were greater in length and number, but were "all mean
miles," too.

The letters show Lummis to be precociously mature. He
knew mining claims could be "salted" with high grade ore. He
notes that Denver had great vistas of the Rockies "when the

abominable smoke does not interfere, as it does about two-thirds of the time." He detailed how to prepare tomato preserves and stretch tortillas, how New Mexicans build their grain mills and wooden carts, and how to "case" a pelt. Little of this kind of detail can be found in his other two publications about the trip. At times Lummis became almost poetic. Of Platte Cañon near Denver he wrote:

Cold as coldest lee-water, clear as crystal, swift as an arrow, it is dashed musically down its steep and rocky bed, turning, foaming and twisting through the sinuous channel it has carved, by the labor of a hundred million years, through the solid granite.

He describes the mountains of the Mohave Desert:

But the strangest of all is their color. The prevailing hue is a soft, dark, red brown, or occasionally tender purple; but here and there upon this deep background are curious light patches, where the fine sand of the desert whirled aloft and swept along by the mighty winds so common there, and rained down upon the mountain slopes where it forms deposits scores of feet in depth, and acres in extent.

Despite these words, Lummis had no love for the dry Southwestern low desert, and he crossed the wide Mohave wasteland as fast as he could. He reached Daggett, California, near Barstow, on January 28, went through Cajon Pass, and saw his first orange grove in Cucamonga, where he described this part of southern California as "God's country and a New Eden."

On February 1, after a hearty late-evening meal with Harrison Gray Otis, who had come out to meet Lummis, the two strode the tramp's remaining ten miles past San Gabriel Mission into Los Angeles. The next morning Lummis was on the job at nine o'clock as the first city editor of the *Los Angeles Times*.

Within a short while, Lummis became a well-known figure in the still somewhat frontier Los Angeles area. About this time Lummis began to wear the earth-toned, wide-waled corduroy suits that became his trademark. At the *Times*, he later said, he put into his work "all the soul and brain I had." He labored "without a thought of late hours or of health." According to Lummis, after putting the paper to bed, he would arrive home at 6 A.M., only to get up an hour later to return to work. "In my three years at the *Times*," he claimed, "I never got more than two hours of sleep in the 24."

He must have had some time off because Lummis did have an active social life. His marriage to Dorothea continued to deteriorate, and he fell in love with Susana del Valle, an aristocratic señorita who lived at Rancho Camulos near Santa Paula, about fifty miles west of Los Angeles. Lummis asked Dorothea for a divorce, but Susana's father, Don Jose del Valle, told Lummis that his daughter could never marry a man who previously had been wedded. Like other Hispanic old-world families, such as that of Amado Chavez, the Del Valles brought him the intimacy, warmth, and conviviality—and a surrogate mother—for which he hungered.

The *Times* sent Lummis to southern Arizona in April 1886 to cover Gen. George Crook's campaign against the Apache chief, Geronimo. Back home, he resumed his frenetic pace and reduced his sleep to one hour a night. "But," he asserted, "I felt like a fighting cock!" On December 5, 1887, he lay down to rest and suddenly discovered his left side was paralyzed.

The paralytic attack forced Lummis to seek a rest, and he returned to the area he favored the most during his tramp—northern New Mexico. Slowly, with "sand" and willfulness, he began to recover. In the fall of 1888, after a lengthy stay at Don Manuel Chavez' rancho at San Mateo, he moved to the pueblo of Isleta, a few miles south of Albuquerque, on the Río Grande. He found a small apartment within the pueblo and gradually overcame his paralytic affliction. While at Isleta, Lummis' divorce from Dorothea became final, and he married Eva Douglas, the sister-in-law of an Indian trader at Isleta. Eventually he and Eva had four children.

Also, while living at Isleta, Lummis wrote numerous stories and articles for different periodicals, and he authored six well-received books and began a career in photography that became what is probably his most important achievement in his lifelong effort to promote and preserve Southwest culture. During this four-year stay at Isleta, he met Adolph Bandelier, and in 1892 the two men went to Peru to do archaeological research.

Returning from Peru to California, Lummis decided to build his own home in the Highland Park district, six miles northeast of downtown Los Angeles. El Alisal, "place of the Sycamores," he called it. Here he displayed his collections of books and photographs, exotic souvenirs, and Indian artifacts, and held discourses on Southwestern culture. He entertained friends by the score at his dinner parties, or "noises," as he called them. At El Alisal, Lummis supported, criticized, and encouraged dozens of artists and writers. From this home, Lummis carried on his crusade to reform United States Government Indian policy, and his friend President Teddy Roosevelt sought his advice on this subject.

In his "Lion's Den," as he called his study at El Alisal, he edited for ten years a monthly periodical first known as *Land of Sunshine* and then as *Out West*, a publication intended to promote all aspects of Southwest culture.

Actually, Charles Lummis' Southwest was limited to places—except for the bottom of the Grand Canyon—higher than four thousand feet in elevation and within seventy-five miles north or south of the main Santa Fe line between Kingman, Arizona, and Lamy, New Mexico. He rarely visited the region of his first Southwest cultural awakening, southern Colorado, and he spent very little time at Taos or Santa Fe, New Mexico, even though the artists and writers of those two New Mexican cultural colonies venerated Lummis as a saint. One of his earliest books about the Southwest, *The Land of Poco Tiempo* (1893), became an enduring handbook and scripture for those Southwest aesthetes. In truth, Lummis had little interest in the bohemian affectations of Taos or Santa Fe.

While at El Alisal, Lummis raised his children, and Eva divorced him.

For years, Lummis passionately wanted a museum in Los Angeles dedicated to preserving the culture of the Southwest. He broke ground in 1911, and the Southwest Museum, close to his home in Highland Park, was opened to the public on August 1, 1914.

From Los Angeles, he continued his travels back and forth to New Mexico on the Santa Fe line. Between 1905 and 1911 he served as head of the Los Angeles Public Library, and he campaigned constantly to preserve the natural wonders of his beloved region.

Alfonso, King of Spain, recognized Lummis for his efforts to understand the Southwest's Hispanic heritage and in 1917 awarded him the Order of Isabella. "Don Carlos" treasured the medallion the rest of his life. For four decades Lummis remained the most energetic advocate of Southwest culture who has ever lived.

In 1926, he made his last trip to New Mexico. His health failed rapidly; doctors diagnosed cancer, "the crab," Lummis astrologically called it. In great pain, he kept busy until his last day, November 25, 1928. He was sixty-nine years old.

Despite Lummis' energy and prodigious tangible achievements, Southwesterners and the rest of the country alike quickly forgot him. Indeed, during his sixties he became, at time, a recluse. Highland Park residents occasionally saw him, stooped and alone, shuffling along Figueroa Street, pulling a wooden toy wagon with groceries in it, headed for El Alisal. It is difficult, in fact, to ascertain the source of his income between 1915 and 1928; apparently he lived close to poverty.

Some say he was a dilettante and buffoon, an egotistical and frustrated would-be patrician who wanted to be called "Don Carlos," but who made a fool of himself in attempting it. Southwest writer Beatrice Chauvenet, in a recent book (*Hewitt and Friends*, 1983), said Lummis' writings "were for popular consumption—enthusiastic, dramatic and often somewhat imaginary accounts of his adventures in the Southwest." This was a charitable view. Historian Leonard Pitt, looking a little more closely perhaps in *The Decline of the Californios* (1966), wrote that Lummis' activities were "one part aestheticism, one part history and one part ballyhoo."

Charles Lummis at El Alisal, 1925(?). Courtesy of Southwest Museum: negative no. 22,932.

These comments give us due reason to ponder the significance of the fact that *The Land of Poco Tiempo* has (always)
enjoyed so much popularity in those Southwest communities
most known for their dilettante nature.

Actually, the expression "land of *poco tiempo*" (in English
"land of 'in a little while'" or, loosely translated, "*mañana*
land") does not reflect in any way Lummis' attitude toward life.
To his dying day, Lummis displayed the old New England Protestant virtues of hard work, punctuality, organization, and
thrift. Throughout his life anxiety gripped him, and he was a
workaholic. He perceived himself as a patron, a catalyst, an
organizer. At his "noises," the only "noise" came from volatile,
animated, show-off Charlie Lummis. He often said that no one
needs more than four hours sleep a night, and he, himself, spent
twenty hours a day meeting self-imposed deadlines. Little evidence exists to show that he ever relaxed. Achievement was
everything.

But why has history neglected him when obviously he craved
so to be immortal? Like most other people, Lummis had a very
complex personality. Filled with ambivalences, competing pri-
orities, a desire for perfection, and an even greater desire for
attention, Lummis needed the frequent recognition and reinforcement that only a quickly and impatiently created product
could bring.

Other contradictions, too, blur his identity. A campaigner for
minority rights, Lummis still hankered to be an aristocratic
hidalgo. A writer who worshipped true scholars like Adolph
Bandelier, Lummis possessed a need for instant gratification
that forced him to publish only "popular" books written off-the-
top-of-his-head. Documentation and originality took too much
time and too much work. His ego always needed a quick fix. His
tourist's gee-whiz, gosh-golly attitude toward so many subjects
eclipsed and discredited his very few sober and legitimate
achievements. Too much of his written work reads like Chamber of Commerce promotional material.

None of his books possess any intellectual depth or true
original scholarship. All of Lummis' work is based only on a

cursory examination of a few secondary sources. More discriminating scholars rarely treat such products with kindness. Among serious historians, he has earned no more respect or recognition than any number of grade B (or worse) movie directors. And his perspectives as well as his sensibilities about any subject appear to be, at best, superficial and romantic.

Moreover, Lummis did not show a philosophical and reflective mind; New England pragmatism dominated his thinking. A man of action, not of ideas, his credibility as a seminal figure was washed away in a torrent of superlatives and melodrama, travelogues and didacticism, hyperbole and simplistic observations. His best book, *Mesa, Canyon and Pueblo* (1925), a well-reworked version of *Some Strange Corners of Our Country* (1892), was definitely written with a genteel New England audience in mind. Thus, like the others, it was very long on colorful promotion and short on original scholarship. Lummis was so deliberate and self-conscious about his rejection of New England that his demeanor presented not so much a *person* naturally at ease with the people and culture of the Southwest as the *persona* of a bourgeois Yankee in revolt. Conspicuously, his desire to escape often dominated and blotted out his ability to affirm.

However, all of these cruel limitations to his image notwithstanding, the sum of his talents and achievements is overpowering. On January 20, 1903, in *The Los Angeles Times*, the esteemed western artist Frederic Remington wrote of Lummis:

He is one of the greatest men in the country today. Positively I never met a man just like him. He's a genius, that's what he is. His philosophy of life is simply great. And the worst of it is, you don't half appreciate him. If he wasn't right in your midst I dare say you would run over him as you do over other men with far less talent than he possesses.

Charles Lummis, the bedazzled tourist, had genius—and he had "sand." These virtues appear nowhere else more than they do in these *Letters from the Southwest*.

LETTERS
from the
SOUTHWEST

CHARLES LUMMIS' physical appearance at the time of his departure for Los Angeles was described by the editors of the Chillicothe *Leader* as an introduction to the cross-country hiker's first letter. Under the headline "Fun in Store for 'Lummy'" the following material accompanied publication of that letter in the September 20, 1884, edition of the newspaper.

Mr. Charles F. Lummis took his departure Thursday for Cincinnati, from whence, after a day's examination of the curiosities of The Exposition, he will enter upon the long and wearisome journey he has resolved upon undertaking, viz., a trip to California on foot.

A Chillicothean, who has seen a great deal of the world for a man of his youth and simplicity of character, and in the accumulation of a portion of which knowledge he spent several years on the plains, in the role of an amateur cow-boy and mule-trader, was discovered by the reporter, on the day referred to, leaning over one of the store-boxes which adorn west Second street, and laughing immoderately.

"Here, old fellow, what's the matter with you; what are you laughing about?" said the janizary, slapping him on the back familiarly.

"Did you—did you—you see Lummis' picture?" was the interrogatory response that came from the ex-cow-boy's lips, between his hysterical bursts of laughter.

The scribe recalled the fact that a day or two before he had seen the cabinet-sized photograph of the pedestrian, taken in the costume he proposed wearing on his proposed trip, a suit that does not vary much from the style of dress so popular among baseball clubs. He recalled the fact that in the photograph, Lummis' pantaloons seemed to fit him unusually snug, so much so that the scribe had wondered whether their snugness would not interfere with the muscular exercise he was about to undertake. He acknowledged to the ex-cow-boy that he had observed these facts whereupon the ex-cow-boy again broke out with a peal of laughter, and again fell over the store-box, as he remarked:

"I was just—I was just—I was just thinking what a picnic those fellows out on the plains would have with the seat of Lummis' breeches. Did you ever see one of 'em handle a bull-whip? Never did? Why, I tell you one of those fellows can stand off a distance of twenty feet and take those breeches off Lummy with one stroke of his bull-whip, just as nicely as he can take them off himself, when he says his 'Now I lay me,' etc. They would probably do it a little quicker and not so tenderly, but they would do it just as well. Why, they will have more fun with the seat of Lummy's pants than they have had before for a year. I don't think he will wear the suit clear through the trip, and the ex-cow-boy again dropped over the store-box."

Nebraska, Indiana
Monday, September 15th, 1884

When 6 A.M. finds me elsewhere than in my virtuous couch, be sure something remarkable turned me out from the aforesaid v.c. That sweet sleep which glues down the lids during the two or three hours after sunrise, is worth all the rest of the night's repose, and I lose it only on compulsion. To remark that any other Chillicothean breakfasted at the Warner House at six o'clock, last Thursday morning might not be at all surprising; but that the nine o'clock boarder should be in his seat at that unearthly hour, meant more. It meant indeed, that I was about to sever the pleasant relations of two years and a half; to say a

long good-bye to the hospitable and home-like Ancient Metropolis, and to the many cordial friends I had found within its
borders. A roving disposition does not always carry with it an
inability for strong attachments. I am the poorest hand in the
world to forget friends; and Chillicothe has established more
claims on my remembrance than any other place of so short
acquaintance.

It was, then, with many a backward glance and genuine re-
gret that I stood upon the platform of Charlie Howard's train,
that morning and watched the dear old city fade back into the
distance. Still, I had good company, and that made things more
cheerful. Chillicotheans George Smith, Hon. Wm. H. Reed and
S. E. Mosher helped to dispel the tedium of a four hours railroad
ride—not to mention friend Juneman's nine-inch cigar, from
which I sucked solace during nearly the whole trip.

Reaching Cincinnati, I expressed my baggage on to Lawrenceburg, laid in a few necessary supplies, and prepared to loaf
away the long afternoon. By unexpected good luck I ran across
Fleetwood Ward on Fifth street, and jumped at his proposition
to go down to his club boat-house a little later. At four we
pranced up the river about a mile and found the boat-house, a
floater. Joe Miller, who needs no introduction to Chillicotheans, was down there in a sleeveless undershirt, chopped-off
pants and canvas slippers. Joe has the sculling fever in the worst
form, and is shooting a slender shell up and down the river
about half the time. We had a good spin in a two-oared working
boat, Ward and a friend on the slides, and myself as coxswain.
Then came a grand swim, a launch of pretzels and pop, and a
long stroll about the city, a good-bye to my companions, and off
to bed.

The Chillicothe *Leader* of Saturday, September 27, included a
short article concerning Lummis' visit to Cincinnati. A Chillicothe friend of Lummis, Fleetwood Ward, told the newspaper
that he and Lummis had visited Schumann's, "a large refresh-

ment saloon . . . which was frequented by the active, energetic business men of the city in the evenings, they having become hot and thirsty following their feverish pursuits."

"When Lummis came down," said Mr. Ward, "I naturally wanted to show him due courtesy, and so I took him out rowing in my boat, in the day time, and in the evening I walked him down to Schumann's. Now while it is true," explained Mr. Ward,

that Schumann's is largely patronized by the intelligent, refined, and cultured classes of society, yet it is also true that America is a great country, and within its domains no barriers of caste are permitted to exist, especially in a public refreshment apartment like Schumann's; therefore it happens, that at Schumann's, one is compelled to encounter all classes of society. Mr. Lummis and I moved among the vast crowd which thronged the hall, until we found a desirable table, when we sat down and ordered a couple of bottles of the essence of Gambrinus. As the waiter moved off to fill the order, I observed that he was attracted by my friend Lummis' novel appearance, he having refused to doff his handsome and unique walking suit, for the evening stroll. On his way to the beer faucet, the waiter turned repeatedly and looked admiringly back, and every few steps would stoop and whisper to some guest with whom he was acquainted, evidently calling attention to my friend Lummis' appearance. The result was that in a few moments our table became the center of attraction, and young and elderly men passed and repassed, gazing with undisguised admiration at Lummis' white flannel shirt, artistically tied at the neck with a blue ribbon, and at the parti-colored stockings which adorned his symmetrically shaped calves. Finally the agony became too intense, and after a moment's whispered consulation with his associates, a youthful looking Plug Ugly, with one shoulder about two inches higher than its mate, his arms loosely hanging straight down from the shoulder joint, his chin protruded, and a prize-fighter's curl to the upper lip, emerged from the crowd and with a 'be-Jesus' swagger, te[e]tered up to the table where Ward and Lummis were sitting, and leaning affectionately over the latter, thrust his face within a couple of inches of the pedestrian's, and remarked in an affectionate soprano voice:

'Say, ole fel, what nine do ye b'long to, any way?'

'Me? I don't belong to any nine,' replied Lummis, looking up inquiringly at his interlocutor.

'Yer don't, why I thought ye did,' and the young gentleman with an amiable countenance and soprano voice ambled back to his friends to report the result of his investigation.

'Can it be,' thoughtfully inquired Mr. Ward of the pedestrian, as the waiter sat the beer on the table, 'that you are going to walk clear to Los Angeles, only to acquire the reputation of a professional base ball player?'

It was 9 o'clock Friday morning when I turned my back on Cincinnati, and started down Sixth street, and thence out upon the dusty "river road" toward Lawrenceburg. Down the valley of the broad Ohio the traveler's path is a charming one. The rounded hills, the wide valley, the fertile bottoms rustling with yellow corn, the deep forests and the shimmering river are his companions. There are fine residences along the western banks for ten miles out from the city. Some of them are almost palatial. The little towns lower down on the hills are less attractive. All bear the scars of the great flood of '84 which stood chin-deep in most of their buildings. I passed through ten of these hamlets before reaching North Bend, where the pike—which has thus far followed closely the tracks of the O. & M. [Ohio and Mississippi] and the C. I. St. L. & C. railroads [Cleveland, Indianapolis, St. Louis and Chicago R.R.]—takes off on a sudden freak and loses itself in the hills to the west. Here I took the O. & M. track, and began, "pounding the ties" westward. There was nothing notable along the rest of the way, save the heat, which touched the limit. The whole wide valley, from hill to hill, is in corn—the only decent corn I have seen since I started.

I reached Lawrenceburg [Indiana] at four o'clock—having walked 27 miles in all since rising—and ambled up to a bench under the depot porch. As I sat there, talking to a little knot of natives, a good-looking young blonde fellow came around the corner and chipped in. It was John Howard, an old Chillicothe

boy, now agent of the O. & M. at this point. He has been
stationed here for about six months, and likes his surroundings.
John has accumulated a wife and three young Howards, and
looks as if domesticity and life in general agreed with him. E. C.
Frederick, a nephew of Capt. Michael Kirsch, has a restaurant
next door to the depot, and appears to be flourishing there.

I left Lawrenceburg at 8:40 Saturday morning and stumped it
down the track to Aurora, four miles below. Here the placid
river makes a sharp turn to the south, and parts company with
my route. Aurora is a little ribbon of a town, lying along the
upper angle of the bend. It does not reach back from the river far
in any direction but sticks closely to the above, resembling in
its shape nothing so much as a boomerang. They make good
nails and poor beer there.

At the depot, I met a mendacious child from Belial, for whom
I invoke perpetual corns. In answer to my queries, he told me
that there was a good pike to Milan, and that it was only a mile
farther than by rail. He also pointed out this desirable highway,
so that I might make no mistake. May he never take a painless
step! I branched brashly out upon that pike. I labored with it;
wrestled with it; tumbled over its rugged stones, and climbed
its interminable hills. The farther it went, the less it seemed to
approach Milan. Finally it petered out into a dirt road, which I
plodded over for several dusty hours. After a day, nearly, I asked
an honest granger how near Milan was. He cheered me by
remarking that if I would take the next crossroad and walk
seven miles north, I'd reach Milan. The road I was now on went
to Versailles. Well, I finally got to Milan, having walked 23
miles to get ahead 21. I didn't care so much about the distance,
but it made me hot to think of that doddering imbecile at
Aurora, who had thus imposed upon my confidence and my
corns.

Up at Cincinnati, Thursday afternoon, I sprained my left
ankle pretty badly. It didn't bother me much for a day or two,
but steady walking upon it began to develop the well-known
cursedness of a strain, and by Sunday afternoon I was pretty well
crippled. Then the extra responsibility thrown on the other

ankle made it rebel also, and my present gait is "half alligator and half hoss." I may add, too, that the walking is not prime. The earth is baked hard, and hot and "green" feet blister readily. Then, too, this road was not ballasted with proper consideration for tramps. The ballast is of course pebbles, from one to three inches in diameter, and if anyone thinks that it is easy to walk on, let him try 20 miles of it. Still, the dirt roads are too vacillating for me. They go about two miles around for every one ahead, and I am done with them for now. The detours of walking are big, too. I have walked 91 miles now, and still am but 83 from Cincinnati, in a straight line. But the weather is good, the air is sweet, and the Chillicothe wanderer plods cheerfully onward.

LUM

Vincennes, Indiana
Saturday, September 20th, 1884

When I left the *Leader* at Nebraska [Indiana], a little hump of houses that look now 5,000 miles off, luck looked a little cross-eyed at me. I am glad to record, however, that the unreliable jade has been duly affected by conscientious snubbing, and now hangs with both arms about my neck. It doesn't do to court her; but if you are indifferent, she can't keep away from you. This proves her right to be reckoned a feminine. Where she got in her work in my case was on the feet. This walking on ground baked hard and hot is a good deal like the old ordeal of pedestrianizing over red-hot plough-shares, with the deal decidedly in favor of the ploughs. But with such troubles as sore feet, the wise tramp never dallies. If you give up to them, they will always be sore.

> Tender-handed stroke the nettle
> And it stings you for your pains,
> Grasp it like a man of metal,
> And it soft as silk remains.
> [Aaron Hill, *Verses Written on a Window in Scotland*]

When walking on nettles the same treatment applies.

So, though a thriving blister embellished the top of each little toe, and two lame ankles creak off at every step, I girded up my loins as soon as that letter was written, and prepared for a long pull, that should make or break my feet. There was no town on the little distance slip I carry which seemed to me an attractive resting place, short of Seymour, and that was 25 miles ahead. I had already walked four, and knew it would be a hard pull to get through, thus crippled, but one can do almost anything if the will is there. Buckling down to the middle of the track, to save every foot, I hobbled along with increasing ease, finally rising nearly to comfort. There was very little along the way worthy of remark.

Seymour is a dull-looking, wooden town of 4,800 people, but it looked fine as silk to me when I crawled in that afternoon. "E. Bruce Sprague, Seymour, Ind.," was one of the entries in my route-book, and he was the object of my first query. I walked around to a neat cottage, not far from the railroad, and found "Bruce" getting on his brass-mounted gear for a trip, having been ordered off to Louisville to take the place of a sick brother-conductor. We had a pleasant chat while he wrestled with his clean linen, and I met his wife, (nee Hamelbach) also a Chillicothean. Bruce has been out here for fourteen years, and is enjoying his life as a passenger conductor between Vincennes and Cincinnati. His brother, George, is also located here. I walked over to the depot with Mr. S., and talked Chillicothe to him until his train rolled in. He threatens a descent on the old home, this fall. While the train was standing there, a stentorian voice from a forward car yelled out my name. It was George Clough, on his way to the Ancient Met. on a visit. A little later, I met Mike Lanton, who was for six years an M. & C. brakeman, living in Chillicothe. He is now twisting the wheel on the Air-Line, with headquarters at New Albany.

Politics in Seymour are hot. The Republicans have a huge wigwam, and are booming things. A large number of old-line Democrats are off on the tariff, and will vote for Blaine. There are eighty such in two townships of this county, who have burned their bridges behind them.

I left Seymour at 9 o'clock, Tuesday morning, and paddled out upon the dirt road. Pikes petered out long ago, and the "dirt" is my only alternative from the railroad. This one lasted but three miles, and then I returned to the track. From Nebraska to Seymour it was rank enough—largely ballasted with coarse limestone—but thence to Medora things were better. At Shields' Mills I struck the White River, and had a good swim, not to mention a big string of fair-sized channel cats, caught from the broken dam. I threw away nearly half the day fishing here, and was horrified to find that I could get no food. All the people were hard pushed to feed themselves. It was 11 miles to the next hotel town, and I expected to starve before getting there. I guess there must be a special clerk up aloft to look out for tramps, however, for about five miles from the Mill, I struck a 10 acre watermelon patch, with the house at the farther corner. I got a melon pretty near as big as a beer keg under each arm, and lit out, with an aged granger shaking his fist in the safe distance. If I had stopped to settle with him, he might have been hasty enough to kill me with shot before I could explain my desire to pay, so I went on. Under a fine beech, not far beyond, I camped with those melons, and later, we all three got up together—a little condensed, it is true. N'yum-n'yum, but they were good.

I had to make a mile and a-half detour at Vallonia, to get my mail, and then pressed on to Medora, where I passed the night with mighty clever people. The little town has 42 voters and thirty-eight hickory poles wave the Cleveland colors from its street corners. There would have been 42 but the poles gave out. Here I made my first acquaintance with the Indiana bugs. There is no doubt about their politics—all are moss-backers, and hungry for spoils. I got no sleep till about three o'clock, when I butchered a small army of them with my hunting knife. Bugs are not a polite topic, I know, but they bite polite persons just as quick as boors, so I shall let this reference to them go.

At Fort Ritner I met an aged watchman, who left his home in the State of Wooden Nutmegs fifty years ago, and has been in this lonely spot half that time. He was enchanted to meet a Yankee, and walked a mile with me, talking with sad affection of his old New England home. Beyond Tunnelton there are several hundred acres of watermelon patches, and I had what the kids denominate "a pudding." From there on, the valley grows narrower, and less attractive, and I was glad to reach Mitchell, the point of junction with the Louisville, New Albany & Chicago R.R.

I got away Thursday morning, September 18, and soon struck snags and the misery began. Imagine a big black-snake with the jim-jams, and you have a faint conception of the next 13 miles on the O. & M. road. It makes three or four pot-hooks to the half-mile, and wouldn't go straight ahead for money. It is the crookedest thing I ever ran across, except, perhaps, Grover Cleveland's private record. Furthermore, it is all rock-ballasted, nearly, and with no little tow-path at the side as a refuge. Down in crooked little Beaver creek, which rivals the sinuosities of the track, I caught a dozen half-pound black bass—real black bass, with big mouths, red eyes and locust-thorn fins.

I believe I am carrying as many h's as the law requires, but somehow, every last soul takes me for a blasted Britisher, to my vast disgust. Perhaps my sun-struck complexion is more torrid and Titianesque than they are used to seeing in this malaria-haunted State. The Irish all look upon me with suspicion, and it takes a deal of talking before I can get them down to a friendly confab of politics. Thank heaven, there are no dynamiters thus far West.

I stayed at Washington, last night, and came on to Vincennes to-day—two hard trips over rough track. As I reached town this afternoon, I saw them carrying a dead engineer to his home. The Calendar grist mill boiler had just exploded, wrecking the mill, and tearing him to shreds.

My jaunts since the last letter, have been as follows: Monday, Holton to Seymour, 29 miles, walked 31; Tuesday, to Medora,

19, walked 19; Wednesday, to Mitchell, 21, walked 25½; Thursday, to Shoals, 23, walked 25½; Friday, to Washington, 22, walked 27½; Saturday, to Vincennes, 20; walked 25. I am now 119 miles from Cincinnati, and 147 from St. Louis, which I hope to reach Sept. 28th. All right up to the present time.

LUM

This letter from John Herlihy appeared in the *Leader* at the end of Lummis' letter from Vincennes, Indiana, September 20, 1884.

Charley Lummis is arousing the natives along his line of march to California to an intense pitch of curious excitement. Mr. John Herlihy, an old Chillicothe boy, and one of the most accomplished athletes developed by the town, writes the *Leader* from Seymour, Indiana, saying that Lummy's passage through that city, just tore up the burg. Six hundred or more people witnessed his entrance into the town, and since his departure, he has been the leading topic of conversation. Herlihy says Lummis was in fine condition, but was looking "awful white, and raised a whirl of excitement." Herlihy is employed in the O. & M. railroad shops at Seymour.

St. Louis, Missouri
Sunday, September 28th, 1884

If that strip of Indiana skirting the line of the O. & M. may be taken as a fair index of the whole, I feel a lively faith that the Republicans will carry the Hoosier State this fall. I talked along the way with everyone accessible: Republican, Democrats, Green backers, Butler men and disciples of St. John; farmers, railroaders, section-hands, merchants, mechanics and editors, and nearly all the straws are blowing in a way to please me. The personal character of the rival candidates excites little interest among these people, and is little discussed. They are concerned

only with the principles behind these men, and of those principles the tariff's almost the sole one at issue. The bosses may
toot as they will, but the people at large do not let go of the idea
that a vote for Blaine means protection to American industries,
and that a vote for Cleveland endorses free trade. The farmers
lean to the latter policy with natural short-sightedness, but the
workingmen, the laborers in almost every branch of industry,
are stiff-necked in their support of protection. This tariff business is costing the Democrats a handsome little bunch of old
allies in every township, and will probably turn the balance of
power against them in the State.

I find, too, that the Irish distrust of Cleveland is rather remarkably strong in Indiana, and will count up big at the poles.
Lawrence is the only county I struck which has a Republican
majority at once large and reliable; but nearly all the towns are
already on the right side, and will be more so than ever in
November. Democrats all along my way have admitted to me a
strong fear that they will lose Indiana. None of them care a skip
for Cleveland, and their work is far less animated and cheerful
than that of the Republicans, who are carrying things with a
whoop.

Once more under way, a half mile took me from the Union
Depot Hotel—of which I shall always cherish palatable memo-
ries—across the iron railroad bridge which spans the muddy
Wabash, and I was glad to feel under my feet once more solid
Republican soil.

For three or four miles there are various faint attempts at
hills; but thenceforward you might almost see across to St.
Louis, for there begin the prairies. I have always felt a weary void
because I had never seen a "purayra"—as the Suckers themselves call it. Well, it took about one hour to fill that aforesaid
void as full as a tick, and leave some fullness to dribble over the
sides. Flat? Yes, verily, flatter than a dude, flatter than a Democratic national platform, flatter than some jokes which mod-
esty forbids me to name. Now and then you strike a little rolling
country; but most of the way from Lawrenceville to East St.

Louis the level is so dead that the funeral should have taken place long ago. The flatness hangs over at the edges. I would have given the heel off one of my shoes to see a good old scraggy New England hill dumped down in the middle of that howling, area of monotony. When the Almighty had baked the rest of the earth's crust into biscuits, doughnuts and loaves of various form, He evidently took down His big rolling pin from the shelf of the celestial pantry, and took the still unbaked dough of Illinois to roll out pie-crust. For that matter, I don't believe He ever put it in the oven at all. If you could see some of the mud I struck between Noble and Odin, you'd doubt about the baking, too.

The land is somewhat feeble, furthermore. On top it is far from bad looking; but its fertile depth is very slight. Anywhere from six to twenty inches down, you come to a burglar-proof clay, hard and impermeable as iron. So the little soil above is either all mud or all dust. Almost all across the State the drouth has marched with withering tread, and its track is broad, brown, and bare.

Farmhouses have been my chief reliance across Illinois, for the stations are so far apart that it is often hard to make the distances fit in right. The beds are generally as hard as husks know how to be, but clean enough, if one be not too dudishly fastidious. Bread and milk is about the only procurable "chuck" there that I can eat, for the general cooking is something to give even an ostrich the nightmare. Everything is solid Republican all the way through, and a Democrat is as hard to find as a good cigar. The Demmies are not making any such fight in this Republican stronghold as the Republicans are making in Democratic Indiana, either. They haven't the "sand" to play so up-hill a game. So I have had little incitement to stop and canvass the situation, but with elevated nose have pranced along as fast as the brevity of my hind legs would allow.

I worked in a pretty fair joke on an old granger, near Iuka, Monday. He was very inquisitive about my business, and swallowed everything offered. In answer to a question as to whether

I didn't get pretty tired, I said that one of my legs did, but the cork one never gave out. "Now, you hain't got no cork leg, stranger, hev ye?" said he, in amazement, and with lifted hands. "Why, cert'nly. Just feel o' that, " said I, poking my left leg where he could pinch it, with the muscles at full tension. There isn't much dough about the leg, and he evidently never pinched flesh quite so hard. Then he felt of the other leg, whose muscles were relaxed, and gave in at once. "Dog on me, if t'ain't. But you're the fus' darn man ever I seed plunkin' along that-a-way on a cork leg." And he hobbled off on his own rheumatic pegs, to tell the neighbors about the cork-legged dude that was walkin' to Californy.

After all the flatness and the drouth; the alternate mud and dust; the hot sun and the long walking, I was glad enough when far off on the Western horizon I saw the smoke that broods over a great city, and knew that I was nearing St. Louis. There were cool clouds and brisk breezes in place of the hot glare of the earlier week, and it was with genuine enjoyment that I swung fast along through the shanty kingdom of East St. Louis, past its thousands of side-tracked cars, and its scores of sidetracks, and up on the great double railroad and wagon bridge which wades, with giant legs of granite, across the Father of Waters. A wonderful bridge is that, and the view from it is worth many a mile's jaunt. Behind lies East St. Louis, that ugly, flat jumble of grain elevators, freight cars and hovels, and one of the "hardest" places on the continent. North and South, with calm and coffee-colored tide, flows the greatest river in this big world. West, on a high and rolling bluff, the spires and towers, the roofs and domes of St. Louis break the smoky horizon in Whistleresque confusion of form and color. The shriek of bustling tugs; the dull droning of the big steamers; the rattle of wagons and the rumble of trains fill the air with discord, but the outlook half excuses that. It is a scene neither beautiful nor grand, but it is striking.

As for St. Louis itself, apart from such of its matrimonial probabilities as interest Chillicotheans, I have been running over it assiduously, but must reserve further notice for another letter. Suffice it that I am here, 341 miles from Cincinnati, in better whack than when I started, and that I have thus far contrived to keep out of both the morgue and the workhouse. And so, *auf Wiedersehen.*

LUM

Kansas City, Missouri
Saturday, October 4th, 1884

On Wednesday [October 1] I slid into Sedalia, [Missouri], not feeling at all tired, but with a frightful headache from the heat, and my clothes wringing wet with perspiration. I got supper, saw the town ten minutes' worth, and rolled into bed for an early start next morning. But I reckoned without my bill. The room into which they stuck me was damp and mephitic as a tomb. Rats scampered through the broken walls, and mosquitos sang arias from Wagner over the barless bed. I cut a hole in the sheet to breathe through, and pulled it over my head. That froze out the mosquitos, but ingenuity couldn't circumvent their yet more devilish allies, the bugs. I rolled and groaned and scratched and fought and—well, call it prayed; that sounds well—for two mortal hours, my head splitting and my temper growing cyclonic. Then in a rage I arose, fired the bedding out the window, dressed, ate the rest of my lunch and started off. The night was glorius—swept with a soft breeze and lighted by a moon not yet a circle, but like the convivial son of Erin, "just full enough to be comfortable like." Anything was better than that inquisatorial bed in that accursed morgue of a room and I felt really light-hearted as I hurried up the track. All night long, till the kindly moon went down behind the low hills, "leaving the world to darkness and to me," I pushed along very rapidly. Then a sweet and well-earned nap bridged me over the waiting for day's first faint streaks, and the march began again.

A few miles west of Warrensburg, that morning, I had my first real, all-wool adventure. As I passed a comfortable little house near the track, a huge black dog of the mastiff-hound persuasion, leaped the hedge and came at me in a way that meant business only. You can generally tell when a dog is monkeying just to hear himself bark. He was not on that track, but after gore with a ten-line G. He was as large and genial looking as Mr. Dufeu's familiar pet, but with more appetite for live meat. I trust it is no disgrace to admit that my heart turned three or four back somersaults when he dashed at me. I have seen two cases of hydrophobia from the bite of dogs not known to be mad, and an ugly canine has no attraction to me. But there was no way of retreat, and the maniac had to be faced. As he jumped at my throat I put out my stick, which he caught in his big jaws, and then with a desperate image I drove my big hunting knife to the hilt up through his throat and brain. It is a very pretty toy, by the way, that knife. Eight inches of keen, double-edged steel from the forge at Wortemholm, with a murderous point and a stout handle of buck horn. I got it at Kittredge's, and have found it invaluable for plugging watermelons, cutting fish poles, and the like, and as for defense—well, if you have telephonic connection with the spirit world as the enterprising *Leader* must surely have, just ask that dog. I had a good revolver in my pocket, but the house was too near—no knowing how many buckshot there might be in their double-barrel, and folks hate to lose a dog like that.

I wished to see a gentleman at Holden, 8 miles beyond Centerview—Mr. D. L. Albin—but when I got there it was only to find that he had moved, no one knew whither. The town was in the agonies of a fair; all the hotels had three in a bed, or thereabouts, and I was fain to push on three miles, where a little Dutch farm-house afforded a good bed wherein a glorious sleep rewarded the day's labor of 46 miles. The difference between these long distances and the short ones of my first week will give you an idea of the effect of a little training even on one in so good condition as your humble servant was at starting. The

chief gain has been in the condition of my feet. For the first 8
days they made it painful for me to walk 20 miles; but now they
are to the touch like a side of a sole-leather, and entirely devoid
of feeling. My ankles, too, are wonderfully toughened, and it
seems impossible to sprain them. I think they have increased at
least half an inch in girth since I started—the low-cut shoes
have given them a vast amount of extra work. I have also inven-
ted a new gait, which is a streak. By skipping every other tie I
can make within a tiny fraction of five miles an hour—Wednesday I did 30 miles of it in 6 hours and 21 minutes—and keep it
up a long time. It is not a square walk, but half run, half hop,
rather tiresome, but not so much so as you would fancy.

Let me tell you how a couple of tramps held me up, yesterday,
between Kingsville and Pleasant Hill [Missouri]. I was ploughing along in the pleasant morning air when two as tough cases
as you ever saw, met me. Either one had 40 pounds the better of
me, and they didn't think it worth while to even take a club at
so small a cuss. The biggest one walked up to me with the
remark, "Say, young feller, yer can't pack all thet plunder alone.
Lemme take it fur you," grasping at my coat. "Well," I said, "I
haven't much, but what there is your mighty welcome to—"
and I gave it to him. The weapons were handy, but he was
standing so insolently close, so loose upon his pins, that flesh
and blood couldn't resist the temptation. What he got was a
liberal left-handed "lead" between the eyes, followed by a right-
hander plumb on his under jaw. His heels caught on the rail, and
down he went like beans in Boston. Then the knife shining in
my hand, I told the other fellow if he had any business to hurry
up, because I wanted to poke along. It was sore ribs to see them
go down that track hot-footed. They couldn't get away too fast,
and looked comical enough with their rags fluttering straight
behind them. There was no danger in the encounter, for I was
fully armed and they were not, but it lent spice to the journey,
and may be mentioned as one of my opening experiences with
hard cases.

I wish to misery, I could find some water somewhere fit to

drink. All across the 283 miles of Missouri I have struck but one
spring and seen but five wells. Everyone relies on rain-water
caught in big underground cisterns, and there are few big wells
at all. But with that exception, and its bitter Democracy, Missouri is one of the finest States I ever saw—

> Where every prospect, pleases,
> And only man is vile.
> [Reginald Heber, *Hymns. Missionary Hymn*]

I shall start out again to-morrow—or rather to-day—if I get
to bed any time, which I believe might well be done now,
leaving a little guff about Kansas City for my next. I am now 724
miles from Chillicothe, 622 from Cincinnati, and have walked
in all 701.

LUM

Bavaria, Kansas
Friday, October 10th, 1884

For 220 miles of the K.P.R.R. [Kansas Pacific Railroad] runs
with few infidelities beside the wide, unruffled Kansas river—
or, as the natives call it, by some Japanese jugglery of abbrevia-
tion, the Kaw. So I had a very pleasant journey Monday morning, through the wide, black bottom farms, catching frequent
and beautiful views of the quiet stream.

It was half-past six, Monday, October 6, when I ambled into
North Lawrence [Kansas], crossed the Kaw to the town, proper,
and began to hunt up some readers of the LEADER, who had long
before written, inviting me to call on them. We had a long talk
together, ran over the long list of mutual friends in Chillicothe,
and I finally went to bed—a rest not unwelcome after my day's
total tramp of 41 miles.

Tuesday morning I should have been off, but the boys
wouldn't hear of it, and they set out to show me the town.

Lawrence has about 12,000 inhabitants, and is growing like the beanstalk of Jack the giant killer. It has a marvelous water power from the Kaw, which is not eternally, but substantially d--d here; (force of habit, contracted on the *Gazette,* prevents me from writing this naughty-sounding word in full). This power, conveyed to town by cables, runs several huge grist-mills, a large barbed wire manufactory, foundries, chemical works, etc. The little city has the finest Blaine and Logan Flam-beau Club in the State, with seventy-five men—the leading young gentlemen of the place—in $15 uniforms for the privates, and $25 ones for the officers.

The Government has just completed a fine school for Indians here, similar to the institution at Carlisle, Pa, and this is barely getting under way about two miles south of the town. It is a most instructive place. The grounds are a half-mile wide, and one and a quarter miles long, mostly devoted to farming pur-poses, and admirably adapted thereto. The buildings are of stone, three in number, and generous in size and equipment. The dormitory is 100 × 60 feet and four stories high, with large, well-ventilated rooms, in each of which are from six to a dozen comfortable beds. The Superintendent also has his office and apartments in this building. Next stands the school-building, two stories high, and about 100 × 40 feet in dimensions. It is a model school-house, inside and out, and there are not too many Caucasian children who get their knowledge boxes filled in so attractive a place.

We visited some of the rooms, and I was astonished at the intent attention of these children of the forest. I never saw such orderly schoolrooms. The pupils range in age from 8 to 23 years, and are of both sexes. Many are stolid and dull-looking, but there are plenty of really bright faces, and the average is perhaps as good as in the ordinary white school. There are now 131 young Indians here, of whom half work upon the farm and about the buildings while the others go to school, the two divisions changing places every week. As to descent, the pupils come from Poncas, Pawnees, Pottawottomies—or correctly, Potte-

watemis—Arrapahoes, Cheyenes, Menomenies, Muncies and
Caddos, with one Apache. One hundred of them are boys, and
the rest girls.

You would be amused if you could hear the names of these
young savages. The native titles are entirely unpronounceable
by English-speaking jaws, but the English translations—by
which the pupils are now known exclusively—are ridiculous
enough. They are given a gratuitous christian name, to which is
appended a translation of their father's name. For instance, we
have Fred Eagle, Frank Buffalo, Joseph Fireshaker, and many
others. The funniest was Moses Bears-ears.

The whole institution is under the charge of James Marvin,
L.L.D., an educator of almost national reputation, and he shows
by deeds his faith that here lies the true solution of the vexed
and vexing "Indian Question." An industrial school will soon be
in operation in one of the buildings, and here the boys will
be taught to make shoes and bread, tin cups and pantaloons,
houses, furniture and other similarly practical things.

The school-room instruction is at present of the kindergarten
sort, as the pupils understand but few words of English. They all
wear modest garments made in full civilized fashion, and are
beginning to get over their first awkwardness in this unac-
customed toggery. It is wonderful how anxious these children
are to learn. The Indian is generally accredited with endless
laziness and stupidity in matters of school education, but after
this visit I find it hard to believe the slander. There was no
fidgeting about on the seats, no throwing of saliva globes, (as
Boston girls would say) no pulling of hair. Every eye was on the
teacher all the time, and every ear attentive. No, not every one.
The dullest-appearing boy in the room looked away for a couple
of minutes, but no more. A big, solemn buck on the very back
seat, arose, walked noiselessly up behind the offender, seized
his head on each side, shot it around to a "front face," and
walked gravely back to his bench without a word.

Thursday, certain signs of approaching wild country began to
meet me, and have been growing thicker ever since. I saw my

first prairie chickens a few miles out of Wamego, and just west of St. George, some game yet more thrilling. A small snake, two feet long, was basking sluggishly beside the track, and I prepared to jump on him with both feet, as I always do with snakes. Just in time, however, I noticed the "brown watch-chain" down his back, and jumped, not on him, but to the other side of the track, cut off his head with my knife, and looked him over at leisure. He was a young "rattler," with his first button just budding. His fangs were well developed, however, and it is quite as well that I didn't rub my thin-stockinged legs up to them. The budding button reposes in my pocket-book.

I came into Manhattan early in the morning, ate, and talked awhile with some of the editors. The whole country is full of Swedes and fine-blooded cattle—principally short-horns. Well-informed newspaper men there tell me that St. John will not get over 3,000 votes in his own State. I have been investigating this Prohibition question assiduously, for the sakes of my Second Amendment friends back in Ohio. They would find very little comfort in the truth, if it could be beaten into them. I am sorry to say, however, that Prohibitionists in general shy away from practical truth as if it were a XXX brand whisky.

Well, no intelligent man can go through this State—so widely paraded as the scene of successful prohibition—and fail to see that prohibition is a sorry farce. Now, I have been traversing the very best part of Kansas—200 miles of it—the richest, most fertile and most thickly settled section. It is against my principles, as well as my tastes, to touch stimulants when on an outdoor trip of any sort, where perfect training is indispensable to perfect enjoyment; but along here I have been somewhat sacrificing myself in the interests of science and truth. The *Leader's* many readers may depend upon my giving them facts as near the bottom as so brief a sojourner can get. Well, then, you can "get what you want" almost anywhere. Take Lawrence, the first place of importance on the K.P. It has less that 12,000 people, but you can get the ardent or the frothy in no less than 38 different places there. I had not been in the city two hours before

I had half a dozen invitations to liquor up. There was some pretty good "budge" there, too. You can get it in any hotel, and in many a sly back door. As it is in Lawrence, it is all along the line. I have found the stuff procurable in every town of over 500. I presume it is also to be had in these hamlets if you know the "ropes"—so they tell me, at least. But take it in Junction City, Abilene, Brookville, and these other places along westward, and the saloons are open and defiant. I have been content with a few drops and the truth, but could have drunk myself blind in a hundred places. That is the way prohibition prohibits in Kansas.

I may add that St. John is the most unpopular man in the State. Of several hundred men from all classes with whom I have talked, not one had a good word for him personally, though two prohibitionists say they will vote for him "for the good of the cause." He is regarded as a fifth-rate lawyer, not strictly reliable, and a sad incubus upon the States. He will not do any damage to the Republican vote, I feel fully assured.

Sunday night, come what will, I shall have walked a full 1,300 miles, though by direct rail some 80 miles less than that from Cincinnati. I shall strike straight for Denver, carrying my rifle from Wa Keeney, and expect to reach the former city Oct. 23rd. I will tell you in my next about the cowboys I saw at Junction City, Abilene and Salina. They are "hot stuff," but I still retain the knee-breeches, thank you, Mr. Wenis. It is a decidedly wild country here, and I could utilize the rifle pretty handily even now. I have averaged 40 and one half miles a day since Sunday, not counting that 24 mile fiasco, for the 5 and one fourths miles I made on a trial spurt in 20 hours Thursday, Thursday night and Friday morning, has pulled up the notch considerably. You see, it was made at a comparatively easy gait—fast walking with numerous rests. The people here and all along are as clever as they know how to be, and every town I pass in the day time has a flurry of pleasant excitement. The dogs sometimes flurry me, in those I pass at night. No more deaths, however. I shall strike antelope the first of the week. I am going to see, the first fine day, how far I can make in 24 hours, just for luck. I believe I can strike above 80. I will let you know, anyhow. Walking is the best I ever saw, and it is a perfect "snap." Send me good news from Ohio, Tuesday—the west is watching you.

LUM

First View, Colorado
Thursday, October 16th, 1884

Editors Leader:
If any hasty remarks in my third letter to the *Leader* appear to insinuate, even so remotely, that Illinois might possibly be deemed a stale, flat and unprofitable State, please assure the solid suckers that I was merely talking in my sleep. I am willing to make affidavit that their territory is paradise and their alleged prairies are in reality beetling cliffs and yawning gulfs. To my misguided eyes it did look a trifle monotonous as I stumped through; but that was before I had seen Kansas. I stand here on the top of a windmill and look over the horizon, which is flat and round as a recumbent cart wheel. See? Why I can see clear into the year after judgement! But though you can look over the edge of this terrestrial ball and see day-after-tomorrow crawling up on the underside, you can't see anything else. The bare, brown plains in their mats of buffalo grass, relieved here and there by little clumps of darker and taller blue-stem, comprise the whole world, so far as your senses can detect.

For ten miles before or behind, you can trace the long array of telegraph poles, growing shorter and shorter in the distance, and perhaps 20 miles away you catch the smoky outline of a range of embryo hills. No trees, no rocks, no nothing. Or rather, I should say, an immensity of nothing. There is enough nothing to build an ell on space. Here, too, silence not only reigns, it fairly pours. The occasional twitter of a snowbird; the shrill chirrup of the prairie dogs, and the rare purring cry of a flock of sandhill cranes (blue herons) are the only sounds you may hear in a whole day's journey—save the rumble of some distant train, audible ten or

twelve miles away. As for animated life, that is represented by
distant herds of cattle; by little ranch buildings far off under the
edge of some bank; by the white flash of a hasty jackrabbit, or
the Centaur figure of a cowboy prancing along the flanks of his
scattered herd. Illinois, here's looking at you. May your shadow
never grow less.

Friday, things began to grow more interesting, and new experiences crowded in upon me with delightful rapidity. All in one
short day I saw my first dog town, my first prairie chicken, my
first sage brush, buffalo grass, cactus and ranches. I reached
Brookville, the western extremity of Kaw Valley Division of the
K.P. about noon, but stopped only a few minutes. Pushed on to
Terra Cotta, a little hamlet of six or seven houses, and there
heard of a big sheep ranch, north-west of there, owned by a
Boston man. Here was a chance to gain much coveted information, and I hied me over there, arriving just before supper. Struck
the foreman, a muscular, keen-eyed but warm-hearted Scot,
who offered to keep me overnight with "the boys."

This little preliminary off my hands, an inspection of the
ranch was next in order, and a mighty interesting place it was.
Here Mr. E. W. Wellington, a wealthy young Bostonian, has a
domain of over 15,000 acres—purchased two years ago, for $7 an
acre. It is fine, rolling land, rather rich with plenty of water, a few
trees, and inexhaustible quarries of solid black sand stone. The
valleys and divides are mossed over with the buffalo grass—now
brown and curly, but still nourishing and highly relished by the
cattle. When Mr. Wellington bought this big range, there was not
a building on it save two little dug-outs. Now the structures are
worth probably $75,000. On the brow of a little divide near the
center of the ranche stands the residence—a stone mansion
which would not look out of place in the finest dwelling street in
any city.

Two hundred yards south, and lower on the hill, stands the
boarding-house for the men. It is about 40 × 20 feet, and very
conveniently arranged; kept by Mr. McDonald, the foreman,
and his wife, a bright-faced, matronly, little Englishwoman.

Then under the shelter of the hill are the barns and sheep corrals. The latter are two in number, about 200 feet long and 40 feet wide; built of stone, and solidly roofed, while big fences shut in about a half acre in front of each. There is a big wool-house, a fine stable, model hen-houses, blacksmith shops, etc., all the buildings being of stone and well made. Several wind-engines dump water from the valley into a big tank on the hill, whence it runs through pipes into all the buildings and en-closures.

We had a great supper in the boarding-house that evening. Beef pie baked in a half-bushel pan; fine bread and golden but-ter; good roast mutton, excellent coffee and prune pie—that was the bill of fare. After writing a few letters I joined the boys out on the porch, where they were grouped around a not too harmonious French harp. Then nothing would do but I must sing them a song; with a vision of a thumping if I refused, and of tar and feathers if I sang, I proceeded to assassinate a rollicking college song for them—the classic "Mush, Mush." Before the first verse was ended, with the threat to "tread on the tail of yer coat," the whole population of the ranche—save "the Boss"—was at my elbow. The women, children, the herders, the cow-punchers, the farm hands, they were all there, and all intent. When "Mush, Mush," was done it was "more! more!" and so we went on through "Michael Roy," "Menagerie," "Sally am de gal," and a score of others, until I could howl no longer.

They had rather classed me as a crank before, I fancy—for in this country a man who would rather walk than back a pony is incomprehensible—but those roughly-rendered songs changed everything, and thence forward they couldn't do too much for me. Indeed, it is not so strange, either. Take their little colony out there in solitude, far from all companionship, and you can imagine how welcome they find anything new.

Well, the "singing" over, it was time to adjourn to bed. The one lack of the ranche is a "bunk house," which will soon be erected however. In default of this, the hands sleep "just where it happens." One of them, who used to live in Columbus and work on the Pan Handle, piloted me to the big haymow in the stable, gave me two of his own blankets and got a third and made a most comfortable couch, where I slept the sleep of the just.

In the morning, after a hearty breakfast at the boarding house, I met Mr. Wellington—a slender, sinewy, keen-eyed gentleman of about 30. I found that he too was a Harvard man—class of '74. Upon this discovery of mutual ties, he trotted me up to his mansion and seduced me into a second breakfast—and a most toothsome one. His old parents and his young wife are now settled here, with every comfort at their command, and the circle has been completed by the recent arrival of a bouncing heir to the big estate. Old Mr. Wellington showed me a cabinet of fossil leaves he had picked up in the neighboring sandstone quarries and "brought out" with infinite care. They are all of the cretaceous period, and I was astonished at their marvelous excellence. There is not a museum in the country which can match them. Huge leaves, ten or twelve inches across, are there in absolute perfection, even down to the delicate veins.

The younger Wellington showed me over the place still more thoroughly, pointing with pride to his black and gigantic polled Angus bulls, his little herd of registered Jerseys, his mouse-colored Swiss cows, and his 400 royal bucks—100 of the latter being worth $20,000. He has in all 8,000 head of fine sheep, 300 blooded cattle, 40 horses and 35 men on his ranche. The whole concern stands him at about $300,000. You might forget that this little colony lay in an almost wild country, as you looked over its elegant appointments; but the fact would come back to you before very long. To climb to the top of a divide and scan a landscape of 40 miles radius without seeing half a dozen houses, would be convincing; but still more so to sit out in the hush of early night and hear the doleful howling and petulant snarling of the coyotes among the hills. The very night I slept there, one of these ravenous but cowardly beasts jumped into the corral not 50 feet from me, and killed a choice ewe. Mr. Wellington is

terribly annoyed by these animals, and has a standing offer out
of $15 for every two scalps. With the county bounty and the
value of the pelts, this would net a man $21 for two shots, but
the hands work too hard by day to care about lying out at night
for coyotes. They are therefore content with tying up the dogs
and scattering poisoned meat liberally over the ranche.

It amuses one fresh from the heavily timbered East to see the
dodges to which people are driven in this treeless land. I suppose Mr. Wellington, for instance, has 30 miles of wire fences
on his ranche. The posts are of cedar, imported from Michigan,
and set about 100 feet apart. To stiffen up the wires between
these are tiny stakes, no larger than walking-sticks, driven into
the ground and then nailed to the wires. The posts themselves
are only 2 or 3 inches in diameter. Soft pine timber there is
worth $35 per M., and the southern pine $55. The wood that is
wasted in Ross county every year would make a man independently rich if he had it out here.

As for winds, Kansas has already established an unenviable
reputation. Over these bare, unbroken and unsheltered plains,
all the air there is sweeps at will. What is here an every-day
breeze would make all Chillecothe hunt for a cellar, and as for
their cyclones—well, you know about them without my inter-
ference.

I got away in very good season from the hospitality of Monte
Carneiro ranche, and proceeded to Ellsworth, here getting back
to my old love, the railroad. Here, too, I met my first all-wool-
and-a-yard-wide cowboy—those back at Junction City and Abilene being merely second-class stock. He calls himself Antelope Bill, and looks as if he might be a pretty hard Bill to settle.
Six-feet-two in his bare feet, and an inch and a half taller in his
number six boots—cowboys don't have very big feet, by the
way, as they hardly ever walk—broad shouldered and brawny,
he would catch your attention and hold it in any crowd. He is a
decidedly handsome fellow, dark as an Indian, but with good,
clean-cut Saxon features and a flashing, devil-may-care black

eye. His right hand has but half its complement of fingers, the others having eloped with a hot-headed chunk of lead, forty-five one-hundredths of an inch in diameter.

But his dress was the center of my admiration. Talk about your dudes in the East—and you will hardly find a thoroughbred west of Philadelphia—why, they don't know the a, b, c of dandyism! If you would see the most finical fop in the country, seek out a western cowboy dressed for a visit to town. Perhaps you would like a pen picture of his gorgeous array? Well, upon his coal-black hair, of course, rests the fawn-colored sombrero. Its crown is high and creased down the middle, while the rim is 8 inches wide and flops up-side down in the passing breeze. A highly ornamented band of fine russett leather, three inches wide, is buckled around the crown to hold it tight to the head, and a small strap hangs to the nape of the neck, as a windward anchor when Bill turns his broad back to the blasts. That hat cost him $20, and is made of the finest beaver. A soft buckskin shirt shows under his open coat, which is of dogskin, lined with wool—water-proof, wind-proof and always soft. His breeches are of the same material, but have a dado of bead work along the welt seam. They are tucked into the tops of costly, oil-tanned boots, which reach fully to the knee. Last, but far from least, are the appendages to the boots, and fully as important in his esteem as the boots themselves—his spurs. These are about the diameter of a silver dollar, and are also of solid silver, beautifully made. The rowells are an inch long, and sharp as daggers. As he tersely said, he could "rip the liver out 'n any d--n hoss with 'em." A tiny-silver bell hung to each spur, and tingled pleasantly as he walked. Nor should I omit to state that from his belt depended a pair of Colt's six-chambered arguments; each as long as a country sermon. Bill was a very clever fellow, withal, though at first inclined to make remarks about my extremities. When he learned my destination, however, he was affability itself, and gave me some very useful pointers about my route. He was familiar with nearly all of it, having "punched cows" all through there. A couple of minutes after I left him, he was on his cow-pony, loping off across the plain.

At Hays City, a comical little town next east of Ellis, I picked up a novel chum. He was a *bona fide* cowboy, who had been "bucking the tiger" [playing the gambling game, faro] there in sorry luck. He had gambled away his money, his pistols, and even his pony, and didn't know which way to turn. A brother in Wallace would "stake" him, he reckoned, if he could only get there. I proposed that he tramp it with me. Nothing could have been more distasteful to this man, who would rather ride an unbroken pony a day than walk a mile, but he seemed to "cotton to" me, and finally assented. So he shared my bed and board for 131 miles. He had come from Caldwell, where they had a pleasant little bull-fight, a week ago last Sunday, and was evidently fresh from pretty tough companionship. But I found him good-hearted, sociable, lenient toward my ignorance in matters where his own knowledge was strong, and altogether a decidedly spicy and agreeable comrade. It was death to him to keep up with my present fast gait, but he was game to the ends of his toes, and hobbled along pluckily in those heavy boots, until I felt ashamed and slowed up for him. We traveled on up to Wa Keeney, whither I had sent my rifle from Kansas City, and bunked at a little hotel which is a marvel of cleanliness for this uncleanly country. I found my cowboy a regular directory, and learned "more than a few" from his pithy discourses.

Naturally, in this unwooded waste, the natives have to depend on stone for most of their buildings, and things seem to have been specially arranged for their accommodation. The divides are full of stone, which is white, and easily quarried. When first taken out, it is nearly as soft as crayon chalk, and they cut it into blocks with an ordinary whip saw. After a few months of exposure, however, the rock becomes hard as fine limestone, and makes remarkably good houses and barns.

We left Wa Keeney three hours before sunrise, Monday, and enjoyed the cool, clear air of the early day immensely. As for the

sunrise itself, seen on these plains, it is nearly as fine as when
viewed at sea. Indeed one feels rather at sea as he looks out over
this strange country. Fun with the rifle began now, too. I had
seen the "villages" of those curious, saucy little rodents, the
prairie dogs, and had watched the frisky villagers as they bobbed
about on top of their mansard roofs. But, now, five miles west of
Wa Keeney, I had my first chance to see one at close quarters. It
was no easy job, however, to get a specimen. I shot three through
and through, but though the heavy bullet tore them almost in
halves, and rolled them over three or four times, they invariably
crawled into their holes before I could reach them. The fourth,
however, was somewhat dazed, and didn't know which way to
go. The ball struck his spine, cutting it off at the loins, and
knocking him at least five feet from his burrow, yet, so remarkable is the vitality of these delicate-looking little fellows, that
he crawled over 40 feet with his forelegs, and would have been
in another hole if I hadn't overtaken him.

The prairie dog—which is as unlike a dog as a rat is—is half
as large again as a fox squirrel, and has fur nearly like that of a
rabbit, but infinitely finer. He would be a beautiful animal but
for his ridiculous little tail, which is short and bristly, like that
of some very lean and aged horse. He lives on buffalo grass,
taking an occasional lunch off the eggs of the owls which share
his domicile. The owls get even by eating the young dogs. This
popular idea, that rattlesnakes also live with the dogs and owls,
is an error. The snakes hang about the villages, but are never
received into society there. Once let a snake enter a dog-hole—
as he frequently will in search of the young—and the outraged
inhabitants vacate at once, and forever. They are even so frank
in their dislike as to stop up the polluted burrow, which they
will never again approach. These dog towns vary in size from
one-half an acre to three or four acres, and contain from ten to
two hundred burrows. The clever little fellows are good engineers, and always locate over water, down to which they drive
their winding wells. Their settlements lie along the railroad
every few miles; generally within 100 feet of the track.

One strikes many curious forms of vegetation, even this far east. It looks droll enough for instance, when the wind is high, to see thousands of big tumble-weeds rolling and bounding over the prairie like so many gigantic yellow balls. These weeds grow up into the shape of an imperfect globe, nearly spherical on the under side, but irregular on top. At maturity, they dry up, the slender stem breaks, and off they go, nature's footballs, kicked about by every vagabond wind. Then, there are also several kinds of cactus in the last 200 miles of Kansas. I have already seen three—the prickly pear, which bears a sickish, juicy fruit, about the size and color of a seckel; the ball, or echinocactus, which is a spiny globe as large as a shaddock; and the Indian soap, whose foliage consists of long, slender, sword-like blades, tipped with a needle point. Its roots are much like soap to the touch, whence the name.

In things to stab and devices to sting, this country is a caution. Here are a few of the things you will run upon and dedicate at once to a more torrid clime: sandburs about the size of peas, and with countless sharp thorns, which pierce you everywhere; bull-nettles, less troublesome, but bad enough to encounter; cockleburs, big and penetrating—and so on for quantity. This doesn't count the prickly pear, which are simply diabolical. I stepped on a bunch yesterday, and the long, stiff needles went through my shoes and quarter of an inch into my foot. Great Caesar's ghost! How infernally they did hurt!

I have seen some new snakes, too. I killed four young rattlers within a week, but have been looking in vain for an old codger with a long string of buttons. Had a long chase, Monday, after a blue snake, or racer. You never saw anything run so, but I finally got him. My cowboy—whose civilized title is Bill Henke—says they are very troublesome to the rancheros, biting the cattle on the feet frequently. Wednesday brought a sensation in the shape of an auger snake, which we surprised at work. He was about two feet long, nearly as large around as my wrist, and had a big muscular-looking neck. Lying in a close coil, and with his head down, he was industriously drilling a hole into the hard soil. He paid no attention to our approach, and we killed him at his work. On examination I found him well adapted for boring. His nose extended into a tough, horny point, half an inch long, shaped much like a duck's bill, and slightly *retrousse*.

I struck a familiar chord when I got just this side of Hays City, and saw a lot of oxteams. The ranchmen and farmers along in the western part of the State use oxen almost entirely for their heavy work, and keep ponies merely for riding, or for driving to town with an express.

I was a good deal puzzled at first to see at every cut a peculiar open fence on the north side of the railroad; but it finally occurred to me that these must be snow fences, and so they proved. Two scantlings are nailed together in the form of an X, and across the one which slopes from the track are nailed the boards, six inches wide and the same distance apart. This fence served to make an eddy in the wind, and the snow therefore drifts into huge hills between the fence and the track.

The fire guards along the track, and in fact all over the country, were also a novelty to me. They have a big plough attached by long side-arms to a flat-car, and an engine drags this along, turning several tremendous furrows 8 or 10 feet from the track. The ranchmen also plough double strips ten feet wide around their ranges, and then burn out the space between, thus opposing an effectual barrier to the sweep of a prairie fire.

The grasshoppers which nearly devastated the state a few years ago, are not in great supply now, but I have picked up specimens at about every mile. They are wingless but wonderful jumpers, brown in color, and mottled with darker spots. Some of them are as large as my whole thumb—one of their hind legs would make a small Ohio grasshopper.

I have still been pushing on in a rush, so as to have time for a little antelope hunting before reaching Denver. From Wa Keeney we tramped to Grinnell, 43 miles by rail, but four miles less by cutting off the bends; Tuesday, we reached Sheridan, saving five miles out of the 41; Wednesday found me at Arrapaho, having left the cowpuncher in his brother's bosom at

Wallace; and to-night I shall spread my bed in a railroad cut at First View whence I write. At Collyer we stopped an hour, nearly choked to death with thirst, and found some luscious watermelons at a little store. Here, too, I invested in a blanket, having found these Kansas winds entirely too permeating to sleep out all uncovered. We slept out that night at Grinnell, a little section house place, in a basket of resin weed, Bill sharing my blanket and nearly snoring my head off.

Had a nice time at Sheridan, a similar hamlet now, but once the terminus of the road, and a bustling place of nearly 2,000 people. At present it contains a wind-engine, water tank, hand-car shed, section house, operator's house, and three or four "dugouts." These "dugouts," by the way, are a peculiar institution. A big hole is excavated in the side of a hill, and roofed over, the walls being left unboarded. Sometimes the frame is raised far enough from the ground to admit of windows, but oftener not. They are cool in summer, and warm in winter, but you can imagine that they are not the cleanest places on earth. We slept in one, Tuesday night, with some Danish section men, who were really nice fellows. To the music of my French harp they danced a number of their dainty dizzy Danish dances—figures which would kill American exquisites of either sex in about four minutes and a half. Here too we saw eleven cowboys bring in a thousand head of cattle to be branded in the yard, where the victims are driven one by one into a high and narrow chute, through the sides of which the hot irons are pressed to their sizzling flanks.

As we started off early in the morning, I caught a glimpse of my first antelopes. They were quietly grazing on the brow of a divide some three miles away, but down the wind from us, so that it was useless to go after them. I saw three jack-rabbits, Tuesday, but they were on the keen jump, and didn't stop running for a mile. Yesterday, however, I got in my work on three of the long-legged flyaways. They were up against the wind, and after running a few rods sat up to look at me. I lugged those fellows three miles to a section house, and swapped two of them for a dinner, reserving the other for future reference. He made me a fine supper broiled over a fire of sage brush, grass and fragrants [*sic*] cut from ties with my all-useful knife.

I have slept out now three nights, and expect to all the way to Denver. These little section houses—erected to accommodate the railroad laborers—furnish good meals at 25 and 35 cents each, but their beds are irritating and not satisfactory. I like buggy-riding, but not buggy-sleeping, so I shall stick to the buffalo grass, which really makes a very nice bed.

I had expected that the railroad would streak through this comparatively level country as straight as an arrow, but I find some of the longest curves I ever saw. The road will run for three or four miles in a bee line, then turn off at right angles and run three or four more, and so on. This is to get over the divides and valleys without cuts or fills, and works well that way, but I save many a mile in a day by cutting off these turns. Ever since I left Kansas City, I have been climbing, climbing, from near the bottom of the vast catchment basin of the Mississippi up toward the watershed. Let me give you an idea of the steady up grade. Kansas City has an elevation of 763 feet above the sea level; Topeka, 67 miles west, 904 feet; Brookville, 200 miles, 1365 feet; Bunker Hill, 252 miles, 1882 feet; Ellis, 302 miles, 2125 feet; Buffalo Park, 350 miles, 2773 feet; Wallace, 420 miles, 3319 feet; First View, 472 miles, 4595 feet. Stations, or rather towns, are a long distance apart. From Grainfield to Wallace, each of which places has less than 100 people, it is 65 miles. From Wallace to the next place of 100 people it is 114 miles. But the section houses make it all right, being scattered along at every ten or fifteen miles, and furnishing accommodations far better and far cheaper than the hotels.

The great trouble here is lack of water. Ten or fifteen miles isn't much to ride; but to walk it in a blazing sun, over parched earth, without a sip of water, is real suffering. I am now carrying a quart bottle filled with water, and it shortens the way wonderfully. Most of the last 200 miles they have to haul their water to the section houses; and you will see whole trains of flat-cars filled up with huge wooden tanks, conveying the precious fluid from some good well to distant points less fortunate. The water as a rule—except what is hauled a long distance—is alkaline, and has a most demoralizing effect upon the internal economy of the stranger. It has bothered me somewhat, but I am getting hardened to it. As for rivers, they are scarcer than whales' hind legs. From Ellis clear here—170 miles—I have seen but two— the North Fork of the Smoky, at Sheradan, and Turkey Creek. It would take 50 of them to make one Paint Creek.

Twelve years ago, the whole country here was black with vast herds of buffalo, but the skin-hunter, the pot-hunter, and worst of all, the soulless fellows who killed for the mere sport of killing, have thinned out this noble game almost to the limit of extinction. Now and then the roving cowboy sees a lonely survivor of these former monarchs of the plain, but it is very rarely. One was killed down at Cheyenne Wells, a week ago, by a lucky hunter. But traces of their occupancy remain in plenty. You can hardly walk half a mile across the plains in any direction without finding one of their deep-cut trails, while at every few hundred yards may be seen the buffalo wallows—bowl-like depressions in the turf, six or eight feet in diameter and one or two in depth. The shaggy brutes, tormented by clouds of gnats, used to roll over and spin around on their backs, thus hollowing out these bowls, which served in turn to catch the rain water for them.

I am robust as a young bison, myself. This sleeping out is a glorious tonic, and when I rise at daybreak from Mother Earth, I seem to have realized the fable of Antaeus. My lungs are expanding, my eyes are good for three times their ordinary range, and every muscle is strung like steel. As for my feet, they are much in the condition of those of the Georgia girl, of whom Porte Crayon tells. Her mother called out, as the girl stood on the hearth, "Sal, there's a live coal under your foot." Sal did not budge, but looked up stupidly and drawled, "Which foot, Mam?" I shall be in Denver a week from tonight, unless the hunting is too everlastingly good. To-morrow will see me 20

miles north of the railroad, where I shall camp, and I hope to get
some antelopes and coyotes. I cannot begin to tell you a half of
the interesting things I encounter at almost every step. This
letter is too long already, and I am just getting fairly started. But
sometime, when it comes to a visit back in old Chillicothe—for
which I already hanker—I can fill you full for all time, if my
jaws hold out.

LUM

P.S. First View is a fraud. They showed me a little white cloud
which they said was Pike's Peak, 150 miles away. If it was, then
Pike's Peak is portable, for I saw that cloud float a mile. Hurrah
for Ohio and Jim Blaine!

"The Windsor," Denver, Colorado
Thursday, October 23rd, 1884

Editors Leader:
    The backbone of the continent! Surely a phrase more accu-
rately expressive was never coined. For six weeks to-night I have
been toiling over the scaly hide of this insensate monster we
call North America; and to-night I look up from my window to
where the crescent moon lies like a tiny silver saddle on the
vast, rugged, rocky vertebrae of the sleeping Titan. The smoke
of the smelters and the rolling-mills has blown away up the
wide valley of the Platte; the dust of the streets and ranch roads
has settled back on Mother Earth; and though the night is dim
and unlit, the eye traces the stupendous bulk of the vast range
which stretches north and south a lofty wall of blacker darkness
than the night's. For three hundred miles you may trace that
wall, from giant Pike on the south to the long and fading line of
lesser giants that lie to the north of Long's Peak. The air is cold,
dry, bracing; the stars seem tipped with an unknown fire, so
brilliantly they coruscate through this rare ether; and the hum

of the busy little city seems strangely out of place amid the supernatural sublimity which environs it. My mind is all the time leaping to those ragged peaks, and it is hard to come down to such a humdrum matter as letter writing. However, here goes.

Friday morning, before the sun had climbed over the brown divides of Kansas, I rolled out of my blanket in a little patch of blue-stem, not far from the First-View section house, danced around a few minutes in the cold morning air to get warm, and then set my chattering teeth into a greasy but warming breakfast. Then, as day just burst into bloom, I filled the long magazine of my rifle with cartridges, slung it across my back and with a quart bottle filled with ice-water in my pocket, sallied out northwestwardly, innocently expecting in this wild country to knock over an antelope every few miles. My course lay diagonally down the long, high ridge upon which First View stands; for I wished to go far out into the wilderness and still get back at night to Kit Carson, 15 miles ahead.

It might be remarked that it is not in the nature of a "snap" to walk across these plains, especially at this season. The grass is as slick as greased glass, and in about ten minutes the soles of your shoes get into the same slip-uppery fix. Then you have a three-ring circus. You reach out your foot for a good stride, plant it on a mossy little tuft of buffalo grass, and start to propel yourself forward. What with the onward push and backward slide, you must be an expert to make out which way you really are going. About as cheap a way as any is to face about and walk toward a point directly opposite to that you wish to reach. Walk hard and the sliding will do the work—you will get to your destination in quick metre. This may seem a little colored to you—it does to me, now that I am on city pavements—but it wouldn't when you were sliding and slipping over those smooth slopes.

Ten miles must have slipped by me in this sort of scramble, before my eyes rested upon the object of my search. Far off on a brown, low divide to the northwest, were four little patches of light gray. They had no apparent shape, nor did they seem to move, but I knew they were antelopes. You can't fool a hunter's eye, even if it's vision has been sawed short by years of burning the midnight oil. Three weeks ago I couldn't have seen those little flecks of gray at half the distance, but one's sight lengthens out wonderfully on these plains. Well, the game was there, and the next thing was to get a little more intimately acquainted with it.

The various modes of antelope hunting, were sufficiently familiar to me by hearsay, and I proceeded to put my theories to practical use. A huge red bandanna was soon transferred from the depths of my pocket to the end of my staff, which I planted firmly in a snake hole. Then leaving this banner snapping in the brisk breeze, I crawled backward on my stomach about a hundred yards, to the foot of the ridge, and then set out on a dog-trot up the ravine, in the general direction of my hoped-for game. The ravine sheltered me about half a mile, and then ended in a long smooth swell, dotted thickly with sage brush. I peeped over the edge, cautiously, and saw that the antelopes had not moved, but were quietly grazing in the same spot, some three miles away.

Now began the hard work. To get behind the little hill upon which they were grazing would have brought me to windward of them, and the keen-nosed, lightning-footed little fellows would have been off like a bullet. So there was nothing for it but to crawl up toward them from the side. Now three miles isn't much of a walk but to crawl it flat on your face, dragging a heavy rifle at your side, and frequently pierced by the daggers of the prickly pear, is an equine animal of diametrically different complexion—(label that Boston).* I suppose none but those imbued with the wild, savage passion of the chase would think of trying it. But your genuine sportsman never stops to ponder such trifles.

---

* "A horse of a different color"; Lummis is making fun of himself with a reference to his Harvard education.

I put my hat in my pocket, knocked a cartridge up into the
barrel of my Winchester, and as flat to the ground as it was
possible to get, wormed along among the dots of sage, through
the thin patches of blue stem and gumbo grass, toward the
distant quarry. It probably took me an hour to go the first mile,
for man is poorly articulated for serpentine locomotion. But
though slow, my progress was sure, and I was finally near
enough to distinguish the forms and movements of the antelopes. It was evident that my flag had caught their sharp eyes,
for they were paying more attention to it than to the buffalo
grass, and in their interrupted grazing kept edging slowly down
that way. At last, after nearly four hours' laborious squirming
and wriggling—half choked for the water which was back in the
pocket of my coat, and stabbed in five hundred places by the
omni-present cactus—I was within three hundred yards of the
graceful creatures.

That was about as near as it was safe to get, and I slowly
pulled the rifle forward, cocked it, and pushed the muzzle over a
little knob of grass. But alas! There must have been a little flash
of light from the barrel, for before I could draw the notches into
line the big buck gave a quick stamp, and the whole four in
another instant, were flying down the wind like a streak. It was
a mighty sore hunter that climbed stiffly to his feet then, shook
his fist impotently at those fast-vanishing specks, now a mile
away, and limped back to his bag and coat, sour enough to curdle
vinegar.

But bad luck never can outweary perseverence, and in two
hours more I had had my revenge. I had just reached the top of
an unusually steep divide, and as my head rose above the ridge, a
sight caught my eye which made me drop to the ground as if
shot. Down there in the hollow, not more than 60 yards away
from me, were three antelopes grazing—an old buck with two-
inch prongs on his antlers; a young buck with prongs just budding, and a sleek doe. By the greatest luck in the world, they
were unconscious of my presence, and I must have lain there
five minutes, watching them through a little tuft of grass, before

I drew up the rifle, took a careful aim at the old buck, and pulled the trigger.

As the smoke shot out from the muzzle, I saw him leap high in the air, run a couple of rods, and roll over on his side. His companions stood bewildered, a second, not knowing which way to run, for I had not shown myself, and the wind gave them no hint. That hesitation was fatal to the young buck, for before he had time to run a hundred feet another bullet broke his spine.

I also sent a leaden pill after the doe, but misjudged her, and saw the bullet kick up the dust twenty feet ahead of her. Before I could reload again she was out of sight.

An expert, armed with a long-range Sharpe rifle, would have waited until two of them got in line, and then sent a ball through both, shooting the other in the run; but I am not an expert, and my gun is not a Sharpe. I was well content however, with two full grown antelopes, and felt more than repaid for the morning's fruitless labor. Beautiful animals they are—graceful and slender as a greyhound, and fleeter of foot. Nothing short of a wolf can run them down, and I reckon it would take a wolf about a day. You cannot conceive anything so agile. They don't seem to run, but fly upon the wind like an exaggerated thistle-down. They stand about three feet high, and weigh from 35 to 60 pounds.

I slung one over my back, with the legs on each side of my neck, and calculated long on the possibility of carrying him in. But by a very simple sum in progression he would have weighed just 26,284,000 pounds before I got him to the end of the 20 miles which lay between me and any station, and I concluded to leave him. I cut off all four horns, however, with infinite trouble, carved about three pounds of juicy stake [sic] from the younger animal, and prepared to get a dinner.

At first flush one would soon think of gathering fuel from the sea as from the bare plains; but after about an hour's work and scouring two or three acres, I managed to get together a sufficient pile of sage brush blue stem and the big, inflammable bulbous roots of the soapweed, and soon had a fine fire. The venison was covered with ashes and smacked strongly of bitter sage, but I think nothing ever tasted better. At any rate, there wasn't a scrap of it left.

I saw no more antelope that day, but a little later in the afternoon had a sensation equally stirring. I shot a large hawk at long range, and went over to look at him. Coming back to where my blanket lay, I passed through a bit patch of tall gumbo thinking of nothing but my blankets, which I left back 300 yards in the grass. I was then carelessly wading along when—ak-r-r-r. I jumped about six feet into the air. I had stepped right across a big rattler, and he had thrown himself into a coil and was waving his broad flat head and a foot of his sinuous length from side to side in a strange, dreamy sort of fashion. His temper was unmistakably bad, as might be shown by his hisses and the dry whirr of his tail, which moved so fast as to look like a yellow plate. I cut his throat slightly with a bullet, but he minded it no more than he did the touch of the grass. At last after much countermarching and maneuvering, I pinned his head to the ground with my gun; and holding this in my left hand, reached around for my knife. Just then he squirmed loose, and as quick as thought made a spring at my face as I stooped over him. His big open mouth came within four inches of my nose, but he fortunately could not quite reach. But there must have been a big dent in the air, just at this gesture judging by the way I flopped over backward. Finally I got him pinned again, and chopped his head off.

Did you ever examine the wonderful adaptations of a rattlesnake's mouth for its purpose of death? The teeth are like those of ordinary snakes, so delicate as to be scarcely visible. At the very rim of the upper jaw, on each side, are the fangs—two tiny points, fine as the finest cambric needle, and about a quarter of an inch in visible length. They are imbedded in a strong, white, elastic muscle, and when the mouth is closed, they lie flat back along the roof. Opening the mouth, however, throws

them forward rigid and ready for action. They still rake backward, and therefore strike far more effectively. Luckily the
snakes have to fall into a coil in order to get the necessary
purchase before they can strike, though if you were to hold one
down with your foot that would answer the same ends. Their
rattles begin to grow after the second year, and one is annually
added to their number. This fellow had six rattles, and lacked
two inches of being four feet in length. About an hour afterward
I killed a tiny rattler of a different variety, only ten inches long,
yet with three rattles. As for the big fellow, he has had to pay for
the scare he gave me. You know everyone in this country wears
a hatband of some sort, generally of stamped and frilled leather.
Well, I have gone the cowboys one better, and devised a band
which is the admiration of all beholders. I skinned my two
snakes at Kit Carson when I got in, and stretched the hide of the
big one over a pair of old suspenders, with the rattle lapping over
where the buckle usually comes. It is great. Perhaps you fancy
that a snake skin is not very ornamental, but if so you are dead
wrong. Those seal-brown links down the light grey background
make as fine a harmony in modest colors as old Nature ever
mixed on her faultless palette. The skin of the rattler is the
prettiest thing I have ever beheld, not even excepting a live
brook trout or a live mackeral. I shall make it into a bracelet one
of those leisure days.

   If you would go through Kit Carson [a town in eastern Colo-
rado] with a fine-tooth comb you might rake up 20 buildings—
not more. The comfortable section house, the station, one tiny
residence, two dug-outs, water tank and a little store where you
can get sugar for 25 cents a pound; beer for 15 cents a "pony" and
anything else for corresponding altitudes—that is Kit Carson.
Twelve years ago the place numbered nearly 6,000 souls and its
tents and shanties and dug-outs dotted the prairie far around.
Then it was the terminus of the Union Pacific, and a vast
amount of shipping was done thence. But the road crept on, the
shippers and squatters and speculators crept on with it, a great
fire licked up the town and it has never risen from the ashes.

It is not such a monument now to the grand old pioneer and scout as it was once fondly expected to be. It is some 300 feet lower than First View, whose two little buildings you can plainly see, 15 miles away. The Big Sandy "flows" through Kit Carson. That is to say, there is a broad bed of parched sand white with alkali dust, stretching along the plain, but no water visible. Scoop out a few handfuls of sand, however, and you will come to water, brackish with alkali and effective enough to purge the ancient Cities of the Plain. That "river" follows the track for about 50 miles, and is the most navigable stream in Eastern Colorado.

I have not seen a real stream since I left little Ellis, 327 miles from Denver. There have been one or two beds with occasional pools in their hollows, but nothing better in all that long arid stretch. There is one little muddy, cattle-infested pond near Kit Carson, whose acre and a half of surface I saw covered thick with fat mallard ducks, of which I managed to get a couple. Here also I killed my first centipede—a hideous fellow, six inches long and a quarter of an inch across the back, and with about a hundred bowlegs, each tipped with a black fang. Let one walk across your hand undisturbed, and he leaves a highly inflamed red track. Hit him during that march, and he will sink those hundred fangs into your flesh, and it will rot away and drop from the bones. At least that is what the natives believe, and they ought to know. I didn't care to verify the story by personal investigation, as I shall need all my flesh until I get through this job.

The spiders out here seem to be built tarantula fashion, though I have seen few huge ones. They are all hairy and devilish looking and all live in little round holes in the dirt. But talk about "pison critters," the people here tell me that their most venomous insect is the skunk! I had often heard of these odorous fellows before, but never quite so extensively. They make no bones of attacking a man, and their bite is alleged to be sure death. I experimented a little, to see if this story was "straight goods" and while talking politics to a lot of section men, I

suddenly yelled "Skunk! Skunk!" There was no fraud about
their terror for they ran like sheep. I trust that no skunk will feel
bound to show me the hospitality of his race.

Saturday night brought me to Bo-ye-ro—a little water tank 9
miles west of Kit Carson—after a long, vain hunt for antelopes.
The only game I saw was one "cotton-tail" (the small ordinary
rabbit) and he was in such a sorry pickle that I didn't try to shoot
him. A huge, dark eagle with swooping wings that must have
spread over six feet, had his big, sharp talons fixed into the poor
little devil's wool, and flopped along over him as he ran. How
the rabbit did yell! In that still open air you might have heard
him a mile, and his screams were almost human in their agony.
Before the great bird had flown away with his quarry, however,
he spied me and soared off, while poor cottontail limped to his
hole to die—for a rabbit never survives even a trifling scratch.

At Bo-ye-ro I fell among some very clever young laborers
working on the section there, and passed the evening with them
in the bunkhouse. One of them had a fine accordion which he
manipulated with a skill that would bring him a good salary on
any Ohio stage. The college songs came in handy here again,
and we sang and danced away the evening in very jolly fashion.
These boys were above the average, had plenty of good reading,
including some standard books and several of the best papers in
the country, and seemed to enjoy life heartily. I saw the steam
ploughs at work, also, Saturday, widening out the cuts, so as to
give elbow room to the snow-ploughs. They turn a monstrous
furrow in this hard soil, which a yoke of stout oxen, even, could
hardly scratch.

Sometimes a fellow has what these eloquent sons of the
plains call "bull luck." I hit a streak of it Saturday morning.
Coming by Little Wild Horse, I stopped at the section-house,
borrowed a needle and thread, and sewed my double blanket up
into a sleeping bag, barely wide enough to crawl into. This
increased its warming capacity about six-fold. It was oppres-
sively hot when I did the job, and up to midnight, in fact was

unusually warm. Then suddenly the wind veered around into
the North and began to howl murder around my unprotected
ears. I was lying on top of the blanket then, but crawled into it
mighty soon, and pulled the top down over my head. Even then
the cold bored through unpleasantly, and I was glad when morning came with its gentle sun. It stayed cold as charity until
Tuesday, and them came up to a decent temperature.

Sunday, I plodded up to Lake, 31 miles from Bo-ye-ro, and
camped out there after a mallard supper. The night again was
abominably frigid, and little gusts of snow danced around my
ears. Saw a coyote for the first time, Sunday, but couldn't get
within 300 yards of him, and took a snap shot as he ran. But you
might as well hope to eat soup with a tuning fork as to shoot one
of them long runners in motion. The name is pronounced ki-
oat, with the accent generally placed on the first syllable. Their
fur is exquisite, and I must have a robe of them. Will have to gun
for them with strychnine however, for it is next to impossible to
shoot them. They are twice as large as a red fox and shaped
exactly like one, but their fur is long, silky, and of a fine silver
gray.

Deer Trail and Byers were my respective stopping places,
Monday and Tuesday evenings, the first after a tramp of 10
miles and the second after a hunting circuit which took me 31
miles around for 13 ahead, but netted one antelope, two jacks
and a cottontail.

Don't let anyone tell you that this is a country for epicures.
The man who would say that shouldn't be fooling away his
wind gratuitously. So able bodied a liar can command any salary
in the lightning rod business. Of all the scaly meals I ever gulped
down by the help of abundant water and keen hunger, those for
the 100 miles between Kit Carson and Box Elder are the toughest. Corned beef tougher and older than S. J. Tilden; bread the
color and flavor of Portsmouth mud; coffee as rich as the water
of the Ohio on a "raise"; fermented molasses; butter which
needs no testimonial from me, being old enough to speak for

itself, but not yet bald—that about fills the bill of fare. Oh, yes, there are potatoes, too, which contain all the water that the rivers lack. For this sort of a banquet you are charged 25 cents; or if it is unusually bad, 35 cents. At Magnolia, however, I found excellent fare. Here at the Windsor the best hotel in Denver, and one which double-discounts the Cincinnati Grand, please feel assured that I am giving my poor belt something substantial to rub against, after its long wandering in search of something besides air to encircle. A song which one of the boys sang back at Wild Horse, describing the sorrows of a laborer in Arkansas, touched a responsive chord in the place where my stomach used to be and is again, thanks to the Windsor. One verse ran:

> His bread was nothin' but corndodger,
>   His beef you couldn't chaw,
> But he charges us 50 cents a meal
>   In the state of Arkansaw!

But amid all the drawbacks of this wilderness of nearly 500 miles, I wish to say a friendly word for a class of men who get about as liberally abused as anyone on earth. I mean the station agents. In a majority of these little stations they are about the only people one cares to assimilate with fully, and so I have come in contact with perhaps 50 of them since leaving Kansas City. If there be any more agreeable set of men to encounter, I have not discovered the fact on this trip. Kind-hearted, liberal in their notions, courteous and well posted, they have been active in making my journey a thing of pleasant memoriam. Their work is exacting and annoying, but they keep cheerful and hospitable, and I believe they will get corner lots in the celestial metropolis, while some of us are trying to find unfurnished rooms on the back alley. There are many of them whom I shall always remember with friendly feeling. I only met one mean man among them all, and he had nothing to do with me, but it made me hot to hear him snarl at his assistant. He is at Wallace, Kansas, and the best-known and worst-hated man on the road. He used to be at Hugo, but offended the cowboys by his meanness, and they gave him thirty minutes in which to leave town. He was just mulish enough not to budge, and would have been named Dennis* in a brief time if his friends had not made an assisted emigrant of him. They bound him, locked him in a box car, giving the conductor instructions to water him oftener than the other cattle, and sent him off into Missouri.

Many kind friends have written me, expressing doleful fears that I will be eaten up by cowboys. They need not be alarmed. These cowboys are among my most hospitable friends, and do their utmost to make my trip enjoyable. Their kindness is rough, and it is honest and earnest, and perhaps not as much less welcome than the salvy, hypocritical show of friendship supposed by society to be proper measure for all alike. When these rough, profane, muscular fellows on the plains, as ready with the trigger as with the tongue, like a man, he knows it directly, and can rely on it. If they don't like him he will know that, too, without the aid of a diagram. Well, if a man has any trouble with such people, it is his own fault. Let him leave off his sirs and frills, keep his nose from tilting upward, mind his own business, take a rough joke in good part and yet let no one bully him; let him know how to mingle with these men as one of them, still preserving his self-respect and my word for it, he will be as squarely treated as ever he was in his life anywhere. If a lot of people who think no dirt of themselves were half as white at heart as these despised cowboys, this world would have a healthier atmosphere.

I am now 1261 miles from Chillicothe, and have walked in all, with these many hunting detours, 1418. I got in Denver at noon to-day, after a glorious tramp in full view of this wonderful range. An attempt at description must wait for my next, this is already so long. Mrs. Roads, Dr. Lummis and Miss Virginia

*Lummis uses the term "Dennis" several times throughout these letters in a reference to death or to a dead man. The expression probably refers to an English literary critic, John Dennis (1657–1734), whose death terminated a bitter feud between Dennis and the English writer Alexander Pope. The expression is most likely Harvard vernacular.

Bereman, of Washington County, Ohio, arrive here from Bur-
lington, Iowa, to-morrow morning at 6 o'clock, and we will pass
Sunday here together. They leave on Monday for San Francisco,
while I strike south for Pueblo. I hope to be on the summit of
Pike's Peak the last of next week. Now a jump to catch the mail.
Will see you later.

LUM

Platte Cañon, Colorado
Thursday, October 30th, 1884

Editors Leader:
    The haste with which I had to rush off my last *Leader* letter
allowed me no room for speaking of the scenery which meets
the traveler's eye as he approaches Denver from the East. The
Snowy Range of the Rocky Mountains is frequently visible
from River Bend, over a hundred miles distant, but a cloudy
horizon froze me out of this sight. The same was true at Cedar
Point, the highest pitch of the road between Kansas City and
Denver, and it was not until Tuesday night that my wishes were
gratified. Passing through tiny Byers, I saw ahead a high divide,
whose summit must certainly command a view of the distant
range. The day was cloudy, but I know that when the sun went
down behind that rugged wall it would show at least a sil-
houette of the adjacent mountains. So I rushed up the long
divide at a breakneck and breathless pace, and reached the top
just as

>   The level sun, like ruddy ore,
>   Lay sinking in the western skies.

    And sure enough, there lay the white peaks of Gray and his
neighbor giants, bluish purple in the waning light, distant and
cold, half their height hidden by the rocky foothill, yet serene
and glorious beyond description.

> Then felt I like some watcher of the skies
> When a new planet swims into his ken:
> Or like bold Cortez, when with eagle eyes
> He gazed on the Pacific—and all his men
> Looked at each other with a wild surprise,
> Silent upon a peak in Darien.*

That was just at the post which marks 600 miles from Kansas City. Next day, when I stood on the summit of Box Elder hill, 21 miles from Denver, and 300 feet above it, the whole marvelous scene was unfolded before me. For 300 miles, that rocky battlement split the sky, with here and there the sentinel towers of loftier peaks upreared. Ninety miles to the South as the crow flies, Pike's Peak thrust its giant shoulders and snow-capped head to the clouds. It stands apparently alone, and is one of the most impressive of all this congress of the Titans. North of it and due west from my lookout, stands Mt. Evans, Gray's Peak, James Peak, Arapahoe Peak, and mighty Long's Peak the last, the grandest mountain profile I ever saw. Besides these greater giants, there are scores of mountains that in other company would be hardly less sublime. I counted 72 peaks, each of which must be 10,000 feet or over. Many people have an idea that Pike's Peak, the most celebrated of all these mountains, is also the highest, but this is a mistake. I append a table of the highest peaks in Colorado: Mt. Evans, 14,400; Gray's Peak, 14,341; Sierra Blanca, 14,464; Long's Peak, 14,271; Mt. Wilson, 14,289; Uncompahgre Peak, 14,235; La Plata Peak, 14,302; Mt. Harvard, 14,151; Yale Peak, 14,421; Mt. Holy Cross, 14,176; Capitol, 13,992; Music Peak, 13,299; Summit Peak, 13,393; Conejos Peak, 13,947; Mt. Powell, 13,308; Macomb's Peak, 13,454; Trincheras Peak, 13,611; Culebra Peak, 14,049; not to count hundreds of peaks whose altitude is from 9,000 to 12,000 feet. When you reflect that the tops of the innumerable "foot hills"—themselves true mountains in formation—are 7,000 and 8,000 feet

*From John Keats, *On First Looking into Chapman's Homer.* Lummis is parading his Harvard education again.

above the sea, you will see that this is a tolerably high-toned
State. The little log cabin in which I write this is away down on
a plain, not a hundred feet above the swift current of the Platte,
yet I am 7,400 feet higher than the sea; and the foothills, two
miles away, tower so high as to shut out all view of the vast
range behind them.

All of the last 24 miles into Denver I had the mountains in
view—an ever-shifting panorama, as if giant "supes" were continuously shifting the scenes. There was a wonderful fascina-
tion in that jagged, savage chaos of rocks and crags, with purple
base and snowy crest, and my eyes would not be kept away from
them. Much of my way was across the plains, and I suppose I
stepped into a hundred patches of prickly pear, and uttered
many corresponding objurgations, Wednesday, just because my
eyes were a hundred miles away instead of on the path.

From Denver itself you may get many fine views of the great
range, when the abominable smoke does not interfere, as it does
about two-thirds of the time.

Twelve miles East of Denver I saw the first signs of cultivation in nearly 100 miles. There were thirty teams at work
ploughing a huge field of good, black soil, through which flowed
many irrigating ditches, blocking off the land into squares of an
acre each. Of the irrigating systems of Colorado I shall presently
have some remarks to offer.

In the very edge of Denver I saw at last a brick building. It was
the first that had met my eye since leaving Salina, nearly 450
miles away. I came into the city on a long, straggling street,
without any signs to tell its name, but before walking half-way
down town I knew what it was—Holladay Street, one of the
most notorious thoroughfares in the Union. Three-fourths of its
little cottages and shanties are given over to vice, and it looks as
if some of our missionary collections might be applied right
here.

The Queen City of the Plains—that is Denver's "store
name"—and not so inappropriate a name, either, as those which
some towns arrogate to themselves, for Denver is a remarkably

fine city. When the insignificant outskirts of the place have been left behind, you stand amid magnificence such as you were quite unprepared to meet in this settlement, under the very shadow of the Rockies. Fine streets, whose gutters are flushed with clear, icy, dashing rivulets, superb buildings of brick, lava, trachyte or soft, pink sandstone; and a general air of "d-m the expense" are all around you.

Denver is only 25 years old, and is a mighty vigorous young-ster. It grew like scandal from '49 to '61, when the great war checked all enterprise. Then it struggled along for many years, till the completion of the Kansas Pacific and Union Pacific railroads to its doors gave it another boost. In 1869, it had but 21,000 people; to-day it holds up its head and brags of 75,000, which is a pretty lively jump for these days. It has become a great railroad point, no less than 13 distinct lines centering here. Of these four are standard gauge lines to the east; two stan-dard and one narrow gauge to Salt Lake, three narrow gauges to the south, and other less important roads. The city is partly illuminated by the Brush* electric light. The lamps are sus-pended from six skeleton towers, each 150 feet high, situated in various quarters of the town. The water-works derive their sup-ply by the Holly† system from the river Platte but its discovery of artesian water last year has rather pied [sic] their form. Since then over 60 artesian wells have been sunk; the shallowest going down 250 feet, and the deepest 919; and these produce a total daily average of 8,000,000 gallons. This water is clear as crystal, and delicious for drinking purposes but pretty expen-sive.

In public and business buildings Denver need take a back seat for no one. Arapahoe, Laramer, Lawrence and other streets have an almost New Yorkish air. The Arapahoe county court house, the Mining Exposition building, the Windsor Hotel, the Tabor

*Charles Francis Brush (1849–1929), U.S. inventor and industrialist, devised the electric arc lamp, first used for street lighting in Cleveland in 1878.

†Birdsall Holly (1822–1894), U.S. inventor and manufacturer, developed pressurized water systems and steam heat in the second half of the 19th C.

Block and other buildings would ornament any metropolis. But the finest edifice in Denver and one of the finest in the country, is the Tabor Grand Opera House, built by $250 night-shirt Tabor out of his own pocket. It cost him the little sum of $800,000, and is said to have but one peer in the world, Napoleon Third's hobby, the Grand Opera House in Paris. This Tabor, by the way, who is a marvelously insignificant-looking man, has been a God-send to Denver, and has left more money in it than any other three people. A few years ago, you remember, he "grub-staked" a dead-broke miner, advancing him about $7 worth of provisions from his little grocery. The hitherto unlucky trea-sure-seeker thereupon struck it rich, and made the fortune of his grocer.

The rarified air of these lofty Colorado plains is sweet and clear and exhilarating, but peculiar in its effects. Everyone—not even excepting the campaign orators—becomes short-winded in a little time. Cattarha and bronchitis are almost universal, though apparently not in very serious forms. You soon experi-ence a burning sensation in the base of your nose; and perhaps also a slight sore throat. But these are trifles which occasion but slight inconvenience, and you soon forget all about them.

My deserted folks reached Denver on time and in good order, and we had a very jolly re-union from Friday morning till Mon-day noon. The only drawback to my happiness was that the selective rates of the Windsor, not tempered by any exercise to speak of, came near knocking me out in four rounds. You see, my internal economy was completely taken by surprise by all the richness after 400 miles of scaly provender. While here I swapped my little .28 caliber pocket gun for a two-foot .44, whose big holster peers out cheekily below my long duck coat. This change saves me the trouble of carrying two sizes of car-tridges, rifle and revolver now being pitched on the same key.

Monday noon, feeling unusually muscular, I managed to carry enough money down stairs to pay our little bill, whose altitude would have overshadowed Gray's Peak. Then I put the three ladies on the Pullman for Cheyenne, whence they strike

across for San Francisco, arriving there this morning, if there
were no delays. I wished to get away at once myself, but had to
lose nearly all the afternoon in visiting a college friend, and
didn't get away until 4 P.M. I have given up the 750 mile trip to
Salt Lake, as I should inevitably be snowed in before I got half
way there. [Evidently, Lummis had considered other routes for
his tramp.] I walked out 11 miles to Littleton, and there sat up
nearly all night getting off three columns of newspaper correspondence, at which I had to take another whack in the morning.

I started away from Littleton at 11:30 Tuesday, and hit the
track hard for twelve miles, getting glorious views at every step.
By the way, I am carrying now 37 pounds of baggage, but shall
not after I strike the next express station, you may stake your
epidemic stomach. I have toted my knapsack from Denver, and
its straps have nearly sawed my shoulders off. It contains my
blanket, duck coat, an undershirt, 100 cartridges, matches, tobacco, and a lot of little necessities for a sojourn among the
mountains. It weighs 21 pounds. The six shooter, loaded, weighs
2½ pounds; the cartridge belt, 3; and the rifle, with its magazine
full, 12½—and all this in addition to my heavy clothing, whose
pockets are crammed with everything but "boodle." I don't
believe I was cut out for a pack mule, however well I might do as
a St. Julien. Now, I have packed my rifle from Wa Keeney, and it
has been growing no lighter fast in all the four hundred miles
and more since traversed. Talk about your 100-ton Krupp guns!
Why, for the first 100 miles this Winchester grew in weight at
the rate of 13½ tons a mile. It hasn't been quite so bad since, and
now only weighs 27,396,241 tons. I don't mind a trifle like that,
so much, for there are a dozen different ways of carrying it; but
that knapsack balls me all up. I shall send the grip on by express,
and trust to Providence (R.I.) for something to take the place of
the blanket. If it gets too beastly cold, I shall probably contract
enough so that I can crawl into the muzzle of my rifle and keep
warm.

When I got nearly to Sedalia, some section men told me of

trout-fishing over in the mountain opposite, and about ten miles away. In ten minutes from the first mention of trout, I was streaking it across the plains at a five-mile gait, forgetful of my heavy load, forgetful of dinner, forgetful of everything but the existence of the sport which would allure me from anything else on earth. I strode away till dark, and then broke for a little ranche almost under the shadow of the foot-hills, where fried chicken and fixin's filled the dinnerless void. Here they told me there was no trout-fishing within 25 miles, and they knew because they had hunted and fished all through these mountains for 20 years. That made me feel sick, you may be sure; and I decided to fly back to the Denver & Río Grande track p.d.q. in the morning. P.d.q., you know, is French for "tolerably immejit." But with the clear, glorious morning came better thoughts, and I went over to see the long cañon of the Platte, anyhow, and also try the river itself for my speckled idols. I walked five miles southwest across the plains, past the "Hog-backs"—a park of huge ledges of red sandstone which crop out from the bare ground and rise from 50 to 150 feet in the air—climbed up and down the precipitous mountain for five miles more; and finally, at 2 o'clock, emerged from the dry ravine of a little brook, and stood beside the shouting river in the bottom of the Platte Cañon.

A splendid stream it is, and welcome doubly to one long bored by the rolly rivers of Ohio and her sister states. Cold as coldest lee-water, clear as crystal, swift as an arrow, it is dashed musically down its steep and rocky bed, turning, foaming, and twisting through the sinuous channel it has carved, by the labor of a hundred million years, through the solid granite. The Denver & South Park Railroad follows the stream closely, clinging to the cliffs above it. I cut a good cottonwood pole, filled the case of my French harp with grasshoppers, and proceeded to business. Just where a huge ledge towered twenty feet out of the torrent, I dropped my grasshopper into the deep eddy. It had not sunk three feet when swish! off went the line sawing through the water, and the limber pole bent half double. It took a couple of minutes to land that fellow; and when he at last flopped beside me on the bank I threw up my hat and danced. He weighed three-fourths of a pound, but had more strength and more fight in him than any four-pound bass ever hooked in Ohio waters. In following down the seven northern miles of the cañon—the Platte flows northward—I caught eight more. All nine were of a size, probably not varying two ounces in weight, and they made a noble string. I felt richer than if they had been so many nuggets of virgin gold.

The cañon of the Platte is about 30 miles long, and though tame compared with the deeper defiles in these great mountains, interested me greatly as the first scenery I found within the walls of the Rocky Mountains. It winds snakily around the colossal feet of mountains sculptured from the solid granite by frost and water. Their wild, shaggy heads rise 700 or 800 feet above the current of the noisy Platte, while their crags sometimes overhang the very water.

Three miles south of the cañon's mouth, and 23 miles south of Denver, where the mountains crowd close together, is the great granite dam of the Northern Colorado Irrigation Company, and here begins the Platte or "High Line" canal. Just above the dam, about ninety per cent of the river disappears. You look for its exit in wonder, and at last notice a low arch in the foot of a mountain of solid rock, 300 feet high. A tunnel 700 feet long, 20 feet wide and 10 feet high, has been cut under this mountain through granite nearly as hard as quartz; and this is the beginning of the Platte canal. That 700 feet cost $100,000. The whole canal reaches far north of Denver, and has a total length of 89 miles. Its irrigating capacity is 59,250 acres, and the land already irrigated by it is 15,000 acres. It carries 1,184 cubic feet of water per second past a given point. I presume it is the costliest irrigation canal in the world—it took nearly $800,000 to build it, over $9,000 per mile. Leaving the rocky mouth of the cañon, it winds away over the long divides, with a width of 40 feet, a depth of seven and an average fall of 21 inches to the mile. This is the largest and most important of Colorado's twelve irrigation systems, and bears about the same relation to the other

"ditches" along the Platte that the Standard Oil Co. does to
smaller lines.

I had of course looked upon this system as a perfect bonanza
to the State; but the natives sing a different song. This big
monopoly, the Platte Canal Co., has acquired possession of
great tracts of land along its course, and holds the thousands of
acres at a ruinously high figure. It has also raised the price of all
contiguous land to a point which shuts out the stockman and
now bids fair to swamp the farmers. I have talked with 79
farmers—not to mention numerous outsiders—and all are blue
as Ohio Democrats. They are bankrupt and despondent, almost
without hope. They have spent their last dollar, many of them,
and do not know where the next is coming from. They have to
pay $17 royalty for the right to irrigate each 160 acres; and then
$1.50 per acre for water rent every year; then comes in all the
ordinary expense of farming. On the other hand they are now
getting but *seventy cents per hundred-weight* for their wheat! If
any *Leader* readers were planning to come out here and farm on
irrigated-land, let them take this as a pointer to stay at home.
The farmers here without exception are in sore distress. The
only money now is in cattle and this part of the State is less
profitable even in that line than a few years ago. The ranges are
overcrowded, and when a severe winter sets in—like the last—
the plains are strewn with carcasses. Last year there were
1,461,945 cattle and 1,526,822 sheep in the State. There is room
for plenty more, but great sections are unoccupied and others
already too full. Think of it, though—only 13,000 hogs in all
this great State!

But Colorado is plucky. As one shaggy-browed old farmer said
to me; "Yes, Colorado has had a tough pull. She has suffered
more than any other state, but she never yawped. She never had
to go outside her own borders, in her worst scuffle for life." And
it is true. For the seven years ending in '76, she was devoured by
the grasshoppers. Her cornfields disappeared as by fire; the grass
on which her million cattle and other stock depended was
stripped to the very roots; her trees stood in leafless nakedness.

The man under whose humble roof I write, drove to Denver one July morning in '75. When he returned next evening his 20 acres of corn was absolutely annihilated; his cattle range was bare earth, and his hay had vanished. He showed me where the ravenous insects had even gnawed the casing of his house. But the mountains were full of gold and silver, the mines poured out a flood of money, and the stricken state "grinned and bore it." Mighty different, this, from braggart Kansas, which was the nation's beggar in her need; and then, last spring, when she had gathered a few un-begged carloads of corn for flooded Ohio, laid to boast for a month—covering the relief train with advertisements of Kansas' wealth and charity, and delaying the train for many days that the people of every town might see at leisure this boastful alms.

The people with whom I shared my trout are clever in their way, but a queer way. While I was off, fishing, they ransacked my baggage, not for dishonesty, but for curiosity. When I sat down to a late and lonely supper, last night, the son put my fish in a pan, sat down at the table, opposite me, and dressed them at leisure. Fortunately I have a hunter's stomach, and am not disturbed by little things like that. Later, while I wrote some letters at the table, the rancher and his buxom spouse retired to their virtuous couch, here in the one room the cabin boasts. I sleep with the son, in a little iron-rock house beyond. They have a few cattle, and make out a scant living by selling butter, cordwood and railroad ties, hewn in the mountains, and hauled by gaunt little ponies over the most horrible roads you ever dreamed of. They are settled on "school lands," which they neither bought nor rented, but simply pay taxes upon. They were just exclaiming over the hard luck of a neighbor, who leased some of these lands and had to pay 25 cents an acre per year. It *is* pretty exorbitant.

Coming home in the dark, last night, I nearly pinched my right forefinger off in a gate, and it is so painful to write that I shall "cut her short." Furthermore, it is 4:30 P.M.—only half an hour more of daylight—and I must tramp six miles across the plains and then eight up the track, to get to a place where I can mail this in time for the *Leader's* use. I don't know at all when I shall get to Colorado Springs—the presence of trout makes it might onsartain [*sic*]. I may, however, strike down there at once, and wait for my fishing till I reach the mountains west of Cuchara—will see how I feel. It snowed briskly in Denver, Sunday, and is fixing up another whirl, which may strike me at any hour. But I am getting acclimated, and don't mind the cold much. I'm glad the Presidential agony will be over next week— folks will be much more entertaining then. This air is hard on the voice, but I shall make a good, big hole in it with three times three for Blaine and Logan.

LUM

U.S. Signal Service Station, Pike's Peak, Colorado
Wednesday, November 5th, 1884

Editors Leader:
Fourteen thousand, one hundred and forty-seven feet above the sea! Two miles and a half higher in the air than you of Chillicothe, who will presently read these lines. Around me lies eternal snow—the same hoary crystals that fell here before Adam was, have lain here ever since. A perpendicular mile below my feet the soft, fleecy clouds are drifting along the scarred flanks of this grim, unmindful giant, and the full moon pours down on them her cold, white glory. Dimmer than the clouds, I trace afar off the faint outlines of Pike's brother Titans as they toss back the snow from their bare brows, and stare solemnly at the round-faced moon. God's tiny carbon-points, the stars, seem to burn through the very dome of heaven, so unnatural is their dazzling luster. The icy wind howls and raves around the corners of this low building, or hurries off to drive hither and yon his flock of cloud-sheep, scurrying down the deep passes of the range. It is one o'clock in the morning, so my

watch tells me, but time does not seem to exist up here. Alive, I am yet out of the world. This might be a planet solitary in all space, so far as any connection with things terrestrial appears. The peak is a vast cairn of jagged red-granite rocks, which are frosted with the snow-crystals, while their points show cruel in the weird light.

I am sitting in the highest inhabited building on the face of the globe; a building stuck up here among the clouds, in 1882, by Uncle Sam, who never grudges expense in carrying out his scientific whims. It is a very cozy place, some 40 feet by 20, with great stone walls two feet thick, lined with two feet more of wadding and wood. There are five comfortable rooms, and barring the loneliness of the winter, the men here must have a rather pleasant time. During the summer, they have plenty of company every day; but after the middle of October they are pretty closely tied down to solitary confinement until spring— sometimes having no communication with the outside world for months at a time. But if there be any appreciation in their souls, as I am sure there is, Nature can compensate them for the lack of society. Mr. John P. Ramsey is in charge here, and I find him a very clever young man. He comes from Hanover, Ind., graduated from the college there, and entered the signal service soon after. His assistant is Mr. O. H. Davis.

I left Manitou at 10 o'clock Tuesday, and started up the rocky fastnesses of Engelman's canyon toward the peak. For a couple of miles a fine carriage road winds up along the tumbling brook. Then at the little toll-house, where they collect a dollar out of every traveler, you cross the stream, and hard work begins at once. This is the steepest part of the trail, and will make the best climber grunt. The gravel is loose, the trail is narrow, and the grade about that of an ordinary flight of stairs. This sort of thing keeps up for three miles, until you reach the alleged half-way house, whence the walking is not bad until you get well above the timber-line. This half-way house and I are strangers henceforth. We never speak as we pass by. I had been told that it was exactly half way to the top of the peak, and I was just fresh enough to believe it. Well, about about 3½ miles of red hot clambering up that steep trail I struck a little shanty in the wood, which rejoiced in the title of the Trail House.

Now this was the "Half-way" house, if I had but known it—but I didn't. I never thought of finding the half-way house quarter of the way up—which was rather dull of me, too, knowing the popular inability to tell a thing straight. They had also informed that the half-way house was at the very timber-line; and as this cabin was about three miles and a half below timber-line I was again fooled. It doesn't grieve me that I didn't recognize this half-way Half-way House for its own sake; but you see I was humping myself all afternoon up that tough old trail, looking in vain for half-way houses, or wondering how under the hinges of merry Hades I had managed to walk ten miles and not reach a point six miles from where I started. I didn't relinquish the fond fancy of hitting that house till nearly three o'clock, but held to the petticoats of Hope like a tin can to a dog's tail. It was discouraging, however, as the porcelain eggs the old hen tried to hatch. I hope never to see the back of my neck if it didn't begin to seem to me that the mountain was bewitched. I certainly wish those Manitouters were.

Within a hundred yards of where the trail leaves the highway, you begin to strike the wintry ear-marks which betoken the high latitude you are entering. Little patches of dry, frosty snow lie all along the trail and the beautiful brook dashes and foams down a bed of ice. The rocks and logs of its course are draped with fantastic sheetings while the neighboring bushes glitter with countless pendants. Did you ever see icicles with the big end down? That is the shape of all that bend these twigs. The spray, of course, is thickest near the brook, and so the icicles are club-shaped or pear-shaped.

Leaving the ravine at that good-for-nothing Trail House, the path climbs a long, gentle slope for a mile and a half, and then turns up along the southern spur of the peak, skirting up closer and closer to the timber-line. Here the snow first begins to be really troublesome, and continues so nearly all the rest of the

way. The trail is dug down along the steep slope, and into this
hollow all the snow around has drifted, until it stands two, and
sometimes three feet deep. There is no dodging it, and it strikes
pretty cold on feet and shins. The day was very comfortable
until I passed the timber-line—just cool enough to alleviate the
torrid heat generated by climbing; but when I left behind the
last scrubby pine, and got around the southern spur, "Windy
Point," a change came over the spirit of my dreams.

A keen, savage, icy wind came cavorting up from the snowy
peaks of the Sangre de Christo range, and struck me all of a heap.
My perspiration-soaked clothing seemed turned to sudden ice,
and my teeth began to chatter. On went the discarded coat; on
went the thick duck over it, and on went I, puffing up the steep,
rocky, snowy trail in a not too successful effort to keep warm.

Such an aggravating path I never before trod. Had it gone bang
up the steepest pitch of the mountain it would have suited me
exactly; but thus to putter and poke along around the side of the
ridge, heading everywhere but to the peak, gave me a pain. The
last two-miles are mighty hard climbing, too; steep as a roof, all
full of snow and ice and sharp rocks. I began to think this trail
didn't go up Pike's Peak at all, but was striking for Leadville,
until, of a sudden, as I came over a steep pitch, the station
loomed up right before me. Didn't it get a cheer, though, from
what wind was left in my lungs? That is the worst of climbing
such a lofty altitude—the way in which you lose your breath. I
have done mountain climbing that was harder on the legs than
this peak is, but never had such a struggle for breath before.

It was 3:30 when I stood before the door of the signal service
station, gazing out upon the marvelous view. Eastward, for hundreds of miles, stretch the bare, brown plains. In the same direction, but at my very feet, lie Manitou and Colorado Springs,
both plainly visible in detail. The Garden of the Gods, Cheyenne Peak, Ute Pass—through which streamed a struggling tide
of men, mules and wagon-trains in Leadville's early days—the
Seven Lakes, and other minor points of interest are also spread
before the observer. Due North, and seventy miles away in a

bee-line, you see the cloudy spot that represents bustling Denver.

Fifty miles to the South, the smoke of Pueblo curls up from the prairie, falls back and trails along the plain in a misty belt, that reaches farther Eastward than the eye can follow. A little pond-like broadening in this smoke river shows the location of La Junta, one hundred miles away. West of South, in long and seried ranks, stand the Culebra and Sangre de Christo ranges, while nearer tower the Southern walls of the Grand Canyon of the Arkansas. Far to the West are the pinnacles of the main range of the Rockies—for Pike stands in regal isolation a hundred miles from any peer. His sole companions are the 10,000 and 12,000-foot "foot-hills" that look up in awe to his lofty throne.

But the grandest sight of all—the sublimest I ever saw— came with the setting of the sun. As the great red orb sank down behind these rocky bastions, the gigantic shadow of the Peak crept up on the foot-hills, leaped across the plains, and at last climbed the far horizon, and was projected high in heaven— vast, pyramidal, ghostly. For a few moments it lingered there, and then died away in the slow twilight. Perhaps the other world has scenes as glorious; this surely has not.

But why attempt description of this place? It bankrupts language. I try to write you the ineffable splendors of this world above the world, but

> In the cold,
> Dead ashes of expression thought's flame
>   dies
> And meaning palls on utterance.
> Let me come down to what I can talk about.

The question of supplies up here is a most momentous one. Everything that is used has to be packed up that long narrow trail on the backs of burros—which is the Western name for mules. Meat, flour, canned provisions and the like, are thus transported all the way from Manitou. The fuel is pine wood, brought from the timber-line, six sticks at a time, on burros.

Uncle Sam owns the wood, but has to pay $23 per cord for cutting it and hauling it up here. This is, I fancy, the highest wood in the world, in more senses than one. It costs about $1,300 a year to warm this one room in which I write.

The observer here, who has to record his gleanings from thermometer, anemometer, barometer and other instruments five times a day, has rather a good time of it. He stays up here two weeks, and then goes down to Colorado Springs to loaf an equal length of time, being relieved by his chum, who comes up as he goes down. The government isn't such a bad master to work for, after all.

I find much less trouble with this rarified atmosphere than I had anticipated. Except under exertion it does not particularly affect my lungs. Its biggest operation is on my stylographic pen; the outer pressure being so much less than usual that, the ink fairly spurts out. The temperature during the day is from 10 to 16 degrees above zero, and about 10 degrees less at night. The air seems to evaporate on your flesh, and leaves a delicious coolness like that resulting from an ether or camphor bath. Now for my experiences since the last letter, and then to bed.

Instead of fourteen miles, I had to tramp seventeen, Thursday evening, to mail that last *Leader* letter. If it hadn't been for that errand, I should probably still be throwing barbed grasshoppers into the clear, green pools of the Platte. It was slightly exasperating, therefore, after that long, dark, prickly-pear-beset trip across the valleys and divides, to find that there would be no mail to Denver for 23 hours. I did think at first of suing Uncle Sam for breach of promise, but concluded to let him off this time. Finally I found that the screed could go by the southern route, and mailed it accordingly. Hope it got through in time.

To my application for a belated supper the landlady of the little Weaver House, Sedalia, asked "An' are yees but wan?" "Yes," said I, "only one, but there's a lot of me." "Faith," she retorted, scrutinizing my small proportions, "the owld carpenter shud 'ave put a pane o' glass in the front of yees, to show where the lot is." It's no use to measure wits with a clever Irishwoman, and I didn't try it; but when I got up from the table she was ready to admit that my tonnage is heavy, even if my deck measurement isn't big. You have no notion how this thin, crisp air which sets the heart to pumping at double speed, makes one devastate the table. A grey wolf would hide his diminished head if he could see me getting in my work. The greasy bacon and potatoes, the bitter coffee and dingy bread of these section-houses taste like ambrosia, and there is no language to denote the absolute deliciousness of really respectable provender—food that would be admitted into polite society.

Truly a healthy appetite is wealth. I wouldn't swap my athletic stomach and my empty pocket for [William] Vanderbilt's dyspepsia and his bank account. In fact, I don't envy the red-faced, red-whiskered, unread billionaire—who looks like a hog and talks like a hostler—in any respect. He never dared have as much enjoyment in ten years as I have every day. Real pleasure never bunked in the same house with heavy cares, and never will. Try to lock them in together, and there will be hair-pulling just too quick.

At Sedalia, Friday morning, I turned the two-ton knapsack over to the tender mercies of the expressman, having previously extracted the duck coat as a sort of compromise. The scales there showed me up at 161 pounds as I stand, which means that I am toting 25 pounds more than the Lord meant me to. The rifle, duck coat, cartridge belt and revolver are chiefly responsible for that.

I removed the light of my countenance from Sedalia at 9:30, and meandered up the track on over the hills to Castle Rock, through a dullish country whose leading industries seemed to be sand and rocks. Castle Rock is so called from a peculiar freak of nature just northeast of town. Here, on the table-top of a 300-foot hill, lies a huge block of granite some 60 feet wide, 40 high and 200 feet long. From a short distance it looks as regular as if hewn from a quarry, and really resembles an ancient castle—the likeness becoming stronger, the farther away you get.

On the way thence to Larkspur, I gently entangled my inner consciousness with about a peck of very toothsome wild plums, and also found enough game to keep my Winchester from feeling lonesome. Rabbits! You never saw such rafts of the light-footed skippers as there are all along this road. With a good shotgun one could load a buggy brimful of them every day. A rifle is a poor tool for shooting rabbits on the wing, but I managed to get three of them in ten minutes that afternoon. The last one rolled down into his hole, and I should have lost him but for a little bit of hunter-craft which it will not hurt some of your sporting readers to know. He lay about six feet down the hole, far beyond the reach of my arm, but I could just touch him with my walking-stick. Wetting the end of this in my mouth, I put it against his silky hair and twisted it 'round and 'round perhaps 20 times. Then when I drew the stick out carefully, the rabbit was on the end of it—bound by a delicately twisted cable of his own hair.

The full moon was high overhead as I wound through the lonely canyon of Plum Creek; and, mid-way of that bare defile, my ears pricked up at an old, familiar sound, for years unheard, and almost forgotten—the long, wild howl of a grey wolf. It is a cry to make the blood curdle under some circumstances; but there was no answering chorus to his yell, and after the first startled grab at the butt of my .44, I plodded on serenely.

I got up to Larkspur late, expecting to find a good bed, but it wasn't their week for beds. The section house was full, there was no other place of accommodation, and I had to turn to the bunk-house of the section hands. I supposed, of course, there would be some sort of covering there, and didn't worry myself further till midnight, when, having had enough of a talk with a lot of bums who were waiting to beat a train, I prepared to turn in—the preparations in such a case being to remove hat and boots and button up my coat. The night was bitter cold, ice stood an inch thick under the spout of the water tank, and the wind howled down the canyon like the ghost of Wagner's pet cat. Fancy, then, my dismay at climbing up to a bunk and finding it as bare as the palm of your hand. The one old fellow who slept there had but a single thin blanket, hardly enough for himself, and I couldn't scare up so much as a gunny sack. I laid me down—not to sleep, but to try to—on the rough boards, with two signal flag sticks for a pillow, and wrestled with Nod for a couple of hours.

I asked the old man why he didn't have a fire. He replied that "it made the bugs too dom'd bahd to have it warrum, but whin it was cowld they wudn't be after botherin' you so much." At last, after three hours of profane restlessness, during which my shins felt like two icicles hanging at the north pole, I went out and scraped up some chips and coal, got the little cannon stove red-hot, and then slumbered sweetly on the floor beside it. I had to get up and skirmish around for fuel three times more before morning; for whenever the fire dwindled the piercing cold would awaken me at once.

When I left Larkspur, Saturday morning, the weather had taken a big flop from that of the day before. It was as cold as oilcloth is to bare feet, and the wind roared down from Pike's Peak as frigid as if it were bringing the whole peak with it. The swift current of Plum Creek was thickly frozen over, and did not thaw out during the whole day. I buttoned up my duck, pulled down my sombrero—a Deer Trail investment—and with hands in pocket and head down, worried along as best I could, utterly unable to make two miles an hour. I tried to borrow an auger, to bore my way up through the wind, but they didn't have any.

The railroad keeps climbing a steep grade all the way to Palmer Lake, which is on the Divide, 8,000 feet above the sea, and all the way that wind grew colder and more obstreperous. I never saw anything to match it, except on Mt. Washington. It was a perfect gale. Two miles east of Greenland—the most aptly named place I ever saw—that mountain zephyr came near writing "Dennis" on my classic brow. I was crossing a longish trestle over Carpenter's Creek, when a sudden rush of wind swept me bodily off from the track and dumped me kerslosh in the sand or ice-water 25 feet below. Ugh! That fall hurt me about as badly as anything that ever happened, and I can feel it yet in about 200 places. Even the sensation of falling wasn't pleasant. Cowper was a crank when he sighed

"Oh, had I the wings of the wind!"

If he had got wafted out on those same wings just once, the way I was, he would have torn his throat begging a kind providence to let him settle down on the legs of the mud-turtle. My heavy octagon rifle was across my back, and the way it scraped my old spine in 27 directions was a caution to doctors. It would have been money in my pocket if I had been born without any vertebrae. Still, I don't complain. Most of these bridges have big dumps of rock or iron slag at each end, and I was pretty well content with my wet, soft sand. It was mean walking, though, the rest of those eight miles to the Divide, with my clothing frozen as pliable as a spruce plank, and every bone in my body aching. But a remarkably good dinner at Palmer Lake and a long spell of embracing the stove, braced me up greatly.

Going down the south side of the Divide, the scene was changed. The air was warm; the wind was left behind the mountains, and a smooth, down-hill road just seemed to fit my feet. I killed four cotton-tails and one jack between the Divide and Husted's—a tiny hamlet where I abode over night with a hospitable ranchero. I slept under four horse-blankets in a little shed bedroom, whose sides and roof let in all out-doors. I never before felt so much respect for my moustache as when I awoke in the morning and found two-inch icicles depending therefrom. I could have taken off my hat to it.

Sunday morning found me pacing off the 13 miles to Colorado Springs, and making the usual detours over hills and down valleys. Here I confidently expected theological accommodations with a minister who moved out from my Eastern home, to take charge of the Colorado College. I gave, therefore, a big brushing up to my biblical lore—which isn't so limited for an unregenerate journalist—and felt ready to tackle the Pope himself. But it was wasted. The reverend gentleman had gone hence, and many there be that grieve over his departure as only those can who cherish unpaid bills. This man's rascality cost me a dollar, for I had to go to the hotel. Why can't folks be honest?

From Denver all the way down to the Divide; over in the mountains and on the prairie trails, I have been almost literally walking on agate. Every day I have picked and then thrown unwillingly away perhaps 500 specimens of this beautiful mineral each of which would be worth, polished, from $1 to $5 in New York or Boston. Of course it is impossible for me to keep them; but if I had a pack-mule he certainly would have to grunt under the load of them. A few particularly nice pieces, however, are at present wearing out my pockets. Most of the specimens are of the carnelian variety, and some are very beautiful. I have found no moss-agates yet, save in veins impossible to break.

Some of the names of towns out in this country are real "corkers." I have passed through Lenape, Menoken, Black Wolf, Bunker Hill, Hog Back, Monument, Co-lo-no, Me-lo-te, Eagle Tail, Wild Horse, Bo-ye-ro, Agate, Deer Trail, Box Elder, and other equally gifted towns in Kansas and Colorado. Other towns yet to be reached are Spiked Buck, Devil's Hole, Good Night, Wigwam, Mule Shoe, Cactus, Cotopaxi, Badger, Volcano, Huerfano, Commanche, and so on. There are still more startling names in the state, as Dirty Devil, Fair Play, Bill Williams, Hard Luck, Exchequer, Jack's Cabin, Dornick, Americus, Harp, Greenhorn, Toll Gate, etc., not to mention the countless Spanish jawbreakers. No need to bother yourself hunting up names for your children—just hire one of these Coloradoans to do your christening. They can be depended upon to give you something unique, if nothing more.

You never saw such a country as this for tramps. I have met or overtaken more of these knights of the brogan in the little railroad I have traversed between here and Denver than in all the rest of my trip and find great entertainment among them. They are what Artemas Ward loved to call "amoosin cusses." Light-hearted and jovial, almost without exception, having no care whether the stock market goes up or down, always looking for work (with a knife and fork) and never fretting if they don't get it, contented to lie in the sun and let the wind fill them. I suppose they have about as good a time in this world as any adults. They are all along the road here, traveling from Denver to Pueblo, or from Pueblo to Denver.

I think most of them must be really looking after work, for this is a poor country to beat a living out of. They don't calculate to walk much, but travel mostly by rail. You will find a knot of them at almost any water-tank, awaiting a train. If it is a passenger, they will try to get a perch on the front of the forward car, which has no exit toward the engine. This is "making the blind baggage." If it is a freight, they will slip in between the cars, into an empty box-car, or even on the truck. They seldom try a box-car unless they have a little spare change, for the train hands overhaul these cars frequently for just such game. If a brakeman finds a bum thus secreted, he collars him and says, "Got any stuff?" If the wayfarer is possessed of "stuff" he hands over fifty cents or a dollar, and gets a ride of 50 or 100 miles. The freight brakemen build up their scanty wages to a pretty handy figure by such schemes.

Once in a while one of these beats strikes trouble, however, for some ungodly braker will take his money, and stow him away in a box-car that is going only to the next station. When Mr. Tramp awakes from his slumber, he finds himself nicely side-tracked in a locked car, his money gone, and nothing gained but an excuse for painting the air blue. There is one fellow whom I encounter at almost every station. He puts up now and then in dollar hotels, and upon leaving, carries off all the towels, bedclothes and other truck he can hide away under his voluminous clothing—and that is a good deal. He thinks me peculiarly dull because I don't follow the same tack, after he has told me how easy it is.

It is truly wonderful how the weather-boss has turned his feather-edge to me all the way. I have been out now 55 days from

Chillicothe, and in all that long time have had but three bad days. Think of that, and talk about luck. Two days it has been cold, and thrice it has rained; but with those trifling exceptions, things couldn't have been better if I had had the weather made to my measure. If I don't have any future falling out with the storm-steerer, I shall not cloud up much myself.

In a straight line I suppose I am now about 50 or 55 miles from Denver; by rail and road about 94; but I have been nine days on the way. You need not think I have been loafing, however, for in that nine days I have covered 267 miles, and much of it the toughest kind of climbing with tooth and toenail. Nearly every high foot-hill, every canyon I have labored over, both to see sights and to hunt. My search in the latter direction has been rewarded by nothing bigger than jack-rabbits, but they are plenty and there is worse sport than killing them, and worse eating than they make.

Now that my engagement at Denver has been filled, I am taking my ease and might never get out of this seductive country at all, but for a lingering, though somewhat vague desire to get back to work and civilization and a home—sometime.

I think I could plant myself pretty comfortably in lovely Colorado Springs, 8,000 feet below me here. It is rather a modest town. Its 6,000 people are almost entirely of the better class, and poverty and the criminal element are nearly unknown. It has no saloons, no hovels, and no apparent haunts of vice. Its climate is claimed to be one of the finest in the world, and its scenery is undeniably sublime. Spread on a high plateau 6,000 feet above the sea-level, it is skirted on the East by the vast plains. On the West, in savage ranks, rise the lower mountains which form the threshold of the Rockies. Through a big gap in these, directly in front of the city's slope, Pike's Peak frowns down in all its awful majesty, its great shoulders dark with indistinguishable pines and crags, and its high brow fittingly crowned with eternal snow.

The streets, stretching north and south, are broad and well-made, and down each gutter, under the countless young shade trees, flows a swift stream of living snow water, fresh from the peaks. The business blocks are not gorgeous, but amply adequate and the dwellings remind one of a bright New England town, in their handsome homelikeness and neatness. There is a little hill just back of town, by the water and 150 feet higher than the main street, which they have sarcastically named Mt. Washington, because it happens to be of the same altitude as the highest mountain East of this range. But never mind. I have seen here no nobler mountain than the old New Hampshire monarch, and I do not expect to. The Presidential Range of the White Mountains would not show beside these towering giants, but where they are they are hardly less impressive.

Manitou—which is, by the way, a name for God, current in nearly all the varying Indian dialects—is a beautiful little town lying seven miles up the canyon from Colorado Springs, and 6,500 feet above the sea. It is like no other town so much as little Bethlehem in New Hampshire, and is equally a place devoted to attending the pocket-books of tourists. Half of its 500 people make their living by keeping boarders. The other half don't need to make a living at all, being wealthy owners of some as pleasant villas as you ever saw. The rugged niches in the mountain wall afford footing for these charming summer houses, and give them a grandeur of setting seldom equaled. There is a humorous saloon-keeper here, whose sign reads "C. F. Albrecht, dealer in Barley Water and Bad Cigars." The last part of that inscription ought to be placed by law over the door of every tobacconist in this western country. A branch of the Denver and Río Grande R.R. runs up from Denver to Manitou, and a road thence to the very summit of Pike's Peak is now under construction, about four miles being already graded. I fear I slandered the O. & M. road back there by Shoals, Ind. This track is by close computation, 36¾ times as crooked. It goes 27 miles around to get 9 ahead.

A mile northeast of Manitou—these folks would never think

of naming a town God in plain English, but it's all right in
Choctaw*—begins the Garden of the Gods. I used to think that
title a little high-flown; but since seeing that marvelous spot on
my way up from Colorado Springs, Monday morning, I beg the
pardon of its godfathers. It is rightly named. The heights of
shaggy Olympus were tame beside this wonderland. Fancy,
walled in by rock-bound peaks, a wild glen of two thousand
acres. In it, among the murmuring pines, a hundred colossal
towers and castles, pinnacles and battlements, hewn from the
deep red sandstone. Perchance fat Bacchus and knotty Hercules,
returning from some godly revel, frolicked here among the then
uncarved cliffs, and while the tricky fancy of the God of Wine
mopped out the imagery of what now is, the brawny arms of the
God of Muscle twisted and tore the great cliffs into their fantastic shapes.

All through its extent the Garden of the Gods is fascinating,
but at the highest point its wonder is the greatest. In the center
of a great amphitheatre, four colossal crags, blood-red and radiant, have pushed their way up from the level ground, and soar
300 feet up into the clear air—thick strata of the old red sandstone, cropping out perpendicularly. They are worn at the top
into jagged points; their thickness is from 50 to 150 feet, and
their length from 200 to 500 feet. After infinite labor and at
considerable risk, I climbed the highest, whose apex is 330 feet
above its base. A narrow cleft at the end of the strata was the
only possible ladder—the sides themselves being sheer as a
wall. This particular crag has a truly marvelous resemblance to
a huge citadel; one can hardly banish an idea that it was carved
thus by animate hands. Its walls are pierced by rain-wrought
portholes, in which the wide-winged hawks rear their savage

---

*"Manitou" is from the Algonquian Indian lingual family, and, therefore,
not necessarily a locally indigenous expression. And Colorado Springs is no
more a "western" or "Southwestern" town than is Saratoga Springs, New York,
another quaint and genteel watering spot. Here and in several other places at
this time Lummis assumes the standard persona of the well-bred traveller, with
frequent classical name-dropping—Bacchus, Hercules, and even Shakespeare.

young. All around, too, are smaller out-crops of the sandstone, worn into yet more striking shapes. At the upper end of the Garden, close to the wilderness of Glen Eyrie, is another group of monuments, the most singular of all. One is about 50 feet high, and no larger around than a barrel.

There has been a deal of money spent on this upper end, in the way of a beautiful hotel with elegant walks and bridges and lodges and bowers; but these things are out of place there. I wish these Philistines could learn that when the Lord lay Himself out on a landscape, there is no need that little man should lug in his microscopic tools and do the job over. If I were the Ruler of the Universe, I should get so disgusted at one or two such performances that I'd kick the earth into a flat bunk and say "There, you mush-headed idiots, fix up your darned old world to suit yourselves, if you're so gee-whizzly smart." And I'd make 'em do it, too. If they didn't like the result of their puttering, they could lump it—they'd get no more help out of me.

In one part of the Garden is a huge ledge of crystalline gypsum—or, as my landlady at Manitou, who had evidently heard the name with careless ears, persists in calling it "Egyptian Stone." I never realized, before, the force of Shakespeare's

"Purer than monumental alabaster."

It is the daintiest, purest, fairest mineral I ever saw. The heart is a soft white, but outside it blushes into tender pink. After eating a prosaic can of Boston baked beans and pork on top of the highest pinnacle of the Castle, I carved myself a pipe from this spotted alabaster. A pretty one to talk about Philistines, am I not?

Coming out of this place of beauty, I met a young fellow just arrived here from Toledo to begin duty in the Pike's Peak Signal Service Station. After a pleasant chat he gave me a note to the boys up here, which has helped me. They charge you 50 cents for a cup of coffee, and $1 for sleeping on the floor; but I shall escape this tax, thanks to the courtesy of Mr. Curtis.

Tell Tom Cahill that he may use my name in vain all he

pleases in praise of my Curtis & Wheeler shoes. They are jewels. I put on a pair when I left Chillicothe, and they are on my feet now—patched, rubbed, torn by the sharp rocks of these mountains, frayed by the sharp gravel of the track, but still sound. They have their fourth pair of soles on, but I believe the uppers will last me clear through. I hope so, for I respect those shoes, and shall preserve them with honor to the day of my death, as befits their faithful service. As for stockings, I should wear out a pair every day, if I would acknowledge it. But one can hardly afford that, and they, or their remains, have to do duty until little is left but the shank.

This noon I shall get about 8,000 feet farther away from heaven by going back down over the snow and rocks to Colorado Springs, whence I make a detour of 100 miles from my route. I shall take the trail for Cañon City, go thence up to Texas Creek, and then follow down through the Grand Canyon of the Arkansas to Pueblo, where I strike my line of march again. This canyon is said to be the finest traversed by any railroad in the world, and I anticipate a glorious trip. I may very likely date my next letter thence, as I shall not hurry over such scenery. Now I must go for a last gaze at the unspeakable glories of this dizzy lookout, and then back to the world below the clouds, so farewell.

LUM

Pueblo, Colorado
Thursday, November 13th, 1884

Editors Leader:

This has been by far my best week thus far—a week crowded with incidents more or less exciting, and all interesting to me. If I could present them to you as graphically as they came to me, you would be interested, too.

Wednesday noon, after as delightful a time on Pike's Peak as I ever had anywhere, the hour came all too soon when I felt I must depart. It was a warm, clear, glorious day, and I had a chance to enjoy the scenery without freezing to death, as I jumped and stumbled down the steep and winding trail—it would be mighty hard on the hold-backs to go down slowly—and slackened my speed only on the comparatively level stretches. Just below the trail-house I met Sergeant H. Hall, the "chief of staff," and Mr. Curtis who were making their way up on mules. I had a very pleasant chat with them, and then went plunging down the steeper pitches of Engleman's canyon. My actual time from the summit to Manitou, 12 miles, was an hour and 51 minutes, which I guess is pretty good. But alas for my poor shoes! That 12-mile run over the sharp rocks and sharper gravel did them more damage than 300 miles of ordinary walking, and I fear their days are numbered. They look as if they had been run through a sausage machine.

I cantered on down to Colorado Springs after a ten minute rain at Manitou, anxious to hear the election news. Little good it did me, however, for no one knew anything about it. Even now we are not much better off down here, though there is a general impression that the Demmies "got thar." Well, if the people of these United States have deliberately gone to work and chosen the Buffalo Bull as their highest representative, I shall for the first time blush that I am an American. I shall wish to resign my citizenship and light out for the Sandwich Islands, where they don't wear many clothes, but still have some decency left.

In default of definite election news, however, the *Leader* was lying, (now don't get hot, gentlemen—wait till I finish) was lying in the post office for me. Chillicothe news is a little pre-historical by the time it reaches me, but it is none the less as welcome as dinner-time.

The two Cheyenne Canyons, about four miles from Colorado Springs, had been recommended to me as not to be missed, and Thursday morning I started out in good season, planning to

explore them and get out 15 or 20 miles along the overland trail
to Canyon City. A noble pile of bristling granite is Cheyenne
mountain—a peak without a parallel. The only mountain in
the world without a base, it thrusts its grizzly head 4,000 feet
out of the prairie, along which for three miles its rocky ramparts
tower in an almost sheer wall.

At the northern flank, split by a great crag, the north and
south branches of Cheyenne creek come racing down the mountain ridges, cold as ice, clear as crystal, foam-decked from their
breathless leaps. I went first up the South Canyon, which is
usually deemed the finer of the two and climbed it from end to
end. It is an impressive spot; although I have since clambered
twice through the more colossal grandeur of the Grand Canyon
of the Arkansaw, the picture of South Cheyenne will linger as
long and as vividly before my mental vision. Passing the two
toll-houses—out here the natives apparently appreciate nature's noblest works as for revenue only—you turn the corner of
a great red granite gateway, and stand in the jaws of the defile.
On either hand is a mountain of rugged rock, seamed and broken: and between their steep sides dashes the noisy stream,
which it seems wicked to call a creek. It is too clear, sparkling
for such a malarial title.

After a few rods of tolerably level road, flanked by walls fast
growing more and more rugged, you reach a spot where the
walls seem actually to meet. Their crags, 500 feet high, are not
30 feet apart; and the sudden angle in the southern cliff beyond
apparently obliterates even this small gap. The whole two-mile
walk to the head of the canyon is a ceaseless but ever-varying
delight. At every step a new crag or cliff or pinnacle peers down
at the beholder, and the great ruddy mountains themselves
change shape from peaks to ridges or from ridges to peaks, as the
point of view is shifted.

Near the upper end of the canyon are the "Seven Falls," really
one cascade in seven leaps of from 10 to 40 feet each. A steep
stairway climbs the water-worn cliff at the very site of the
narrow fall; and on two dizzy pinnacles of rock, 200 to 300 feet

above, are two little observatories, scarcely visible from below, but commanding a glorious view of the canyon and its encircling peaks.

Seeing the brown flash of a trout in the clear pool, I cut a cotton-wood pole, corraled some grasshoppers, and began fishing. I caught a small string, and then got caught myself. At the top of a fine fall I stepped on a treacherous rock, and went down with a sharp thud (please take notice that it wasn't a dull one) into a hole ten feet below. Of course I got wet nearly all over in that icy water, but that wasn't half as bad as the sprain my ankle got. The fish along the brook must have thought some one was using dynamite, for they wouldn't bite any more, and I gave them up more in sorrow than in wrath.

I took a limping look at the North Canyon, which doesn't differ essentially from the South, and then struck off across irrigating ditches, wire fences, gullies, scrub-oak thickets and similar landscape ornaments, to the Canyon City road. It was mighty poor walking on that lame ankle, however, and when I struck the road at last I was glad to get into the first ranche.

It was an uncommonly interesting place that I thus stumbled into—not so much for its own sake as for that of its proprietor, a tough, battered, grizzly old miner. He got home a few minutes after my arrival, from where, away back in the mountains, he had been working one of his claims since February. He has 18 prospect holes that he is working by turns, leaving his young boys to run the ranche as best they may—and they do it pretty cleverly. When he makes anything on the ranche he "puts it into a hole," and his numerous holes pan out about enough to keep him alive and hearty. One of us would grunt terribly at going up some of these peaks in silk tights; but this shaggy-browed, tangled-bearded old man puts his heavy pick, three or four three-foot drills, two blankets, and some provisions on his thick but bowed shoulders, and stumps clear across the range as carelessly as if he were carrying nothing but Alice Oates' wardrobe.

The veteran has been out here for twenty years, and with the observation common to these fellows who have had to carve

their way through starvation and disappointment, through suffering of every sort, among wild beasts, wilder Indians and
wildest outlaws, he has laid up a wonderful store of reminiscences. It would do you good to hear him growl away in some
tale of the days before Colorado was a state; days when the three
great Ute tribes—the Utes, Paiutes and Uncompahgres—were
as thick over these foothills and plains as the grasshoppers are
now; and when through the winter snow of the wild mountain
passes pressed a long, gaunt train of excited men chasing their
dream of the Eldorado; how some struggled onward grimly under their heavy packs, while others dropped in the great white
drifts and sobbed like children; how a few "struck it rich," while
the forgotten thousands strained all day vainly at the heavy pan,
and every night had to show for it only the few tiny flecks of
yellow. Ah, there's where the poetry of these Rocky Mountains
comes in.

It's easy enough to recount the Tabors and Floods and Sharons
and Mackeys—the golden accidents of fortune; but that is mere
jingle. It were an epic to tell of the great motley throng—the
scum of great cities, the brawn of the farm, the gamblers, the
ministers, the lawyers, thieves, bankers, beggars, college boys,
cowboys, lads and old men—that plodded across the vast barren
plains, struggled wearily but hopefully up the wild mountain
sides, waded the heavy snow and the icy streams, froze and
starved, yet never despaired. How they ran hither and yon as
delusive hope blew her golden bubbles about: how they toiled
over the heavy sands of the wild mountain stream, shoveled
them into the flaring gold-pans or the long sluice boxes, washed
and dug and scraped, forgetting to eat and sleep—all crazed for
the sight of those little yellow scales that might blink up at
them from the bottom of pan or rocker. How young men grew
old and bent in the feverish chase—some of them still roam like
uneasy specters among the gulches of the farthest ranges—and
old men laid their weary bones to bleach beside the lonely claim,
the little buckskin bag of "dust" clutched in their gaunt fingers.
How men made fortunes in some golden placer and then

dropped the last cent into a worthless hole. How paupers became princes and princes paupers, and the man whose claim to-
day was worth its hundreds of thousands, to-morrow turned a
beggar, to strike it again among the hills. How that hetero-
geneous mass of humanity, akin only in the one absorbing
passion, battled with cold and hunger, with disease and death,
with beasts thirsty for blood and desperate men still thirstier for
gold—ah, my friends, it is the greatest, longest, strangest tragedy the world has ever known.

It sends a thrill through my veins to meet out here in some
lonely cabin a gray-haired remnant of those old heroes—for
heroes they were, that fought the death against such odds,
though that aim was ignoble—whose tireless vigor opened
these western states and territories to civilization; the men
whose average of ill luck buried twenty dollars in the ground for
every dollar in gold that was taken from it, yet paved the way to
a surer and more substantial prosperity—the prosperity of solid
business.

But to-day they are half forgotten. The mountain brooks
tumble down to the rivers unchecked, their bars and beaches of
shifting sand are undisturbed by the greedy shovel, and the fine
grains of gold that still lurk beneath, rest at last after their long
hiding from covetous eyes. For the days of gold-washing are
over. You can still "strike color" in almost every running stream
along the Rockies, but that is about all.

Perhaps some of you do not know what "color" is. Well, you
take your shovel and gold-pan—a flaring dish some two feet
long and made of galvanized iron—and strike out for some
brook. From the sand and gravel of its bed—digging from one to
three feet down—you throw a couple of gallons of stuff into
your pan, and then work it to and fro in the running water. The
lighter particles are washed away, and on the bottom of the pan
at last you may see a few tiny yellow spots, scarce coarser than
dust—the time-filtered particles of gold. Each of these spots is a
"color." Perhaps you fancy that this is not very laborious. Don't
deceive yourself. It is the very hardest work in the world. I have

tried it and I know. Half a day of it will make every muscle in
your body feel like an aching tooth.

Well, I stayed with the grim old miner Thursday night, and
slept in his heavy blankets, ate his pork and potatoes, and
listened to his epigrammatic talk. In the morning, when I asked
to pay him, he said "No, sir. A miner always feeds all that come
along, but not for money. If you come to his cabin when he is
away, you will never find it locked. Go in and be at home. If
there are any provisions, eat what you want and welcome, for he
expects it. But you don't want to offer him money."

He told me, too, before I left, of a little episode in the Leadville of '77. One Stevens, a wealthy mine owner, went back to
his home in Detroit, and bragged rather broadly of his big enterprises. When he returned to Leadville, two or three hundred
misguided men followed him, hoping to share in the great bonanza. It was at the time when washing had already given way
to shaft-mining, and the place was crowded with hundreds of
unemployed men. They were fed by the miners and slept where
they could—always cold, always hungry, always penniless.
When the Detroiters told how they had been led out here by
Stevens' talk of abundant work, the rough but honest miners
gave Mr. Stevens a characteristic call. They stretched a long
rope over a cedar branch, and worked one end into a tight-fitting
cravat which discommoded the Stevens neck. "Now," said they,
"you fooled these men out here to starve by your damned blowing. Give them $50 a piece to go home with, or you'll dance on
nothing in two minutes." It is almost needless to add that the
money was forthcoming.

A similar dose might have been administered very appropri-
ately in another case that has come to my knowledge. A few
years ago, the quarter-section on which the little city of Colorado Springs now stands, was owned by a convivial Irish miner,
"Judge" Baldwin, whose only enemy in the world was whisky.
Well, General Palmer—the genial shark, who has, until recently ousted, been President of the D. & R.G.R.R.—along with
other grabbers, took a notion that here was the place for a town.

They got the old, simple-hearted miner drunk, provided him a
perpetual pass over the road, and a corner lot, and induced him
to deed his whole 160 acres to them for nothing. He never got so
much for it all as a free ride to Manitou. This Baldwin had a
strange life. Twice he was scalped by the Utes, once on his
ranche, in the very spot where the present natives scalp the
pocket-book of the summer visitor. He ended his romantic
career in an element for which he had in life but little use. They
found him one morning in a shallow well, drowned in two feet
of water.

Friday I was almost too lame to walk, but managed to hobble
ahead 18 miles to the banks of waterless Turkey creek. A young
rancher was chasing a stubborn cow around a corral, trying to
argue her, through the logic of a big cudgel, to "go there, you
brute." When she finally "soed" and the milking was over, he
took me into the house, fed me full, and made me as comfortable as a king. He had been a rough boy, running wild through
the big territories with the hardest kind of company; but he had
the right stuff in him, and knew when he had had enough. Now
he is quietly settled on the ranche, with his aged parents and
sharp-eyed little girl, making a home for the rest of his family.

The old gentleman was in Pueblo, but the white-haired
mother made the stranger wonderfully at home, and beside the
big fireplace, that night, gave him the first praying-for that he
has heard in many a long day. It does a man good, after this
roving, irresponsible life I am now leading, to fall now and then
within homelike influences. There is many a place and many a
face I shall forget sooner than Charlie Bixby and his ranche on
Turkey.

I was a good deal surprised, just before entering Dead Man's
Canyon, that day, to come upon a big rattler basking in the sun.
At this time of year the snakes are almost invariably in their
holes for the winter, but the noonday sun had brought this
fellow out for the last time. His skin and handsome string of
rattlers have gone to Los Angeles.

Leaving the Bixby ranche after dinner, Saturday, having

passed the forenoon in grinding out three columns of copy, I struck over across the hogbacks—as they call almost every ridge in these mountains—toward Canyon City. My ankle was still painful, and I got only as far as Beaver Creek, 9 miles away, before darkness came. All the afternoon I was picking up countless pebbles and fragments of the prettiest quartz in the world— rosy, snow-white, smoky, yellow and many another hue.

By the way, all this quartz is emigrant. It is not native here at all—you will not find a vein of it in all the mountains. The gold-bearing quartz is of a dingy color. But these specimens dot every prairie, every foot-hill, every highest mountain top. They came down here thousands of miles from the arctic north, borne on the crest or ground under the bulk of the vast glaciers that marched from the North Pole to the Rio Grande in prehistoric days. And such clouds of blue-jays as fill the cedars! These Rocky Mountain jays are larger than the eastern kind; blue all over, with a big top-knot and are as handsome a bird as one may find, but atrocious thieves. Along through this country, too, I saw my first magpies. They are as heavy as a pigeon, but far longer, with a tremendous tail, and big white patches on their black sides and wings. They learn to talk readily, and are often called "the Rocky Mountain parrots."

I put up Saturday night at a delightful ranche in the fine Beaver Canyon—the best part of Colorado I have thus far seen. The proprietor is a great hunter, and frequently takes "mountain lions"—cougars—bears, mountain sheep (or bighorns) and elk to the Colorado Springs museums, where they fetch fancy prices. Hanging in his front hall is a beautiful cinnamon bear skin, yellow as gold. He killed the brute, a few weeks ago, within sight of his house. The cinnamon bear rivals the grizzly in size and ferociousness. Some of them attain a weight of 1,600 pounds. Fancy a savage beast as big as an ox, armed with two-inch teeth and five-inch claws, with brawny forepaws whose single stroke will brain a cow!

The mountainous foot-hills are close to this house, and after breakfast Sunday morning I made a side raid about six miles back into the wilderness to see what I could. A little flock of bighorns led me on a long and fruitless chase, leaping along the inaccessible crags far above me, or peering down from the edge of some lofty cliff, beyond the reach of any bullet, the impregnable buttresses of their heads outlined against the blue sky. They are strange animals. Take a large ram, double the size of his head, plate his skull with four inches of hardest bone and increase his horns five-fold in size, and you approximate the bighorn. I know of no finer frontlets than these wild animals possess. Each ponderous horn curving three or four times upon itself, is as large around at the base as your thigh, and all of one solid armor with the skull. Let one of the cimarons [sic], as the Mexicans call them, fall 50 feet and strike upon his head upon a mass of rocks. You rush around to pick up his mangled carcass, and behold! he is far up the cliff, leaping from narrow ledge to ledge, unhurt. They do not jump from cliffs and alight on their heads purposely as some careless observers assert, but even such sure-footed leapers will sometimes fall, and for such accidents nature has built them to order.

Back in a little dry canyon near the "Buffalo Sloughs" I found a tiny cabin—the home of a grey-headed hunter. He hobbled out on a crutch as I drew near, and shared my tobacco on a sunny rock. "Old Monny," as they call him, is but a wreck of his former self. His right leg, from knee to hipjoint, is practically gone. He showed me the roughly-spliced bones, with their scant fringe of rough flesh; and pointed back into the hills to a wild ravine from which he was carried by rough but tender hands, four years ago, crippled for life. Monny and a comrade were going up that gulch, one spring day, their rifles across their shoulders. They had just passed a deep fissure in the rocks when suddenly, without a second's warning, a huge brown-yellow beast, bigger than a fattened steer, lumbered out upon them. Monny was ahead. A despairing shriek from his chum turned him about; and there he saw the cinnamon bear—for such it was—standing over a still palpitating corpse, while from his great fore paw, with its deadly armature, dripped the bright

blood and warm brains of the ill-fated man. Monny threw his
long, heavy barrel to a level, and sent its leaden messenger
through the lower half of the monster's heart. But a bear dies
hard; and before the hunter could reload or clamber up the steep
rocks the bear was upon him. Felling him to the ground with a
single sweep that crushed his shoulder, the dying beast seized
his thigh in its ponderous jaws and chewed the limb out of all
semblance to aught but mince-meat; and at last dropped lifeless
upon him. And that is why the old hunter carries a crutch. He
showed me the hide of his foe—11 feet, 7 inches from nose to
root of tail, with the little round hole that had at last let out that
great, savage life. It sent a strange chill through me to look at it
hanging on the walls of that lonely cabin—inanimate relic of
that bloody morning among the black rocks—while the only
living witness of that death-struggle sat maimed before me.

A couple of miles over the hills from Monny's cabin I saw
three black-tailed deer—the buck a royal fellow, larger than any
red deer, and with six years counted upon the spikes of his sharp
antlers. I got him by a lucky snap-shot, and am even now looking for a remittance from the rancher who agreed to haul him
out to Canyon City for me and send the receipts—minus $2—
by mail. If it doesn't come, I am only a cent and a half out on the
cartridge, and $100 ahead on the fun. Of course I shouldn't have
shot him on Sunday, but who would think of that at the time? It
is a mighty thick Sunday that will turn a bullet from a buck's
hide!

All the way from Colorado Springs, save when an intervening
foot-hill shut me in, I have been in full view of the snowy range
of the Sangre de Christo—or, as most of the natives here call it,
the Sandy Christo—about 90 miles away. It is the most serrate,
jagged mountain outline I ever saw. Nearer lie the high, brown
battlements of the Greenhorn range, stretching along the valley
of the Arkansaw. Now the bareness of the plains is exchanged
for vast, scattering forests of inconceivably twisted red cedar
and low, spreading pinons—pronounced like pinyun. These latter trees are a curiosity. A true red pine, the pinon bears in the

end of its cones a genuine nut, the size and general shape of a beechnut, but far richer. The crop is an inconstant one, however, as the nuts come but once in six or seven years. Monday, after getting back into Eight-mile Park—a park out here is a broad, levelish, plain-like valley among the mountains—I saw the curious buckhorn cactus for the first time in its natural state. You have seen the canes made from it—Commodore Ireland has a fine specimen—all hollow and lattice-like. The cactus itself has a strong, thick, prickly skin, in curious knobs like those on a buck's antlers. They peel these sticks and let them dry, when the pith comes out easily, and there is your cane.

By the way, did I tell you in my last that burros were mules? That was a stupid blunder. They are a race by themselves, breeding readily, and not hybrids like mules. One good mule would cut up into two of them. I believe they come originally from Mexico.

I saw a thing that amused me a good deal as I passed a ranche near Canyon City, Sunday. A little boy about two years old was tied to the end of a long rope, which was attached to the door, and played contentedly about, in no danger of being lost, strayed or stolen. I asked his mother the reason for this tethering, and she said, "Oh, the cattle's so bad that we dassent let him run loose, so we lariat him out." A lariat, you know, is a rope for picketing horses or other animals. There is a peculiar sameness about their interments out here in Colorado. They have no such things as cemeteries, but here and there on some little bluff you will notice a grave or two, each surrounded by a board fence.

Sunday night, at late supper time, hot and dusty from my 30-mile tramp over the mountains, I pounded away at the door of the Canyon City section house. Got supper and breakfast there, and slept in full dress, revolver and all, on the floor beside the bunk house stove. I got an early breakfast, left my rifle, and started up through the little city, of 4,500 people, toward the Grand Canyon of the Arkansaw. Half a mile beyond town, and a mile east of the portals of the canyon, I noticed a big stone building half hidden by the smoke of a dozen lime-kilns. Getting closer I saw here and there a man pacing about with a double-barreled gun on his shoulder, and swarming about the lime-kilns or engaged on other work, a great crowd of fellows in the black and white stripes. Then it dawned upon me that this must be the penitentiary, and so it was. I trotted placidly along the sidewalk, like the chuckleheaded ass I was, looking curiously at the vicious faces of the hundred convicts who were at work along the two-foot wall close beside me. I probably should not be writing to you now if it hadn't chanced that the sun was behind my back.

It did occur to me that my dress excited considerable curiosity among these fellows, but I couldn't take the hint, though they looked at me like hungry wolves. A group off to the left, near the railroad caught my eye, and I was half-back to the wall, when something on the sidewalk at my feet made my blood stand still. It was only a shadow, but the shadow of a bull-necked ruffian, whose uplifted right hand held a heavy stone-hammer. To jump halfway into the street, jerk my revolver to a "halt," and see the convict and his fellows jump back to their work with studied innocence—all that didn't take two seconds, but it wasn't a tenth of a second too soon. One of the mounted patrols, with two six-shooters strapped outside his coat, rode up in a hurry. "Why, you God d——d infernal fool, don't you know any better than to walk along within reach of those men with a revolver sticking out like that?" (I had restored it to its holster.) "There are 19 life-termers in that gang you passed, and that pop o' your'n means life and liberty to any one that gets his fingers on it. Another second and your head would 'a been mush, and we'd 'a had a break here for the hills. A man might just as well be in hell with his back broke as pack a shooting-iron around here where these ——— ——— can down him with a rock behind his back. Now get out into the middle o' the road there, d——n ye, and keep as fur from anything striped as you know how." And I shivered a little and went out into the road, realizing how closely I had escaped a fate my idiocy deserved. Put yourself in the place of one of these desperadoes, condemned to hard labor for life. Think how good the butt of a .44 would feel in your hand with the mountain fastnesses a few hundred yards away, and freedom among their rocks—and congratulate me.

There are now 350 convicts, chiefly murderers, horse-thieves and "rustlers" (cattle-thieves) in the Colorado State Penitentiary at Canyon City. They all work outside the walls by day at various employments. Thirty-eight guards, armed with Richards' breech-loaders, nine buck-shot in each barrel, and a six-shot, .44-caliber Colt's revolver, are scattered about among them. Then three mounted guards, without guns, but having two revolvers, ride around the place continually. In the little stone sentry-boxes along the high wall of the building, are stationed expert marksmen, each furnished with a long-range Sharpe's rifle, good, in their hands, to bring down a man at 800 yards every pop. Under such circumstances, there is little inducement for the unarmed convicts to attempt escape. Yet they do make a break now and then. Last spring, fourteen of the most desperate cases employed in the limestone quarries "jumped" their walking-boss, and showered down a volley of rocks upon him. Strangely enough, he was not hurt, and managed to beat them off so that they didn't get his two revolvers—the object of their attack. Three of them started up the steep hill-side, unheeding the warning of the guards to halt, but two gave in as the buck-shot began to patter on the rocks about them. The third kept on to the top of the bluff. In another moment he would have been safe, but crack went a Sharpe away down in the corner tower, a full thousand yards away, and the convict fell back dead upon the cold rocks. I don't think I should care for a job as guard here—the atmosphere is a leetle too exhilarating.

Well, having escaped the convicts more by bull luck than good sense, I went up to the Grand Canyon, which begins about a mile and a half above the city. I shall not attempt to do justice to the terrific gorge, for tongue nor pen can tell its awful glory. It is enough to say that for nine miles the raging Arkansaw seethes over the granitic debris at the bottom of a gloomy gorge which seems cut into the very bowels of the earth. The cliffs are those of the Greenhorn range, which dammed the river till at last—aided, I fancy, by a terrible earthquake—it tore down its way to the broad plains beyond. The mountains rise three thousand feet above the howling torrent; generally in steep and rugged slopes, inaccessible even to a bighorn, but sometimes in beetling cliffs which overhang the very track. The windings of the canyon are innumerable, its red crags and peaks bewildering in their majesty and multitude; and even the river is terrible. The stoutest swimmer cast into that white current were as helpless as a fettered babe, and would be ground to meal in half as long as it takes you to read this sentence. The Royal Gorge, 4½ miles from the eastern entrance to the canyon, is its highest pitch of grandeur. The sheer walls are a thousand feet high, and some of the crags jut out over your head as you creep like an ant below. I think it is a pretty good nerve that doesn't keep a man looking up to see if some of those loose boulders are not getting ready to drop on him. At the western end of the gorge is the famous iron bridge built on iron bars set in the face of the cliff, and suspended by four A-shaped spans bolted to the rocks above. The bridge is about a hundred feet long, and a fine piece of work, but to my fancy the best of the Royal Gorge is a few rods east of it.

Went on up to Parkdale, at the head of the canyon, and then down back the railroad alongside the river, pausing again at the Royal Gorge and then on to Canyon City. I planned to strike directly for Pueblo by rail, but the section boss, when I went back for my rifle, told me of a little trail over the Greenhorn Mountains which would take me through a fine hunting and mining country, and still not much out of my way to Pueblo. So I struck across the range past Coal Creek, whose striking miners are now scouring the country in search of fish and game to stave off starvation, and as darkness was coming on, Monday evening, I spied a lonely little cabin far up the side of the Wet Mountains. There was no other habitation near, and I steered straight for it. It was empty, but only temporarily. The short-

handled pick, the battered gold-pan, the hard-worked drills all
told me that the owner was a prospector, and that he was even
now pecking away somewhere at Mother Earth's hard breast. So
I went in and made myself at home, built in the big fireplace a
roaring blaze of the fragrant cedar, ate the pocketful of wild
plums I had found along the way, smoked a few pipes, and
finally rolled myself in my host's blankets and went to sleep
with my feet up to the fire.

The one window-opening had no sash, and the miner's few
aged hens had free access to the rafters above my head, where
they sat in a dumpy row. Along sometime in the night—my
watch has struck on me now, and I have to guess the hours—I
was wakened by an unearthly uproar in the room, and jumped to
my feet in sleepy confusion. The hens were terribly excited over
something, and as my eyes got a little open I could see the
reflection of the dying fire in a pair of big fierce eyes that burned
like coals away up on the rafters. I may remark that the eyes of
any wild beast will never show at night without the aid of some
illumination any more than the moon could shine if the sun
were quenched. The gleam so commonly supposed to be a positive light is of course only a reflected one.

Well, this is straying. I didn't then stop to think whether that
ugly light was positive or borrowed; I knew that there were two
eyes up there and a wild beast behind them. Up went my revolver, and bang! There was a tremendous screech; and something dropped heavily at my feet and then started for the window. I pulled the trigger again, but there was only a dull click. I
had forgotten the afternoon's shooting of magpies, and the subsequent neglect to reload. But a .44 makes a terrible club, and
without waiting to get my rifle, for fear the intruder would
escape, I pitched in with the butt of the old Remington. Once
the beast caught the grip in his big teeth, and as the novelists
remark, it "will carry the scar to its dying day." But a few
desperate blows on head and ribs settled my mysterious foe, and
he dropped back on the rude floor with the blood and brains
streaming from his nostrils.

Then, in great relief, but still shaking so with excitement
that I could hardly do anything, I stirred up the embers, threw
on more wood, and by the springing blaze dragged my game to
the hearth and looked him over. Just as I had suspected, it was a
wildcat; but his size terrified me. Yes, actually, though, he was
dead as Adam is. Why, if I had known he was as big as that, I'd
have crawled under the live coals sooner than tackle him, for I
am not fond of wildcats. But as it was safely over, I felt more
than a little elated, and was glad he had called. It really was a
very easy job to kill him, too, big and powerful as he was. My
one bullet shattered his right foreleg, and the first welt on the
skull practically settled the matter, though he showed battle for
awhile longer. I came out of the fight without a scratch, save a
short hole in my duck coat, and feel lucky. He had a venerable
cackler in his jaws when I killed him, and as she was already
dead I broiled and ate her. My jaws are several times as strong
since then.

In the morning I packed that brute on my shoulders—his legs
on each side of my neck for handles—down to the next settlement, a small ranche where they had some scales. He weighed
53½ pounds. You ought to see his long, white teeth, his needle-
pointed, sickle-shaped claws, and the marvelous muscularity of
his frame. I weighed nearly three times as much as he did, and
my arm is not badly developed, but the great knots of his biceps
and triceps measured an inch over mine. About two-thirds of
the time since Tuesday noon I have spent in removing and
scraping the hide, and there is still a day's work ahead before I
can put it in the shape I desire. Then, when it is cured, I shall
send it to Los Angeles as a souvenir—and it will probably be the
most beautiful one of my trip.

I stopped at a queer little ranche up in a canyon of the Greenhorn, Tuesday night. A white-haired blind old lady was there,
and interested me much. I don't know her name, but I know she
is a good woman. If there were more like her, the country would
be in a better fix. After breakfast in the morning she gave us a
prayer which was a new one on me. After invoking a benediction

on mankind in general, she said; "We don't know yet, O Lord, how the tide of our country's interest has turned, but we fear *those nasty Democrats* have seized the reins of government. But we beseech Thee, Great Ruler that if it be consistent with Thy will, Mr. Blaine may be our President, and that wicked man Cleveland be rebuked." Wasn't that a corker? I said amen! as heartily as any old deacon.

I got a glimpse, afar off, of the famous Bassick mine, one of the richest in the world—stocked up at two million and a quarter. It is in the Silver Cliff district, and has a romantic history. Years ago in the full finish of the gold excitement, a fellow, whose bad luck would have driven Job crazy, sank a big hole and never took a cent out. At last despairing he gave it up and drifted off to other fields. In the little settlement there, lived a doless [*sic*], drunken old man named Bassick. He pattered around prospecting, while his wife took in washing. A year or two later he wandered down into this deserted shaft one day. The frost had been at work on the walls, caving off big patches, and the old man saw a golden glitter. He dug his short-handled pick into the wall and turned out a golden nugget half as big as his thumb. That hapless miner had sunk his hole within six inches of the richest lode in Colorado; and who should find the treasure but worthless old Bassick! That afternoon the old man refused $100,000 for his claim. Isn't that the very mockery of fate?

Since leaving you on Pike's Peak I have traveled only 200½ miles—nearly all in a big circle about the mountains. Am now but 50 miles from the Peak, but the roaming has been fraught with pleasure. By Monday I shall have tramped 2000 miles, and will be among the Sangre de Christo mountains.

I struck down from the mountains last night, hitting the river at dark, some 15 miles west of Pueblo. Walked a mile down the track and got supper at a section house, but at 9 o'clock they cooly informed me that I couldn't stay over night. So I tramped back to the bridge, crossed the river and went down on the other side. I soon found a ranche, but it was locked and unoccupied. I went on two miles more, despairing of accommodation and prepared to walk on to town. At last, however, I came to a section-house on the Coal Creek branch of the Atchison, Topeka and Santa Fe. They wouldn't let me in here, either, and the score of Americans on a sided construction train were equally hoggish. It was desperately cold, and I was getting ruffled, when a gang of Italian laborers offered me room in their car. I looked at them rather sharply, for Italians don't bear the best reputation in the world, and then accepted their offer. One of them, a frank-faced, broad-shouldered young fellow said to me, "No hav-a but three-a blanket. Me give you two." And I'll be shot if he didn't do it, too. I was glad to find one "white" man in the God-forsaken place. I expect to reach Cucharas Saturday, and get my first letter mailed since leaving Denver. I will see you again somewhere about the Veta Pass. Till then, in the language of the plains, "so long."

                                                                    LUM

Alamosa, Colorado
Tuesday, November 18th, 1884

Editors Leader:

Well, I have been striking it rich again, in the last few days, and though the events of the week have been less thrilling perhaps than those of the last, they have not lagged behind in interest—to me, at least. Now that the Río Grande lies behind me, I begin to feel, too, as if I were "gettin' thar or tharabouts." To-morrow, if my usual luck keeps up, I shall be over the line into New Mexico, with only one whole state and halves of two others between me and my Mecca.

There was nothing to keep me in that cutthroat little iron city of Pueblo—paradise of sand baggers, thugs, and everything down to cheap thieves—and after getting out of the way my *Leader* letter and other correspondence, I skipped out around

the tremendous curves of the Silverton branch of the D. &
R.G.R.R., and once more had my face turned southward. The
only interesting thing in the afternoon walk of ten miles was
Bessemer, a little town given over—as its name implies—to the
manufacture of steel. The works are mammoth in extent, and
looked bustling enough with their swarms of grimy workmen,
their great blast pipes spitting white smoke, and their vast hills
of ore. An infernally sore heel, however, detracted much from
my appreciation of this industry. Did you ever hear of feet
getting so tough that the toughness made them sore? Well, that
is what ails my tie-pounders. The skin on my heels is about as
thick and hard as a mule's hoof; and where this half-inch horn
joins the tender flesh of the ankles, there is a crack two inches
long. It has bored me more than a little, but is yielding to
treatment.

I got down to San Carlos section-house in time for supper. As
I drew up there a beautiful greyhound, tall and trim-built as a
clipper, flew out at me with inhospitable bark. One of the section men gave him a kick and a curse, and said "d——n the dog!
Anybody that'll take him can have him." "Do you mean that?"
said I. "Bet yer life I do," was the answer. That settled it, and
since then I have had company. The poor little devil had been
maltreated all the six months of his short life, and didn't dare
think his bark was his own. It took me three hours to get him up
to me, but half my supper established an understanding between us. There is nothing at San Carlos but the section house,
but one of the men shared his blanket with me, and I got along
very well.

In the morning I had a great toot with Shadow—the dog—
trying to tow him along at the end of a string. For about ten
minutes the frightened creature plunged and snapped and
howled, and then his dog sense triumphed, and he came along.
A fine fellow he is, black as coal, nearly, if not quite a thoroughbred, and a runner from Runville. His owner had died
there, and left Shadow to the untender mercies of the section
men. He has cost me enough already, however. That very day, he

lost me $15 or $20 besides a deal of satisfaction. I was coming along the railroad, a mile or so east of Salt Creek section house, where the creek comes within 100 feet of the railroad. Two or three hundred head of cattle were poking their thirsty muzzles into this, the only water in 20 miles. I chanced to look over to the opposite bank, and there trotting along slowly, broadside toward me, were four big black-tailed deer, not 100 yards away. Off came the rifle from my back, and down I went on my left knee, dead sure of the stately buck ahead, and almost equally so of two more running, for they had a full mile to go to any cover. The white front sight fell into the rear notch, and both lined full on the left side of the buck as I pulled the trigger. Just at that instant Shadow—whose rope was tied to my wrist—caught sight of the deer, and he made a terrific spring aside. I saw the ball kick up the dust a hundred feet away from aim, and off went the blacktails in a quadruple streak. There was still time to drop one or two of them, but that accursed pup, made frantic by the report, was dancing and howling right and left; and before I could get him civilized the deer were looking back at me from a ridge a mile away. It was as aggravating as burdocks in bed, but there was no help for it. Probably none of your hunting readers will believe me when I say that I didn't kick the ears off of that dog, but it's a fact. Nary a kick. I hope the head entry clerk up above will give me one credit, anyhow.

Looking south from Bessemer, Thursday, I saw two great blue islands rising from the level distance of the plains, lonely and glorious. They were the Spanish Peaks, a twin pair exiled from their brethren. For three industrious days I pushed along toward them, and then got no nearer than 10 miles from their frowning fronts. They are about 12,000 feet in height, and seem to have been thrown off from the great range of the Sangre de Christo, fifteen miles away. Their isolation and rocky cliffs give them an impressiveness entirely their own.

West of Salt Creek, where Shadow and I shared a big jackrabbit, we struck the crookedest track yet—just crooked for pure deviltry. There is no more need for that road to stagger around that way than there is for me to shave the soles of my feet, but I reckon the engineers knew I was coming along here sometime, and calculated to raise my mental temperature about 200 degrees. If so, they succeeded like money in a legislature, for I got so hot I had to take off my shoes and wade in the ice-water of the creek. Finally I saw a line of telegraph poles about six miles southeast, and exactly parallel to my course. I struck across and saved two miles, but could just as well have economized five more, had I but known it.

Right in the midst of this wabbling way, at an unnamed little place, was a superb eagle in a little pen. He was as handsome a specimen as ever flew, and appeared to be living on the fat of the land, for the tattered hides of a hundred rabbits strewed the ground around him. He yearned for a whack at Shadow's ribs, and the fool pup would have given him the best chance in the world, but for an admonishing yank at his collar. The great bird had got entangled in chasing a rabbit through a wire fence a few weeks before, and was easily captured.

I would mummur gently in your ear that this is the godforsakenest country around. The soil is about as rich as Paint Creek [Ohio] gravel, and raises grand crops of sage brush and soap-weed, the only timber being on the mountains. Times are tough, wages as low as the deuce—which is always low, you know—and not enough work obtainable to keep a flea from the dyspepsia. I know of but one industry that pays here, and that is—walking. A man can earn big wages along this road by hoofing it, and it is the only way he can earn much of anything. I stopped in the station at Graneros, Friday, and chanced to see a schedule of distances and fares. What do you suppose this Denver & Río Grande R.R.—whose initials might well stand for Down-Right Grab—has the undying gall to charge local passengers? The trifle of ten cents a mile! That is all—I guess none of it got away. That rate obtains everywhere south and west of Pueblo, there being no competitive road thenceforth. So I begin to feel pretty well heeled, having earned a clever week's wages since leaving smoky Pueblo, though it hasn't been paid over to me yet.

I had calculated to put in the night at Huerfano—pronounced Wharfano—but Shadow snaked me along at such a cannonball gait that we struck Cucharas at 7 o'clock, after a spin of 40 miles. I found my mail awaiting me, took in a good cargo of internal ballast, and slept like a top—that is according to Hoyle,* but I don't know why "like a top"; why not like a bottom?—in the bunkhouse, having got my blanket back from brothers Wells, Fargo & Co.

Saturday, we plugged away over to La Veta, which lies apparently at the very foot of the Spanish Peaks, but in reality a tremendous day's march from their summits. The day was full of interest to me, for in it, I stepped across the line from an alleged American civilization into the boundaries of one strangely diverse. Two miles out from little Cucharas, and on the willowy banks of Cucharas creek, I ran across a big plaza of Mexicans— Greasers, as they are called out here. A westerner would no more think of calling a "Greaser" a Mexican, than a Kentucky Colonel would of calling a negro anything but "nigger."

This plaza is a big, rambling, many-ended and many-roomed, mud shed, ten feet high, and several hundred around. In it, in lousy laziness, exist 200 Greasers of all sexes, ages and sizes, but all equally dirty. The building, if it can be dignified by such a title, is an adobe. A multitude of crooked cedar posts are set into the ground, and across the top of the enclosure thus made, are laid others. Then, mud with hay kneaded into it is slapped two feet thick over these posts and left to dry in the sun, which soon bakes it nearly as hard as a brick. That is an adobe. These dwellings are not pretty enough to violate the ten commandments, but are tolerably comfortable, the thickness of the walls making them cool in summer and warm in winter. I have seen

---

*Lummis is obviously using a familiar expression of protocol and authority here ("according to Hoyle"), but stumbles over his own effort to be clever.

but little else in the way of houses since leaving Cucharas. All
along the way, little adobes—the word is pronounced "do-by"—
are almost the only visible habitations. In Wahlsen, a little coal-
mining town, 7 miles west of Cucharas, are several very pretentious adobes two stories high, and with shingled roofs.

Around all the ranches I saw, too, for the first time, great
herds of white goats, with long, silky hair. One had the finest
head of horns I ever saw. They were three feet long, spiral, and a
transparent white. The Mexicans themselves are a snide-looking set, twice as dark as an Indian, with heavy lips and noses,
long, straight, black hair, sleepy eyes, and a general expression
of ineffable laziness. Their language is a *patois* of Spanish and
Mexican. These may be poor specimens along here. I hope so.
Not even a coyote will touch a dead Greaser, the flesh is so
seasoned with the red pepper they ram into their food in howling profusion.

Along near Wahatoya, I had the luck to kill, by a running
shot, a small fox of the kind known here as the swift. A tenderfoot, seeing a jack-rabbit or a coyote run, would snort at the idea
that anything could outstrip them, but this little fox, the speed-
iest quadruped on the plains—and, I presume, in the world—
can do it like rolling off a log.

After a soul-satisfying supper at La Veta section house, I
trotted to the bunk house and applied for a chance to spread my
blanket and my bones on the floor. To my surprise and conster-
nation, the boss refused. He had taken in two strangers, a few
nights before, who tried to rob him, and he had "swore off" on
all such hospitality. It took me a long time to convince him that
I was a white man, but he finally came around and let me stay. I
tell you the permission was a big relief. The Lord only knows
what would become of a man sleeping out on the hard ground
these nights, when the wind roars down from the snow-clad
ranges, freezing the creeks three inches thick—and He won't
tell.

From La Veta the railroad twists and squirms from pitch to
pitch, in a 20-mile endeavor to scale the Veta pass. I concluded

that was a little too much generosity for my feet—20 miles to
go 14—so I struck in on an old trail leading straight over the
mountains. It gave me 12 miles of mighty stiff climbing, and
toward the top of Middle Creek Pass, as it is called, the knife-
edged wind cut through my perspiration-soaked garments till I
felt like a whole dissecting room, saws, scalpels and all. Half-
way up I turned Shadow loose from the leading string, and he
verified his name by tagging along at my heels in solemn gratitude.

On the summit of the Pass I had the pleasure of wading
through a fierce snow-squall, which was unlooked-for and un-
wanted. I hadn't lost any snow, and wasn't looking for any. But
misfortune is fickle as her brighter-faced sister, and the top of
the range once crossed, walking was as easy as lying abed in the
morning. We hurried down the valley of Wagon Creek, spying a
snowy ermine as he scurried along the ice-bound brook, but
looking in vain for a house. At last, just at dark, the smoke of a
little log cabin curled up the wooded hillside ahead, and we
were soon at its door. The sole occupant was an old miner,
prospector, and generally ore-struck seeker after wealth. He
took us in to the grateful fire, and while he chopped up a big,
dead pine he had just dragged down the hill, I cooked my supper
in the big fire-place. Good frying-pan bread, fried potatoes and
pork, coffee, and can of baked beans I had packed along with me,
made a meal fit for anyone, and Shadow and I did it full justice.

Just in the midst of supper, I heard a deep, mellow voice
outside, which had the New England brand, sure pop. In a moment, its owner, dressed in a fringed buckskin hunting suit,
came in, and proved to be a wanderer from old Plymouth Rock.
Maybe he didn't help me bury those beans. He is a professional
trapper and hunter now, and has been out all over this western
country for many years, as placer miner—gold washer, that is—
government scout, freighter and much more. We sat and talked
by the fire a long time, his conversation as vivid as a romance,
and then he went off to bunk at a cabin down the creek promising to call for me at sunrise, and take me down to his camp, 24
miles below.

Then "the old man"—H. D. Chase, Russell, Costilla Co., is
his name and address—turned into his narrow bunk, while I
inserted myself into my sleeping bag and camped on a piece of
burlap, spread on the dirt floor. He entertained me for hours with
descriptions of his dozen or more of mines in the gulches round
about, and in the morning, loaded me up with his best specimens of gold, silver and lead-bearing carbonates, and of the iron
ore he has found in bewildering abundance. Then, when Lora
Washburn, the fine-faced, square-shouldered, thick-chested,
sinewy, young hunter, came for me, we went over to take a look
at these wonderful mines. You never saw such a sight. The
shafts run from the very surface through huge ledges of mineral,
95 per cent ore—the finest iron in the world. It carries 72 per
cent pure, magnetic iron, $20 to $40 per ton gold, and a little
silver.

One of the outcrops is 60 feet wide. I took a piece of that ore
from the mine, and with a hammer pounded out a flat, smooth
surface on it, as if it had been malleable iron. What do you think
of that? The whole hillside is full of that ore, and the old man
has a dozen mines there staked out. One shaft is sunk 80 feet,
but the others have only the "assessments" done. The assess-
ment is sinking a hole ten feet a year, and perfects a miner's
title. Mining law out here, you know, takes precedence of everything. If you had a dwelling or a farm in one of these valleys and I
found "mineral"—ore-bearing rock—there, I could sink a thousand shafts on your premises, tunnel through your yard, under-
mine your very house—and if you tried to stop me, I could shoot
you. All I would have to do would be to pay the damages done
your property. The man who finds mineral owns it, on
whosoever land it may be. So, though Mr. Chase doesn't own a
foot of land there, all the vast mineral wealth is his. A three-
mile branch could be run up the valley from the D. & R.G.R.R.,
with light grades, to the very dump. The man that will put up a
furnace on that creek can have an interest in the mines and an
independent fortune. Here is a chance for some of you bloated
newspaper men. The only lion in the way is a present difficulty
with some big corporations which are trying to freeze the

miners out—but the miners will not be "friz" and "will stay with it" as long as their lungs pump air.

The East has her monopolies, and they are big and dangerous; but they have grown with our growth, and we do not realize their full menace. But out here in this new country of sudden fortunes, monopoly has sprung full-armed from the ground almost in a day, like the dragon's teeth of Cadmus. Colorado, the foremost bullion producing state in the country, is at a standstill, instead of on a boom as she should be. Monopoly has her by the throat, and I know not how she shall arise—unless the poor laborer turns to the last resort of lead and hemp. I have been finding this more and more apparent all through the state, and at every turn there is that which must make thoughtful men look grave. Everything is monopoly, and the poor man has no rights that these great grabs respect. The cattle business is in the hands of great pools, and the small rancher is going to the wall. If he homesteads or pre-empts his little range, some day the thousand steers of a great cattle king are driven in and eat every blade of his grass. The streams are fast being fenced in; and that means more than you think. Out here land is worth absolutely nothing—it is the water that sells; and with that shut in, the surrounding country is and must remain a desert. In mining, the same state of things prevails. Let a poor man strike it rich, and a hundred hands are turned to oust him from his claim. The big pools do not care to buy his mine—it is easier to freeze him out. Hired spies sneak in to note the value of his "lead"; bought desperadoes try to "jump" his claim, even at the expense of killing him; and his whole life is a perpetual warfare.

Now the Colorado Coal & Iron Co.—"the C.C. & I."—of Pueblo, is one of the biggest and cruelest monopolies in the State. It is in practically the same hands as the D. & R.G.R.R., and what the two can't steal between them is locked pretty tight. Now for an example of the way they treat the man who is impudent enough to be a poor miner. This Wagon Creek iron is far ahead of any possessed by the C.C. & I.—they admit it and I know it, for I have handled both ores. They want the mines the

worst way, but they do not offer a cent. It is their calculation to
wear out the miners and get the claims for nothing—as they
have gotten most of their mines. So their pal, the railroad, helps
them out. These Wagon Creekers apply for terms on hauling
their ore to a furnace, and are politely informed by the railroad
officials that that ore will not be hauled for them on any terms!
That is a very fair sample of the way things are doing all over the
State. But there will be a change somewhere and somehow. The
mutterings of a mighty discontent, a savage though suppressed
wrath, are heard all over Colorado. These miners are not boys;
they are rough, earnest, hard-muscled men, accustomed to
hardship, danger, and daring. Their very patience is a menace of
what will be when the last straw is laid upon them.

Perhaps these monopolists do not know that they stand on a
mine whose fuse may be already lit, but it is so. No man with
attentive eyes and ears can go through Colorado and not see it.
Nearly all these corporations have got their wealth by theft.
Their lands—sometimes hundreds of thousands of acres—are
largely obtained by illegal means. Men are hired to homestead
or pre-empt a place, and all the places go to swell the company's
acres. This is notorious. I don't know that France has a copyright on the commune. There are things in this country that
may kindle less fiery blood than hers. To illustrate the extent of
the ill-blood between miners and monopolists. A respected and
well-to-do miner from a section that is being "frozen out,"
chanced to meet in Denver, not long ago, the president of the
C.C. & I., who is also a high official of the D. & R.G.R.R. "Well,"
said the president, "I may come down to your place, by-and-by.
Will it be all right?" "You might git down thar," replied the old
miner grimly, looking his oppressor in the eye, "but you'll never
come back, only in a box." The capitalist decided that the
Denver climate suited him well enough, and he stayed there.

Well, Lora and I snapped off the miles in lively fashion, Monday morning, down Wagon Creek, across Sangre de Christo
Creek, and along the old government road to Fort Garland. The
stupendous bulk of Sierra Blanca—the tallest and grandest of

Colorado's congress of Titans—loomed up on our flight, far above the clouds. A spiteful snow-squall hissed in our faces over the high divide, and the wind all day was marrow-chilling.

But Lora's reminiscences of an eventful life made the way short. I must give you some of them, some day. Running away from home at 16, to ship before the mast on a New Bedford whaler; cruising among arctic ice-fields and tropic sea-weed; leaving at last his berth as second mate on a San Francisco orange schooner to join in the rush for gold; scouting in the far territories during the troublous Indian times of 1876—the time of the Custer massacre—trapping and hunting and prospecting in the same wild country—that is a life that seems like a romance to you in the sleepy, fallow east. If this Cape Cod boy could write out the true tale of what he encountered in thus roughing it in the far west, it would discount in interest any fiction ever concocted.

Now, with his brother Carroll, he is trapping beaver on these creeks, catching coyotes, otters, and every kind of game here, for pelt or bounty or flesh. That is fall and winter work; and mining keeps the pot at a boil during the summer. He already has a claim in one of those rich Wagon Creek iron mines—"the Bay State"—and is only awaiting means to develop it. Meantime, next summer, he will go to placer-mining in Wagon Creek. That is the way one hand has to feed the other in this bare country.

About four o'clock we came to the brothers' camp on Trincheras Creek. There I met Carroll, or "Cad"—a short, quiet, determined-looking man, with the build of a Hercules. He had just brought in the biggest antelope on record, a splendid buck of 130 pounds, with a head that would adorn a palace. We went in to the cozy adobe ranche in which the boys are camped, had a supper of antelope heart and liver, potatoes and frying-pan bread—the best bread that ever was made. I never ate a better or a bigger supper anywhere. Then, after a long smoke, and a still longer chat, we camped down together on a luxurious bed of hay, with blankets under us and good old New England quilts over us, a big wagon sheet capping all.

If you will ever find honest hospitality, a blunt cordiality that makes the cockles of your heart warm, it is in the hunter's camp. You are always welcome to share his invigorating grub, and he will "whack up" his last blanket with you at night. He has his bag of flour at hand, with a pail of fermented batter in place of yeast, and in ten minutes he will have a giant flapjack of bread that beats the Vienna bakeries. His wagon sheet—the canvass cover of a freighting wagon—serves him by turns as tent and blanket. His pack-saddles, with their X shaped sticks, lie in the corner with the pack-ropes; while the patient jacks themselves graze contentedly without.

Around the walls hang big, round, shield-shaped affairs, looking worthless enough, but each standing for eight or nine dollars in Uncle Sam's gold. They are beaver skins, stretched to dry on willow hoops, some three feet in diameter, numerous thongs holding them to the hoop. It looks comical enough to see a circular hide, but that is the natural shape when the animal is skinned in a certain way. These beautiful soft pelts sell at $3.50 to $4 per pound; and a good big one weighs three or four pounds. The furriers pluck out the long, coarse hairs, and leave for the market only the short, velvety fur with which you are familiar. The creeks all about here are full of the strange beaver dams as soon as the mountains are left behind. All through the meadows you will see quiet ponds, substantial dams, and chiseled stumps of trees and bushes, all chopped down by these wonderful engineers. They can fell a tree, 12 inches through, as exactly to the line they desire as an old lumberman. Should it chance to fall wrong, the beavers leave it and turn to another. I have never known pleasanter days than the many passed in spying upon the work of a beaver colony as they dam strong streams, cut down the green clubs for winter food, or mud-plaster their comical lodges with their trowel tails.

Now to round-skin a beaver, so there will be no waste of that precious fur, there is but one way. The big flat tail is cut off, and then the feet. Then a split down the belly, and the hide comes off round as a flap-jack, the legs being pulled through without splitting. A deer, bear, or similar large animal is split down

without preliminaries, and the hide taken off like a coat; but a
coyote, fox or such like is "cased." Casing is a fashion of skin-
ning that would puzzle you, for the whole hide is taken off
without cutting a hair. Loosening the skin about the jaws, the
hunter draws the hide back until the entire animal has passed
through its own mouth. The pelt is then loosely filled with
grass, to keep it in shape, and dries exactly in the form of the
animal that once wore it. Casing prevents a waste of about ten
percent of hide—the trimming of a pelt that is split and pegged
up, every peg leaving an unsightly tag.

Now let me tell you one of Lo's adventures—in the hearty
camp on the Trincheras it was not "Mister" or "Stranger" or
"Pard," but "Lo" and "Cad" and "Charlie"—and then we'll push
on.

"I was trapping in the Little Rockies, back in 187–," said Lo,
in his deep chest-tones, "and taking out a good many beaver
pelts a week. One day I ran across a den in a deep canyon—a sort
of natural cave—and found grizzlies in it. At its mouth the hole
was too low to walk into, and I had to crawl on my hands and
knees; but a few feet in, it opened up into a high chamber. Away
at the far end, 40 feet from me, I could see where the nest was,
down a few feet below the general level of the cave; but the
brutes were lying down and wouldn't come out, and kept growling away in the dark. Presently a cub lifted his head above the
side of the nest, and he fell back with ball through his brain
from my old Sharpe—a buffalo gun, .50 caliber and 115 grains.
By and by up came another cub, and down he went; and then
another. But the old she [she-bear] wouldn't raise, but laid there
growling among her dead. I threw rocks into the nest, and she
would snarl and move, but never expose her head. At last I got
sick of that, and said to myself 'Well, old girl, if you won't come
my way I'll have to come yours.' So I stuck my pine torch in a
crack above my head, and stood up on my feet. Then I could see
into the nest, but it was just a mass of fur, and I couldn't tell
t'other from which, for the old one had her head down among
her cubs. Well, I couldn't afford to wound her, and it wasn't a

very rich light to shoot fine by, but I was bound to have her. So I picked up a rock in my left hand, threw my cocked rifle to my shoulder with the right, and then tossed the rock into the nest. I saw the great head lift from the mass and wave from side to side an instant suddenly, and before it could drop back, there was a big chunk of lead buried in the brain, and I was flying down the canyon.

Finding that she did not follow, I went back to the hole and crawled in, with the Sharpe clutched in my hand. But that nest I didn't care about tackling. All was quiet in it, but that didn't signify anything. A bear is a devilish brute, and a foxy one, and nothing was likelier than she might just be laying for me. So I stood there for a quarter of an hour, chucking the biggest rocks I could get hold of over into that nest, always with the rifle at a ready. Then, as there was no stir, I ventured up, and found them all four stone dead—the old she and her three big cubs. I dragged them out into the canyon. I had seen her out in the hills and broken a fore leg for her the day before, and that is the reason she wouldn't come out to me."

That is one of the many stories Lora Washburn told me, simply and unaffectedly, as if the lonely entering of that dark and bloody den were not a heroism. It was impossible to look into the narrator's frank, manly eyes, and doubt the truth of every word. It is a pity, I think, that we have got into this habit of deeming every man a liar just because he has seen more of the world than our narrow lives take in. Simply because we are timid stay-at-homes in a tame country, it doesn't follow that everyone else has led as dull an existence as ours.

Monday morning, after a hearty meal of venison and bread, fresh pork and potatoes, Cad went off in the dim, cold light to overhaul his beaver traps. Lo and I chatted awhile, with the feeling of life-long friends, while Shadow gorged himself with antelope liver and steaks, the biggest meal of all his poor, starved little life. Then with warm adieus and a heart-felt grip of hands that would have made the blood spurt from dude finger-tips, the hunter and the tramp parted—not forever, I hope. It would be a keen pleasure to me at any time and place again to meet the manly trapper from Cape Cod.

For three or four miles Shadow and I tramped across the sage brush and soapweed to the railroad. How I did long for a shot-gun; the brush was too thick for a rifle to be of much use. In that short walk we started up no less than 119 jack-rabbits, and I don't know how many cotton-tails. It was a four mile laugh for me. As soon as Shadow spied one of the John rabbits scurrying through the brush, off he went in hot-footed pursuit, yelping like mad. On open stretches the long-legged pup could hold them about level, but they dodged him behind the tall bunches of brush. One tremendous jack rose just before the dog and ran 600 yards in a beeline, Shadow's nose within two feet of its tail. Then Brer Rabbit found he had too warm a dun, and took an angle off into the sage. That brush was three and four feet high, but I hope to be pulled for a horse-thief if he didn't sail along with two feet of horizon showing between the brush and his stomach. You actually couldn't see him go down at all. It was much like a big white bird skimming along level with the ground. Those who have ever seen one of these fellows hard-pressed by greyhound or coyote, will know that I don't exagger-ate; those of you who haven't, must take my word for it. Wait till this pup gets a month older, though, and toughened up by the trip; then if he doesn't pick up these kangaroos of the plains, I'll eat gravel. He runs already like a Democratic candidate in your Sixth Ward.

We struck the railroad in due season, and there I spent half an hour pulling the prickly pear thorns out of Shadow's feet and my own. We were now in the great, circular looking valley of San Luis, a basin 50 miles across and twice as long, all walled in by a circling sweep of the Sangre de Christo range. And here I find my finest mountain view. I told you at Colorado Springs that I hadn't seen a nobler mountain than old Agiochook (Mt. Washington) but it is true no longer. The pride of New England, Pike's Peak, Long's, and all their kindred, must bow to mighty Blanca. Seen from the west, the vast, white, frowning peak, gouged into a chaos of clefts and precipices, towers over the level plain, unhemmed by foot-hills. It lies at the very end of a fork in the broken range, and is simply terrific in its wild grandeur. I would walk a thousand miles to see such another sight. Every day that I have seen it the great white snow clouds have been driving across its shoulders, thickening the white robe that wraps them—and I have seen more or less of it for the last 200 miles.

At Baldy, a little section house, I picked up another "busted" cowpuncher, and tramped in with him to Alamosa. He comes from Galion, O., and his father is, or was, a conductor on the "Three C's & I." The boy, who looks to be 22 or 23, is a tough young case, and will never do much good for himself.

I got in here at four o'clock P.M., after a rough day's tramp through the iciest wind you ever saw. Lordie! How it does howl down across this level plain! For 24 miles—all the way from Ft. Garland—the railroad is one straight line, and I had that wind in my face all the time. Ugh! I have hardly got thawed yet. My mail tells me that "the folks" got through to Los Angeles O.K., which is good news.

By the way, before I forget it, let me tell the *Leader*'s lady readers something that may interest them. Through Colorado, I have been eating a delicious tomato preserve, that would probably be a novelty in Ohio. I have never seen it on any Eastern table. The housewives out here take ripe tomatoes, peel them, weigh out two pounds of sugar for every pound of fruit, put in enough water to dissolve, and then, when the sirup [sic] comes to a boil, put in the tomatoes. Some take only pound for pound of sugar and fruit, and even then the sauce is good. Suppose you try the recipe.

To-morrow, I expect to strike into New Mexico, and after a little hunting and placer mining, I shall hit Santa Fe some time next week. So when you read this you may think of me in the hospitable clutches of "Phon" Ireland. There is nothing to keep me in dull Alamosa, whose only interesting point I have seen— a sign bearing the alliterative firm name of "Dubberton & Duddleson." That sounds like Dickens. Well, Shadow and I must turn in. I am glad to be out in the wilderness, where I can't hear these darned Democrats cavorting around. *Adios.*

LUM

Santa Fe, New Mexico
Tuesday, November 25th, 1884

Editors Leader:
   Hello yourself! Here's looking at you from the quaint plazas of New Mexico's Ancient Metropolis. If you feel half as well-suited to be in the Ancient Metropolis of Ohio as I am to be here at last in the City of the Holy Faith, you are indeed content. This flat little town of dry mud looked as handsome to me as the New Jerusalem, when I crawled over the sandhills into view of it. And I may as well make the most of it, too, for it will be a long day before I see again anything as civilized as even Santa Fe, except Albuquerque. In one way, my long journey is nearly two-thirds done; in another, it is hardly commenced. For ahead of me lies more than 1,000 train miles far worse than all the many I have already traveled. That 1,000 miles will lengthen out to 1,300 or 1,400, with all these detours of hunting and fishing and seeking after sight and specimens. The railroads along which I have come measure off but 1,813 miles from Chillicothe—1,745 from Cincinnati; but my pedometer, accurate as a tapeline, shows me that I have walked 2,202 miles.
   Had it not been for countless short cuts across bends and mountains, those figures would be a good deal bigger, but as I have increased distance in one way, I have lessened it in another. If it is just as convenient, please believe that this 2,202 miles represents more or less hard work, some hardships, immense instruction and boundless enjoyment. I don't think you really comprehend what 2,202 miles means. It looks pretty well on paper; it is a long and tedious ride by train; but the full magni-

tude of that distance can never be realized save by those who have measured it off a step at a time. Now, let me give you a pointer or two. My steps average exactly 34 inches in length. This means that since I left Cincinnati, 74 days ago, I have taken *four million, two hundred and seventy-one thousand, two hundred and nine* (4,271,209) steps. Calling 143 pounds a fair average—and it is a low one—my old feet have lifted the trifle of 785,962,156 pounds, or nearly 393,000 tons, three inches from the ground. There are 22 telegraph poles, and 3,150 ties to the mile, on an average, and if there had been track for all my detours, I should have passed 73,344 of the former, and 7,219,800 of the latter. Just you try to walk off one million ties, instead of seven million, sometime when you feel in first rate trim, and you will begin to have a slight conception of what I have been doing.

I shall remember Alamosa chiefly for one man—the boss swindler. When I came to leave his ornery little shack of a hotel, and paid my bill, he collared another full rate for poor Shadow, who had enjoyed the usufruct of a few bare boiled bones, and a strip of rags beside my sheetless and dirty bed. When that pirate dies and goes to his reward, he will charge up as fuel, to his fellow sufferers the fire that burns them. I hope the head stoker down there will ram Mr. Jones, of the Inter-Ocean, right under the grate.

When I shook the dust of Alamosa from my feet, it was with the intention of sleeping in Antonito that (Wednesday) night. But two miles out, my eye caught an unusual glitter on the ballast of the track, and I picked up a fine moss agate, two inches square. Well, I didn't rend my underclothing in any rush to get away from that place. In fact, I was right around there the better part of the day. The whole great sage brush plain, for six miles, is one bed of pebbles, mostly water-worn fragments of lava, but about every tenth pebble is an agate of some sort. Most of them are dull and worthless, but I filled one of my huge duck pockets with half a peck of agates, a majority milk agates, but some moss, and a good many carnelian. Also found two imperfect opals, some smoky topaz, and a fossil wolf's tooth. It was away after dark when I pulled into little La Jara, half-way to Antonito, but I didn't begrudge the lost distance with that pocketful of beautiful stones.

Thursday I went in much the same way, bringing me to Antonito at 4 o'clock, weighted down with a few more pounds of agates. I went into the station, and sat down at the operator's desk to scratch off some letters. I had been there but a few minutes when a disturbance in the doorway made me look up. A well-dressed man was standing inside the door, about three feet from me, and facing outward. Four feet in front of him stood an excited tough, pouring out profanity by the cable yard, and shaking a great .44 in his face. "You ——— ———," he said, "You'll shoot me, will ye? D———n your eyes! I believe I'll kill you, anyhow, just for luck. Yes," as the victim made a move for a similar weapon, which I could see bulging under his coat, "you pull that gun on me, and I'll pump enough lead into you to patch a mile of hell!" And so on. He was throwing that big self-cocker up and down, with his finger on the trigger, and the muzzle—which looked big enough to crawl into—bore just as dead on me as it did on the man he was bully-ragging. My legs were under the big desk, and it was such a cosy-looking place down there that I just went along under to keep my legs from getting lonesome. If he fired, the bullet was sure to come my way—one man doesn't stop a ball like that—and I didn't think it would be respectful to interfere with its course, especially as I wasn't acquainted with the man. He might take it as an impertinence.

Well, he didn't shoot, after all, for the other fellow "took water" and slid off on a passing train. "Who is that shootist?" I asked the quiet agent. "That? That's G. Myers. Keeps a saloon across the street. He's constable—been constable four years." "I guess he didn't want to shoot very bad," I ventured, feeling a good deal better since emerging from under the desk. "Don't you fool yourself," was the reply; "Myers'd just as soon shoot as eat. That's what he's constable for—we have to have a pretty tough man for constable out here. If Dalton hadn't kep' his hands up, you'd seen some fun." And I concluded that maybe that desk was a pretty good scheme, after all.

After a spell of writing, and a supper at the section house, I went over to the bunk house, chatted awhile with the men, and crawled into my sleeping bag, which was spread on the soft side of a plank, with the foot to the fire. Two bum looking strangers came in to pass the night, and a merry dance they led us all. One was enjoying a plain drunk, while the other had arrived at a higher luxury, and was on the ragged edge of the James Preserves—I never could shock the well-bred readers of the *Leader* by saying jim-jams. This latter fellow lay down with his shaggy head, about a foot from mine, and if he didn't give me an earache, my name is Spoopendyke. He would lie still three seconds and then snort "Oh, God, but I'm sick as a dog! Oh, if the good Lord will only let me get over this night. Ouch! Catch that rat!" And so on until you couldn't rest. I did think of moving to the other side of the room, but the plain drunk was over there, and the incessant, business-like scratching he kept up made me rather bear the ills I had than fly to others that I could guess only too well. Then one of them would get up and thunder across the floor, in his ponderous, hobnailed boots, after a drink of water, and so it went till an irritated section man, himself plainly a tough case, rose and shook the front teeth of the disturbers loose, with a threat to murder both if they didn't "let up." After that they were a little less uproarious, and we managed to get a few winks of sleep.

Bright and early in the morning, Shadow and I were hoeing it down the track in the cold air. About five miles south of Antonito we passed the stone post which marks the state line, and were at last on the unprepossessing soil of New Mexico. Almost directly after leaving Antonito the face of the country undergoes a great change. All the way from Alamosa you find the tiny pebbles of lava, ground smooth and round by the swift current of the Río Grande; but below little Conejos creek it is all one

vast lava bed. The plains are strewn thick with great, jagged
blocks, while huge ledges of lava, red and black or whitewashed
with deposits of lime, crop out everywhere.

The railroad winds about in horrible curves, but there is no
cutting across lots. I tried it, and found that a mile would cut
iron shoes to pieces. All went well enough for ten miles, but
after I had passed the Palmilla section house the meanest wind
that ever blew got up and howled in my teeth all the rest of the
day. It was bitterly cold, strong and fierce, and the clouds of
alkali dust it bore gave me a sore nose, sore lips, sore eyes and
sore throat in less than no time.

Once in every little while I had to get down in the ice of some
big rock or sage-brush, and get warm enough to go on. Thirty
miles of this was a hard pull, and when, after the desperate
struggle, I saw the wind pump of No Agua ahead, I was as happy
as a boy with top boots. That name No Agua (pronounced No
Ahwa) doesn't mean that they have no ague there—though they
don't—but is simply Spanish for No Water. And the name is
well bestowed. It is about the driest place you ever saw, and the
little alkali water raised from the deep well is about the color of
coffee.

I saw my first mirage, that day. Some little volcanic peaks, 30
miles away, showed high in the air with a broad strip of horizon
below them. That was back at Antonito, where there are also,
by the way, enough Mormons to sink a ship. The whole river
bank is lined with their settlements.

Mrs. Dunne has charge of the No Agua section house, and a
great case she is. The men all call her "Mother Graball," and
have countless rows with the old virago, who always comes out
victorious. Such a dirty house and dirty woman I hope cannot be
found in all Ohio. Charcoal would make a white mark on her
face.

About half the section hands from Cucharas down are Mexicans, and white folks anyhow are in the minority. But I find the
"Greasers" not half bad people. In fact, they rather discount the
whites, who are all on the make. There is only one sociable

thing about the white folks all along the D. & R.G.—they will share your last dollar with you. A Mexican, on the other hand, will "divvy" his only tortilla and his one blanket with any stranger, and never take a cent.

When I rolled out of the bunk-house at No Agua, Friday morning, the ground was white with three inches of snow. I plodded up to Tres Piedras (The Three Rocks) and there sat down in the station to write while the snow should go off. It went off, and I started on, but hadn't tramped a mile when the clouds came up, and all the rest of the way to Servilleta a blinding snowstorm drove in my teeth. Six inches must have fallen, but it didn't lie long. Poor Shadow had never seen such a thing before, and kept up a piteous whining all the afternoon. I didn't like it any better than he did, but couldn't do better than grin and bear it.

I had a good time at Servilleta, where a clever Frenchman feeds the hands in gorgeous style. It is a long way between stopping places on this New Mexico branch of the D. & R.G. Except the tiny towns of Antonito and Española, there is not a house in 75 miles but the section buildings and they are some 20 miles apart. To go only from one to the next is too short a day's walk, and to hit the third one is almost too long.

And such a one-horse road! One day a train goes down from Alamosa to Española, and the next day it goes back. That is the limit. The rolling stock consists of two locomotives, one freight car, and one coach, half express and half passenger. If you mail a letter at Española for Santa Fe, 26 miles distant, it goes clear back to Pueblo, and thence down here by the Atchison, Topeka & Santa Fe R.R.—somewhere about 400 miles.

I started from Servilleta for Barranca, Saturday, a 21-mile trip without any water save one indescribably filthy sheep pool. At this pool, Shadow, who was running ahead, scared up four deer. I got a flying shot at one, wounded him, and followed the bloody trail for ten miles—nearly to the river—and then unwillingly gave him up. I could have got him by persevering, but did not wish to lose a day in getting to Santa Fe. When I finally dropped the trail it was cold and raw, and Shadow and I were famished. By great luck we found a little prairie dog town—rare enough out here—and managed to secure one of its citizens. I cleaned him, took him back to the railroad, and filled our hollow ribs. A battered powder can served as kettle, some snow furnished water, and well parboiled and then roasted, Mr. P. D. made a very good meal. These animals are hardly ever eaten, but I don't know why. There is no cleaner beast in its food and habits than the prairie dog, and parboiling removes the slightly strong flavor and leaves the meat as good as rabbit.

A good supper at Barranca made things all right, and I decided to keep on to Embudo, seven miles below. So in the early light of a quarter moon, Shadow and I started down grade. Just below the station of Barranca the track, which for many miles has been climbing the plateaus, takes a sudden jump toward the river, and for eight miles slopes down a wild, lonely canyon with a 200-foot grade. We were having a very pleasant, rapid walk down among these wild rocks, but just as my ears caught the hoarse roar of the river, far below and faraway, my pleasure was suddenly and lastingly spilled. Shadow was trotting along behind me, when like a shot he dashed between my legs, and lay there cowering and crying in abject terror. The onset nearly upset me, and startled me not a little, but when I caught my balance and looked around there was a sight not calculated to reassure me. Poor dog!

He didn't come into camp a bit too soon. We were in a deep, dark cut, with wild rocks and tangled thickets all about. Twenty feet away, a great, dark form was crawling stealthily up behind us, without a sound of warning. The light was too dim to distinguish much, but there was no mistaking that motion. You have seen a cat stealing after a bird through the grass? Well, that is what I saw—that slow, alert, noiseless, treacherous movement which no other animal can counterfeit. Yes, it was a cat—but such a cat; the great cat of the Rockies, the largest of the feline species in the Western hemisphere; in other words, the cougar, or "mountain lion." My heart stopped beating for a moment and then down came rifle and revolver to full cock.

The terrible fellow—he would probably weigh 300 pounds, and measure 8 feet from tip to tip—stopped and lay crouched flat on his belly, with a low, deep, growl. It is a wonder that I didn't shoot, for I have been praying for a cougar. I would rather have had him than a $100 bill.

But luckily I had a little sense left. He was only after the dog, for the cougar will not attack a man save when cornered. But to wound or not kill that great creature at the first shot—that were simple suicide. By day, it would have been different; but in that gloom I could not see the sights on my gun, and it was a thousand to one against making a fatal shot. And though my fingers itched on the trigger, I did not fire; but with rifle leveled, and revolver grasped in my left hand along the gun barrel, I stood and yelled until the huge cat turned his head, and with one incredible bound landed in the bushes far up the hillside. The rest of that walk was done with a cocked revolver in my hand, and Shadow sticking close against me. Some of your readers may think they would have belted away at the brute anyhow, but they would not. And if they did, it would be because they were fools, not heroes. A man might better turn a razor to his throat than come within leaping distance of a wounded mountain lion.

I reached Embudo ("the Funnel") at 8 o'clock, and camped on the floor beside the big stove. That last seven miles, by the way, is a fine bit of road, and partially apologizes for the idiotic engineering to the north. On the plains that D. & R. G. track is simply ridiculous and the engineering would disgrace a high-school boy. The road was built by a construction company at so much a mile, and whenever they got a chance to double the necessary distance, they did it.

Last winter there was a big snow blockade, and this branch of 91 miles was abandoned for two months, every section man being sent up to the Silverton branch to "buck" snow. The women were left to their own resources, and a hard old time they had. Three of them at Barranca had to come clear to Embudo—seven miles—after water, which they brought up on a little push-cart propelled by a burro. They nearly starved and nearly froze, and you may well imagine they are not particularly in love with the management of the road which exposed them to such hardships.

At Embudo we returned to the river, from which we parted away back at Alamosa. El Río Grande del Norte—the Great river of the North—is truly a beautiful stream all its length and particularly where, as at Embudo, it comes tearing down between the cleft walls of a mountain range. It is about the size of the Scioto, but runs three miles while that deliberate stream is running one, and discounts it in every way. Its color is an emerald green, and as it roars among the great lava boulders, it is something of which the eye never wearies. A little below Embudo, the canyon opens out into a pleasant valley, and the quaint Mexican plazas begin to dot the banks at frequent intervals.

Down here I ran across a Mexican mill and roared at its narrow-gauge scheme. All the mills are exactly alike and would be mistaken in Ohio for covered pig pens. Each is about 12 feet square, and so low that even I have to stoop in it. The millstones are about two feet in diameter, and rounded curiously on top. A spout runs from a little canal to the wheel, which is set flat instead of vertically, and is no larger around than the millstones. Fit accompaniments are the agricultural implements you may see every now and then.

The clumsy carts have solid wheels, each a cross-section of a big cottonwood some three feet in diameter, and without hub, spokes or tires. The rims are 6 to 8 inches wide—the same thickness as the whole wheel. A peg through an auger-hole serves to keep wheel and axle together. I was coming down by Alcalde (which means Mayor), when an indescribable shrieking and howling smote upon my ears. "What in thunder sort of a wild beast has got loose now," I thought; but lo and behold, it was only one of these carts coming down the road. I don't know what kind of nerves a Greaser must have to drive one of these infernal machines without cotton in his ears. It would put a white man in his grave after just one turn.

Down here, too, I saw one of their aboriginal ploughs—
the same pointed stick, with two branches for handles, that
scratched up the soil when Cortez landed. Most of these Mexicans along here, however, have Studebaker and other farm wagons, and modern ploughs, and are slowly coming to modern
modes of agriculture. Their fields are tiny, but well worked, well
irrigated, and marked off by the funniest little ridges.

Oh, I must tell you how an Aleck played a joke on me, just
below Embudo. He was an American, apparently a sort of land-
shark, and was driving along with a good span and a new plug
hat. Seeing in me some one to buzz, he drew up and fell into a
conversation, chiefly directed to giving me a little quizzical glu-
cose. Finally he said, "Say, that rifle of yours don't look as if it
would·shoot much. What'll you take for it?" I resented the
imputation, and said "I'll swap it even with you for your jaw—
that's sure death at a mile and the rifle is good only for 500
yards." "Sort o' smart to-day, ain't ye? I tell you what I'll do. I'll
put this hat at 50 feet, and bet ye a dollar ye can't hit it." "Well,
I'm not much of a gambolier," I replied. "But I guess I'll have to
go you one on that."

There was a plaza near by, with a few stumps around it. The
sharper took off his hat, stepped off 50 feet, and put the tile—
behind a stump! Then he turned around to me with a mean grin,
and said, "Shoot away, Cap." I was stumped, and just about to
knock under when I saw something that stopped me. "Say, how
many shots will you give me from where I stand?" "Oh, all you
want." I went over to an adobe, against which leaned a modern
steel plow, and this I toted down to the stump. "What's that
for?" queried the sharper, anxiously, but I only said, "Wait and
see." I leaned the plow up against the post at what I fancied
would be about the right angle, stepped back to the mark, took a
judicious aim and fired. But the ball didn't touch the hat. I
altered the position of the plow twice, and at the third shot the
bullet glanced around the curving share, hit the $12 plug amid-
ships, and made the sickliest wreck of it. My too smart friend
looked very tired, and refused to pay over the dollar. "That's all

right," said I. "I don't want any of your stolen money, my Christian friend, but let me give a straight tip. Next time you go
fishing for suckers, don't throw your hook into Yankee waters."
And he answered "I'll be d——d if I do, young fellar."

At Alcalde I trotted over to a neat, whitewashed plaza, to
prospect for dinner. A good-looking Mexican came to the door
and bowed politely with some remark that sounded to me like
an alphabet gone mad. "Da me tortilla, señor," said I, as sweetly
as I knew how. Then he rattled off a long string of what were
probably polite frills, from among which I could catch only the
words "Entre V." I "sabied" that and entered at once. He gave me
his chair and rolled me a cigarette, at the same time sending a
pretty señorita out to get some provender. She took down a leg
of mutton hanging in the porch, and disappeared. In a few moments she came in with a big pot of coffee, flavored with aguardiente (Mexican brandy, literally "burning water"), a platter of
mutton fried in inch cubes and three big tortillas. Perhaps you
don't sabe what a tortilla is. It is a thin sheet of unraised bread,
cooked in a frying-pan, indestructible as leather, but very good
eating, withal. The word is pronounced torteeah—the Spanish
"ll" being sounded like the French ditto.

Well, I made a very gratifying meal, and enjoyed a good look
at the house. The señor and his wife have a bed, but the rest of
the numerous family sleep on the floor. A huge roll of such
blankets as you never saw in the East—each big enough for a
carpet, and half an inch thick, reposes against the wall by day,
and at night makes a most comfortable bed. The old gentleman
was so cordial that I dared not offer him money—indeed, they
tell me that all these Mexicans will do their best for you out of
simple hospitality, and spurn the idea of pay—so I said, "Mil
gracias, Senor. Adios," and came off. I can stand it as long as they
can.

It would start your ribs to hear me talk Spanish. I have sworn
in a posse of about twenty words, and handle them with the
easy grace of a cow shinnying up an apple tree tail first. But
small as my awkward squad is, it is invaluable to me. I should

starve to death, and get lost in these vagabond roads, if I hadn't picked up enough to ask for food and the road. Why, even the dogs out here—and the Mexicans have more dogs and meaner ones than any other people on earth—can't understand English. I try to drive the howlers away, and I verily believe they think I am inviting them to come and get a bone. As for burros, you will see more of these comical brutes here in an hour than you could count in a day. Nothing could look cuter than these solemn little fellows, with their huge heads and ears out of all proportion to the rest of them, their big, wise eyes, knock knees and insignificant tails. They are of all hues, the handsomest, to my notion, being a fine, mouse color. The burro is slow, but sure. He can climb anywhere that a man can, and keep it up all day. He needs no more water than a camel and as for feed, he thinks himself in clover if he can get a few rags, papers and old boots under his girth. I don't know but I shall get one of these handy animals to pack my traps and water keg across the vast deserts I am so soon to enter. Burros sell here at from $8 to $15 and are worth it, too. Pack saddles cost about $1.50 more.

I got down at 4 o'clock, Monday afternoon, to Española, the end of the railroad. To look at the D. & R. G. map, one would take Española to be about the size of New York. In reality it has about a dozen buildings, including two stores. These were jammed full of Pueblo Indians, with their gay-colored blankets. Bucks, with bottles of whiskey or plugs of tobacco in their hands, squaws with their big papooses slung across their backs, and youngsters of all sizes were crowding the counters and keeping up an incessant jabber. Coming down from Embudo I had passed the pueblos of San Juan and Santa Cruz, but they were on the other side of the river, and I didn't stop for them.

I got my knapsack again at Española, laid in some provisions, and ploughed across the Río Grande to get a good start toward Santa Fe. Well it was that I did so. I walked seven miles down the river, and anchored in the delightful pueblo town of San Ildefonso. Pueblo seems to be a mighty useful word out here. It means a certain tribe of Indians, the Pueblos. One of their towns

is also a pueblo; and pueblo is Spanish for "people." San Ildefonso contains I should imagine, 400 or 500 souls, but is
tenfold more compact than an American town of the same
population. It is built in the shape of a hollow square, the
houses and walls all of adobe, and facing inward. Most of them
are very neat and attractive, some even attaining to two-storied
dignity. The second story stands well back, on the roof of the
first, and is reached by a ladder outside. There are about a dozen
Mexicans here, and the rest all Pueblos—the best looking Indians I ever saw. They are not tall, but are well-built and sturdy.
They have light, copper complexions, and good features.

I struck the adobe of Alonzo, who must be a sort of High
Muck-a-Muck among them, and never was more kindly treated.
The old fellow took me in, set me a chair by the fire, and was as
courteous as any one could have been. He wouldn't let me eat
my own lunch, but made his rather handsome squaw get me a
hot supper of mutton, tortilla and coffee, with some matchless
cheese. I have eaten cheese from almost every quarter of the
globe, but never any other half so delicious. The squaw had
about three pounds of silver rings, bracelets and anklets, and her
crow-black hair was dressed in the heaviest and most becoming
"bang" to be found any-where. What with Alonzo's little stock
of English and my poverty-stricken Spanish, we got along nobly,
and had a very interesting patch-work conversation. I had a
down-at-the-heel mouth harp, which I play like a cat with false
teeth, and it took immediately with my hosts. My host took a
whirl at it and tickled himself nearly to death.

He showed me some buckskin he had been making, and it
was a good job. The whole big skin was soft as velvet. Ask Tom
Wilson if he ever tanned a hide with sheep's brains. That is the
method employed by hunters and Indians all over the country.
After the skin is dried and scraped, they put it in a big earthen
dish, pour on the brains, and rub and scrub the hide until it is
perfectly pliable. After that you may wet it all you will, and it
remains soft as ever. Take a piece of American-tanned buckskin,
and one wetting spoils it forever. I'm going to have a suit of it

before long, or I'm no Yankee. After a long chat with Alonzo, he made me a luxurious bed on the floor, where I reposed beside the half-grown boy and girl, the latter a real beauty, while Pa and Ma Alonzo climbed into an American bed at the head of the room.

In the morning I had a good breakfast of venison, red hot with chili peppers, frijoles (beans), coffee, tortillas, and a queer preparation of wheat, tasting like the New England "Indian pudding." They call it "panacha." A few good fishhooks and lines made Alonzo happy, and at 8 o'clock we bade each other a fond farewell, as I started out for Santa Fe.

If ever you come to Santa Fe, don't take the D. & R. G. R. R.; and if you have to come that way, don't walk across from Espanola. I am still interested in you all, and would hate to think that your bones were bleaching on these dodgasted sandhills. That shameless D. & R. G. folder says it is but 25 miles from Espanola to Santa Fe. At Espanola they told me it was a long 28 miles. I got out seven miles to San Ildefonso, and found it still 26. I have done many a hard day's walk, but none harder than that. A Greaser—the only man I met in all the way—misdirected me, and I grunted up the hills for ten miles out of my course. Finally the road petered out, and there I was in the howling wilderness of sand and scrubby trees, dying for water, night only three hours off and not a bite of food. I climbed the highest hill in sight, took the bearings of the mountains, and struck for them, fortunately remembering that I had seen at Commodore Ireland's a photograph of Santa Fe with peaks in the background.

After a few miles of this, I sighted a good road over a distant hill, and was soon on it. It didn't seem to go anywhere in particular, except up-hill—you can't walk in any direction here without going up-hill—but I had faith that it would wind up in Santa Fe, and I kept on though half dead with thirst. I should have dropped by the roadside, but for a simple little scheme—a small pebble rolled under the tongue. This keeps the salivary glands at work, and has saved many a hunter from dying of thirst. Hunger is endurable. You hear of people who live a month or two without food. But thirst is a different thing, and the stoutest must succumb to it in a day or two. I began to despair of Santa Fe, and was about to dig a hole in the sand and bury my blanket and myself for the night, when a light two miles ahead made me throw up my hat and whoop like a commanche.

At 8 o'clock Shadow and I were drinking a well dry at the very first house in all our roundabout tramp of 38¼ miles; and a few minutes later I stood in the plaza or public square of Santa Fe. *"¿Donde son Fisher y Cia., boticarios?"* [Where are Fisher & Co., druggists?] I asked a Mexican, and he showed me. In I went, and in three minutes more was shaking hands with Mr. A. C. Ireland, Jr., or "Phon" as he used to be in Chillicothe. Without any disparagement to the kindness of many other friends, I have not been, since I left Chillicothe, so thoroughly and pleasantly at home as here with "Phon" and his charming wife. A shave, a big scrub, a big bunch of mail, and a bill of fare fit for a king, make me feel like a civilized being once more. The hospitality of these friends, the crowds of cordial ex-Ohioans I meet, who have been reading the *Leader* and looking out for the Tramp, and the oddities of this strange old city—all are at my finger ends, but all must wait a week. I shall be here for two or three days, "do" the town thoroughly, catch up on my correspondence and then on to Albuquerque and the wastes of Arizona. *Buenos noces, amigos.*

LUM

Cerrillos, New Mexico
Monday, December 1, 1884

Editors Leader:
    Probably you think that I am monkeying around somewhere near the Arizona line tonight. Well, I ought to be, but am not. You know those old pictures advertising "Spalding's Glue"—

two men with a dab of the "stickum" uniting their coat-tails, despite their desperate struggles to tear apart? Label one of the men "Santa Fe" and the other "Lum" and you will have it straight. That is the hardest place I ever saw to break loose from. Stick? Why, you stick to Santa Fe like a fly to the bunghole of a molasses hogshead. The quaint old town holds on like Potiphar's wife, and to get away I had to be a Joseph, and leave my garment in her hands—metaphorically, of course, for I need all my garments in this climate, just now.

But in sober fact, I doubt if one could exaggerate the cordiality of Santa Fe folks. All my life I have been finding clever, warm-hearted, hospitable people, and not least on this trip— which affords the best of chances for learning what men are made of. But let me tell you that you can scrape this country from end to end with a fine-toothed comb, scour it with a posse and search-warrant, and if you find a better set of people than those I have met in Santa Fe, come out to Los Angeles next February and see me eat my old shoes, admission free. That is why I write to-night, from Cerrillos (Ser-ree-ose) 20 miles from Santa Fe, instead of from a point 200 miles ahead. When I struck the ancient city, it was with the expectation of cooling my heels there just two days. As a matter of fact, I stayed nearly eight, and then tore myself away only by brute force. It is a wonder to me to find myself alive; for if I hadn't been pretty tough, they certainly would have killed me with kindness.

La ciudad de la Santa Fe—the city of the Holy Faith—is in itself probably one of the most interesting places on the continent, and certainly the most unique. You know, of course, its great antiquity—last year it celebrated its tertio-millenial. It claims to be the oldest settlement in America, and; though this assertion has always been contested by St. Augustine, Fla; and is now, I hear, by Tucson, Arizona, I fancy Santa Fe has a pretty good "call" on the title. Away back in Fifteen Thirty-something, when Cabeza de Vaca got tumbled upon the Mexican coast and meandered up through what is now New Mexico, Santa Fe was already an ancient city of the Pueblo Indians. There are dumb witnesses to-day of the prehistoric-town—ruins and relics of the inhabitants of perhaps a thousand years ago stretching for five miles along the Santa Fe River, or Río Chiquito ("Little River"). Then came in Coronado in 1510 [Lummis is inaccurate here; the date was 1540; may be a *Leader* typo], and after him other conquistadores by odd fits a few years apart.

These old Spaniards appear to have been Southern Democrats, every mother's son of them, for they stuffed the ballot boxes, bull-dozed the majority, and kept the poor Pueblos down in regular slave fashion. Then the Pueblos arose on their ear—in 1680—and ran their oppressors out at the end of a pointed stick. I can just imagine what a fat time these Pueblos had, making the big plaza hot with bonfires of archives, papers, sacred images and vessels, and knocking the very stuffing out of all the churches. That is why the early history of the city is shrouded in a sort of mosquito-netting of uncertainty—all the records were destroyed in the great insurrection. Still it gives the historian a better show to trot out his imagination and let it prance at will, so we will not bemoan the lost records. Well, things went on for 12 years, and then the Spaniards came back and gobbled the town once more, under the lead of Vargas. Since then it has poked along in much the same channel until a few years ago.

In 1804 some Yankee, hot-footed after the mighty dollar, came out from the East in a trading wagon, marking out, by the faint tracks of his wheels, that which was to become the most famous wagon road in the world—the old Santa Fe Trail. Of course the city has had its full Spanish share of insurrections and revolutions, but they never amounted to much, so far as I can learn. I believe the Territory became part of the United States in 1846, during the Mexican War, when Gen. Kearney marched in; but I can find no definite information about any of these things in the alleged "guides"—which are pretty low-grade ore, carrying about 5 cents' worth of information to the ton. In 1879, however, the Atchison, Topeka and Santa Fe R.R. got out to Las Vegas, some 30 miles [Lummis is in error here; the distance is 60 miles] away, and the Americanization of the dull Pueblo-Spanish town really began then.

There has evidently been a wonderful change in Santa Fe in the last few years, and the change has been for the better. The boom is petered out now, but it lasted long enough to sprinkle the little city thickly with modern buildings, some of which are very creditable, and to graft a modern and progressive civilization upon the dead old trunk which had not grown an inch in two hundred years. Now you might stand in some parts of the city without seeing anything to prevent your belief that you were in an ordinary American town.

It seems to me that the traveler who would get a thorough idea of Santa Fe should first of all hie him to the commanding adobe walls of old Ft. Marcy, or to the cupolas of either the hospital or the college. From any one of these points he will get a bird's-eye view of the city and all its surrounding country— and a remarkable pleasant view it is. Behind are the snow-powdered crests of old Baldy—the southern extremity of the Culebra (Snake) mountains—some ten or twelve thousand feet in height. Far off to the right is the long and impressive range of peaks forming the western wall of the Río Grande valley. Across the great plateau to the south, are the blue ridges of the Cerrillos, Placer and Sandia (Watermelon) mountains, from 8,000 to 11,000 feet in altitude. And at your feet lies scattering Santa Fe, in a huge natural basin, sheltered on all sides, and probably 200 feet below the surface of the plateau. The altitude of the city is 7,017 feet.

Right in the center of the city is that most important fixture of all Spanish and Mexican towns, the plaza, or public square— a respectable park about 300 feet each way. When the natives ran the town, this square was a general stamping-ground for burros and trading caravans, but the American settlers filled it with trees and walks, fenced it in, stuck up a fountain and a band-stand—which they call "the pagoda"—and otherwise turned the old arrangements inside out. There is a soldier's monument in that plaza which should be framed—not because it spells February with only one r, but because of one good Anglo-Saxon word that I never saw on a monument before, the

word "rebels." It occurs three times in the various inscription—
for instance on the south side; "To the Heroes of the Federal
Army who fell at the battle of Valverde, fought with the rebels,
February 21, 1862." [This monument still stands in Santa Fe's
plaza.]

Around the four sides of the plaza are most of the leading
business houses—some in rather handsome blocks—and outside these lies the residence portion of the city. These New
Mexican dwellings look odd enough to Eastern Eyes. Nearly all
are adobe, and a majority only one story high, though there are
some three-storied adobes. But don't let yourself be fooled by
nincompoop correspondents who write back home about "mud
houses." These adobes are made of baked dirt, it is true, but so is
your Ross County Bank Block. The sole difference is, that you
roast your clay with a fire, and these people let the sun do their
brick-burning. An adobe out here, knocks the socks—pardon
my territorial elegance of diction—off of any brick or frame
building, so far as anything but looks is concerned. The thickness of the walls—from two to three feet—insures comfort all
the year round, and an adobe is cool in summer and warm in
winter.

These houses are not generally very gorgeous outside, but
within they are as capable of decoration as any other kind of
buildings. You get into one of those large, handsome rooms, 18
feet high, finely papered and furnished, carpeted with Brussels,
and you will laugh at your prior conception of "mud houses."
Even the ruder dwellings of the lower class are very comfortable
and pleasant. It would be a good scheme if the board shacks of
Eastern shantytowns could be replaced by these neat little
adobes. The more pretentious houses here are built in a square,
with a placita (little plaza) in the middle, and many have remarkable fine gardens besides. One thing strikes you as you look
down upon the city—the universal flatness. Probably there are
not 20 pitch roofs in the whole place, and but few mansards. A
Mexican, you know, always has two stories to his house—the
roof serving as floor to a sky-thatched attic as big as all out-
doors.

The U. S. military post here takes up a big part of the city's western side, and is the life of the place. The military band toots in the "pagoda" on the plaza every afternoon, to the great comfort of the citizens—and justly so, for it is a pretty good band.

The narrow, unpaved streets—most of which are little, if any, wider than Chillicothe alleys—are full of interest. You meet so many different types of humanity—and some of them types that are new to you. And in a bunch you may run across Yankee, Frenchmen, German, Mexican, Spanish—for there are a few real Castillians—Indian and Negro, not to mention English, Irish and Scotch representatives. By the way, why are there so few colored men in the West? In the last thousand miles of my tramp I have not seen 20 Negroes, and they were all at Denver and Santa Fe. The Indians will catch your eye often enough, however—plenty of Pueblos every day, and now and then a Navajo.

Then the countless burros, driven through the streets by Mexicans or Pueblos at a reckless gait of half a mile an hour, and generally loaded with wood, will look queer to you. It must be a semi-science, loading these little fellows. The wood—in crooked sticks of cedar, about two feet long—is laid in a kidney-shaped pile as big as the burro, across the pack-saddle, and held in shape by an adroitly-wound rope. I'd like to see a tenderfoot pack one of these loads—bet he couldn't make three sticks stick. So what with the people, the burros, and the queer little houses that pay no more attention to alignment than a dog does to catnip, one finds here street scenes as unlike as possible to all American ideas.

As I remarked before, Santa Fe is on the downgrade. Its boom was founded on nothing substantial, and therefore went the way of most booms—*viz*, up the flume. You will find any quantity of good buildings unoccupied, which seems a pity in this ancient capital, and business even with the best firms is not what it was a few years ago. You see, the sole recommendation of Santa Fe has been its real attractiveness as a health and pleasure resort; and that is a basis that one cannot build upon for any great length of time. It is good, but inadequate. Now, the climate of

Santa Fe is unquestionably one of the finest in the world, too
bracing, indeed, for those who are very feeble. And this same
climate is what Santa Feans swear by. The first thing they all
ask the new-comer is, "Haven't we a glorious climate?" and if
the stranger doesn't wish to be mobbed by an outraged popu-
lace, he had better answer "yes" like a little man.

Fortunately, he can do it with a clear conscience, for it would
be impossible not to feel the exhilarant twang of this, high, dry,
champagney atmosphere. It makes a man feel as if he would like
to be all lungs. You could almost count on your fingers and toes
all the stormy days in a whole year, and one begins to think the
Lord must be running pretty short of bad weather, by the scar-
city of it in Santa Fe. It would seem good, I should think, to have
a real old rip-roaring storm there, once in a while, just to break
the monotony of perpetual sunshine. The days are warm in the
middle and decidedly cool at both ends, so that fires and blankets are nightly necessities all the year round. Folks use the
same amount of bed-covering in winter and summer, so they
tell me. All this delightfulness of climate makes Santa Fe attractive both as a home and as a sanitarium—for those who
come in time.

But such things, though not to be sneezed at, cannot give a
city substantial prosperity. I have been looking over this country heedfully, and it seems to me that the only future for Santa
Fe lies in artesian boring. The soil all about is excellent, and
could be made to grow any kind of crop profitably if irrigated.
The city lies at the very foot of the mountains, and there can be
no doubt that abundant water would gush out responsive to the
artesian drill. In a few years this whole surrounding desert of
sage-brush and cedar could be made to blossom like the rose;
and as for fruit, I suppose there is no better fruit country in the
whole great west. Now that is where Santa Fe must turn for
lasting prosperity. Mining is good in its way, and has been the
making of many a city—as witness Denver, which owes to the
mining camps nearly all she is.

But the best leads will run out, and the best mines last but a
few years. Furthermore, Santa Fe has no particular mineral

*Palace of the Governors, Santa Fe, New Mexico, n.d. Photograph by
Charles Lummis. Courtesy of Southwest Museum: negative no. 1067.*

wealth, so far as heard from. But give a city a good agricultural
country roundabout, from which to draw, and there will be a
city there forever. It makes a business basis less brilliant than
that of mines, but sure as taxes and reliable as the rock of ages.
Streams are scarce and small in this part of the country, and
irrigation must depend on artificial fountains. One of these days
some Eastern capitalists—for the moneyed men of New Mexico's ancient metropolis are something like those of Ohio's
ditto; they are well enough fixed, and don't care to stir up new
enterprises so long as they can sit still and loan their money at
12 per cent and upward—some Eastern capitalist will come in
and punch the earth's crust full of holes, and then you will see
here one of the garden spots of the world.

It is just as well that I have gotten away from Santa Fe at last.
There would be no living with me if these hospitable folks had
kept me among them much longer. I had just a triumphal procession throughout my stay there, and haven't fully recovered

yet from the big dinners and little exercise. After all my roaming through a country where the chief end of man seems to be to
skin his fellows, it was good to hit a city where you are made at
home in ten minutes. Of course I owe the bulk of my pleasure to
"Phon" Ireland and his wife, who were unremitting in their
kindness. Phon is right hand man in the leading drug store here,
that of Fischer & Co., and is mighty popular. He is snugly
domiciled in a pleasant up-stairs suite two doors from the store,
and has a home it warms a man's heart to see. You folks back in
Chillicothe, who remember the hilarious boy that used to help
Cliff Douglas, *et al.*, in various schemes against the peace of the
neighbors and their pigs, ought to come out and see the sedate
business man now, as he toasts his feet at the domestic fender,
or jabbers Spanish with Indian or Mexican customers. As a
general rule, I think a man doesn't amount to much until he
gets married—and too many are not much force even then.
Well, Phon has taken the right road, having been married some
eighteen months, and has won the sweetest, most sensible and
most unaffected little wife in the whole country—east of Los
Angeles, I mean. I hope you'll see her one of these days—it will
give you new confidence in Chillicothe luck. Their home was
my home during my stay in Santa Fe, and I never enjoyed a week
more heartily.

But Mr. Ireland and his wife are not the only Santa Feans in
whom you are interested—for there is a whole nest of good
people here who are tied to the Ancient Met. by bonds of kin-
ship or friendship. Among the first I met was Capt. J. R. Hudson,
a well remembered ex-Chillicothean, who is thriving and popular in this old town. He is carrying on his old business—that of a
watchmaker and jeweler—in the handsome store of Hickox &
Co., on the plaza. Thanksgiving evening, Mr. and Mrs. Ireland
and I enjoyed a bountiful Thanksgiving spread at his house, and
there I met pleasant Mrs. Hudson and the children. Miss Mary
has grown to be a really beautiful young lady, and there are two
sturdy boys who are hustlers. The Captain was a valuable ally to
me, and with his practical knowledge of the city and surround-

ing country gave me a stack of information which has been good
as gold. He took me over to see Mr. Cole, brother-in-law of the
Territorial governor, and there I reveled in a wonderful collection of aboriginal pottery and stone and bone implements. I
wish John Selp or Dr. Leslie could see that layout—it would
make their eyes pop out.

The Captain and I also passed half a day looking over the
great collection of minerals which Judge W. B. Sloan, Commis-
sioner for New Mexico, is about to take to the New Orleans
Exposition. He has several tons of the finest specimens that ever
made my fingers itch. If you go to New Orleans don't fail to
hunt up his exhibit and Judge Sloan, who is a very pleasant
gentleman and an epitome of mineralogy. He used to hold down
a professor's chair at Delaware, Ohio.

It will just knock you silly with amaze to see the illimitable
and diversified mineral wealth of New Mexico by sample. Nature, like a watch, has always a compensation balance, and this
arid, desert territory is a perfect treasure house of hidden riches.
Gold, silver, copper, iron, lead, tin, zinc in every possible form
and combination; amethyst, turquoise, ruby, calcedony, corun-
dum, garnet, topaz, agate of a dozen kinds, opal, emerald and
even diamonds, are all found here, many of them in bewildering
profusion—not to count petrifactions of every sort. The Judge
loaded me up with about 30 pounds of handsome specimens,
including a whole raft of petrified wood, which will polish up
handsomer than a diamond, to my taste. I am also indebted to
him for much information about, and a chance to see for myself,
this Cerrillos-mining district, from which I write.

One of my most interesting visits in Santa Fe, was to Senor
Don Pedro Sanchez, the Indian Agent, a very refined and courteous Mexican. Unlike the average Indian Agent, whose highest
use for the red man is to skin him alive, the Don is very plainly
putting his whole energy and attention to such honest endeavor
as is doing vast good. I don't have to take anyone's word for
this—the thing speaks for itself. The remarkable respect and
regard in which the Indians hold him, shows that they deem

him their solid friend, and you can't fool an Indian. Don Sanchez has been in charge of the Pueblo Agency for 18 months,
and it is to be hoped that he will stay, in spite of the general
shaking-up that will come next March. He is devoutly interested in the education of the Pueblos, and after long, up-hill
fighting, has succeeded in making a very handsome beginning.

According to old archives still extant, there were once 50,000
Pueblos in this territory. Now, there are only 8,000, 1,000 of
them are of school age, and 800 are now at school, which is a
good showing. The old element of the Indians naturally sticks
in its ruts, and is opposed to all these innovations, but the young
people are solidly with the Don, and like him, wish the Government to make the education of its wards compulsory. Many of
these young Indians are at Carlisle, Pa., and more at the 3-year-
old training school in Albuquerque. There are also seven social
schools, scattered among the Pueblos. The latter are hardly
successful, however, for the people do better when entirely
removed from the home influence and customs.

I have several letters [written by these students]. One, from a
16-year-old girl, who has been in the school but two years,
would do credit to an average white Miss in your grammar
schools, and is beautifully written. It strikes me that the present Indian policy, of which the above letters are among the first
fruits, is rather an improvement on the old one of getting the
poor savages crazy with tanglefoot [cheap whiskey], and then
butchering them for their consequent misbehavior. Major
Sanchez takes great delight in these epistles, and answers them
at generous length. There are 19 pueblos in this agency, including about 8,000 people. It ought not to be long before this
schooling of the young leavens the whole lump.

Saturday, Mr. Ireland, Father Farini and other friends es-
corted me out to the interesting pueblo of Tezuque [sic], seven
miles north of Santa Fe, and we explored every house in it. The
pueblo is, of course, a hollow square, but its houses are double,
back to back, one row facing out and the other in. Most of them
are two-storied. You will see no doors—merely a few small

windows—below, and to enter the lower rooms you must climb one ladder and go down another through a hole in the roof. The upper houses open by ordinary doors to the roof. All are adobe, small but well made, and have from one to three rooms— generally two. They are white-washed with gypsum inside, and are neat as wax. In the corner of each room is the conical—but withal incomparably convenient—adobe fireplace, common to all Mexican and Indian houses, and in it stand the knotted sticks of cedar, for in this country wood is always burned up-right instead of horizontally. In the hearth, in all probability, you may see sundry rude images of red clay baking, or well-made pottery, of peculiar polish and decoration, and charac-teristic shape. Now some very excellent but still greener people who come out here from the East, buy these fantastic images and take them home as "Indian idols." Thereby they become a laughing stock.

These Indians are all as good Christians as you are—per-haps a good deal better. They are devout Catholics, and their churches and homes are alike full of the symbols of their faith. They make these "idols" simply to sell to greenhorns, and they do sell both by the hundreds. Nor are pottery and earthen dolls their only resources thereunto. On their walls hang Springfield and Winchester rifles, double-barreled shot-guns and the like, cartridge belts and reloading tools; but they sell to these fool tourists any quantity of bows and arrows and raw-hide shields, and these tourists carry off the relics as something really used by the red men! They pay five or six prices for them, too, for the Pueblos have learned that little scheme from the Jews, who trade with them.

Well, there are fools and fools. The venerable proverb says "there's no fool like an old fool." Western sufferers would amend this to "there's no fool like an Eastern tourist"—and they are about right. I don't know why it is that folks who have good horse sense back at home in Boston, New York or Cincinnati, can't get out here without turning to doddering imbeciles—but it seems that they can't. Such exhibitions of ill taste, bad manners, ignorance and gullibility are to be met nowhere else, I trust. Why, these frank folks out here, and they are not unkind or uncharitable, either, have a contemptuous pity for Eastern tourists, who have become synonym for all that is ridiculous and disagreeable.

Now when a Westerner sees anything novel and surprising, he takes it all in without moving a muscle. He "always comes down stairs that way." But an Eastern tourist will throw up his hands and open his mouth and slop over until the very dogs have run around to the drugstore for something to steady their stomachs. Right on the streets of Santa Fe intelligent and refined looking ladies have been seen to stop in front of a half-dressed Indian buck, gape at him, talk about him, and even pinch him to see if he was honest flesh—unmindful of the spectators who looked on in contemptuous wonder.

There is absolutely no story so ridiculous that you cannot ram these tourists full of it, and of course the natives take malicious pleasure in filling them with guff. I am sorry it is so, for I like the East and its people; but if I stay out here much longer and see many more of its transient representatives, I shall have to lock up my respect or it will get lost. People of sense who come to a strange country will keep their eyes and ears open, and their mouths shut. However, this is not exactly a direct description of Tezuque.

In every house at Tezuque, as in other pueblos, the visitor will find the cooking arrangements among the chief points of interest. At the side of one of the rooms—usually that also is used as a store house and granary—is a wooden trough, a foot deep, from three to five feet long, and three wide. In it are fastened from one to three curious rocks, shaped something like a bracket, slightly concave, and sloping from the edge to the bottom of the trough. They are about six inches wide and 18 long, and would probably weigh 50 pounds apiece. These are the Pueblo mills, and on these, with smaller, oval stones, thin enough to be easily grasped, the squaws rub down their blue maize into a muddy-looking pulp. This dough is then slapped by hand into a flattish shape, laid on flat, round rocks before the fire, and there baked into tortillas. Jerked meat—that is, meat cut into thin strips and dried in the sun on lines—hangs on the walls, and there are other provisions stowed away in various corners.

Now when you go to visit an American friend of family, the chances are that his young hopefuls will pull your hair, break your hat, split your ear with their howls, daub you over with molasses, and in all ways irritate—not to say irrigate you. But among the Pueblos, people have more sense as well as more manners than to turn loose on you a pack of devastating infants. Go into one of these little "mud huts," and you will see the baby strapped hand and foot, and wound so about with cloths that it cannot stir. A small board swings from the low rafters by buckskin thongs, and on this board the papoose lies serene as a summer dream. I have seen about 300 tiny Pueblos, and I never heard one of them screeching. There are some mighty good-looking youngsters among them, too. Perhaps the tourists have done some good, after all.

The adults of Tezuque are not particularly bad looking, but incomparably inferior to the Indians of San Ildefonso, who are noted—and especially the women—through-out the territory for their attractive appearance. The Tezuqueans are, however, intelligent, rather neat, and industrious after their own funny fashion. The Governor was away from home, but the others were good enough. I am told that all these Pueblos have a Republican form of government, electing by ballot their own Governor, Secretary of War, etc., for each town. They raise small crops of grain and vegetables, and get more or less game, but make their living mostly, I fancy, by the sale of pottery, images, bows and arrows, buckskin—whole or made up into leggings and moccasins—pelts, minerals and other commodities, of which they are not slow to learn the market place, among their friends, the tourists.

We made a long, entertaining and instructive stay at Tezuque, and there was but one cloud upon the day's enjoyment—

the zeal of Padre Farini in trying to work off some aggressive
temperance tracts upon us, at the low figure of $33.00 for a
thousand. I may mention that he is the duly authorized agent of
their sale in Santa Fe. If you should wish any, I have no doubt he
would be pleased to send them to you C. O. D.

I ran across Major Bailhalche, son of one of the first proprie-
tors of the *Scioto Gazette,* and thereby struck richness. After a
pleasant chat, he took me over to the office of Señor Amado
Chaves, a young and polished gentleman from one of the most
noted New Mexican families, and ex-Speaker of the Territorial
Legislature. Señor Chaves has recently discovered on his big
place by the San Mateo mountains, a remarkable buried city—
an American Herculaneum—and by his invitation I am to visit
and explore it when I get out there—which will probably be in
about ten days. This is apt to be the richest find of my whole
trip, for the place has never been described nor even visited by
scientists.

Well, now I have told you the good of Santa Fe. There is a
little bitter with the sweet, of course, though mostly in small
doses. Some things are very high—the servant girls, for instance, run from $25 to $35 per month and their board, and then
they are not worth a mill dam. A shave costs two bits—25
cents—and a hair-cut four. Postage stamps sell at two cents,
however, so there is a silver lining to the cloud. Gas is $3 per
1,000 feet, furthermore, this place is rough on scalps, somehow,
everyone's hair drops out like men between the acts, and nothing but clinching will stop it. However, that is all I have been
able to rake up against Santa Fe, and that isn't much.

A description of this wonderfully interesting Cerrillos mining district must wait a week. I go down to the ancient pacer
mines of Golden Tomorrow, and across to the A. T. & S. F. R. R.,
again at Wallace, where I hope to see Mr. Roads a few minutes
on his way to Los Angeles. Then on to Albuquerque, with a
short stop for more agates, and out on the line of the Atlantic &
Pacific R. R. toward Arizona. Bye-bye

                                                              LUM

Golden, New Mexico
Wednesday, December 10th, 1884

Editors Leader:
  I begin to feel something like a Forty-niner myself, and am
coming to understand, partially, the craze which made men
forget home and everything else in the pursuit of these little
yellow rascals I have been digging from away down under the
ground and washing in a little puddle of muddy water. It does
feel queer to know that the ground you walk on is full of this
precious dust, and that the barren gravel carries a richer crop
than man ever planted. But I am getting a little too previous,
snaking you clear down to Golden before we get out of Santa Fe.
Let's go back a little.
  I am proud to say that I did finally elope from Santa Fe—
proud because it took a great deal of nerve. It was as hard as
breaking away from your best girl at 11:45 P.M., when she puts
her soft arms around your neck and says: "Oh, George, it is *real*
early yet. Please don't go." I presume you know how hard that
is—if you don't, the sooner you find out the better. The eventful
day was Wednesday, and a pleasant one it was. I got away about
9:30, and struck out along the road leading to Cerrillos—for it
didn't suit me to make the long railroad detour via Lamy. Santa
Fe, you know, is on an 18-mile branch of the Atchinson [*sic*],
Topeka & Santa Fe R. R., and Lamy (which is no relation to our
old friend, "Now I Lamy"), is the point of junction with the
main line. There is a good cross-lots road down to the railroad at
Cerrillos, however, and this I took. It was a warm, dusty and
thirsty 24 mile tramp down to Carbonateville, which lies on the
southern slope of one of the Cerrillos mountains, but I didn't
mind it. Thoughtful friends at Santa Fe had filled me up with
canteens, maps, directions and everything else essential, and
the Pilgrim's Progress was not troubled by a single Bunyan,
though a stiff ankle had to take its whack at me.

Golden, New Mexico, n.d. Photograph by Charles Lummis. Courtesy of Southwest Museum, negative no. 3011.

I reached Bonanza in the afternoon, but did not stop long in this first camp of the district, for it was pretty well deserted. Carbonateville, six miles beyond, and in about the center of the Cerrillos mining district, was what I was after, and just as I was beginning to think the camp must have gone prospecting—for the miles seem longer when you have no milestones—I turned a little corner in the hilly road and there was a house looming up right over my head in the twilight. I found a Virginia welcome in the first house I struck, which was the comfortable dwelling of Mr. Geo. L. Wyllys, who has strayed out here and is doing contract work on the mines. With him I raised my Ebenezer, and abode there till Friday morning, visiting the various mines of the camp and covering a lot of paper with ink.

Carbonateville, like most camps in this region, is of comparatively recent date, having been started in 1879. It boasts about twenty houses, all comfortable and rather substantial buildings, and only awaits reduction works to begin making good money. It is a low grade camp—that is, its mineral, as a rule, does not give fat assays—but there is any quantity of it, and that means wealth for the owners. The mineral is principally galena—though there are some carbonates—and all runs paying quantities of silver.

The leading mines are about 20 in number, but there are prospect holes everywhere, and most of them have struck more or less valuable bodies of ore. Near the town is the now deserted Mina del Tiro (mine of the shaft) worked by the Spanish the Lord only knows how long ago. A tangle about title keeps it idle at present. In it are still some of the primitive ladders used by its early owners. They are simply tree-trunks with notches cut deep enough for a toe-hold, and reaching down from ledge to ledge, clear to the bottom of the 200-foot shaft. I should prefer to be excused from climbing them—they look as though an eel would be sand-paper beside their slipperyness.

One dry fact about Carbonateville is that she has no water. Wells have been sunk 150 feet in vain, and all the wet the Carbonatevillians use, they have to haul from Bonanza in barrels. I think the little town will pull through, however. It has abundant mineral at its very doors, and only needs a few honest men with courageous money.

The most interesting thing in that whole neighborhood, however, lies about a mile south-east of the village. A walk down the zig-zag road, Thursday afternoon, brought me to a swelling dome—only a few hundred feet above the road, but 7,000 feet above the sea—whose top and sides had a whitish cast totally different from anything I have seen elsewhere. This Mt. Chalchuitl, whose rocky heart is pierced by the countless drifts of one of the oldest and most famous mines in the world—the Great Turquoise. From this mine, hundreds of years ago, was taken the largest turquoise ever found, that which adorns the royal crown of Spain. The story is that this great gem was given to Cortes by Montezuma, but I cannot just remember whether this is so or not. My memory is failing on these events of my boyhood. Anyhow, it is certain that the Aztecs and Mexicans worked this mine long, long ago.

I presume it is a thousand years since the first rude stone hammer was swung against these white rocks, and the first little azure nugget of turquoise taken out. The evidences of antiquity are unmistakable, and lie on every side. The great hill is fairly honey-combed, and on the west side is one excavation big enough to swallow your court-house without a strain. All around are vast heaps of debris, covering in all about 33 acres, and upon these heaps great cedars, twice as large as my body, have grown thickly. In this dry climate it has taken them hundreds of years to attain their present size. So you see these great dumps could hardly have been made yesterday.

If it hadn't been for this mine, Santa Fe might have retained all her old archives and beehives and other hives, for here was the scene and the cause of the great uprising of 1680. The Spanish conquerors made peons (slaves, practically) of the Indians, and among other things kept a big gang of poor devils hard at work in this turquoise mine. In 1689 a big chunk of the mountain took a tumble, and buried a great number of the Indian miners under a few million tons of rock. I presume they are in there yet, but no one seems to bother about letting them out. Well, perhaps they are dead by this time, so a relief party would do no good.

I could go on and tell you the chemical composition of the mountain—how the decomposition of the feldspar of the trachyte, and the imposition of the phosphoric acid of apatite, and the deodorization of the thing-a-mabob produced the present state of things. I could also remark that the turquoise is a hydrous aluminum phosphate. But it wouldn't lengthen your life or enable you to beat the assessor to know all this, so I refrain. It is enough to say that the mountain is full of turquoise, but that valuable specimens are extremely rare. You know the correct color for a turquoise is sky blue, and most of the veins here are greenish. On almost every broken rock of the dumps you will see the color, but it is generally in veins of paper-like thinness. I did see one or two veins an inch thick, but they are inaccessible without blasting. The gem also occurs in little nuggets, though less frequently.

I pottered around a few hours with a heavy hammer, battering the outcrops, poking over the dumps, and crawling the whole 300 feet of the longest drifts now open, and found about a dozen pieces of fair stuff, some of it pretty good color. The latest real working of this mine was in 1890, when Tiffany, the great New York jeweler, sent out an expedition to dig for "chalchuitl" (the Mexican name of the stone). They didn't exactly connect, however, and soon gave up. But the place is by no means deserted. You can't go up there anytime without striking a lot of Indians pecking away at the rocks with dude hammers. They are harmless, however, and won't strike back. All these Pueblos use turquoise as currency among themselves, and sell a good deal to tourists. For every tourist that buys a piece of real turquoise from an Indian, however, three buy a polished chunk of a copper ore which much resembles turquoise. Who says the Indian isn't getting civilized?

After winding up my last *Leader* letter at Los Cerrillos, which means "the *pole-cats*," I believe, I waded the icy Galisteo and started up the sandy arroyos (ravines) toward the south. Cerrillos is a rambling little railroad town, supported by the many adjacent mines, of which the most important are the coal banks. Right here comes in another sample of the beauties of railroad economy. Santa Fe has here, close to her doors, an inexhaustible supply of the finest coal in the world, both anthracite and bituminous, yet she has to pay $7 per ton for her fuel. The Atchison, Topeka & Santa Fe R. R. has coal of its own up at Raton, and freezes out these Cerrillos coal banks by charging an extortionate freight. Just now there is a strike at Raton, and Cerrillos is permitted to ship a few carloads a day; but as soon as the strike is over, things will go back to their old channel.

Coming out of Cerrillos I was perplexed by about 13 different roads branching off in all directions, and had to take one by guess. Meeting a teamster soon after, I asked him if this was the road to Golden. "Yes" said he, "and you've got a big afternoon's walk before you. Golden's 12 miles from here." That didn't rattle me, and I tramped three miles up the hills until I met two men in an express. They informed me that I was now 14 miles from Golden, and on the right road. A mile and a half beyond, two ox-teams loaded with coal hove in sight, and the drivers said, "Yes, straight road, 16 miles." That began to give me a pain, and when I found a man working at a coal bank, a hundred yards further on, I asked him the distance to Golden, in a voice that would have drawn tears from a turnip. He mildly but firmly replied that it was just 18 miles.

Then I sat down on a rock and felt of my feet, to see if they hadn't got turned around somehow. A long-bearded bush-whacker came loping along on a little broncho, and to him I appealed; "Say, Mister, don't impose on an orphan, but tell me how far it is to Golden. If it's 50 miles, just spit it right out, for I want to know the worst. They've been breaking it to me gently all the way, but I want you to tell me the whole bitter truth." He looked at me compassionately, doubtless thinking me a mild-eyed crank, and told me it was not quite 20 miles to Golden. I went and wept great salt tears over a buckhorn cactus—you can still see them, I reckon, strung like beads upon the thorns—and struggled on.

Perhaps you think this is fiction, but it is bedrock fact. The conversations occurred exactly as I have reported them. The only thing that puzzles me is, how they were all so unanimous in sticking on two miles each time. There must have been a conspiracy to impose upon my virgin confidence.

I suppose the reason none of them knew the distance is, that the road had not been surveyed; but if any of you should ever want to walk it I can tell you that it is just 20⅔ miles—I measured it that fateful afternoon. And mean miles they are—sandy, hilly and dull, at least I found them so. There is some very pretty scenery, too, as your way winds among the rough Ortiz mountains; but by the time you have walked ten miles through the deep sand, on a tiresome up-grade, and still have not reached the height of land, the beauties of nature have lost their charm. If it hadn't been for my canteen filled with muddy water from the vile Galisteo—a Gal. I am glad to have left behind me—I never should have got out, for it is the driest road I ever pounded. With every "snifter" of that water I swallowed a tablespoonful of iron rust and sand, but it tasted sweet as honey. Clear water lacks body, anyhow, and iron is good for the system.

At last the highest pitch was reached, and Shadow and I started on the long delayed down-grade. Luckily it was a cold day, or we might have stuck on this pitch. As it was, we touched it without being defiled. Just at sunset a young fellow on horse-back informed me that it was still two miles to Golden. I hurried on for half an hour and met a Mexican who said Golden was three miles away. I'd like to have a pair of suspenders made of that road—it is the most elastic thing ever made by the hand of man.

But finally, after a mile climb up the wooded hill, I heard the welcome toot of a big dog, and a moment later caught the dim lights from a score of windows. A man doesn't know what feels good until he gets in from a long, cold tramp, which has been aggravated by uncertainty, whether he was on the right one of a dozen different roads running off through the darkness, and sits down to a good hot supper beside a ruddy base-burner with a pleasant hostess attending to his wants.

I expected Mr. Roads to be going through on Sunday, and decided to go over to Wallace to intercept him. This was almost the same thing as going back to Cerrillos, but the Golden schoolmaster offered to take me over and back, so I left my things here and went on Saturday. After that long cold ride, fancy my disgust to learn that the train I wanted wouldn't be along till some time on Tuesday, and that this 40 mile trip had been thrown away. It was impossible to wait all that time in pokey Wallace—a town for which I have about as much use as a dog has for two tails—and equally out of the question to break away thus quickly from Golden, a brief glance at whose rich placers, that morning, had completely caught me. So there was nothing to do but to stay over night and come back here next day. Wallace, it should be remarked, though only an insignificant, brown railroad village—the terminus of a division of the A. T. & S. F. R. R.—is somewhat noted as the only turquoise market in the country.

The pueblo of Santo Domingo is not far away, and the Indians come in to every train with chunks of turquoise, or of malachite counterfeits which they have ground on a grindstone. One buck took a marvelous fancy to my Apache leggins, and had the gall to offer me "cuarto [sic] reales" (50 cents) for them.

I should tell you that the knickerbockers are "froze out" for the present, and will hardly get a show again this side of the Mohave desert. They are mighty nice to walk in when the weather is fit to eat, but what shall it profit a man to gain the whole world and freeze his knee-caps off, especially when he don't kneed to? So with all due respect for the knickerbockers, I have supplemented them with a handsome pair of buckskin leggins, made for some Apache dude, and am proof against any wind the territory can scare up. These leggins come to the hip-pocket, fit like my own hide from the ankle up, are soft as velvet, white as kid, and have a fringe of thongs two feet long, running down each welt seam. The wind might just as well try to blow open a burglar-proof safe as to get through these things, and that is no small scheme these bitter days. I'd just like to walk into Chillicothe, though, with my recent outfit, and see the small boys skin over the back fences holding on to their scalps with both hands. These leggins saved me from being used for an ice-cake to cool claret with next summer. I certainly should have frozen on the way back from Wallace, Sunday, had it not been for them; and as it was I had to run at the wagon tail two-thirds of the way, to keep alive.

The wind came down from those Ortiz mountains with an edge on it that you could have shaved with. I expect it must have been the effects of that cold day the Republicans have had, just getting this far west. I had planned to get down to Albuquerque in time to meet Mr. R., but the first big storm of the season came on Sunday night, and lasted all day Monday, and I wasn't going to try a strange trail through 36 miles of snow.

So I am for the present located in Golden; and though I expect to get out again to-morrow, it wouldn't take a gun at my head to induce me to send for my possessions and stop right here for good. For I know that this little camp has an 18-karat future before it, and that that future, though long delayed, is now coming on the keen jump. It is as sure as death. I have been tramping over the mountains that hem it in, catching my toes on their innumerable outcrops of rich ore, blinking at the brilliant revelations down in their many mines, and handling the heavy yellow lumplets from their inexhaustible placers—and I know what I am talking about. If you could walk through the bowels of Mt. Logan and see that it was all one great body of copper and silver and gold, you would call it richness, but I have seen better than that. There are whole ranges of mountains here—not single pigmy hills—whose rocks are cut and seamed with huge veins of mineral wealth in many forms, and whose washings, now great gravel banks covering thousands of acres, are all rich in golden sand.

A place with that to fall back on cannot be kept down, and Golden is coming up. Through all the five years of her life, her neck has been under the heel of the most rascally set of cutthroat robbers that ever went unhung. But the political overturn this fall means life to New Mexico. You have always known me as a solid Republican, and I am one still, but our late defeat doesn't gall me as it did before I understood the situation out here. Let me give you the matter in a nutshell, and then you will understand why nearly every Republican who comes out here, (save as an official,) turns Democrat within a year and why this Republican territory is fairly standing on its head with joy over the election of Cleveland. A big ring of unscrupulous and wealthy scoundrels have for years had everything their own way, and their way came near being the ruin of this great and should-be-prosperous territory. Many of them were officers in the Rebel army, but they have been Republicans out here because it paid. Most of them have government positions, and all have 'fluence. Steve Elkins is the boss thief of the lot, and he is a choice one. He is universally detested and feared throughout all New Mexico, and his life wouldn't be worth much if he were to venture into this part of the country. The Chief Justice of the Territory, Judge Axtell, is his ready tool and some of his acts are almost incredible. I am glad to see by the papers that the government is making tardy amends, and that this thief's resignation has been called for and his successor selected.

I couldn't stop to name to you all who are in this ring—whose crimes are countless, and cover the whole list from larceny to murder—and you would not be interested. Suffice to say that the "Santa Fe ring"—including the Chief Justice, the Attorney General, surveyors, lawyers and many more—with a few outside monopolists like Elkins and Senator Chaffee, have been trying to steal the whole Territory and carry it off in their vest pockets.* They came pretty near succeeding, too, but the late election knocked them crazy. Their name is Dennis, and that is my one consolation in Blaine's defeat. I believe that a majority of the people in New Mexico preferred Blaine to Cleveland: but Blaine had allowed Elkins to be his chief promoter—a mistake which I think we all recognized from the very start—and they feared that Blaine's success would probably put Elkins in the Cabinet as Secretary of the Interior or at all events confirm his strength and do them harm. Such a result, they believe, would have been the death-blow of the Territory—and I believe it, too. I suppose nothing is much better understood throughout the country than that Steve Elkins is an unscrupulous shark, and I cannot be sorry that they have pulled his leash.

*Stephen Benton Elkins was a New Mexico banker and lawyer from 1865 to 1890 and the territorial delegate to Congress, 1873–77. He used frontier politics as a stepping-stone to success in national business and politics. Jerome B. Chaffee was Elkins' Colorado counterpart; he came west in 1860 and made his fortune in mining and banking, and he served as both territorial delegate to Congress and U.S. Senator, 1871–1879.

You ask how these things have worked to oppress the people. Well, it is very easily told. You will remember that in a letter from Alamosa I had something to say about the audacity and appalling power of monopolies in Colorado. The nether mill-stone which has been tied about New Mexico's neck has been the "land grants." You know the Mexican government, when this territory was part of Mexico, used to make grants of large tracts of land to certain citizens whose service made such gifts fitting. The grants are respected by our government, under the treaty with Guadalupe, and many fictitious ones have been manufactured. They were made solely for grazing and farming—"for agricultural and pastoral purposes," in the language of the documents—and can be used only thus.

The Mexican government didn't give away mines, you may know from your early reading, but kept all such under its own thumb, with a few unimportant exceptions. Now of course comparatively few of these grants remain in the hands of the original grantees. Indeed, I do not know that any of them do. Most, if not all, have been bought up by syndicates and speculators. That is all right, of course, but not so the perversions which have arisen from the greed of unscrupulous, and powerful men. The sharks have not only turned the lands—given for agriculture and grazing, and as such only available in law—into vast mining monopolies, into which the poor prospector cannot come, but whenever there was valuable mineral land anywhere near them, they have fraudulently gobbled the whole business, suborning surveyors to run false lines, and buying judges or juries over to make their robbery safe.

Take the case of Golden. Just south and west of town lies the small triangle of the Cañon del Agua grant, made by the Mexican government in 1839 to Don Jesus Miera and others, and orginally containing 3 × 4½ miles square of land. It included one old silver mine, about a mile south-west of town; and the rest was for farming and grazing. In 1866, Elkins and several fellow sharks bought this grant from the then owner, and got a deputy surveyor out to put the lines where they would do the

most good. In 1844, one Barrillo had discovered and opened
what is now known as the Great San Pedro Copper Mine—one
of the largest and most valuable mining properties in the world.
This lies about two miles east of the east lines of the original
grant.

The first step of the robbers was to have their surveys made
so as to include a great tract of land whose lines run from
Golden to the top of the mountain on which the copper mine is
situated, then to the Cañon del Agua Spring and back four miles
to Golden—a triangle containing several times as much land as
the original grant, and in addition to it. This gave them the
copper mine—a fabulous fortune in itself—and a great area of
wonderfully rich placers. A little later they concluded that they
hadn't stolen enough, so they ran new lines and took in several
thousand acres more of rich mineral land. Some years ago,
parties struck a tremendously rich lead of gold quartz in the
Delgado mine, which is on a mountain a few hundred yards
outside the lines of the second steal.

Perhaps you remember seeing, at the Centennial Exposition,
those specimens of quartz from which the wire gold bulged out
so blindingly. Those specimens came from this Delgado mine.
As soon as the rich find was made, Elkins and his gang remembered that their last line had been run a few hundred yards too
far to the south, and they had a third survey made, of course this
time taking in the Delgado. Now you understand that all this
stolen territory—which has grown from a few hundred acres to
35,000—was and is dotted by the cabins and the claims of
hundreds of honest miners whose title to them was as perfect as
yours is to your home—obtained in a different but equally legal
way. But that made no difference to the sharks—they wanted
the land, and the squatters must go. But the squatters wouldn't
have it that way.

In 1880 the Copper Mine was sold to a Boston company, at
whose head was the notorious Geo. William Ballou. This "San
Pedro and Cañon del Agua Mining Company," so it was called,
bought the mine, fully understanding that it was stolen, and

was to take the whole expanded "grant" if the squatters could be fired out. If it had not been for the brains, honesty and indomitable pluck of Col. R. W. Webb, a pioneer journalist who has been for years the champion of the miners, and is the idol of every poor man in the territory, the firing process might have succeeded; but he never slept.

Suit was finally brought against the company for false survey. It came, after long delays, to trial this fall, and though the miners had all the evidence, a case as clear as the nose on my face, Axtell rendered a decision against them. Meantime, the company had begun, in April 1880, to work the big copper mine. They blew in a million dollars sinking and timbering miles of shafts and drifts, building a 25-stamp ore mill, two copper furnaces, two smelters, a town for workmen, reservoirs, roads, and everything else on a princely scale. They spent $500,000 in bringing water by pipes from the Sandia mountains, 15 miles away. This latter enterprise was a fair sample of dude management. That pipe, 8 inches in diameter, was only an eighth of an inch thick, and was expected to withstand the pressure of water from a head of some thousand feet! Of course it burst at once. Then to freeze out the squatters, they refused to employ miners living here, but imported Swedes and other cheap laborers to work the big mine.

Well, all this was snide enough, but no one cared to kick. If the company had been content with its big stolen mine, it would be running today. But it had to hog the whole district, and enjoin the miners from working their own claims, and at last the natural result came. The long-suffering miners could brook the wicked oppression no longer; and one day in May, 1883, just as the hundred workmen came out from the big mine to get their dinners, eleven quiet, resolute-looking men from Golden, stepped into the mine and said, "Guess we'd better run this thing a while now." And as each of them had a Winchester and a brace of six-shooters, they had their way. The imported foreigners couldn't see any money in standing up as targets at $1.50 a day, and they departed. The tools, spies and officers of

the company got off at long range and did some deadly shooting—with their mouths—but they didn't care particularly
about running up against that big hole, within which were the
eleven brave fellows. "Well, we'll starve them out anyhow," was
the company's refuge.

However, the little guard stayed in the mine away into July,
and somehow they always had plenty to eat. I reckon it must
have been another case of the ravens. Now don't misunderstand
this. The men of Golden did not want the mine. They were
willing that the company should work it, though it was a steal;
but their forcible capture of it was a last resort to show the
thieves that the stealing must stop with this mine. They had
tried the law, and found judges, lawyers and juries all bought
over by the enemy; and who shall blame them for at last asserting their rights by quiet force. The thinness of the company's
claim is well shown by the fact that even after Axtell's infamous
decision—the decision which has caused his tardy removal—
they have not come out to take the property they alleged to be
theirs. I may also add that U.S. Inspector of Surveys Treadwell,
came out here from Washington, last winter, surveyed the
"grant," and put it back to its original place and size, leaving out
the whole vast tract now included by the steal. It was in the face
of this fact and many others Axtell gave the thieves their 35,000
acres. This San Pedro company is the one which was to have
Gen. Grant for President. But Grant came out, saw the ground,
discovered the rascality, and washed his hands of the whole
business.

The schemes to oust the rightful owners of these lands have
been countless. Time and again the miners have been notified
to clear out or take the consequences, and as to what consequences would be, they had no cause for uncertainty, for murder, through proxies, of course, does not stand in the way of
these monopolists. I could tell you, had I the space, a tale of the
American Valley that would make your hair bristle, and it is a
true story, too. Oh, you don't believe such things can exist! Well,
you will pardon me for saying that if you don't, it merely shows

greenness. You will recollect, if you think a moment, that the American colonization of this Territory is recent; that as in all new countries, the element which was outlawed in the East has drifted here at once; and that in such a place a clever knave gets to the front. It is something so in the East, where the biggest rascals are frequently on top; but you cannot hold a population of several million up by the tail the way you would one of a few thousands; and a thinly settled country is the rascal's paradise.

That such almost incredible wrongs have been done as I have described, I know absolutely. It is notorious throughout the whole West, and among all classes. Why, if I were to tell you one-half the infernal outrages perpetrated by those in power— by money or position—it would take more space than the *Leader* has in one year. "But," you say, "these miners are igno- rant and prejudiced, probably in the wrong, and have a natural antipathy to those above them and the information you get from them is doubtless colored."

Well, my information comes from all classes, not miners alone, and is all exactly harmonious; but right here I want to stop and disabuse your minds of another Eastern bit of igno- rance. The Ohio miner and Western miner are two different men. You have been used to the ignorant, besotted, dull, im- ported laborer for wages in the coal mines of Ohio and Pennsyl- vania; and I find that hosts of pretty smart Eastern people have a notion that all miners are very much the same. But when you go to judge the Colorado or New Mexico miners by Cornish or Italian standards, you are going to be left in the hole. They are a different breed of pups. Let me tell you, my dear sir, that in these little prospect holes or down in the developed shafts; picking away at the stubborn veins or tilting the gold-pan, you will find your peers or your betters at almost every turn. Some of these earth-stained, ragged men are better educated than you or I, and the majority of them are fully as shrewd and fully as honest.

I believe that for that matter you will find less dishonesty of any kind in a western mining camp than anywhere else on earth. Remember, too, that these men are not coolies. They are not here as day laborers, toiling for a pittance of some other man's money; but they are men who left perhaps better chances back East than you have now, and came out here to make fortunes. They have no master, and what they have is their own. Perhaps it is only a little hole sunk a few yards into the hard rock; but that hole may mean more money than you ever handled in all your life of business.

Of course, on the other hand, it may not be worth a continental cent, but a miner is willing to take his chances. It might rub your complacency a little if you could know how he pities you fellows for your dull penny-profit lot, and how he despises your business sense. And he hasn't such a bad excuse, either. Once in a while a lot of you will get enthused over mining, and will slap $50,000 or $100,000 or $1,000,000 into a company to develop some rich metal. When the all-important work of choosing a president, board of directors and other equally interesting wax figures is done, you proceed to get a superintendent. Do you hunt up an old miner, whose hair has grown grizzled in practical experience among the rocks and veins and lodes and deposits? Oh, Lord, no! That would be too good sense. Some young dude just from college, where he has picked up a smatter of mineralogy and chemistry, is appointed superintendent, and runs the whole enterprise and all your boodle into the ground in about six months. Then you rear up on your hindlegs and cuss at everything connected with mines, call the whole thing a d——d humbug, and declare you've been swindled, and the mine's a fraud. And meantime the old miners in the camp will occasionally wander up past the ruins of your costly buildings, chip off rich chunks from the very veins your dude superintendent took for moss, and say with a laugh, "If these Eastern fellows would quit sending out fools and tenderfeet to manage their mines, and get someone that ever saw a mine before, they'd find that mining isn't such a bad thing after all."

You have had a pretty bad streak of this sort of thing back in Chillicothe, in the sewing-machine enterprise, where the only man who knew his business was gagged and hand-cuffed, while a lot of people who couldn't tell a sewing-machine from a hole in the ground, unless both were labeled, ran the arrangements, and came near killing the whole enterprise as dead as Job's relatives. I'm glad this order of things is changed now, and that the man who has spent his life inventing the machine, is at last allowed to know something about how it ought to be made.

But you are farther along than the mining companies. They never do seem to learn. Why, last March, an Ohio corporation—the Cincinnati Gold Mining and Milling Co.—blew in a big pile of money to erect a ten-stamp ore-mill here. Of course the dude superintendent was included with the other machinery and he certainly—to quote an expressive nautical phrase—"played h——l on his watch." Probably you are aware that a stamp mill cannot run without water, and also that there is no surface water here. Well, what do you suppose that dude did? Why, nothing much, only that he went and picked out a dry gulch far up in the mountains—where you wouldn't strike water if you were to bore half a mile—and built that costly stamp-mill up there! That's just what he did, and there it stands to-day, though I believe they talk of moving it to some place where it can be run, if they can raise the money. That is a sample of the way such enterprises have been managed, but far from the only one. I could fill you plumb full of instances.

Such things have hurt this mining country dreadfully, for stockholders back East, not knowing the circumstances, and re-alizing only that their money was hopelessly gone, have blamed it all on the mines, and fully believe today, that there is no money in mining. But there is money in it when people go at it in a rational way and not like simpletons. There are a hundred, perhaps a thousand, fortunes right in this very camp, simply awaiting men who will come here and put in capital honestly and sensibly. There is incalculable wealth right here, lacking nothing but capital to bring it out. It takes money to sink these great holes, put up works and all that, but a man can see for himself the treasure ahead, and that treasure is his if he has the brains to use common-sense business methods to get it.

As I remarked, the future of Golden is great, and not long to be deferred. The wealth is here in endless profusion, and it will not long lie undeveloped. Capitalists have been scared off by this land grant business, because they didn't understand it—for those who do know the real situation don't care a snap for the grants. The grants—or rather the stealing extension of them— must go and go now. Fancy what nuts it will be to the Democrats to uncover these rascalities of men who have robbed under the guise of Republicans. There will be no quarter shown, and when this nest is broken up, the whole Territory will have a tremendous boom—and no part of it more than Golden. There is no possibility that the steals can stand—their atrocity is too monstrous. And then the bugbear which has needlessly frightened capital away will have been removed. Works will go up, the great veins of mineral will be torn from the mountains, and money will flow as it did in the old days of California.

In three or four years from now, Golden will have 10,000 people—you hear the trill of my wild bazoo. Why, the gold alone here would create a perfect furore anywhere else. I wish you could see some of the specimens I have gathered. The place has wood for a century, endless deposits of coal near by; and abundant and excellent water from wells, ordinary and artesian. Now is the time to come in here, too. Interest in some wonderfully promising claims can be bought for a song, for money is scarce here now. A year hence you couldn't touch them with a 40-rod pole. I should smile to see myself lying back and getting two per cent interest on my money—if I had any—when I could just as well put it in here.

Monday morning, amid the flying snow, a former Chillicothean, Mr. George Smith, started out to pilot me through the mines near by. Up on the side of the nearest of the Tuerto (crooked) mountains, only a mile from town, we passed over so many of his prospect holes—some well in and showing up in good shape—and then came to the Black-Hawk mine—his most developed work! If anyone were to give me a share of it, I wouldn't kick it out of bed, for it is good property. He has about a hundred feet of development work done on it, and at the bottom of his last shaft, 28 feet deep, is striking fat things. At the surface begins a fissure vein six inches thick, of gold and silver bearing carbonate, slanting back obliquely into the hill and widening all the way with surprising rapidity, until at 20 feet it strikes the big "blanket," lying horizontal it is here five feet thick, and will run handsomely in silver, with considerable gold. It is soft and easily worked, and one man can take out a ton or so of mineral in a day without tearing his undergarments, with further developments the Black-Hawk is a fine thing to have in the family, as sure as you are born.

Passing three or four other good mines, and the deserted works and village of San Pedro, we struggled up the steep hill beyond, and at last stood at the entrance of the great San Pedro copper mine. "Jim" Cheves and John King, two clever miners and also old-timers here, who were stopping in one of the empty buildings and working on their claims near by, accompanied us in our tour through the miles of drifts and inclines, and aided me materially in getting some beautiful specimens. Shadow trotted along too, and acted as if he always had lived underground.

I shall not attempt to describe the richness of these tunnels— a man must see them for himself before he can form the remotest idea thereof. The mine is superbly timbered, and it must have cost a big fortune to put in just the great props. Many hundred yards are fully boxed, walls and roof being framed solid with ten-inch timbers. You can fancy the thickness of the veins when I tell you that there are three levels in it, one above another, and each passage high enough for the tallest man to walk through. Through these levels run drifts in every direction, with plank floors and iron tramways leading to the outer world. A drift, you know, is a tunnel run out horizontally; and a shaft one that is sunk perpendicularly or nearly so. The extent of the drifts, shafts and inclines must be reckoned by miles— and we went through it all. From every wall and roof a dazzling display of mineral wealth stares at you. Most of it is copper, in all the varying forms—and there is nothing richer looking than the combinations of this metal, whether in the flaming or pea-cock-colored pyrites, the deep indigo sulphides or the bright green carbonates.

No walls were ever decorated by human hands so gorgeously as nature has decked the sides of these dark tunnels. Besides the inconceivable quantity of copper ore, there are great veins of reddish, free milling ore running heavy in gold. There is also plenty of silver in the mine, along with the gold and copper. With a pick we dug out an ore-sack full of such elegant speci-mens as would make your eyes pop out. I wish you could see them. Now, this San Pedro mine is the only thing of its kind in this section, but it will not be so for long. The whole Tuerto range is full of the same stuff and the only advantage of the big mine over hundreds of holes, is that it has been developed and they have not. If a man wants a San Pedro of his own, all he has to do is to dig it—the material is there, and nothing lacking but the hole.

After spending some hours in the San Pedro, and visiting the Rob't E. Lee, Lucky and other valuable miners, we came back over the mountains past the placers—pronounced *plass ears*—to town. These placers are all around the mountains—wher-ever the spring torrents from the cañons and ravines have washed down the debris from the mountain sides. This wash has formed great beds of boulders and gravel, covering hundreds of acres, and varying in depth, between surface and bed-rock, from 20 to 40 feet. The diggings which gave this camp its former name of "The New Placers," are situated half a mile east of town. The Old Placers which have been worked by the Mexi-cans for unknown generations, are on the eastern slope of the Ortiz Mountains, 9 miles northeast of here. Walking through the New Placers, one sees countless well-like holes, 30 to 40 feet deep and about 4 feet square. Over each is a rude but effective windlass—a peeled pine tree set on two forked sticks and with a stout branch left on for a crank. An inch rope of sufficient length lets down the miner into the untimbered shaft, at whose bottom he begins to "drift out" horizontally until he strikes a "pay-streak." There is gold everywhere, but not in quantities to pay for working with pick and shovel. But in these pay-streaks the gravel is rich with yellow flakes and nuggets. Particularly fat strikes are being made now, and work is humming.

Bob Carley and Bob Torace, two mighty clever young miners, are having the biggest luck. In three days and a half, last week, they took out $48.80, and on last Tuesday, their wash netted $19. The Mexicans are the best placer miners here, for they have been brought up to it from childhood, understand the lay of the land better, and can stand bad air that would put out a candle and kill most Americans. On Tuesday, by the kindness of the Messrs. Carley and Torace, I was enabled to try my own hand at the business. Swinging astride a little cross-bar on the end of the windlass rope, I went dangling down into the deep hole. At the bottom I lighted a candle, took a double-pointed crowbar, and crawled back 30 feet to the end of the low drift. The pay-streak here lies on a sort of cement bed, and here I petered [sic] away until I had enough gravel to fill two raw-hide buckets shaped like a gripsack, each holding nearly a bushel. Then I sent up the bags and went up myself. The next business was to wash. They have dug a shallow hole, about 6 feet long and 2 feet wide, and keep it filled with water hauled from the wells in barrels. In the middle of this is the rocker, a box 4 feet long, 18 inches wide, and a foot deep, set on rockers. A couple of cleats are nailed across the bottom inside, and at the hind end, which is closed, is the apron—a square foot of canvas set slanting backward on a frame, with a cleat at the lower end. Over this apron fits a smaller box, with a sheet-iron bottom full of one-fourth inch holes. The gravel (or "pay-dirt") is shoveled into this top box, and water is continually poured on from a dipper as the rocking proceeds.

Presently nothing but the course pebbles remain in the top box to be thrown out, most of the sand and gravel has been washed out down the sloping sluice-way of the rocker, and against the apron cleat rest a few handfuls of finer sand. This is taken out and put in a gold-pan, and the operator thrusts one edge of the pan into the pool and swashes it around with a rotary motion. You would expect every last particle to be swept out of the pan, but it isn't. After a few such sloppings nearly all the sand is gone, only a little remaining on the lower edge of the pan; and up behind it in a little cluster lie the yellow particles for whose sake all this delving has been done.

From my two buckets of dirt I amassed a heap of "yaller" that I shall be glad to show you if you ever come to Los Angeles. Probably I should have got three or four times as much, for this is rich dirt, but the apron happened to be upside down, and most of the gold got away. However, I shall have another chance at it as soon as there is a little less weather. In all the little stores here gold dust passes current, and each can show you a bottle heavy with the beautiful stuff. It isn't quite as handy as green-backs, but it looks a heap better. Wait, though, until some man with brains and money comes out here, and with water from the artesian well goes to hydraulic mining. Almost every foot of this ground will pay for working in that way, and there is a princely fortune for those who do it.

And now before I close this long letter, there is one thing I want to ease my mind of, and if I work in a little of my slang, it isn't because I think the subject a trifling one. It is a little sermon to the girls of Chillicothe. I have often said, and I believe it now, that the old metropolis has a larger proportion of beauti-ful girls than any other city in the world, and as for their virtues I can say nothing better than that I found my own ideal and mate among them. Now perhaps it would be proper to pretend that all these lovable young ladies are besieged with hosts of lovers; but not being a society liar, I shall not pretend so. I know, as well as you all know, that the conservatism—in English, old-fogyism—of a certain class has kept Chillicothe down so that her boys are driven away from home to make a livelihood, and that the eligible young ladies outnumber the eligible young men about five to one. This is a cruel state of things, and an unnatural one, for the Lord meant that every girl should have one bean anyhow for keeps, and maybe several more for luck. He cut her out, too, for a happy wife and mother, and she knows it. Now get out your arithmetics and see what sort of a show a girl stands of getting married where she is five next to the boys' one. It isn't very hard to reckon.

The West, on the other hand, is full of men—mostly young men—who have come out here from the East, where they were just as good as any of us—and become the makers of this strong, new country. They are men, fine men in body as well as in mind and heart, sturdy, honorable, self-reliant, full of energy and strength, yet tender as only such men can be when it is the time for tenderness, they have become almost a new race. Girls are rarer than other angels, and when one does fold her wings and light down in one of these towns, she can have her pick from the whole population. These men, long separated from mother, sister and home, are not weaned from the human longing for womanly sympathy and companionship, and the desire is intense within them for a home of their own. Why, I could show you, right here, one sweetfaced little New England girl who came out to teach the young Golden ideas how to shoot [sic]. She taught school just three days, with the whole male population at her feet, and then married a smart young fellow to whom her preference turned. If you will show me a happier little mother and wife than she is today, I'll agree to turn bachelor myself.

Now I shall not give any advice, for that might be impertinent; but if I were a Chillicothe girl without someone that I thought was a powerful sight better than a brother, I'd make a break for the territories too quick. I'd come out to a place where I was dead sure of a chance to marry a man, and not stay back East and run my slim show of catching on to a dude. Instead of tarrying where the ague would make me shake out of my false teeth when I came to wear them, I'd elope for the finest climate in the world. I'd locate in New Mexico—perhaps right here in Golden—find a man to suit me, let him have me, make him build me a good adobe cottage which I'd fix up as a woman can, and then enjoy life. If he came home some night a millionaire— and that sort of lightning is apt to strike anyone here at any time—it wouldn't worry me; but if he didn't, we could be happy anyhow. There, that's what I'd do—you can do as you like; it's none of my funeral.

The weather which has held off for me for nearly three months, has come at last. I am moved in here, and even as I write a howling storm is raving around the house. It may shut me up longer than I had planned, but winter here is a patchwork affair, and the bad streaks are short in duration. So by the time this reaches Chillicothe I shall probably be plodding along west of Albuquerque. *Adios, amigos. Deseo a V. una feliz noche.*

LUM

Albuquerque, New Mexico
Friday, December 19th, 1884

Editors Leader:

When a man is going anywhere, he doesn't generally like to be snowed in on the way, but I begin to fancy worse things might happen. That has been my experience, anyhow. When I got into Golden, the evening of December 5th, it was my intention to light out for good the next day. I did light out the next day, but not for good, and in 24 hours was back in Golden. That time a stop of two days more was about my figure, but just then a snorting snowstorm got in its work, and knocked all my plans bang in the head. The storm commenced on Sunday night of last week and hung on like a bull pup for six days. It would clear up awhile and look encouraging, but it was only spitting on its hands to take a new hold, and in about an hour the air would be white again. About two feet of snow fell up there in the moun- tains—Golden is over 7,000 feet in altitude—and you may just salt it down as a solid fact that that didn't make remarkably luxurious walking. I tried three or four short six and eight mile tramps around the mines there, in my low-necked, short-sleeved shoes—Tom Cahill's shoes still—and concluded that about the richest place I could stick to was the fire-place. New Mexico snow, I find, is just as cold as any other snow, and just as binding on feet practically bare.

The short road from Golden to Albuquerque runs through some pretty rough mountain country, and the snow along that unbroken trail was mighty b-a-d. I didn't want to go 'way up north to Wallace again, if it could be helped, so I sat down blandly to give the snow a chance to thaw off. I might have been waiting yet, so far as the snow seemed to appreciate my polite desire to let it go first. It wouldn't have thawed an inch if you had offered it a gold medal. I regard that snow as a judgment upon the people of New Mexico, who have been bragging to me for the last month about their glorious climate. There isn't any discount on the climate, that's a fact, but shoot the snow! I waited a week on it—not the climate, but the snow—and then had to wade it after all. It was a case of want in the balance and found wading.

But it's snow use to act as if I were mad about it. That storm was a good friend to me and any man that lifts his hand against it has me to lick. If it hadn't been for that storm, I should be out in the San Mateo mountains. If I had been out in the San Mateo mountains, I shouldn't have been in Golden; and if I hadn't been in Golden I should have missed one of the pleasantest weeks of my life. Consequently here's my regards to the snow. George Smith is as much to blame as the snow, too. Whenever he'd see me getting ready to make a break, snow or no snow, he'd say, "What 'n thunder's the use in rushing off so?" And so between them they bulldozed me into having a glorious time.

Of course, the deep drifts shut me out from seeing a good many things that would have been available in pleasant weather, but there was enough and more than enough to keep me fully entertained. To gurgle the straight truth into your ear, I am "stuck" on Golden, and if I am not back there in a year from now it won't be my fault. Of all the many places I ever saw, it is the place for a young man to locate in. Just now it is down and a fellow can climb right on top, but in a little time it is going to rise and shine, and the men who are on board about then will have a solid thing of it.

Wild-cat enterprises are pretty well played out in the west, and people who want to come out here and become millionaires in a month had better stay at home. But the man who will settle here, do a legitimate business in a legitimate way, go slow on the mine question—for a mineral crazed greenhorn might as well go to the poor house to start with—but keep his eyes open. For chances can do handsomely. This country wants honest business men, and it will pay them well. No bummers, cranks or sharpers need apply, however.

The twelve days of my pleasant imprisonment in Golden were not idle; and in spite of snow and *decolette* shoes, I managed to see and do a good deal in that time. You may think this little hamlet would soon be exhausted, so far as sight-seeing is concerned, but I know of no great city whose points of interest are so many and so striking. Thursday, after the *Leader* ceased to weigh upon my conscience, Mr. Smith and I started off up into the mountains through the deep snow, bound for the two principal gold leads of the district, those of the Delgado and Old Timer mines. It was a tough old trip, but we rather enjoyed it. Plunging through knee-deep drifts, grunting up the steep hill-sides, hammering away by dim candle-light at the rich subterranean walls, straining our eyes to catch the yellow glints of golden particles in the rusty, disintegrated quartz, and filling our handkerchiefs, pockets, and oresack with specimens—that took up the afternoon.

Both these mines are fine properties, and well developed. The Delgado is in about 300 feet, with prospects still flattering, and the ore in sight a high grade. The Old Timer is one of the best mines in the camp, and a daisy. The length of the various drifts and shafts is 500 or 600 feet, and all into a fine vein of soft, decomposed quartz which is full of free-milling gold. I have two handsome specimens from which the little nuggets bulge out very enticingly.

We brought back several pounds of this ore—some assays of which have run as high as $30,000 to the ton—and while George wrestled with his frijoles, biscuits and potatoes for supper, I yoked myself to a gold pan and a big sledgehammer and proceeded to "prospect" my booty. If you think it is a picnic to pulverize a lot of that stuff to flour-like fineness, just try it on. It took me about five hours to dessicate [sic] three or four pounds, and gave me a blister for each finger of my right hand, which engineered the sledge. Then when the lot was reduced to what looked like a pan of iron rust, we poured on water, wibble-wobbled the pan about in proper fashion, and finally got out a little heap of fine gold-dust for our pains.

Friday was the meanest day in the whole outfit, with a keen wind, laden with cutting particles of snow. There wasn't much inducement to ramble about extensively, so after finishing our prospect of the Old Timer I contented myself with a visit to Mr. Emmert's store—the respectable loafing-place for "the boys" when they get lonely in their petticoatless homes—writing a few letters and other similarly quiet matters. But that visit to the store fixed a programme for the morrow. I met Messrs. Carley & Torace there, and they talked of having been at work, during the day, on their placer claim—and washing at that!

You will hardly need to be told that gold-washing in winter is about the coldest work a man can do. He sits there all day in the weather, without any shelter, his hands and arms constantly in the icy water, and his exercise insufficient to keep up much animal heat. They had washed out two ounces of gold—$40— that day, amid the flying snow. No wonder they kept at it! 'Most any man would stand "a few" of weather for that sort of a stake.

Saturday wasn't distinguished for Italian balminess, either, for the tail end of the great storm was just flirting by; but if Carley & Torace could stand it, I could too, and after an 11 o'clock breakfast—no use getting up at rooster-time, such mornings—I made tracks up to the placers. For awhile I watched the boys as they tilted the rock or made a clean-up with the pan; and then, as per invitation, dangled down the shaft again to get *uno prospetta* [*prospectiva*?]. The drift had doubled in length since my first visit, and it seemed as if I never would get to the end. But after bumping my head against sundry rocks in the low top, I arrived there Elias, and pecked away for an hour at the pay-streak.

It was a good deal slower work than before—partly because I took only the fine gravel, and didn't again fill my bucket with rocks—and it took me about an hour to get a load. Then, Great Nineveh! what a wrestle I had to pack that 200-pound bucket to the shaft! That is a pretty good load to tote; anyhow, and when you can't straighten up to more than about half your height, 200 pounds weighs a ton. However, we made it finally, the bucket standing the racket a good deal better than I did; and George ground us up, one after the other, to daylight again. This time you may be sure the rocker apron was fixed according to Hoyle, and the gold had no show to elope. So when the one bucketful of pay-dirt had passed through rocker and pan, the bunch of golden scales—with one nugget—that nestled in the remaining teaspoonful of fine black sand (fragments of magnetic iron) was twice as big as the outcome of my former two buckets, and made a very pretty showing. This Golden gold is of remarkable purity and weight, and if anything can look handsomer or more alluring than a little pile of it, I'd like to be introduced to that anything. I notice the weather didn't bother me much there, though when we started home it did occur to me that my feet— soaked for hours in snow-water—were about frozen. However, properly clad, one never suffers here, and there is never a day in the year when the boys don't work—some of them, at least—for a good many let up on Sundays.

Speaking of the placers reminds me to tell you that if anyone comes monkeying around with stock in a certain "Golden City Placer Mining Company," of Chicago, you want to keep your hands off. This concern has got hold of some land on El Tuerto Creek, four miles west of Golden, and consequently so far from the mountain veins—whence, of course, all placer gold originally comes—that the pay-streak is played out before it gets there. You know gold is the laziest of metals, and goes no farther that it just has to. (This is a bad send-out for me after I have come so far.) The first handy riffle he strikes, down sits Mr. Gold, and nothing short of a freshet will make him move on. Of course, the finer particles are the last to stop. They are young and giddy, and may roam a good way from home—even as far as the grounds of the above-named Company. But digging for them is like kissing a female infant when you might just as well go along a bit farther, and get a lip-sample of sweet sixteen.

I speak of this Company, because it is trying to come [bring?] the funny business on the public. Its placers will give colors, and not much else, but they have been salted to bait suckers, and rather successfully, too. Why, the very nuggets which these fellows are displaying as the product of their claims, were bought right here in Golden, and are worn smooth from being carried long in the pockets of the boys who found them in the New Placers. That is a sample of the way many a mining stock is boomed, and so many people have been thus easily victimized, that the prejudice against investment in mines is easily accounted for. If you use common sense, take no one's word, investigate for yourself, and are not too brash, mining is one of the best money-making schemes in the world, but most people take none of these precautions, and then when they get bit they abuse mining for their own asininity.

Saturday evening I had the pleasure of a long call upon Mrs. R. W. Webb—wife of the gallant Colonel. She is a charming little Louisianian, with a pound of dynamite in each black eye, and is as gritty as she looks. The Colonel came into the Territory with her, six years ago, to make a home. As soon as his eyes were opened to the infernal misrule and robbery that was going on in New Mexico's high places, there was but one coarse open to a man of his nature, and that was to peel his coat, roll up his shirt-sleeves and pitch into the official scoundrels with tooth and toe-nail. For three years he edited and published the cleverest, brightest and most meat-axy paper in any of the territories—the little 4-column *Golden Retort*. It was a paper, and don't you let it escape you. A buzz-saw would have been more salubrious to fool with, and it wasn't long before folks began to get up on the fence when the *Retort* went by. How it did dissect the rascals of that Santa Fe Ring and their big-bug backers! Webb never jumped on any man who behaved himself, but the public robbers—and New Mexico had the woods full of them—got custom-made fits right along.

I suppose no other paper in the whole country contained such an overwhelming proportion of editorials, and there wasn't any mush about it, either. For a while a good many of the other Territorial papers—which were almost without exception, truckling to the Santa Fe Ring—let go at Webb as hard as they knew how, but he knocked them all silly in a few rounds, except one or two that hadn't sense enough to know when they were buried. From letting the Colonel alone, nearly every paper in the Territory has at last come over to his side, for he has waked the people up so that ring organs [newspapers] are no go. It has been due solely to Webb's skill and valor, too—for in this fight he has held his life in his hands every hour—that New Mexico is at last on her feet, ready to shake off forever the strong clutch of the garroters.

Last winter he went to Washington the 7th of December and was there till the following July, trying to waken the sleepy authorities. All this time Mrs. Webb was left in Golden, and fighting the Ring heroically. It would not do to let the *Retort* die at that crisis, for it was the one medium through which could be presented to the public the cause of the people against their oppressors. Mrs. Webb knew nothing of running a paper, and there wasn't a typo or press-man within 20 miles, but this delicate little lady went at the obstacle and cleared it. She learned to stick type herself, and taught a green young miner; and between them they got out a well-printed, creditable paper, with editorials that burned like fire, and never missed an issue during the Colonel's absence.

Webb was no slouch on feeding the foe with brimstone, but

that 90-pound wife of his went him about twenty better. In that day of excitement and deep danger, when every man in Golden packed a six-shooter under his coat; when several attempts were made to assassinate Goldenites who had been particularly obnoxious to the Ring, and no one knew what the day would bring forth, the sight of that quiet, fragile but thoroughbred lady defying the power that handled the whole Territory, and exposing the whole range of official villainy, is as true a picture of heroism as I know of. That was sand, and no mistake.

The Retort ceased publication this fall, its mission fulfilled, and Col. Webb is now editing the Las Vegas Gazette. He is idolized by all classes save the politicians and monopolists, and is without doubt the most popular man in the Territory. It is a lucky thing, in more ways than one, that none of the many schemes to compass his death succeeded. If that brave champion of the people had been foully dealt with, there wouldn't have been enough left of Santa Fe to swear by, and the dwarfed piñons around that valley would have borne many a ghastly pendant. Through the kindness of Mrs. Webb, I have a goodly pile of Retorts, which I shall preserve with honor. The Retort was to New Mexico what the little Monitor was to this nation in the rebellion.

It did me good to see those black eyes flash chain lightning as the pleasantly modulated voice spoke earnestly of the wrongs of New Mexico and the fight of two brave souls against such overwhelming odds. But as the speaker got deeper into the subject, and the eyes grew one steady flame, I felt like hitching my chair over to the other side of the stove for fear that some pieces might fly off and hit me. Well, she told me of these outrages until I got hot myself and rushed off, up to George's adobe, to give the Ring a turning over. There was no trouble about getting the documents in the case—I can go over Golden for an hour and scare up enough unimpeachable evidence to hang the whole Santa Fe Ring. There are papers there that would bring a mighty heavy lump of money, if the men who hold them were on the sell.

What fools these mortals be! Now Elkins, Catron and their gang never did me any dirt. I never saw most of them; and as I have learned to keep on the other side of the street from Penitentiaries, I probably never shall. None of them ever did so much as to kick my dog; and yet I put in Saturday night, Sunday, Sunday night, Monday and Monday night, getting together the evidence and writing them up to the extent of six or eight columns, and took a fiendish delight in doing it, too. Well, as I get older, probably I won't become so hot over other people's funerals.

Tuesday, still unthawed, slipped away in more writing and in winding up my social duties in Golden. I don't know where you will find a more cordial and intelligent little community than in this oppressed—but soon to boom—town. A catalogue of the pleasant folk would include almost every citizen, and that is too long a list to quote; but I must mention a few with whom I was thrown more intimately in contact.

Among the most clever is Mr. W. R. Limpert, a tall, smart Buckeye. He came from Groveport, near Columbus, Ohio, in apparently the last stages of consumption. The boys at Cerrillos, where he got off the train, didn't expect him to get over to Golden alive; but he fooled them all, himself as much as anyone, and is to-day in rugged health—a living proof of New Mexico's good climate. He is a clever chemist and assayer, a good neighbor, and an unusually level-headed and well-informed man. Then there are Messrs. King, Peirsol, Morrison, White, Smith, and others more than you could shake a stick at, and all as clever as the law allows. To all of them in partnership I owe the pleasure of my visit.

I had been hoping to get over into the Ortiz mountains to see some fine mines there, but it was too much of a trip for such weather. On Tuesday, however, the man whom I particularly wished to see there rode into Golden—Col. George Crosson. The Colonel is a genius, and I had a very pleasant confab with him, in the store. His home was in Pleasant Plain, Warren county, O. [Ohio]. In 1851, he went to the Pacific coast, and has since been here and there all through the West. He was for a year a resident of Chillicothe, living in the old Clinton House, and managing a stone-yard for some Cincinnati Company. He spoke of going one day into the old stone court-house—this was in 1850—to see some trial that was in progress under long-haired Judge Whitman. Milton L. Clark, then a young lawyer, was making a plea while Allen G. Thurman sat busily writing at a table near Clark. The late Judge Keith was there, too, with his ringlets, as a looker-on in Vienna—and just spoiling for a chance to play a joke on some one. Mr. Clark made some remark. "Yes; that's what Thurman says," broke in Keith. "Oh, I know. Thurman has to have a finger in everyone's business," retorted Clark, a little nettled at the interruption. Thurman jumped up from his writing, said "You're a liar, sir," and started for Clark with a chair. There was a very hot fight before the bystanders could separate the heated young men, and both of them were pretty well "done up." Our present dignified Judge— and by the way, here are my congratulations, even if it be a little late; I didn't learn the result in the district till 20 days ago—was in very sorry whack. His new frock coat had parted with a tail and a sleeve during the melee, and blood flowed freely down his face and clothing from several cuts inflicted by Thurman's chair. The Colonel couldn't remember the exact damage suffered by "the noblest Roman of them all," but I'll warrant he got an even dose of it. Both the young men tendered their apologies to the Court, in a few minutes, Thurman first—but it was some time before the *entente cordiale* was restored between them. Well, if we never were young we'd never be fools, but we'd miss a heap of fun.

Colonel Crosson has been out in Golden only a few years, but the grass has had no show to grow under his feet. He has, over in the Ortiz Mountains, a fine and well developed mine—the Emma—sunk on an incline 100 feet in a big and rich vein—the prevailing blue carbonates of copper, also bearing the precious metals to a gratifying degree. A clever young Yankee named E. H. Sampson is associated with him, and both have reason to feel contented.

And while we are on the subject of mines, it will not do to

omit proper mention of George Smith—Charlie, as everyone
here calls him. Besides the valuable Black Hawk, of which I
spoke last week, George has more claims than any other two
men in Golden, and they are good ones, too, nearly all. While
most of the boys are taking a little respite from work, and
swapping jaw at Emmert's, George is off every time, poking
around in the mountains; and now and then stumbling on
something fat. That boy will die rich, sure as you're a sinner.
Now here's a pointer for some good girl to profit by. George is
straight goods, solid wool and 36 inches across, even-tempered,
industrious, prudent and a general favorite. He has a trim little
adobe cottage, which he has built himself, and is about to
double in size. A girl with any taste could make a mighty cosy
home right there, and I think George is willin'.

There's one thing, too, that I want to impress on you. Most
people back East have it glued into their heads that this is an
awfully tough country, and that a lady would be anything but
comfortable in such a place. That is where they are away off
again, as in most of their notions about the West. There is
probably no other place in the world where a lady will be treated
with such uniform and thorough respect as in a mining camp.
There will be no dudes or loafers on the corners to gape at or
insult her as she passes, as is the fashion in every city of the
polished East. Nary! If anyone were to try that business in a
mining town, he'd never know what hit him. The lady can go
and come at any hour, anywhere, in perfect security. Every man
in camp is her friend, and would spill his last drop of red to
defend her.

I think that rather caps the East, where half the male population, whom we call black-guards, devote their whole time and
energy insulting our wives and sisters; while the other half,
who call ourselves gentlemen, stand by and brook it all. True,
there are rough cases in every mining camp—a good many in
some—and some about as hard as ever trod dust; but every
mother's son of them is a gentlemen in the presence of ladies.
Somehow, our civilization has always seemed to me to civilize
backwards. Its whole tendency is toward laziness, for it is al-

ways inventing something to supplant work. The dude is the natural outcome. He (or it) is not a separate species, but merely the prototype of what we are all coming to in a few generations. He is simply like almost all our young men, only a little more so. Yes, civilization is mighty fast ruining the race physically; and the mental and moral decay are inevitable corollaries of the bodily. No, I'm not a pessimist. I'm as far from that as anyone you ever saw. But facts are facts—and I am glad to be out of the dudebelt, and [in a place] where men have staid [sic] men.

So much for the comfort of a lady out here. As for social enjoyment, she can find a little but congenial circle in Golden now; and before long there will be all the society one could possibly wish. And society out here isn't like the Eastern atrocity which is called by the same name. People here don't abrade their physical foundations sitting still and lamenting because there is nothing going on to enjoy—the way they sit and lament in Chillicothe. If they want a good time they get up and rustle around and have it—which is unquestionably more rational. I like you folks and am mightily attached to your old city; but I'm powerfully glad I'm not a Good Time with headquarters in Chillicothe. I should hang around the streets and starve to death before anyone would take the trouble to open the door and let me in. I'm not abusing you for my own sake—I always enjoy life anywhere—but because of the countless among you who weep over the dullness of the city when it is their own fault. I should just as soon think of going out and waiting for the cow to come and milk me as of sitting down and expecting a good time to come up and collar me and lug me along without any work on my part. Accept all this with the honest compliment of Truthful James.

You observe, doubtless, that my Transcontinental Female Importing Scheme sticks in my mind. Well, I have no apologies to offer on the subject. Some such plan is bound to be adopted one of these days, and it will be the happiness of hundreds of lives which are now incomplete and always will be except for such a move. It will solve two very important problems—the surplus of women throughout the East, and the dearth of women throughout the far greater West. It will be a profitable deal for both sections, and it will be made, one of these days, too. There is plenty of historical precedent for it, as the experience of several early American colonies—and the modern experience of California—will remind you. Put these things in your pipe, and smoke.

And smoke naturally sets me off on another tangent, I don't know whether you ever noticed it, but I sometimes smoke myself, and thought I had the business down tolerably fine. But we live and learn. It took these Mexicans—who can't even say pipe, but call it "pee-py"—to give me a new wrinkle in this greatest, cheapest and most profitable of luxuries, smoking. There was a year—a good while ago, however—when I wasted my energies on cigarettes and averaged in that time 87 per day.

But I never learned to smoke in Mexican till I struck this country. Among all the thousands of Mexicans I have met in Colorado and this Territory, there have not been twenty pipes—visible, at least. They all smoke cigarettes, and all make their own. Taking a little piece of paper or cornhusk, they lay, in a little crease on one side of it, a pinch of tobacco—which has been winnowed of dust by turning it from one hand to the other and blowing gently—and with an adroit motion, which takes but a second, the thing is rolled into a neat cylinder, one end being pinched to keep the tobacco from falling out.

Now there have probably been tenderfoot visitors who have told you that the Mexicans wrap their "cigareets" in brown wrapping paper like that in which the butcher enfolds your beefsteak. Well, the paper is brown, but it is not beefsteak paper. It is made purposely for cigarettes, and is as much purer and pleasanter flavored than the arsenically bleached truck you smoke in the East as you can think. It is really good—much better indeed to my liking than what my Mexican friends put inside it—their "poncha." This peculiar tobacco is a native product, and I don't believe anyone wants to transplant it. It is strong as a bull, has a wire-edge that reminds me flagrantly of under-cured Louisiana perique, and for making itself felt in a room completely outranks Pat's 'dogleg' [tobacco of poor quality marketed in twists]. The Mexicans seem to like it, however, and they like a good many other things that would give a sausage machine the cholera morbus.

Everyone smokes, here. At Carnuel, last night, I had a grand smoking party which included my clever host, the host's thoughtful wife, the wife's mighty handsome young sister, the six-year-old boy and the four or five male relatives. And it was a characteristic scene. All through this country you will see the same thing, running from children just toddling, who roll the cigarettes and whiff them as adroitly as anyone, up to old men whose palsied fingers can barely make a go of it. I had to catch on, of course, and am now so proficient as to make the cigarettes as well as the inventors—in no time and two motions. I manage to smoke 30 a day, too, without any serious hardship.

I presume some of your Spanish scholars back in Chillicothe have been displaying my ignorance in regard to the Spanish words whose pronunciation I have parenthesized in a few of later letters. Well, folks are not always as green as they look, and sometimes the critics get fooled. I have a sneak-idea how Spanish ought to be pronounced; but the Spanish of Castile and the Spanish dialect of New Mexico are two different things—as different as the French of Paris and the *patois* of Canada. If you were to talk about ahgwah, cabahlyo, tohrtillyah, and all that sort of thing, or vairdath, keen-thay or so on, in this part of the country, no one would understand you. A man might just as well talk good English in Lancashire. But when you say ahwa, cavayo, torteea, verdad and kinsee, the Mexicans sabe right away. Of course it is all very fat to talk Spanish like a leaf out of the booktionary, but I'm just fresh enough to prefer talking *patois* and getting grub and lodging, to speaking thoroughbred Castillian and sleeping out in the snow and on empty stomach.

Some of the peculiarities of this dialect are as follows; the *g* is never sounded in words like agua; *ll* is not pronounced like *l-y*, but like yalone—Bernalillo, for instance, is always called "Bernali-yo"; *b* and *v* are commonly interchanged—*veinte* becomes "bainty," and *libro* is "leevro"; the double vowels are usually slurred in a heartless way—*quien*, for instance, becoming plain "kin"; the lisp is entirely discarded and in all this time I have not heard a single *d*, *c* or *z* sounded like *th*. Everyone says "waino" for *bueno*; "muncho" for *mucho*; and the *d* is generally dropped in such words as Colorado, Delgado, which are transformed to Colora-o and Delga-o.

Another institution here deserves notice, namely the baile— "biley" in common parlance—or ball. These comical "hops" come around as often as the natives can crowd them in—and that is pretty often. They had one at Golden Monday night, and a good one, too. In a little 20 by 40 room—a deserted store— with a rough floor, bare walls, and a few chairs, most of the adult population gathered and ran their fun far into the morning. Three or four of the boys are good musicians, and I have heard worse orchestras right in Ohio. Nearly all the ladies are Mexicans, and there are also plenty of male representatives of that amusement-loving race. They all dance well and untiringly and it is a true festive occasion all around.

The only real excitement Golden has had in a good while— outside the various antics of the Santa Fe Ring—came last October, in the shape of a lively little battle. Five young fellows living in the village were accused—with how much justice I know not—of "rustling." There are a good many ranches in this section, and a lot of the cowboys got together to clean out the alleged thieves. Early one morning they rode down to Golden, 16 of them, all armed to the teeth. The rustlers had been warned of their coming, a week ahead, but were nevertheless caught napping. Two of them were in a saloon getting an eye-opener, when two cowboys who had ridden ahead of the main body, drew up to the door. The rustlers saw their pursuers first, and "threw down" their guns on them while the cowboys naturally and wisely threw up their hands and took to flight. While the main body of cowboys was hurrying to the spot, the two rustlers aroused their partners, and all five started up the hill. The cowboys got within range, and the fun commenced. For a minute or two the lead flew like hail, something like 150 shots being fired in all. One of the rustlers, with more nerve than his companions, stopped running, knelt down on the open hillside, and emptied his six-shooter deliberately at the foe. His clothes were cut by bullets in a dozen places, some of the spiteful pills passing between his arm and side. The rustlers had one Winchester, with which they could doubtless have done execution, but a shell stuck, and the gun was of no further account. The battle ended ignominiously, with no one hurt. The rustlers surrendered—having become rattled—except one, who made his escape, and has not since been heard from. The others are now out on bail.

I feel a sort of proprietary interest in Golden, beyond the natural liking for so clever a place. If I don't see what I want there, all I have to do is to ask for it. I am already a silent partner—or perhaps rather the noisy one—in more claims than you could shake a stick at—provisional upon my going back. Some of those claims will be worth fat money, one of these days, and I guess it will be best not to let them get away from me. Then there are other snaps which it will not do to expatiate upon at present, though you shall hear of them some day. I don't know of any other place that is as anxious for my company, and Golden and I will have to hitch.

I did finally feel obliged to break away from Golden, despite the strong attractions there; and after many stout handshakes and hearty good-byes, I turned my face south-ward at 10:30, Wednesday morning. When I started it was with the intention of going out northwest to Wallace, where I could write this letter and then strike down the railroad track next morning. But the boys at the store, where I stopped for a few more partings, strongly advised me to go down through Tijeras (Tihayras) Cañon, thereby saving 21 miles and seeing a more picturesque country; and I took their advice. Confound them! I wish they had had to make that trip here with me, every last mother's son of them. George Smith accompanied me for half a mile, and then branched off to go to work on the Black-Hawk. His kindness to me at Golden was great and doubtless has something to do with the very extreme opinions I formed of the little town.

Then Shadow and I trudged on alone up the long, gentle slope and through the deep snow, which grew heavier and deeper at every mile—as we got to higher altitudes and the sun waxed more powerful. Of course all vestiges of a road were buried; but a buck-board had been along this way, and its tracks led us deviously but surely in the direction of Albuquerque. I had tied up my feet and ankles in strips of canvass, which supplemented the shoes and kept my hoofs warm, if not dry. I never should have got through that awful day if it hadn't been for those rags. The first ten miles were hard as any forty I ever before traveled, for it was violent work breaking through that heavy foot-and-a-half to two feet of snow, with my forty-five pound load. I wound in and out among the little Ysidro and San Francisco mountains, most of the way up-grade, and at last came down to the little creek at the foot of the lofty Sandias.

Here was the scene, four years ago, of a horrible tragedy. One Dr. Potter—I believe that was his name—had stopped over night at the hotel in Tijeras and had carelessly exposed there a considerable sum of money and a fine gold watch. He rode a valuable horse, furthermore. A gang of Mexicans—some of whom now live in Golden—spotted him; and next day as he crossed the creek near the old church of San Pedro, he rode right into an ambush. The Greasers, who are as a rule poor marksmen, succeeded at the first fire in merely killing the horse. The doctor was armed, and fired, at his assassins, but in vain. He fell pierced by many bullets. The murderers robbed him, and then cremated his body and that of the horse. For a long time no one knew what had become of him; but at last his brother, who came out from the East to make search, found his watch in a pawn-shop at Bernalillo, and through this clue traced out four of the murderers. The whole quartetto was hanged by an Albuquerque mob.

I stopped a moment in the old church to cool off—for every rag on me was wringing wet with perspiration—and then I started on again, hoping to make Tijeras by night fall. But an ominous change had taken place in the weather. For an hour the sun had been hidden, and a stiff wind had sprung up. It was not many minutes before the damp snow was dry at the top, and the

little particles began to roll and tumble over one another trying
to go north. Well, you think a little thing like that isn't worth
putting into type at all. But I tell you it made me nervous when
the first fine snow-flour began to rise. It meant a pretty serious
situation for me. Here I was in a trackless plain, without more
than the remotest idea of where any human beings were located
or how far off, the day well along, no food, my only guide a
single wagon trail—and the snow drifting.

As soon as I saw the situation, there was no more thought of
rest. I shut my teeth, pulled down my hat to save my eyes from
the snow which already flew blindingly, noted the general direction of the trail, and plunged along with all the strength in me.
In ten minutes from that time, my fears were realized. The
flying particles had obliterated every vestige of a trail, and I was
left to luck and guess-work. Poor Shadow crawled under a low,
spreading pinon, and crouching there with doleful cries refused
to go farther. I had to take a rope from my blanket, hitch it to his
neck and tow him along, with all my other load. In the two or
three minutes I stopped to tie him, my own tracks faded entirely out, clear to my feet; and the whole big plain was one
markless sheet of deep snow.

For a little while we kept on the road, as my feet informed me;
but before long even this satisfaction ceased, and we were stumbling and plunging through the big drifts, heading southward as
well as we could, but plainly out of our way and in rough
diggings. Every few feet we would fall into some little arroyo or
hole—and it was hard work to flounder out. One of these places
was a full six feet deep, and I thought we never would get out;
Shadow evidently thought so, too. Quarts of fine snow had sifted
down my neck, in [at] my belt, and up my sleeves. My wet outer
garments froze solid, as the wind grew more and more bitter, and
my nose and ears burned with cold. The drifts, too, grew deeper
and deeper, and from the peculiar lay of the land and the direction of the wind, there were very few intervening shallows—for
the whole valley was getting piled with snow from the mountains. If there is harder work than wading through three and
four-foot snow-drifts, loaded as I was, I don't want any part of it.

In spite of the icy wind, steady rivulets of sweat poured down my face and body. I don't know how long this struggle lasted. It seemed a year, but was probably not more than three hours or three-and-a-half. At all events, just as the sun was setting, I gave a great yell of joy to see on a distant hillock, two little black specks which moved as only men move. I couldn't have told them from horses, so far as form is concerned, but every animal has a characteristic motion, and their motion told me they were men. Even then it seemed as if I could never reach them; but it was a groundhog case, and though the holes grew more numerous and more rocky, and the drifts bigger—for I was now on a large clearing cut into countless arroyos by the water of neighboring hills—I staggered on. "*Esta uno Americano aqui?*" I asked a Mexican boy at the common well, and he pointed me out a big adobe at the upper end of the little village. Anyone who knows me doesn't need to be told that my endurance is good, to say the least; but when I crawled up the hill to that store in the cold twilight and sank down on a chair beside the glowing fireplace, I was "done up." A hundred dollars to walk another mile would not have been an instant's temptation.

The storekeeper was a bluff but clever German-American named Chas. H. Walther. He drifted out from his home in Cleveland, O., soon after the close of the war; and after a few years at Albuquerque, settled down in that little Mexican plaza of San Antonito, where he married a Mexican girl. He got me dry and warm, filled me with a good supper and a bottle of pleasant native wine, and kept me entertained all the evening by his spicy remarks. While my weary bones were getting the ache out of them, and my strained sinews slowly snapping back into place, we passed away the time in a game of cold poker—no money to heat it—with some Mexican customers. Such fellows for luck I never saw. As sure as I amassed "*dos paras*" they would bob up with "*tres cuatros*"; and if I struggled to the altitude of a full hand, they were there looking down at me from the top of "*cuatro* aces." However, they were an amusing crowd, and we had a good time. But you never saw folks so easily tickled. One grimace would set them in a roar: and when I crowed *a la* chanticleer, over some good hand, they went into convulsions. And when this was over, Mr. Walther's best bed embraced me, and in two minutes I had forgotten all the miseries of the day.

I made an early start from San Antonito, Thursday morning, for it was beginning to be a problem when I should get back within reach of the postal service and be able to write and mail my customary broadside for the *Leader.* For the first three miles the road was steadily up hill, and the depth of the snow something frightful. It took me three hours to make that three miles, and there was no loafing in it, either. Then I stood on the top of a divide certainly 8,000 feet above the sea, and in another moment began to descend its southern slope. The sun was bright and hot, and the snow grew steadily—but very slowly—shallower. By the time I had passed the little plazas of Canoncito and San Antonio, and reached that of Tijeras, there was less than ten inches of snow, with a good many bare patches, but a horrible and almost fathomless conglomeration of slush and mud. All the rest of the day things improved, but too slowly to do much good. I enjoyed, however, the seven or eight mile trip down Tijeras Canyon, which affords some of the finest scenery in New Mexico. The mountain walls rise a thousand feet or more above the little creek, and are very wild and rugged. The stratification—which is nearly horizontal, apparently—shows with remarkable clearness on the steep thickly-wooded east wall of the canyon, where there are three or four score of strata visible, and these are individually matched on the west wall, a mile away.

At 5:30 I stood just at the western outlet of the canyon, and could see the smoke of Albuquerque, 13 miles away. The big intervening plain looked brown and bare, but I had had enough for one day, and lost no time in getting inside a little "cantina" or Mexican store, the last house in the plaza of Carnuel. And I struck it rich. The proprietor was a tall, good-looking Mexican named Ramon Arrera. I informed him in a wholesale assassination of Spanish that I was hungry and wet, and didn't want to go any further; could I stay here all night? "Si, Señor," he said cordially, and took me in to the fire, and filled me with wine. The Mexicans make a very agreeable wine almost colorless and drinkable in any quantity. In my travels I have not seen one drunken Mexican. One would have to be pretty industrious, however, to get "biled" on this native wine. In a few minutes more I had a good supper of carne, chili colorado, cafe, y tortillas—roast beef; a stew of onions, red peppers and meat; coffee and bread. This was my first venture on chili colorado, and will be my last. One not used to eating fire might just exactly as well chew up a ripe red pepper raw and swallow it.

But the tortillas were marvelously good. In every other place I have seen, the tortillas are cooked like flapjacks; and though "filling enough," they are generally pretty dry eating. But these Carnuel tortillas are of a different style of architecture. My host's wife's handsome sister—to whom I have before alluded [?]—took a little pat of snow-white dough, about as big as my fist, rolled it into a perfect ball, pinched it into a thick flat disc; and then laid it on her apron—an old gunny sack—and with a little, round short stick, rolled it out to a quarter of an inch in thickness. Next she laid it over her knee and with both hands stretched it—as you would stretch a sheet of rubber. By this time the elastic stuff was a disc about 14 inches across and an eighth of a inch thick. A square pan full of fat was sizzling on the stove and into this went the tortilla, remaining there until thoroughly browned. When done, they are good enough for a king. I can remember nothing better in this line, since those fat red doughnuts I used to steal from my grandmother's pantry, some 20-odd years ago.

There were no forks in the table outfit, and everyone was expected to furnish his own knife, but otherwise no fault could be found. After supper I sat down to do some writing, to the great wonderment of the household. The whole crowd stood, looking over my shoulder for two hours, never recovering from their amaze at the action of my stylographic pen, nor ceasing to exclaim "muy bueno!" None of them could understand a word of English, and it put me to my tramps to scare up enough

Mexicano to suit the occasion; but I am catching on tolerably fast and managed to pull through. There was a burro caravan stopping there over night, and the half-dozen Mexican drivers made good company. I kept my watch and scanty "boo" carefully out of sight, but felt rather ashamed of my suspicions when Señor Arrera made me a bed on the floor in his store and left me there alone—where I could have got up in the night and walked off with everything he had in the world. Still, this is a cold country for a stranger to exhibit valuables in; and it's better to be over-prudent a hundred times than not prudent enough just once. If a man wakes up in the morning and finds his throat cut or a knife through his heart, it makes him wish he had been more careful.

This morning, I had an uneventful walk in from Carnuel to bustling Albuquerque, making the 18 miles into 20 in a vain hunt after agates. I shall stay here tomorrow, to finish some letters, and then on Sunday make a break out along the A. & P.

There is very little snow here, though plenty of mud, so I shall not suffer. It is now about the fitting time for me to be wishing you all a merry Christmas, and I do it with all my heart. I would not object to spending the day with you, if I could be back out here next morning. *Buena suerte a todos.*

LUM

El Rito, New Mexico
Thursday, December 25th, 1884

Editors Leader:

It was a decided change to get into muddy, bustling, brick-and-frame Albuquerque after the long weeks in the adobe wilderness. I don't think I quite liked it, either, for the whole country is full of Albuquerques back East, and there is something restful about the adobe. But it never would do in the world to hint such a thing where the Albuquerqueans could hear you.

If there are any people alive who vaunt themselves and are puffed up over their town, it is they. This little city of perhaps 7,000 people seems to its inhabitants the most wonderful place on this foot stool, and they never weary of its praises—unless when they stop long enough to abuse some rival town, and particularly Santa Fe. Why, it would be as much as a man's life was worth to go down there and begin complimenting Santa Fe! The outraged inhabitants would string him up so fast it would make his head swim. They can never forgive the City of the Holy Faith for being older than their alleged Metropolis; and still less for being the Territorial Capital. It just makes an Albuquerquean sick at heart to think that anyone could have stuck the capitol and penitentiary of New Mexico "up in that dull old hole without electric lights, street-cars, or anything else, when they could just as well have picked out a fine, lively, modern city." That is the one central dream of his life that the seat of government will one day be moved down the river there to Albuquerque; and to fulfill that dream, he bends all his energies.

The Duke of Albuquerque was Governor and Captain-General of this region, about 175 years ago, and the city takes its name from him. The old town is largely Mexican, and is situated on the banks of the Río Grande; but the new town hangs to the coat-tails of the railroad, a mile or so east of the river, and looks like a busy, enterprising place from York state, carted out here and dumped whole upon the plain. There are several manufactories there, and the shops of the Atlantic & Pacific R.R.

I wasn't particularly stuck on the place, which is about half a mile farther from heaven than Golden—being only 4,949 feet in altitude. If I were going to live in an American town, I'd pick one back East; and if I were to hang out in this Territory it would be in some place that had some originality about it—an old plaza or a mining camp. Still, I met some very pleasant folks in Albuquerque, and should have seen a lot more—to whom I had letters—if my time hadn't run short.

The office of the *Daily Democrat* was my headquarters throughout my stay, and I got rid of a lot of writing and had plenty of chin-music. The proprietor of the *Democrat*, Mr. John G. Albright, and his brother, George, the foreman, are both Chillicothe boys. They came out here several years ago and seem to be flourishing like two green bay trees. Their editor, Mr. Dixon, is a recent importation from the back-country mines, whence he tramped hither, recently. He is a big, brawny, bronzed fellow, and looks a good deal more like a cowboy than a journalist. There is nothing slow about him, however, and we had a very jolly time together. While I wrote correspondence he told me stories; and when he got too drunk to waddle I ground out editorials for him. So we got along as handily as a wagon with five wheels. While I was sitting in the *Democrat* office a pithless-looking elderly man came in and had a long consultation with the bosses. I didn't notice him particularly, but when he went out they asked me if I knew who that was. Upon my confession of contented ignorance, they informed me that the galvanized cadaver was ex-U.S. Senator Ross of Kansas, whose vote saved Andy Johnson from impeachment. After this record of service to the country, I need hardly add that Mr. Ross is the leading Democratic candidate for the Governorship of New Mexico. My chief impression of him is that he looks like a last-year's persimmon.

Well, by Sunday morning I had got away with about 14 columns of copy, and started south having no further use for Albuquerque. The mud which still swamped the town was spread so thick there that there was none left for anywhere else, and there was good walking down the partnership track of the A., T. & S. F. and A. & P. railroads. It was not lost on an unappreciative tramp, either, for after the two weeks of snow and mud I knew what it was to have dry ground under my heels. Shadow was glad to get out, too. I don't think he was cut out for a metropolitan cur. Like the trousers-seeking Yankee Doodle

> "He couldn't find his tail or shop,
> There was so many houses."

He makes a break into every open door, gets bullyragged by every city dog, little and big—for they all see that he is "country"—and as for markets, he simply thinks they are special snaps. "Lord," he says to himself, "how clever these rabbits here are! So much more accommodating than those long-legged rascals out in the sage-brush. Ki! Yi! Yow———ow! Whatcher hittin' me for? Ain't rabbits made for greyhounds I'd like to know?"

But how I did petition Congress for a double-barreled shotgun ballasted with Number Ones, going down from Albuquerque that Sunday morning! From the time of leaving the corporate limits of the city, until the long bridge over the Río Grande 12 miles below, my ears didn't have a minute's rest from the eternal honking of innumerable wild geese. Sometimes I could see a dozen flocks in the air at once, each containing from 20 to 100 birds. I must have seen two thousand geese, for all the broad meadows were black with them. They would fly within 100 feet of me frequently, but it was hard to get near them sitting, though I did knock a pillow out of one fat fellow. A man with gum boots and a good gun could kill more in an hour than he could carry in a day. I'd rather have a tooth pulled than go by such a place again without the proper armament. I might have bagged a lot of tramps—for the woods were full of them—but it seemed unbrotherly to pepper them.

I got over to the A. & P. junction early, and made myself solid with the two operators, that I might tarry here and do some more writing. There is nothing of the Junction save the section-house and the little box of a telegraph office. But the large Indian pueblo of Isleta is close by, and the office is constantly fringed with girls and squaws who come to sell cherry-sized apples and piñon nuts. They have a game too, at which they pass away the time between trains. It is a sort of stagger at quoits, dornicks taking the place of the iron rings. One good-looking squaw was playing in very hard luck. She would come into the office where her pan was, gather up a fistful of apples and go out. In a minute or two these would have been gambled away, and back she would trot for more apples—until at last she was completely cleaned out, and went home weeping. These Indians

Isleta Pueblo, New Mexico, n.d. Photograph by Charles Lummis. Courtesy of Southwest Museum, negative no. 56.

Pueblo Indians, 1890. Photograph by Charles Lummis. Courtesy of Southwest Museum, negative no. 353.

are a great attraction to the tenderfoot excursionists who go through, and whenever there is an excursion coming, the railroad authorities telegraph ahead to the agents at the Junction to see that the Indians are on hand.

I went over to the town of Isleta to get some tobacco—good to kill moths with, you know—and walked around pretty extensively. The pueblo is not different from others in the territory, save in size, but it is tolerably interesting. The big Catholic church of adobe, with two dry-goods box towers, occupied one side of the plaza. My visit was made at about sunset, and I had to snicker irreverently when they rang the bell for vespers. A big Indian climbed up into the eastern tower of the church by a ladder, and there took a hammer and gave the bell such a comical going-over as you never heard. He would whack away three or four times very rapidly, and then sort of rub down and carry off the bell with his hammer. The whole thing was the hardest sort of a joke as the gong at a railroad eating house. After dark a lot of the young Isletans had a grand firefight. Two parties built fires a few rods apart, and then pelted each other with the blazing brands. It was a very pretty sight in the darkness as the little comets flew about thickly through the air, in sportive bombardment. Nobody seemed to get hurt particularly though a good many must have been more or less singed.

With W. W. Tew and John D. Seiken, the two operators at the Junction, I had a great time. They are both as full of oats as a fly is of tickle. After my writing was done, we had a grand whirl of congregational singing, and made the little box station shiver until after midnight; and again the college songs came in as handy as a pocket in an night shirt. I never was much mashed on my own basso-bull-froggy voice, but it begins to seem as if Patti wasn't a circumstance. The boys couldn't get enough, and when I got up to Río Puerco, Monday night, I found they had telegraphed to the operator there that he must get me to sing "Mush, Mush." Well, I shall not go on the stage yet awhile, in spite of all. The section-house and ranche are better suited to my peculiar style of air-smashing.

This Junction section-house was the first at which I had eaten since away back in Embudo, a month ago. Thirty-five cents was the highest I had been called upon to pay, and when the hash-pirate at the Junction stood me up for 50 cents, for the scaliest supper the Lord in his long-suffering mercy ever allowed a man to see, my hair stood on end. I am a little near-sighted still, but I could mighty easily see to the end of my short pecuniary rope at that rate. But one needn't be stuck like that, as I have since discovered. If these millionaire section-house-keepers find that they can't get but a quarter out of you, they'll take it so quick it'll make your eyes water, and give you the same provender as for double the money. I met an old friend at the Junction—another Ohio man. Our first meeting was in Columbus, when I struck that town in April, '82. We recognized each other at sight, and shook hands on it. It was the butter on

Mr. Delaney's table. The boys identified it under oath as the same that had been on the table for a month, so it is no tenderfoot out here. Well, it relieves the monotony of a journey like this to run across old acquaintances. It made me feel quite at home.

Monday morning Seiken borrowed an old musket—a relic of the Mexican War—and came up the track with me about ten miles to hunt jack rabbits. We had a splendid hunt, but saw no game. However, I stumbled upon a big deposit of fine moss-agates, and gathered about 20 pounds of them, some perfect beauties. Also found no end of petrified and agatized wood, of which I am packing a pocketful. This is the greatest country for specimens I ever saw. You can pick up something valuable at almost every step. On the east side of the Río Grande there is nothing of the sort, but as soon as you leave the A. & P. Junction, the whole face of the country becomes volcanic; great black lava flows lie all around, and the sandhills above them are sown thick with agates of every sort. Not far off from the track are several small extinct volcanoes, and I climbed over one. It has been dead, probably for ten thousand years, but all around are the evidences of its once destructive power.

I wasted most of the day in this mineral hunt, and late in the evening landed at Río Puerco (Muddy River) after a tiresome jaunt of 35 miles. I weighed myself at the station there, and found that my load had grown—what with the agates etc. to 51 pounds. That is too much. When a man has to pack a carload like that, it would be money in his pocket if he had never been born. Just weigh out 51 pounds of something and pack it five or six miles for a sample. Then you will know how it is yourself. There, at Río Puerco, I found another sociable agent, and had a pleasant evening, and there, as at the Junction, spread my blanket upon the floor of the station at night, and slept as snug as a bug in a rug.

To quote an eloquent section-hand, "this is the bigoddest country for water on the face of the earth." You can find the wet by boring a few feet, but it isn't water—rather a rich, rare and racy combination of sulphur, alkali and salt, just damp enough to run. The Río Puerco is the only stream I have seen in about 50 miles, and it would kill an insurance agent to drink two fingers of it. They have to haul water to all these stations from distances of 50 to 80 miles, and keep it in barrels half-buried beside the track. I don't know whether the Lord feels ashamed of himself for having made such a country as this, but he ought to. I could dig a better one out of a saw-dust heap.

No one stays out here unless they have to, and there is a continual exodus of station agents, section bosses and hands. Lonesome? Why these people out here would jump out of their boots with pleasure at seeing so much as a yaller dorg. Let the commonest kind of a bum tramp come in here and they talk him blind, they are so glad to get hold of anything that can speak. Three months is a long time for a family to occupy a section-house, or for an operator to hold down a station out there. The last boarding-boss at Río Puerco was there about three weeks, and then managed to get away alive with his family. They were too lazy to fetch water from the barrels and therefore used the pump beside the door, and the water came near being the death of the whole outfit.

There is a little Mexican plaza not far off, and there, in spite of the universal dryness, they raise some of the finest vegetables you ever saw—beets as big as your head, onions nearly as large, and cabbages the size of half-bushel. All along the Río Puerco seems to be a good grazing country, and I have seen a great many large herds—though how the poor devils of cattle manage to get along with that water, is more than I can tell. They can't need pickling after they are butchered, for every last one of them must be corned beef while yet on the hoof.

Tuesday morning I lifted my load with a jack-screw, got my back under it, and moseyed along very slowly. The agates were the last straw for me, and made walking as hard and painful as it is to tell the truth. I had to stop every mile and let that load rest. I always was a merciful cuss, and don't propose to begin now a heartless career by abusing a poor dumb pack. I prospected some more for agates, but it wasn't their day. The only interesting thing I found were two other belated tramps—a rattlesnake

with his string lost, and a tarantula. The latter was a handsome
bird, and made the cold chills run down my back, just to look at
him. He measured eight inches across his extended legs, was
covered with brown hair a quarter of an inch long, had legs as
large around as a lead-pencil, and a body as big as my thumb.

I'd sooner be bitten by seven rattlesnakes, two dogs and a
book-agent, than by this fellow. He could jump about three feet
at a lift, and make me jump about 30 just as sure as God made
little apples. The rattler was sleepy, and I chopped him in two
with my knife, but the whole Territory couldn't drive me that
near to the tarantula, and I shot him to death with my .44 at ten
feet away. That was close enough for me. I can stand about
anything else in the world, but when it comes to a spider—no,
thank you. Good-day, I have business down town. If I wanted a
truthful likeness of the devil I wouldn't paint him with horns,
hooks and tail—there's nothing appalling about a mooly-cow—
but in the shape of a tarantula. It would be a mighty cold day
when that sort of a devil got any chance to clap his paws on me,
unless he caught me asleep.

It was about three o'clock when I hove in sight of the San Jose
section house, where I calculated on getting some provender.
Just as I drew near it, however, a Texas Jack looking fellow came
riding up with a 30-pound buffalo gun across his saddle. He fell
into a chat with me, and in a few minutes bade me over to the
ranche, close by, to pass the night. Go? Well, now you just want
to remember that I went! Ranche hospitality is something not
to be kicked out of bed. In a few minutes more, that long-haired
cowboy and I had lain off our harness, and were smoking a social
pipe in the large, substantial frame residence of the boss, who
was in Albuquerque.

My entertainer's name was James R. Taylor, and he was a
good one. A native Texan, he has been all over the country, and
is almost as familiar with many of its big cities as with the
ranche. I found him the very liveliest of company, and a most
intelligent and instructive talker. Pretty soon three other cowboys came in, and proved equally sociable. We passed a jolly
evening together, after a good supper cooked by Taylor, smoked,

sang, talked and played pedro till a late hour, and then turned
into the comfortable bunks.

In the morning I had the felicity to get rid of my rifle, swapping it for an elegant new Colt's improved, with the finest belt
in the Territory. The rifle has come in handy enough a few
times, but I have had to lug it 25 miles for every shot, and that is
a little too much port for my shilling. It was abominably heavy
and more awkward still, I felt mightily the difference in my load
when I started off Tuesday afternoon, after a morning of scrib-
bling, and climbed the long, straight grade to the El Rito. Instead
of having to stop at every mile to splice my backbone, I sailed
along without a break, and didn't feel it—though a mulish head
wind blew all the loose stuffing out of my ribs.

The only game I saw was an unusually fine skunk, and a
lucky shot with my new pop—which is a dandy—plugged out
it's eye before he could waste his sweetness on the desert air. I
cut out his little vinaigrette, and brought him along to skin at
leisure. What do I want with a nasty skunk's pelt? Why, that
n. s. p. is one of the handsomest in the country, though coarse.
And it is about one chance in three, my dear madame, that the
very furs you wear so contentedly are made from this same
despised animal, plucked and dyed. If the scent-bag is properly
removed, there is no more odor about a skunk's skin than about
a cat's.

I hit El Rito in due season, looked over the tiny Indian town
and settled down in the telegraph office. This is, I suppose,
the smallest pueblo in the Territory, but the houses I entered
showed the universal neatness and comfort which mark all
Pueblo towns. All these Indians, by the way, dress a great deal
more expensively than you or I would ever dare think of doing.
Most of them wear a Navajoe blanket worth from $15 to $75;
leggins of smoke-tanned buckskins, and moccasins of the same,
over white cotton drawers. But it is in the ornaments that they
shine. Silver is their favorite metal, and they can put on a burro-
load of it. One strapping buck had 20 quarter-dollars made into
buttons handsomely engraved and sewed down the seam of his
calcones (leggins). All that put on any style at all have silver

belts, and most beautiful ones, too. Some contain a hundred dollars' worth of the metal, not to mention a great amount of skilled labor in the making. The prevailing pattern is of from ten to twenty big silver ovals, done in a sort of coarse filagree and strung on a fine leather strap. Then their rings, ear-rings, and bracelets; and the women, furthermore, wear ponderous bracelets and anklets of the same metal.

But with these little varieties—common to the entire race— the Pueblos have uncommon merits. I do not believe there is a christian American community in the world, which can approach in morality one of these little towns of adobe. A loose woman is a thing unknown among the Pueblos—different as are most other Indians—and the laws of property are strictly respected. Packages and bundles of value may lie on one of these lonely platforms at out-of-the-way stations for weeks, and they are safe as under lock and key. Just about half one night they would stay unstolen in an American town. The Pueblos are sharp but honest traders, good neighbors to each other and hospitable far beyond the average white man to the strangers who come among them. I wish they would send out missionaries to their American brothers.

At supper I made a rush for the section boss—A. C. Phillips, one of the well-known Pennsylvania oil people—and after a few preliminary skirmishes he said, "Say, young feller, where you going to spend Christmas?" I told him I expected to pass the day counting ties, with maybe a dinner of bacon and potatoes. "No," said he, "you'll stay right here. We boys have chipped in and got the fixin's for a big Christmas dinner, and you shall stay and help us bury it. Plenty of egg-nog, Tom and Jerry [rum, egg and spices drink], turkey, oysters and pies—that'll beat sow-belly and murphies [boiled potatoes] all hollow." That's exactly what I thought, too, and he didn't have to put handcuffs on me to keep me from running away from this cheerful prospect.

It comes particularly hard on one who used to hang his boyish stocking beside an old New England fireplace, and enjoy all the unparalleled jollity of a New England Christmas, to give up the day altogether, but I had made up my mind to it and was in the same fix as the Dutch man's wife. "Say, Hans, I hear your frau is dead." "Ya-aa, she vas died last nacht." "Was she re-signed?" "Resigned? Mein Gott! she *had* to be resigned." And that was the way I stood when Phillips' kindness to a stranger set it all right. "You'll stay here with me," he said, "do what writing you want to, eat all you can, and it shan't cost you a cent." That settled it, and I stayed. I was in a considerable hurry to get along, too, and a whole day lost was a good deal to me; but it isn't every day we kill a pig and give the bristles to the poor, and I let my hurry go on ahead.

In pottering around El Rito, Xmas morning, I met the most serious setback of the whole trip—the loss of my pet stylo-graph, with which I have done nearly all my writing for a year and a half. That broke me up worse than almost anything else that could have happened, but I have managed to pull the pieces of myself together, and shall survive as long as I don't lose this other stylo. I wrote away most of the forenoon, and then sat down to a gorgeous Christmas dinner good enough for anyone. It was the tiredest looking turkey you ever saw, though, when we got up. I believe part of it is sticking to my ribs yet. After this means of grace was over, the whole section gang, with the operator and myself, jumped on the hand-car and pumped up to Laguna to see the Christmas dance of the Indians in that strange town. They were not ready to dance when we got there, and wouldn't be till midnight, so we had to come home.

But the trip was not fruitless. Hearing that the coyotes were thick around a dead steer, two miles up the track, I made a lap-board, took it up there and set it by the carcass as we went by. Don't know what a lap-board is? Well, I took a two-inch plank, four feet long, smoothed on a side, bored half a dozen holes with an inch auger, making each an inch deep. These holes I filled nearly full of lard, laid on a little strychnine in each, and then smeared the whole thing over with lard, flat with the top of the plank. That is a lap-board; and its advantage is that a wolf or coyote will stay and lap at it until he falls dead in his tracks; whereas if you were to poison a bit of meat, he would lug it off the Lord only knows how far, and you might never find his

corpse. Well, I set my lap-board, and we went on. When we came
back, a few hours later, a whole gang of coyotes were snapping
and tumbling around the board, and fled at sight of us. We took
flying shots of them, and I broke one fellow's hind leg, but he
kept on with three legs at a cannon-ball gait, and escaped into
the lava-beds. But the board had got in its work. Near it we
found one fine, large fellow, dead as a herring. He had crawled
toward the creek, a few yards away, but even his all-consuming
thirst was less powerful than the innocent looking drug, and he
had fallen dead within three feet of the coveted fluid.

After supper I "cased" him, to the great wonderment of the
boys, who couldn't believe that such an animal could be skinned
without touching a knife to his hide. It took me about two hours
to pull grass enough, on this sandy valley, to stuff his skin out,
but it was done at last, and now he hangs over my shoulder,
natural as life. The grass, loosely packed, allows the circulation
of air inside the skin, and it will be cured in a day or two, when it
will be worth four or five times as much as if I had split it in the
ordinary way. If he doesn't make a daisy rug, I am no judge of
white mice. I may get a whack at some more, to-morrow, when I
shall be plodding on again. Have now walked 2,563 miles, and
the old shoes still hang on, though they have to be tied up with
cords to keep them on my feet. I wish all my friends were as
reliable as those tattered shoes.

LUM

San Mateo, New Mexico
Thursday, January 1st, 1885

Editors Leader:
   Buenos dias, amigos! ¡Como lo va V? (Now, compo., if you
don't put in that interrogation point before the *"como,"* I'll start
right back to Chillicothe and be the death of you.) (The Spanish
don't want any mistakes made when they ask a question, and so
they put it in type double-barreled.) This is New Year's Day, and

I trust you are all having a dandy time and swearing off from your numerous vices. For my own part, I have none to swear off from—except journalism—and there is but one new leaf I shall turn over in opening the ledger of 1885. That is, having too good a time. It is a pernicious practice, and would keep me forever on the road if I didn't tear off its baleful clutch. Here I have been ten weeks coming from Denver—a journey I might have made in three weeks and 600 miles—and all because of this habit of having a good time.

I begin to have a sneaking suspicion that the true reason why the children of Israel were 30 years in the wilderness, was that they struck some such snaps as have been flying up and hitting me in the face at almost every step. Needn't tell me that they were lost and couldn't get out. D———n! I won't have it. They struck some Arabian Santa Fe, where all the inhabitants nearly paralyzed them with good dinners; or some mining camp where the boys let 'em wash for gold—else where'n thunder did they get the gold for that calf they set up for a class-leader? That's undoubtedly just what kept them in there so long. Yes, Moses tries to make out that they couldn't help themselves, but I reckon that is one of the mistakes of Moses. He probably stood in with the boys and wouldn't give it away. What could you expect, anyhow, of a man that owns up to having broken all the ten commandments at once?

I shall be in this wilderness 40 years myself, unless I pick up my heels and carry them out of here; and I shall do that same just as fast as the law allows. There are a few more places where a stop must be made, but this getting into a town and waiting there for a generation or two to grow up, the way I have been doing, must be gently but firmly repressed; and I have three or four represses in my pocket all ready for use.

But the temptations to "pause, rash youth" are getting stronger and more numerous every day. In the first place, the longer a man is a tramp, the easier it is for him to stay one; then, too, the country keeps growing more wild and more interesting; and more and more Jordan becomes a hard road to travel. If I belonged to that unhappy throng who are troubled and worried by physical discomforts, my name would have been Dennis some time ago; but luckily it doesn't rattle me to be hungry, wet, half-frozen and nearly out of money. If a man knows how to use the lemon-squeezer of philosophy, he can punch a power of good juice out of even such adversities. I never did think much of Virgil as a judge of human nature, but he hit it on the nose for once when he made Pious Aeneas say to his companions, who were all broke up over their discomforts: "Forsan et haec olim meminisae juvabit"—a remark which I shall venture to translate, rather freely. "Yes, I know it's doggoned tough now, but it'll be a darned lot of fun to remember it, one of these days."

C'rect, Mr. P. A., shake! Now, if I had wanted a soft snap, I should have either stayed in Chillicothe, or gone west on a Pullman—or a cattle car, I don't know which. But what fun would there be in thinking about that ten years from now—or in doing it, either? No. I'm out to corral whatever experience there is lying around loose, and it wouldn't be experience if there wasn't some gall with the honey. If the Lord were to ring me up, right now, and call down through his big telephone, "Say, Lummy, you're having a rough deal out there. Hold on a minute, and I'll spread you out the best weather I've got in the store, and give you a 'pudding' all the rest of the way," I'd just say, "Take it away, pardner, this is good enough for me—I'm no hog." And I'd mean it, too. Just so there is a little grub left in the country, I won't starve, and if everything else gives out, I have the dog to fall back on. He may be a little tough from so much running, but I can just shut my eyes and fancy it is bologna. If the snow doesn't get more than three feet deep, I can plough through somehow, and if it does, I shall merely stop and whoop me up a pair of snow shoes. Oh, there's nothing in this world like taking things as they come. It's a day to freeze mercury when a contentedman gets left at the tail end of the procession. Discomforts I am having in plenty, but I can stand 'em as long as the Lord can spare 'em to send down, and I wouldn't have it any other way if it were all left for me to boss.

In fact the mud, snow, cold, hunger and other frills which at present adorn my wanderings, couldn't possibly be spared, for they bring me an endless fund of amusement. It's richer than goose-grease to hear the wails, howls, growls, snorts, imprecations and lamentations of my new chum, Aleck Phillips. He is the section-boss who treated me so cleverly at El Rito—a good-natured, enthusiastic visionary, up-and-then-down sort of a fellow, the first one who has cared to share my trip beyond sharing it with the mouth. He got completely mashed on the idea of going along, becoming more and more rapt as he pumped information from me; and finally threw up his job, pocketed his pay-checks, and lit out with me on Friday afternoon when I left El Rito. I fear, however, that he is not "a stayer." These little monkeyings of Providence with the weather, these starvation seances and shivering matinees, pierce his heart with grief as readily as a gimlet permeates new cheese. If he does stick it out with me, he will get to Los Angeles a walking skeleton. No man can be bothered as much and as easily as he is, and keep anything on him but bones. But it isn't graceful to rail at him—I wouldn't take $20 for him as a mirth-provoker.

We didn't leave El Rito ("the creek") until two o'clock, Friday P.M., for I waited to let Phillips get ready. Then we started westward along the abominably crooked track. The Atlantic & Pacific R. R. advertises itself as "running along the 35th parallel," and as "Kit Carson's old trail." All I have to say is that if the 35th parallel is to be held responsible for the crazy wanderings of that track, it ought to be put at once in an asylum for inebriates; and if Kit Carson ever laid out any such trail, he ought to have taken the pledge as soon as he got sober enough to see what he had done. If there is any point of the compass at which that track doesn't take a dead aim in the course of ten miles, I'd like to have that point framed and hung up. From El Rito to Laguna it goes six miles around to get two ahead. I'd sooner be a China dog with a kinky tail than carry about such a sense of crookedness as that road must have.

The whole section gang went up to Laguna ("the lake") with

us, pushing the hand-car ahead of them, for the wind was too fierce to permit progress by pumping. They were a gloomy set, for they hated to lose Phillips, who had been pretty clever to them. Half a mile east of Laguna there is a tolerably long bridge across San Jose creek, and here we had an adventure. Shadow was trotting on ahead, but about the middle of the bridge he concluded to come back and see me—and back he started. First thing he knew, he collided with the hand-car, and one wheel actually ran over his body, throwing the car from the track while his hind legs dangled down between the sleepers. I thought he was sausage-meat, sure; but do you know, when I pulled that fool pup from between the wheels he didn't seem to be hurt a bit. I guess he has picked up a piece of my luck. It ought to have killed him, but a fool is awfully hard to murder, whether he goes on two legs or four.

We got to Laguna in good season, bade good-bye to the section men, and posted directly over to the Indian town, where the holiday dance was in full blast—as the hair-lifting songs, wafted a mile by the wind, plainly informed us. This pueblo of Laguna is one of the most unique in the whole territory, and one of the most interesting. An enormous ledge of solid rock—a very hard substance—bulges out from the northern bank of the San Jose, and runs back up the hills for a quarter of a mile. At its highest point it is probably 400 feet above the creek. Upon this ledge and chiefly upon its summit, stands the pueblo of Laguna, huddled in a picturesque confusion. The strong, compact houses cling to the steep slopes or nestle upon the rounding top of the ledge, and the whole scene presents the idea of a strongly fortified citadel. A few determined men could hold Laguna against anything short of cannon.

The railroad sweeps in a long curve about the base of the great rock, in one place cutting off a little segment of the town, whose houses stand on the very brink of the cut on both sides. From the coal-station on the railroad a tiny foot-path runs up the longest slope of the rock to the village. The feet of the Indians and their burros have worn in the hard stone a little channel a foot wide, and in some places of nearly equal depth. That is as much as to say that there has been a town here for several hundred years. On the summit of a lofty mesa, many miles away, one may see from Laguna an ancient watch-tower, whence the Indian sentinels could overlook the whole surrounding country and detect the approach of a foe in ample time to warn the town. I reckoned that there were about two hundred houses in Laguna, all made of adobe, attractive without, and wonderfully neat and pleasant within. Indeed, I don't believe it possible to find a dirty, shiftless-looking room in all the 19 pueblos of New Mexico. There is a look about them that discounts many of our boasted American homes.

On the southeastern side of the ledge, in a natural depression, is a plaza or corral, about 100 feet wide and 300 long, hemmed in by a square of houses broken only by a narrow entrance at the lower end, and thither we went our way. The walls and house-tops were brilliant with a gaudily appareled throng of men, women and children—breathless spectators of the drama in the square below. There must have been 500 in this attentive audience. My nondescript appearance as I climbed up a house and sat down of the roof, captured the whole outfit, as well it might. The sombrero with its snake-skin band, the knife and two six-shooters in my belt, the bulging duck coat and long-fringed, snowy leggins, the skunk skin dangling from my blanket-roll, and last but not least, the stuffed coyote over my shoulders, looking natural as life, made up a picture the like of which I feel sure they never saw before and never will see again. They must have thought me Pa-puk-ke-wis, the wild man of the plains. A lot of the muchachos and muchachas (boys and girls) crowded around me, and when I caught the coyote by the neck and shook it, at the same time howling at them savagely, they jumped away, and the whole assembly was convulsed with laughter. An Indian appreciates a joke, even if it be a rather feeble one.

Such a gay-looking crowd you probably never saw anywhere. The Indians are fond of bright colors, anyhow, and on this festal occasion—the biggest blowout of the whole year—they had out-done themselves. The four sides of the square looked like a big hedge of flaming poppies and dahlias, with those deep ranks of brilliant-hued blankets. The prevailing color was a straight scarlet, but there were other hues, too numerous to count, and only less brilliant.

In the center of the corral, stood the stars of the occasion, the observed of all observers—the dancers. There were 30 in number, all fine-looking, robust bucks, togged out in most unearthly fashion. Their faces were smeared with a wasteful profusion of vermillion paint, with dark lines drawn here and there to give them a more cordially fiendish expression—a design which was eminently successful. Each had a war headdress stuck full of eagle feathers, and all carried weapons. Some had powerful bows, with the necessary arrows, some bore elaborate tomahawks, long spears and shields, and yet others swaggered around with big revolvers or rifles. They wore no blankets, but had each a tanned buckskin girded about his loins, reaching to the knees and gathered in at the waist by a ponderous silver belt. Some, evidently the big bugs of the community, had also similar belts over the shoulder and across the breast, and most of these sported little circular mirrors as pendants from neck or chest. Their legs were covered by calzones, or buckskin leggins—not brain-tanned like mine, but cured in smoke, and of a dark, soft fawn-color—and the white cotton drawers, which they all wear, flopped around the ankles of several, doubtless shaken down by their prancing.

The belle of the ball, or leader of the ballet, was a superbly formed Indian about six feet three inches in height, and straight as an arrow. His long raven hair was done up in a curious wad on the top of his head, and stuck full of eagle feathers. Heavy silver ornaments hung all over him, and around his muscular throat was a necklace of the terrible claws of the grizzly. His leggins were the most elaborate I ever saw—one solid mass, behind, of exquisite bead-work. He carried in his right hand a long, steel-pointed lance, decorated with many gay-colored ribbons, and he used this much after the fashion of a drum-major.

When we first arrived upon the scene, and for half an hour

thereafter, the dancers were formed in a rectangle, standing five abreast and six deep, jumping up and down in a sort of rudimentary clog step, keeping faultless time, and all the time chanting to the "music" of two small bass drums. I was surprised at the real harmony of their singing. The words were not particularly thrilling, consisting chiefly of "Ho!o-o-o-h! He! Ho! Ah! Ho!" but the chant was a genuine melody, though different in all ways from any tune you will hear elsewhere. Then the leader gave a yelp like a dog, and started off over the smooth rock floor, the whole chorus following in single file, leaping high into the air and coming down first on one foot and then on the other, one knee stiff and the other bent, and still singing at the top of their lungs. No matter how high they jumped, they all came down in unison with each other and with the tap of the rude drums. I don't care what clog dancer you scare up, he cannot keep any more perfect time to music than do these queer leapers.

The evolutions of their "grand march" are too intricate for description, and would completely bewilder a fashionable leader of the German. They wound around in snake-like figures, now and then falling into strange but regular groups, never getting confused, and never missing a step of their laborious leaping. Talk about endurance of lung and muscle! Why, these fellows keep up their jumping and shouting all day and all night. An hour of either exercise would paralyze you or me, if we do think no dirt of ourselves as athletes. During the whole of this serpentine dance, the drums and the chorus kept up their hurrah, while the leader accented the chant by a series of yells, worked in at regular intervals. All the time, too, while their legs were busy, their arms were no less so. They kept brandishing aloft their various weapons in a significant style that would make a man hunt tall grass if he saw them out on the plains. And as for attentive audiences, no American star ever had such a one as that which watched the Christmas dance at Laguna. Those five hundred men, women and children all stood looking on in decorous silence, never moving a muscle or uttering a sound.

We tarried a couple of hours here, enjoying the strange spec-

tacle; and then the sinking sun warned us to press on. It was a
very fair sort of day, and Phillips was in high feather as we
pushed along up the track. "Oh, you'll find I'm no slouch of a
walker," he kept saying (and he did take a pretty long stride).
"I'll show you how to do it. I used to walk 40 miles a day on an
average, and carry a surveyor's chain. Won't it just astonish
those folks at Los Angeles when they know about my trip?" I
didn't say anything, but kept up a power of a thinking about this
"Me and Betsy killed the bear" style; and was just mean enough
to resolve to see what this walking prodigy was really made of.
There wasn't time to do it that day, but I got in my work later.

Soon after dark we reached Cubero, a section house some
four miles from the Mexican plaza of the same name. This
railroad, by the way, has an ungodly fashion of stopping in the
wilderness anywhere from one to six miles away from the town
after which the station is named. I suppose this is to encourage
Americans to build up towns at the stations; being near to, but
not in actual contact with, the Indians and Mexicans; but it is a
decidedly aggravating trick. There isn't much fun in getting to a
supposed town late in the evening, after a hard day's walk, and
find that you'll have to go four or five miles from the station to
find a store where you can get the tobacco or cartridges your
spirit craves.

The section hands at Cubero are all Mexicans; but we
couldn't afford to be too fastidious, and spread our blankets on
the floor, having first swept up a little place for them. After
eating our lunch of mince pie and frosted cake—remnants of
the Xmas dinner at El Rito—we made ourselves agreeable to the
Mexicans, through the medium of cigarettes and fragmentary
conversation.

It has already unhinged three ribs for me to hear Phillips talk
Spanish. The only words of that language that he knows are
"vamos" (let us go) and "bueno" (good) but he makes them do
yeoman service. He'll say "which way are you fellows going to
vamos in the morning?" "That blanket of yours is very bueno,"
and so on, and expects the poor fellows to understand him

perfectly because he has one misused Spanish word in the whole sentence. They evidently take him for a brash crank, and stare at him in mild wonder. He has been out here a year, with three Mexicans working under him, and surrounded by a population which understands nothing but Spanish; and how he has failed to catch on is a wonder to me—especially as the language is so wonderfully easy, both in pronunciation and construction.

Saturday morning when we awoke, it was to find the ground blanketed with six inches of wet snow, and more coming. That wasn't very cheerful with a 25-mile walk before us, but kicking would do no good. So after finishing up our El Rito lunch we shouldered our packs and set out. It was certainly abominable walking. The snow was little more than slush, filling my low shoes full, and with just enough consistency to form four-inch stilts on my heels; so that I slipped back about six inches at every step. The wind was cold and blew the still-falling sleet square in our teeth, and our feet felt like lumps of ice. We managed, however, to get up to McCarty's in time for a hearty dinner, which did much to refresh us. Then off again through deeper and deeper snow, and sharper and sharper wind.

I noticed by the time we were about 18 miles from Cubero that brother Phillips was not quite so brash. He lagged behind considerably, cursing the weather at every breath, and every now and then breaking out with, "Say, don't you know this is an awful big undertaking to walk all the way from here to Los Angeles?" "Why, you've walked only a little way now," I said; "what do you think now of making 40 miles a day?" "By gosh!" said he, "they used to tell me we had walked 40 miles, but they must have lied. I don't believe there's a man alive that can do that much in a day." Well, late in the afternoon we struck the hand-car, five miles east of Grant's, and got the boss to carry our blankets to the station for us.

Thus lightened, I set out to try the metal [sic] of my companion, and streaked it up the track as fast as I knew how. From the five-mile post to the station took me just 59 minutes, which is pretty fast walking. Phillips didn't say anything, but kept falling in a long way behind and then running to catch up. It was sort of mean to run him so, but I knew that if that day's trip didn't sicken him, it would be pretty safe to count on him as a companion clear through; and I wanted to know what to depend upon.

I shouldn't have gone to Grant's that night, except for your plaguey *Leader* letter. A very jolly cowboy met us seven miles east from Grant's; and when he learned my mission, was very pressing in his invitation to stay at the ranche over night. I was sorry to decline, for I knew by experience that a ranche is one of the pleasantest places in the world to put up at; but that letter burned in my pocket—already 36 hours late—and I was bound to get somewhere and mail it. Grant's is the first post-office west of Albuquerque, and *only* 98 miles from it. So if the letter got to you late, you will savoy the reason why.

Once arrived at Grant's, Saturday evening, we found things waiting for us. Hon. Amado Chaves, whom I mentioned in my Santa Fe letter, had warned the people of my expected arrival; and they gave me a cordial welcome. E. Bibo and his brother, two intelligent and agreeable Germans, have a store close to the station, where I passed the evening. A clever young cowboy, the station agent and the Bibos made as good company as I ever want, and we sat and chatted until well into the night. Sunday noon, a servant of the Chaveses started for San Mateo with a wagon load of groceries, and I accompanied him. It was a 30 mile trip up into the mountains, through the snow, without a single house by the way, and I was not sorry to have company and assistance. Part of the way I trotted along beside the slow going wagon, and part I crawled into my sleeping bag to keep warm, and rode sleepily. On the way we met Señor Amado, who had been called away on business, and he gave the driver some jaw-breaking charge to treat me well during his absence.

About 5 o'clock, I was awakened from a nap by the abrupt stopping of the wagon, and the abrupt starting up of the driver's tongue, which had been moderately idle for some time. The horses had pulled the wagon safely across a tiny creek, but in going up the steep bank on the opposite side it got stuck, and there we hung. The Jehu kept whirling his "black-snake" around his head with great dexterity, and bringing it down with a pistol crack upon the flanks of the "malditos cavallos," with a steady stream of an anathemas upon them. There is a fresh originality in the way a Mexican or Spaniard curses anything, and I heard a fair sample that night: "Cursed horses! Cursed be your mother! Cursed be your father! Cursed be your grandmother and her sisters! Cursed be your uncle and your aunt, with all your cousins! Cursed be your children and your children's children! Cursed be the whole family of you, large and small, old and young, now and to come! To the devil, all of you!" Now there's nothing small or mean about that, to my notion. It is generous, comprehensive and pointed. If any of 'em got away it was not the fault of the swearer.

Well, by the time the driver had got to the end of the family, and was just beginning his genealogical profanity at the root once more, I had crawled out of my blanket and was tugging at the wheel. We strained at the wagon and argued with the horses for about a half hour, meantime unloading the entire cargo— something like a ton—but it was no go. The horses were tired out, the hind wheels were hub deep in frozen sand, and we were plainly stuck. The driver couldn't understand or speak a word of English, so my poor, hard-worked Spanish had to come to the front. After a short palaver he said he would go on to the plaza, and get a fresh team, if I would stay and watch the goods. I assented, for there was nothing else to do, and he took one of the horses and rode off, with the cheerful information at parting that it would probably take him three hours to get back with help. It was very cold, and a bleak storm was just getting under good headway; but there was no material near for building a fire. How I did thank the lucky star which had prompted me to bring along my blanket! I got into the wagon, took Shadow in—to his vast relief, for grey hounds are extremely thin-skinned— crawled shoulder deep into my sleeping-bag, and wrapped around my head the small but heavy cloth we had been sitting upon. I smoked a good cigar—thanks to the thoughtfulness of Mynherr Bibo—and prepared to go to sleep.

But fate would not have it that way. As the storm waxed fiercer, the poor, weary horse grew wild in his attempts to escape its fury; and in a short time got so tangled up in the harnesses as to tumble down. Then I had to get up and put on my shoes, unhitch him and tie him to the tongue of the wagon—the situation rendering it impossible to fasten him to the wheels. Then I went back to bed and was just getting warm again when he renewed his thrashing. The wagon was so precariously perched that it wouldn't take much to tip it over, and I dared not go to sleep as the nag kicked and tugged away at the tongue, often balancing the vehicle on two wheels. Every minute or two I got up and thumped him around into a position where he could do no harm, and then went back to get thawed out. Shadow was invaluable, and I should have suffered with the cold but for his warm coil at my feet. I had had nothing since early breakfast except a few figs, and was powerful hungry, as you may fancy; and whenever I got my head out from its covering, the sharp sleet cut face and ears like a knife.

I forgot to tell you that I had left Phillips to the tender mercies of the section-boss at Grant's; but it was true, and so I didn't have even the amusement his growling at such a position would have furnished. It was a long, cold, hungry watch I kept there alone until ten o'clock. Then, just as I was getting desperate, ready to go to sleep anyhow, and let the horse tip us over if the Lord wanted to be mean enough to let him do so, I heard the welcome clatter of horse-hoofs; and in another minute the driver drew up beside me, followed by a wagon containing two stout allies. We hitched the fresh team to the mired vehicle and yanked it out; reloaded the cargo, and in a few minutes more were breaking away toward home. Then, with a clear conscience, I crawled back into my blanket, laid my head upon a box of soap, and slept the sleep of the just, as the wagon thumped and jumped and bumped over the rocks and gullies.

Not much before midnight, the driver shook me awake with "*Aqui esta la casa*" (here is the house), and I crawled out in sleepy delight. It was good enough to get into that pleasant and hospitable mansion, fill myself with hot wine and a good supper, toast my cold shins before a roaring fireplace, and then crawl into bed under blankets worth $100 a piece. I felt as if prosperity had really struck me—and I could stand it to be struck that way right along.

Now for nearly a month the fact that my face was a regular stubble-field had not troubled me a bit, and from Santa Fe to the coast I did not intend to have any dealings with a razor. But the minute breakfast was over, Monday morning, I rushed back to my room, peeled my coat, painted my face white and began to chop off that unsightly beard. It took me about two hours, for the razor was dull and my face as tender as an aching tooth, but I was dead-set to do it and the deed was finally done. Of course you can easily guess the reason for this sudden burst of anxiety about my looks. Right at the end of the table, not six feet from me when I sat down to breakfast that morning, was just about the most beautiful girl I ever saw, and two others who would be extremely handsome if she were out of sight. It just took away my appetite to see thòse three señoritas. The true Spanish type of beauty was theirs, and if there is any type more seductive, you may keep it—I don't want anything better. Blue eyes are sweet and alluring, but for solid magnetism it takes two orbs of jet, framed in lashes and brows still darker, and showing the sparks of a fire that is apt to blaze up at any minute. There is *un chiquito diablo* in the corner of such eyes, and I suspect that part of their attractiveness is due to the hint of danger lurking in their depths.

Well, this is rather a risky line of literature for a sober old Benedick, but I wouldn't give much for any man, whatever his condition, who wouldn't warm up a little under the demure glance of such beauty as lights up the casa of Don Manuel Chaves. The Lord didn't make lovely faces just to get rid of a job lot of damaged flesh, but to have 'em looked at, and far be it from me to fly in the teeth of Providence in this respect. I don't look much like a dude, now but as far as a clean face could make a white man of me I was bound to "get thar." Thus it is that a pair of bright eyes make damphools of us all. It gave me a pain, later to learn that the bright, particular star for whose special sake I had flayed my face, was just on the eve of marriage to a tall, good-looking young Mexican who was visiting at the house. Of course, I didn't want her for myself, but there is an inherent hoggishness in mankind which makes us all feel a trifle abused when we see some other fellow carry off such a prize. However, I'll be generous and wish Señor Don Francisco joy of his luck. There's one thing I'll gamble on, and that is that he will have the handsomest wife in all New Mexico. The wedding takes place the 7th Inst., and I had to decline—much against my will—numerous and pressing invitations to remain for this interesting event.

I hated to give it up, for in the first place a Mexican wedding is something not to be kicked out of bed, being one of the most absolutely jovial and lavish affairs on earth; and in the second place, I could have lingered at San Mateo for a year or two, very happily, even if there had been no wedding. Talk about hospitality! I have sampled a good many brands of the article in a good many different places; but I never found any ahead of that on tap at San Mateo—and but few to equal it. I was treated like a king—yes, verily, like the king of trumps. The best room in the fine house was mine. "You are in your own house," said Don Manuel to me, in a fashion which indicated that he meant it. And though the language of the household was alien to my ears, I was made as much at home as ever anywhere.

Monday was mostly devoted to explorations and excavations in the strange buried city of San Mateo—the American Pompeii. It is a wonderful spot, that. New Mexico is full of ancient ruins, but none so far as I know, at all comparable to this in archeological interest. Señor Rodolfo Otero, a very intelligent young cousin of the Chaveses, piloted me over to the spot in the morning; and as he handles English very readily—having been educated in Santa Fe—his guidance was very valuable to me. The ruins lie about three-fourths of a mile north of the Chaves mansion, and are in the form of a low, irregular mound—suggesting at a slight distance nothing of the wonders hidden there.

Hacienda of Don Amado Chaves, San Mateo, New Mexico, n.d. Photo-
graph by Charles Lummis. Courtesy of Southwest Museum: negative
no. 556.

Approaching the mound, one may see at the south-west corner
a remarkable stone wall cropping out a foot or two. Here lies the
key to the discovery of the hidden city. A savage wind-storm
swept away the sand from a little corner of the wall, and Hon.
Amado Chaves stumbled upon the clue thus revealed. A little
excavation has already been done under his supervision, with
gratifying results, but there is a vast amount of work to be done
before the place will give up to science the full value of its
mysteries. I spent nearly a whole day there, Monday and Tuesday, with a spade for company, and richly was I repaid.

The buried city of San Mateo lies—as nearly as may be
determined from the outlines of walls already exhumed—in the
form of an irregular rectangle. There are probably 100 or 150
rooms or houses in the rectangle, which surrounds, as in all
Pueblos and Mexican towns, a plaza. In several places the walls
show above the surface of the mound—which was formed by

the drifting of wind-driven sand against and over the ruins. The walls are perfect, as far as they go, with tops as level as a sidewalk, but I discovered that they were merely the remains of the lower story. The town was, like most pueblos, and unlike all Mexican towns, composed of two storied houses, but all the upper stories have fallen, and their ruins choke the rooms below with rocks and mud-mortar.

The thing which first strikes the visitor as remarkable, is the building material employed. I feel pretty safe in asserting that there is not another town of any sort in the whole Territory which is built of stone throughout; but old San Mateo is—and superbly built, too. There is not a mason in the country who can take the same material and make a handsomer or more substantial wall than the aboriginal people of San Mateo made here many hundred years ago. The rock used is very hard, light-colored sandstone, split by natural cleavage into blocks averaging 10 inches long, 8 inches wide and 2 inches thick. I don't know where this stone was found, but the builders certainly brought it from a distance, for it is not native to the locality. It is laid in simple mud mortar, but with an artistic precision that is simply marvelous. Those walls have been there for centuries; but where they have not been destroyed by human force, they stand as perfect as the day they were laid.

I say by human force; for the ruins reveal their own tragic story. The little town was a victim to the fate of war; and its homes and its people alike fell before the relentless wrath of some savage foe. The fallen walls of the upper stories, blackened by fire; the charred remnants of roof and rafter which may be found deep buried in every room; the dismembered skeletons and scattered household utensils, all point to the same inevitable conclusion. My digging was confined to a room on the eastern side of the plaza, and I got it about half cleaned out, making a hole six feet deep and six feet square upon the floor. It was hard work, for the debris from the upper walls was extremely heavy to handle; but I finally got a small shaft down to the floor, and then ran out along the hard-packed clay as far as I had time to.

After the first four feet of digging, the relics came thick and fast. All through the heavy sand were charred fragments of wood, with here and there a crumbling rafter half destroyed by fire and half by the slower combustion of time. Then I began to encounter pieces of pottery—at first, all of the rude but curious patterns I distinguish by the name of fish-scale; unpainted, grimy with soot and sometimes still smeared with grease—that most indestructible of articles. Then came a great many human bones, much scattered, and mixed with the remains of small animals which I took to be rats. On about the same level, also, were a few pieces of flint and red moss-agate, partially fashioned into arrowheads. This was a point of considerable importance, as an evidence of antiquity. I believe that no metallic relics of any sort have ever been found there.

Reaching the clay floor, I began to find a much higher grade of pottery, whose fragments were scattered among the embers. It was finished smooth—some with a fine glaze like porcelain— and painted in fanciful stripes of black and white, on a background either white or red. Some of the designs are not only extremely tasteful, but also very accurately executed; and I have specimens of it which rank above any Indian pottery of the present day. The last find of my hunt was perhaps the most interesting, though it would be hard to put it above some of the "tepulcates" or pottery. It was a bead from a necklace, three-fourths of an inch long and a third of an inch in diameter, made from an extremely hard and fine-grained bone, and highly polished. It had been so rounded off at the ends as to be elliptical in form.

I tried hard to find more, but the facts were against me. The weather was very severe at this high altitude—San Mateo must be 7,500 or 8,000 feet above sea level—with snow and sand drifting hard in my eyes, and the cold nearly freezing my hands and feet. Furthermore, it is a slow job to dig out such a big mass of earth and rock, and my time was inadequate to the task.

My excavation also disclosed one of the characteristic doorways of this pueblo (I have seen nothing similar elsewhere), a tiny entrance level with the ground, three feet high, 18 inches wide, and carefully cased in stone. Just at one side of this I exhumed an insignificant looking little piece of sandstone, which was perhaps as important as anything I found. It was a segment of a six-inch circle in shape exactly like a small piece of pie. Its value lies in the fact that it is the only hint of the use—by the inhabitants of this mysterious city—of implements other than those of stone and bone. Unless I am sadly in error, it has been used as a whet-stone; and if such were its use, then the people had implements of iron or copper. You can see, very readily, therefore, that plain and worthless as it appears, it may carry a key to the buried secrets of San Mateo.

I may mention that the rooms of this pueblo are all very small, averaging about 10 × 8 [feet]. Each has one tiny door, no windows. In the only room which has been fully excavated, the fireplace was found built almost in the middle of the floor— another point of radical difference from all other known pueblos. Señor Chaves, in his explorations discovered the skeleton of a woman, with her long black hair in excellent preservation. In many localities this would indicate that she could not have been buried long; but in the climate of New Mexico nothing decays. He also found a necklace of beads similar to mine, and other minor relics.

The *Leader* is the first and only newspaper to contain any description of this most unique, most interesting and very likely most ancient ruin in all New Mexico. I trust you will call the attention of Professor Putnam to the matter and also that of Professor Baird of the Smithsonian Institute.* There is here an indubitably rich field for scientific research, and explorations can be prosecuted under peculiar advantages. Hon. Amado Chaves, who is a cultured gentleman, will extend every assistance and when the spring brings good weather, the work of excavation would go on without the slightest hindrance. This

*Frederick Ward Putnam (1839–1915), late nineteenth-century U.S. naturalist and ethnologist, did archaeological work in southeastern Ohio in the 1880s. Spencer Fullerton Baird (1823–1888), American zoologist was director of the Smithsonian Institution, 1878–1888.

city covers about two acres, but there are several other ruins in the immediate vicinity, of scarcely less importance. I fully believe that there should be sought the clue to that most obscure problem, "who were the original occupants of New Mexico?" The city is 30 miles north from Grant's Station, on the Atlantic and Pacific R. R., and can easily be reached from Albuquerque in a day. I trust that this interesting locality may soon be forced to reveal to science its valuable secrets.

It may not be uninteresting to you to hear something of the domestic and social life of the Mexicans "upper-crust," as I saw it in the charming household of Don Manuel Chaves. The casa is a very large and finely built adobe, divided by a hall 12 feet wide running from east to west. The rooms are large and well-lighted, tastefully furnished in American style, handsomely papered and carpeted. The windows are hung with lace curtains, while the rugs and table-covers are precious Navajo blankets. Heat is furnished by the delightful fireplaces peculiar to the Mexicans, and unequaled by any other sort in the world. Pictures, mirrors and various knick-knacks complete the pleasant picture.

Their table is lavishly bountiful, and the viands admirably prepared, though unfamiliar to eastern folk. A fine stew of mutton with rice; beef cut into cubes of three inches and thus roasted; more beef cut into shreds and cooked with the red chili—which looks more like stewed tomatoes than anything else; frigoles [sic] prepared nearly in the American style; white and graham bread, baked in little cakes which they call "galletitas"; wine, coffee, and canned pears or peaches—that will give you a very fair idea of what is to be found upon the table in great abundance. The service and table furniture are plain but neat and the preparation of the food is all that the most fastidious could desire. There are half a dozen or more native servants about the premises, and one or two kept at Grant's.

Monday evening I had my first chance to become really acquainted with the family, as we all sat around the cheerful "fogon," or fireplace, in the sitting room. It was a large, as well as pleasant circle. I believe there were 16 of us, and two or three

of the folks were away, at that. We had a little singing by the
congregation—"Sweet Bye and Bye," and a Spanish lovesong to
the air of "Home Sweet Home," with various other Castillian
melodies. Some of them were very sweet and plaintive, all
pitched on a minor key, and all amatory. There is one thing you
will notice about a Spanish song, and that is the supreme indif-
ference of the music to the words. A Spaniard can take any air
and cram any meter into it, long or short, spondaic or dactylic,
and act as if he wasn't doing any violence to his feelings or his
jaws. Now I tried to sing "Adios, Adios," (air, "Home Sweet
Home") with them; but it was like covering a pair of 49 inch legs
with a pair of 20 inch trousers. I found that they were working in
about four words to my one, and I couldn't crowd the notes to
that heartless extent.

For instance, in a line like "there's no-o place like home,"
their words would be about as generous in number as in the
following English sample: "There can be discovered in the
whole boundless universe no locality at all comparable to the
felicitous home residence." I should expect to have the lock jaw,
if I attempted to ring in any such gang of words on one or two
unsuspecting and unprotected measures. It doesn't look like
fair play, either. But those sweet-faced señoritas sat there and
sang away in low, soft tones, wagging their little jaws like
lightning, and acting as if it were the most natural thing in the
world for a measure to have 56 notes in it. Still, I like their
Spanish songs. There is a plaintive sadness about them that is
particularly fascinating. Then I had to sing for them and chose
"Three Black Crows"—a fool song containing frequent imita-
tions of cawing. It tickled them wonderfully. They could understand it, for the words are easy, and the flapping and cawing
were a new deal to them. There seem to be no really comic
songs in Spanish, though plenty of humorous ones.

After the singing came some queer games. The favorite
seemed to be "Molina" (the mill). We were all ranged around the
room in chairs and each was given as a title the name of something pertaining to a grist mill. Señor Lorenzo Sanchez, a cousin
of the family, was the miller, and after giving us our names he

sat down and began to relate a story descriptive of the miller's life. Whenever he mentioned the name of any part of the mill or its belongings, the person christened after that article had to rise, turn around and sit down. If one rose at the wrong word, he or she was out, and had to leave the circle. Then suddenly the miller would cry "the mill is broke!" and all had to change seats, amid general scramble. One was sure to get left out for the miller changed his seat also, and it was not allowable to sit in the chair he had just vacated. This went on until all had been counted out one by one. Then the miller passed his hat and collected rings, knives and other articles as forfeits from the losers; and the company went into a session for passing sentences. Holding up a forfeit in his closed hand, Señor Lorenzo would ask one of us "what sentence shall be upon the owner of this?" and the person appealed to would give some penalty, which the culprit was bound to pay.

All the sentences were very simple—as "to make a speech," "to make a courtesy," "to give three sighs for the one he loves best in the world," etc. A favorite one was to place the culprit against the wall, where he must blow out a candle which Lorenzo passed rapidly back and forth in front of his face, uttering at the same time some jargon. Most of my sentences, a clue having been taken from the crow song, were to imitate various animals; and if the mimicry was feeble the reception of it was appreciative. The Mexicans, by the way, are the greatest people for compliments—something like our own barbers—who tell every man that enters that he has the finest head of hair, or the heaviest beard, they ever saw. There were no kissing forfeits, to my vast relief. It would have broken my heart to fall on the neck of one of those señoritas, of course.

Another game closely similar in character, was called "Cocha" (the coach). In this we were named after various towns in the Territory, and Lorenzo told about a journey. When he spoke of going from Bernalillo to Las Vegas, the persons named for these two places had to exchange seats, and when he cried "the coach is broke!" there was a change all around. In its other details the game is just like "molina." Then a saucer was brought in, and one of the party gave it a spin upon the floor at the same time calling the name of some one else, who must jump up and seize it before it ceased spinning, or give a forfeit. They kept "Señor Char-less"—which was their pronunciation of my name—jumping lively fashion, and he reciprocated with calls for fair Señorita Rosita, as well as Señoritas Luz, Lola, Beatrice, Vicentita, and Cleopas, and Señora Juanita Sanchez. Then there was a Mexican version of "Button, button, who's got the button?" We all sat down on the floor joining hands and singing a verse whose purport was

> The ring, the ring is hidden,
> Is hidden, is hidden
> In the hands of the Señor,
> You have to guess who has it,
> Who has it, who has it,
> Soon as the song is over.

The ring of course was constantly in motion, and it was hard to guess its whereabouts. As soon as the song was ended, all pounded upon the floor and cried "Floron! Floron!" (the ring! the ring!) and the person seated in the center of the circle had to guess where the ring was, or stay there till he did hit it right; when the person in whose hands it was discovered had to go into the circle and take a turn at guessing. The last game of all, and the one which created the most merriment, had some name which I do not remember. A large plateful of flour was brought in and placed upon a chair, where Lorenzo molded it up into the form of a cone, upon whose apex was placed a large bullet. With a case-knife we all took turns cutting away a small slice from the flour and the one whose cutting caused the bullet to fall had to pick it out of the flour with his or her teeth. Of course that made some very white faces, and no end of fun. I purposely burrowed my whole face into the flour, and they went into convulsions of laughter over my droll appearance.

I never passed two more pleasant and mirthful evenings than those of Monday and Wednesday, which were consumed in such amusement as I have described above. And the reckless fashion in which I slung Spanish about! At some of my sentences they would gaze upon me with a mild and reproachful wonder, but generally I managed to make myself understood. One doesn't want to be a dumb post in such a gathering, so I kept the mutilated Spanish flying anyhow, hit or miss. I believe I could make a pretty good Mexican in a little while more. I have already conceived a great affection for the throat-consuming chili colorado, and can eat as much of it now as anyone, though at first it nearly knocked the top of my head off.

A French padre came up to the casa, Monday night, I suppose, for the wedding. He shared my room, though not my bed, and proved a pleasant chum. He spoke French and Spanish fluently but only a very few words of English, and our conversation was decidedly polyglot. We would start off in Spanish and go to the end of my rope and then branch off into French. By filling up the verbal gaps with plugs of English, Latin, and even Greek, we managed to get along very comfortably, though with all these resources I was often stuck.

I had many interesting talks with Don Manuel Chaves, the father of Amado—an erect, powerful old man of 65. He was one of the pioneers of this part of the Territory, and a history of his eventful life would read like a romance. He has had countless bloody encounters with the savage Apaches, Navajos, and Utes, and their autographs are all over his body in the shape of wounds, some of them ghastly ones. I have space to relate but one of his adventures. Some 40 years ago, he was on one of his many trading expeditions among the Navajos, and had exchanged his goods for a great quantity of blankets, etc. Just as he was starting homeward with his 8 men, 300 Navajos surrounded him, and began to rain down arrows and bullets upon the little party. The first fire wounded him in the arm and body and killed two of his companions. The fight lasted for some hours, but at nightfall the Indians withdrew; Don Manuel was nearly dead from his wounds and the last one of his companions—including a brother—quite dead. He would have perished there but for the appearance of a Navajo who had been a servant in his employ, and who helped him to Fort Wingate, where he lay on the verge of death for three months. On his way home from the fort he was wounded again, and the Navajo was killed. It was only after almost incredible exertion and suffering that Don Manuel reached the top of the San Mateo mountains. Here a friendly Indian found him almost dead, and carried him to the casa on his back.

Later—I have got out to Grant's again (Thursday night) after a frightful cold trip. Just as I expected, Brer Phillips weakened and took the cars the morning after I left him. His pedestrian career was short and sweet; and instead of "astonishing the natives of Los Angeles by coming in on them from a 1,000 mile walk," as he proposed, a day and a half's tramp of 38 miles exhausted his sand. Well, I don't lament. No company at all is preferable to company that is weak-kneed. I am only glad he skipped before getting into me any deeper. Here I am enjoying the hospitality of Messrs Bibo, who are lavish in their kindness. They have supplied me with a beautiful selection of Acoma pottery, and many other valuable relics, which I shall freight to Los Angeles tomorrow along with a lot of my precious load. The weather is extremely severe—to an extent almost unknown here—but I do not fancy it will last long. If it does I shall grin and bear it; if it doesn't I shall not kick. I expect to reach Coolidge Saturday night, and revel in a big stack of mail. Thence out to Fort Wingate and Zuni for a week; and then on into Arizona with all possible haste. *Deseo a V. un muy feliz ano nuevo!*

LUM

Manuelito, New Mexico
Monday, January 5th, 1885

Editors Leader:

I guess the Lord is taking me at my word on that weather question, and has let go all holds to give His undivided attention to dumping all the meteorological cussedness of the winter in this immediate vicinity. If that isn't the case, some dude engineer has hold of the throttle, and is turning the old machine loose for all there is in her. I guess you haven't been having any weather, back East, for there couldn't be enough to go around after supplying New Mexico this liberally. Talk about your mean walking—why, this is mean enough to stop a clock. For the last 150 miles I haven't had three decent steps of walking, and it is doubtful if I shall in the next 300. The snow lies several inches deep, even upon the track, just wet enough to make an abominable, slippery, slimy mud underneath, into which one sinks half ankle-deep at every step. Oh, it is rich. However, I am still on deck, and can, as I remarked before, stand it as long as the weather can. One of us two will have pretty soon to make an assignment for the benefit of creditors, and I flatter myself it will be the weather and not I. The only thing that bothers me is that it makes me feel mean and selfish to be hogging all the storms thus, and not leaving enough to go around to those who would enjoy them just as much as I do.

Well, anyhow, I am just beginning to appreciate the true gilt-edged and aesthetic beauty of a fire, and the man who doesn't know how to appreciate that blessing has only half lived. To wade through the snow and mud all day, and at night snuggle up beside a roaring fireplace or red-hot stove—that is genuine bliss. Fire means nothing to a man who has never been half frozen, nor food to him who has never been half-starved. So the situation is by no means entirely desperate as long as there are two perpetual sources of enjoyment left. I reckon I shall survive and keep cheerful if I manage to find two feet of bare ground between here and Los Angeles.

Another of my can't-get-away fits struck me at Grant's, and it did look for awhile as if I were planted there for good. The Bibos caught me on the fly as I came in from San Mateo. When I finished my writing and visiting, the next thing to delay me was the packing of a box of trophies—and it took a solid afternoon. My agates, turquoises, pertrifications, furs, San Mateo relics, etc., made quite a bunch by themselves, and the Bibos filled me up with a beautiful assortment of the strange Acoma pottery, a

peck of rich pinon nuts and other articles too numerous to
mention. It made a fat box, and the only drawback to my satisfaction was the discovery that the freight to Los Angeles would
be only 11 cents a pound! This godless railroad wants the whole
country for hauling one grain of sand a little way. I'd like to have
them compelled to run over some road of mine just once, and if I
didn't salt them to a queen's taste, it would be because I didn't
have ink enough to make out the bill.

I didn't finish packing that box till Friday evening, and then
had enough writing to do to fill out the night, along with the
social interruptions of the place—which were many. There is an
Apache bridle there, which would make a sensation if you could
see it in Ohio. The leather work is well but simply done, but it
hardly shows anywhere. The whole looks one mass of silver
plates, some circular, some oval and some oblong, all heavy and
all well engraved in simple lines. The silver on that bridle is
worth $30, and the whole affair has a most striking barbaric
beauty.

Before starting westward again, Saturday morning, I picked
up a new chum—and one who seems to stick a little better than
his predecessors. He is a Pennsylvania book and sewing machine agent, who got off the cars at Grant's nearly broke, and
says he is going through with me. In case he does, I don't know
which will be the more to be pitied, his legs or my ears. If ever
the Lord put a double-back-action, reversible heel, twist barrel,
bar-lock, good-shooter-or-no-sale tongue in any man, my new
patience-tester was the lucky recipient. A mute's ear would
evaporate under the fire this lock-stitch talker would pour into
it in half an hour. And as for cheerfulness, he knows about as
much of it as a fly does of saying grace. I could supply the whole
indigo market of the country by boiling down one hour of his
conversation. We left Grant's at 9:20—folks in this country do
not have very early breakfasts at this time of year—and before
11 o'clock, lugubrious Lockard had told me all his family history; how his wife had deserted him; how badly he wanted to
commit suicide, and so on forever. I offered to lend him one of

my guns, remarking that I always liked to accommodate a suffering fellow-mortal; but he looked injured and said I was heartless. Strange, how ungrateful folks are; and how many are just
pining to go to the golden shore until the train is just ready to
start—and then they give away their pass and conclude to stay
at home.

The snow was not very bad for the first few miles, but we
were fast climbing the eastern slope of the continental divide,
and at every step the situation grew worse. At noon we paused
near Bluewater, built a fire of chips hewn from the ties, and
cooked some dinner. Then on through the ever deepening snow
and the ever colder wind, up as lonely a stretch of track as ever
bored the eye. The only amusement was to watch the antics of
Shadow among the countless rabbits, off which he made a regular boa-constrictor meal. I thought I had seen rabbits before, but
it was a mistake. The snow here for miles is so thick with their
tracks that one could hardly set down a bushel basket on an
unoccupied spot.

All along the way, too, are immense piles of ties and cordwood, and these piles are literally alive with cotton-tails. A jack
never trusts himself in such a place. In one place we counted 15
rabbits at once, running from one long woodpile to another. A
man with a good shotgun and plenty of ammunition could kill
here in a day enough game to last him a year. But in spite of the
rabbits, the day was long and cold and dreary; and red noses,
cold, wet feet, and chapped hands got in their work in expert
style.

Brother Lockard had been a wonderful flyer at the start, but
after 20 miles of this sort of walking, his melancholy mind
transferred itself from family sorrows to matters personal—and
every step was enlivened by a heart-broken groan, or a curse
upon the weather. At last, an hour after dark, he dropped upon
the end of a tie and flatly refused to go farther. In vain I told him
that there was a station only three miles ahead, and that he
would inevitably freeze to death where he was, and that a little
more sand would carry him through. "Don't care," said he,

"don't care. I've got to die anyhow, and I might just as well die here as anywhere."

I was about to give him up, when I spied the light of a ranche among the trees about half a mile to the left of the track, and made a break thither, with my doleful partner dangling along in the rear. The snow was half knee deep out on the plains, but that ruddy light made the way short, and in a few minutes we were standing before the open, fire-lit doorway which proclaimed the owners Mexicans. Those fellows are wonderfully fond of abundant ventilation, and while the cheerful fireplace roars loudly, will have their doors wide open a large part of the very coldest days. A big, good-looking man greeted us, and in reply to my statement that we were very wet and hungry, bade us enter. He whooped up the fire, brought us some good coffee and tortillas, and fell into a pleasant conversation.

My Spanish has braced up tolerably fast since leaving Santa Fe, and I had by this time got so far along that I could be pretty sociable by hitches. Señor Juan Arragon, proprietor of the Rock Spring ranche, is a good sort of fellow, and his wife—an enormous mountain of flesh, about four feet in diameter—was equally clever. Lockard was nearly dead, and in a few minutes went off to bed, still groaning and wailing as if our day's reverses had not been happily ended. Then when the family was ready to retire they showed me to a bed-room well furnished and exquisitely neat. By the tiny window I could see that the adobe walls were fully three feet thick. In the center of the room stood a fine new American stove and in the corners were half a dozen guns of different patterns. One thing amused and mystified me a little. Upon the walls were four or five little bronze statuettes, representing Christ upon the cross, naked save for the customary cloth about the loins. Somehow, though, this doesn't appear to have been quite up to the Mexican ideas of propriety, so around the waist of each figure they have put a funny little frilled calico shirt. Fancy Christ on the cross in petticoats!

Well, we had a pleasant and restful time at this little Mexican ranche, among whose other attractions was a bright boy rejoic-

ing in the startling name—common enough among his people—Jesus Maria. They gave us a great breakfast in the morning, including coffee flavored with whisky, and the finest bread I
ever ate—and I come from a bread country, too. There was
something rather fine in the air with which Señor Juan waved
me away when I offered to pay for our entertainment. It was real
hospitality with him, not a commercial transaction. There was
nothing mean about him except his dogs, one of which nailed
mine as we were about to depart. Poor Shadow thought he had
fallen among thieves, and lay flat upon his back, shrieking
helplessly until I pulled off his assailant. I am afraid the dog,
despite his good qualities, will always be something of a dude
and tenderfoot. The native dogs have all their own way with
him.

From Rock Spring, Sunday morning, we soon reached
Chaves, and here filled the canteen at the dirtiest section-house
in the world. The city of Cologne, even if as foul as painted by
Coleridge, would make a white mark on the section-house at
Chaves, N. M. The snow kept growing deeper and more abominable at every yard, until at last it entirely covered the track
except the tops of the rails. At noon we stood upon the crest of
the Continental Divide—that vast watershed, 7,297 feet above
the sea, from whose eastern slope the raindrops find their way to
the Gulf of Mexico, while those upon the western side are borne
to the Pacific ocean. I didn't see any water there, nor any shed;
but knew right well that they must be around somewhere—else
why the name? Going down the western slope of the divide—for
it is down-grade from there clear to Winslow, 160 miles—we
looked for Italian summer, owing to the change in altitude. We
are still looking for the aforesaid I.S., but it is summer else. (Say,
now, don't kick. This is very far from being a no-pun winter.)
Instead of growing better, the weather grew worse; and even up
to the present writing the doctors see no chance of its recovery.
Well, if it would only get up and die, I don't know of any
mourners.

We struck Coolidge at 3 P.M.—the end of the first division,

and the biggest metropolis in the whole 136 miles from Albuquerque. I suppose it probably contains about 100 people. Here
my heart was gladdened by an armful of mail—practically the
first I had had since leaving Santa Fe a month before. I was glad
to hear that all my friends were still in the land of elections and
taxes; and felt so good over it that I camped down, right then
and there, to read the whole stack of letters, instead of pushing
on to Wingate before night. I discovered thereby that owing to
the sickness of one of the editors of the *Times*, the pleasure of
my company was desired in Los Angeles February 1st. This will
be quite impossible to accomplish with the present weather,
but I sent them word to have dinner ready for me on the 7th of
February

Coolidge is a great place for cowboys to congregate, by the
way, and a jolly crowd they are. They were in a little sour humor
just then, however, on account of their inability to get their
mail—after which some of them had ridden 30 miles in the
cold. If the Coolidgites could have their say, I fancy the postmas-
tership there would change hands with dizzy rapidity. I was the
guest of Charlie Flinn during my brief stay in town, and met
very clever treatment at his hands.

I didn't get started till 10:20, Monday morning, on account of
delays in breakfast, and then scuffed up the snow in lively style
westward—declining the offer of a clever railroader to carry us
on to Winslow, 150 miles ahead. I reached Wingate at 1:15, after
a quick walk, and decided to go over to the fort, 3 miles distant,
as I had a letter of introduction to a young fellow there. May
good luck always pursue that fort—and never overtake it! It cost
me a solid half-day, at a time when half-days are valuable and
mighty cold, and was about as poor a bargain as I ever made. I
went over and presented my letter, and was favored with a
handshake and no more. Not as much as a chair by the fire to
dry my wet feet; not a word of information about the post and
its surroundings.

The only result of the trip was a disappointment—the discovery that I couldn't go down to Zuni. That most interesting of

all Indian towns lay 45 miles distant across the mountains, and the only road three feet deep in snow. I did manage to buy, however, a good specimen of the curious Zuni pottery—a canteen in the shape of a turtle—and sent it on ahead by Uncle Sam. Ft. Wingate—more like Lose-gate it was to me—is a little settlement by itself up on the hillside where there are abundant springs. Water is carried into all the buildings by pipes, and things in general are equally comfortable. The fort has its own post-office, store, tailor, and cobbler shops, etc. There are eight companies of soldiers stationed there, and a dull time they have of it—except the many who pass away their time in gambling and getting drunk on beer under Uncle Sam's complaisant nose. The officers, such as I saw, seemed rather of the dude stripe, and I fancy would a good deal sooner fight the tiger than the Navajos. There are several Indian bummers who hang about the fort to drink and gamble, but they are poor specimens of their warlike tribe.

I staid around the fort a few hours, getting a little poor provender at an exhorbitant price, and then waddled off down the muddy road toward the station. I found a clever operation there—as at nearly all such places—and passed a cosy evening, in the course of which we enjoyed a call on the boys of the U.S. Geological Survey, just now encamped there. I got a good supper at the section-house, and later spread my blanket on the ticket-office floor, while Lockard snoozed on a bench in the waiting-room. I was cheered and soothed here by learning that the Durango branch of the D. & R. G. R. R. is hopelessly snowed in. The mail is carried on horses from Ft. Wingate to Durango, 125 miles across the northern mountains. I used to have an idea that the climate of New Mexico was tropical; but am obliged to conclude that I was just a leetle off my bias. There is about as much weather here as I am hankering for at present.

Tuesday morning was a trifle warmer, and we got away early. It was lucky we did, for the mud and slush soon became awful to contemplate, and we had to walk all day upon the ends of the ties, which were generally clear on the south side of the track. I

had a good time all the morning picking up beautiful petrifica-
tions, both of shells and wood, and again my pockets begin to
appear like anvils in size and weight. We passed the little town
of Gallup, famous for its great deposits of bituminous coal, and
sustained entirely by the miners. The shafts are some three
miles north of town, and are reached by a track whose grade is
over 300 feet to the mile.

Here we left behind the remarkable red sand-stone mesas
which skirt the road all the way from Bluewater, and which
form a glorious panorama that is aptly termed "the New Garden
of the Gods!" It does indeed recall the Garden at Manitou, being
of the same radiant hue and much the same formation, but is on
a vastly more stupendous scale, though less grotesque in architecture. For 50 miles the red, rocky wall runs on, usually parallel with the track, and one to three miles from it, in picturesque,
broken ever-varying bluffs, 500 to 800 feet in height. Their usual
form is that of rectangular or square blocks, hundreds of feet in
each dimension, and fronting toward the track almost as reg-
ularly as a row of business buildings. A few, particularly at the
eastern end, are eroded into terraced castles; and others have
assumed more strange and irregular shapes.

But the finest freaks of this strange gallery are a short distance west of Wingate. From the fort itself one notes two small,
peculiar, twin pinnacles, rising above an intervening ridge. As
one walks on down the track from the station, the baffling ridge
slowly fades away, and soon one stands in wonder before that
strange piece of nature's architecture—"the Navajo church."
Back half a mile from the dress-parade of red-coated giants it
stands—a vast cathedral hewn aptly from the solid rock by
Time's patient hand. You see it all there; the vast bulk of nave
and transept, of pillar, arch and dome; while in the middle front,
exactly as human art could have placed it, soar aloft the dizzy
tower with its slender pinnacles.

It is the easiest thing in the world to gaze upon that wondrous monument and believe it really an artificial temple, even
then resounding with hymns of praise. Here the soft-grey sandstone comes out in exquisite contrast to the deep prevailing

red. Just beyond the church is "Pyramid Rock," a curious, conical peak, highest of all the mesas, and beautiful in hue and
contour. This strange wall leaves the railroad, as I remarked,
near Gallup, but by no means ends here. Its ruby cliffs run
across clear to the big Colorado River, hundreds of miles to the
west. Very few indeed are the roads from whose car-windows
you can see such strangely beautiful walls as those of the New
Garden of the Gods.

Tuesday afternoon found us climbing the steps of a large
stone building which, with its outhouses, constitutes the town
of Defiance. I wished to do up some writing; and, as we had
already traveled 20 miles of hardship, concluded that we could
afford to "layover" here until morning. Gladder'n thunder that
we stopped; for here, in this lonely spot, was the man I have
been looking for for the last five years—the typical blow-hard
and ba-a-ad man of the whole west. And I found the animal right
there, large as life and twice as ornery. "Ya-as," he said, when I
asked permission to use his table, "siddown and hump yerself as
much as ye damplease." Whereupon I sat, and began to take an
inventory of the cuss, who was, as one might see at first glance,
a real specimen. A man about five-feet-ten in height, of heavy
and muscular frame, a face with regular but hard features, the
neck of a bull and the underjaw of a terrapin; dressed in a soiled
percale shirt and bell-bottomed pants fringed with solid silver
buttons down the outside of each leg—that is about what we
saw. We heard a swaggering, arrogant, "whaddo-you-soy" voice,
laden with complicated oaths and calculated to strike terror to
the heart of the unsalted. As soon as I heard that bejesus tone, I
sized the man up for about the meanest, windiest snide in the
country; and subsequent events showed that even then I rated
him too high.

D. M. Smith, for that is his name, keeps at Defiance an
extensive, heavily-stocked Indian post; and if he doesn't skin
poor Lo there daily, then my name is Nicodemus. A Navajo will
enter and accept an invitation to play monte with Smith, who
as likely as not will remark to some bystander, "Watch me
down the —— for that pony of his," and down it is, every

time. He is a skillful sharper with the cards; and the Indians acute as they are about all such things, stand no show at all. They are terrible gamesters, and will gamble away their horses, their squaws, and the very clothes from their backs. Taking advantage of this, the shark robs them at every turn. I soon wearied of his blood-smeared conversation, but there was no way out of it. He was bound to be listened to all the time. You have all heard the braggadocio of the eastern thug and bully, with his projecting chin and cigar tilted upward. Well, that thug belongs to the same genus as Smith, but a little different species. The one is the "holy terror" of the East; the other the ditto ditto of the West. You have seen samples of the latter type in the papers; and believe me, the most exaggerated of them all fails to do justice to the real flesh and blood article.

The Georgia fire-eater is nowhere, the New York plug-ugly not a marker beside this chap. His only conversation was of shooting and cutting, and of "what a jesusly time" he had killing off enough Navajos to keep the rest humble; illustrating how he would pump anyone who molested him so full of lead that some tenderfoot would come along and locate a claim there; and in general letting us know what a hell of terror he was on wheels. He showed us some startling schemes, which might have paralyzed a freshman, and did fill Lockard with horrified awe. "By G——d!" said he, "yer can't ketch me nowheres, —— —, in this —— store, but what I'm —— good and ready for business. Sposen I was standin' here, fixin' these lemons, an' a feller was to come in to hold me up. See?" and quick as fire he snatched two cocked six-shooters from under the counter and "threw them down" on us.

We saw very plainly. Well, sir, that animal had more that 100 big revolvers, not to mention magazine and long-range rifles, lying at full cock all over his store, at places accessible only to himself. That was enough to fix his status. He is some eastern tough who has been out here three years, and lives in constant terror of the Navajos and tramps—a terror which he endeavors to conceal by murderous talk and braggadocio.

A few Indians came in to trade, and he bully-ragged and browbeat them unmercifully. A rather handsome young Navajo named John, employed to herd his cattle, came in from the cold day's ride, and was abused and reviled as few men ever were. Then Smith told me how a former servant had upon being discharged, broke into the store during his absence and stole $300 worth of goods. Smith and a companion saddled their horses and set out in pursuit as soon as a traitorous Navajo, tempted by reward, revealed the hiding place of his fellow. They came back with the stolen goods and a blanket rolled around a vest and pair of pants, stiff with gore. They had "found the cuss where he got sorry and committed suicide." "What," said I, "a Navajo commit suicide for remorse at stealing?" "Ya——as," answered the bad man, "an' I'll give some more of the —— the same chance to kill themselves if they ain't careful." Then he had the gall to show me that hideously besmeared clothing, with a round hole on the left flap of the breast and back. There was not a grain of powder in it, and that showed that the fatal ball came from a distance.

The truth of the story is as I have just learned, that Smith and his chum overtook the young thief, and with a single bullet settled both him and his horse. They cut off the Indian's clothes, leaving the poor devil on the frozen ground—this was only about two months ago—still he lived for nineteen days, having been found by Indians and taken to his hogan or house. The Navajos understand the situation perfectly well, and one of these days, they'll catch Bully Smith where his barrel full of six-shooters will do him no more good than nothing at all, and then these red men will have a big crow to pick with him. No wonder he is skeered. He didn't dare to let us sleep in the store, so we went over to a little ranche building hard by along with his very clever assistant, Wes. Hess. The wind whistled through big cracks, and I could see the sky in a dozen places overhead, but we slept very warmly nevertheless, under many blankets and an old wagon sheet spread upon the floor.

In the morning, after further oral blood-letting by Smith and

a scant breakfast, we went on to Manuelito, where I had to stop
to write. Manuelito is the head chief of all the Navajos, having a
dozen lesser chiefs under him, and despite his 75 years still their
ruling spirit. He has two brothers, too, both fine specimens of
manhood in bronze. Klah (left-handed) the elder, would command respectful attention in any crowd, with his large, well-
shaped head, strong face and herculean frame. The younger,
whose name I forgot, is cast in a smaller mold, but an equally
good one. He is an expert silversmith, one of the two in the
tribe, and some of his work—though of semi-barbaric design—
is wonderfully well done. But I shall have to wait to tell you
more of this place in my next; and this present necessity for
haste is apt to shut off my epistolary wind somewhat, anyhow. I
shall cross the line into Arizona in one hour. *A mas ver.*

                                                        LUM

Winslow, Arizona
Saturday, January 10th, 1885

Editors Leader:
  Well, I've been and gone and done it. Yes, verily, done it two
times. Truly a man never knows what he may do, and it's just as
well that he doesn't. Now if anyone had told me before I started
on this trip that I'd wind up with broken bones, I should have
laughed and told him it was very likely, but had he prophesied
that I would, of my own free will and accord, sell my pet meer-
schaum, I should have deemed and called him a measly idiot
and a long-legged liar. Yet he would have struck it straight on
the head in both instances. I have sold my pipe—a transaction
over which I have felt ever since as guilty as a young mother
who should barter off her first-born—and I have snapped a bone.
The one, however, has its compensations; the other hasn't.
Some elegant stuff consoles me for the dhudseen [?]; but if you
think it fun to tramp a heavy road with a ponderous pack and a

broken arm, just try it once. It's a regular picnic to be crippled that way when you're at home, with all the folks to wait on you and coddle you up; but to be out in the wilderness here, with nothing ahead but bare track and now and then a section-house, no one but yourself to rely upon, and every step a stab, that's a different breed of pups. However, broken bones will knit, so there's no use growling.

Well, first to the pipe. Mr. Clarke, the intelligent and pleasant post-trader at Manuelito, took a wonderful shine to the meer-schaum, which was the one presented to me by the Louisville Leaf Tobacco Co. He was not the first that got mashed on it during this trip; but he was the only one that talked seductively enough to move me. I had been looking at his Navajo truck, the beautiful blankets and quaint silver jewelry, and was getting as badly stuck thereon as he was on the pipe. So when he offered me my own price to trade, I clinched. And what do you suppose I acquired? Well, a big Navajo bed-blanket, woven from the native wool in their own inimitable style; a ditto saddle-blanket, of brighter colors; which will make an elegant table-cover or rug; and the following silver jewelry, which has a characteristic, semi-barbaric beauty; two graceful bracelets, a rude, heavy ring, two unique ear-rings, several wrist and leg ornaments (big discs of silver) and about 25 buttons made from dimes, quarters and halves. The silver alone in the jewelry weighs about 20; and the articles themselves are worth many times that. I could sell the whole outfit in the East for $50, any time; so we are both well satisfied, for on the other hand, Mr. Clarke has the finest pipe in New Mexico. All the jewelry by the way was made by the skillful brother of old Manuelito—the leading silversmith of the Navajos. The small blanket I sent West, but the large one—which weighs ten pounds and is pretty near a quarter of an inch through—is keeping me warm o'nights, and looks a deal tonier to pack than did the dingy looking article—now deserted—of American manufacture. On the whole, I feel as rich as a hog with two mouths.

A strange people are these Navajos. Living among the Pueblos, they are as different from them as night is from day. In place of the comfortable, neat, substantial Pueblo cities, they have no fixed and enduring habitations, but dwell here and there among the hills and valleys in *hogans,* or rude shelters built of pine branches and dirt, with one or more sides fully open to the weather. The Pueblos speak tongues of their own, and are also almost universally conversant with Spanish; the Navajos have only their own language, and it is a scanty one. The Pueblos live chiefly by a very fair scheme of agriculture, are cleanly (for Indians), honest, hospitable, and chaste; the Navajos are hunters and stock-breeders rather than farmers; dirty, thievish, treacherous and revoltingly licentious. In fact the one people are civilized beings, the others are still mere savages.

The Navajos number 18,000 and have a big reservation—mostly godforsaken desert, of course—lying half and half in north-western New Mexico and north-eastern Arizona. They are extensive stock-raisers and count among their possessions about 1,000,000 head of sheep and goats, 75,000 horses, and a few thousand cattle. They do not make pottery, but buy it from the more skillful Zunis and other tribes. Yet with all their barbaric condition, there is one industry in which they very easily lead the world, and that is—the manufacture of blankets. And when I say lead the world, I mean it. No other weavers on earth, with machinery or without, can touch them when it comes to making blankets. Blankets of every sort, for the saddle, the shoulders or the bed, they weave with their primitive looms; all colors from the dingy hue of the native wool to the brilliancy of imported fabrics. The materials vary as well. Some blankets—the cheapest—are made from the native wool, twisted by the Navajos themselves; and some from fine imported English yarn. But the finest are made from a thread obtained by raveling a brilliant red Turkish cloth called Bayeta. This costs them $3 per pound, and as some of the blankets made from it weigh from 15 to 20 pounds, you can see that it takes money to make them. A good Bayeta blanket costs from $10 to $100, according to size, color, weight and pattern.

And it is worth it. You never saw fabrics so brilliantly beautiful as some of these Navajo blankets, and surely none as durable. One cannot be worn out in a life-time; and you may fill one up with water and carry it a thousand miles, and not a drop will leak through. There are six blankets in Arizona, not one of which could be touched with $150.

In jewelry and silverware—they have no use whatever for gold—the Navajos fall far short, of course, of civilized artificers, but their work is well done, unique and highly interesting. You can buy their ordinary jewelry from them at—and often less than—its actual weight in silver; but if you order an article made by one of the silversmiths, of whom there are two, you will have to pay double that, a dollar for the work on every dollar of weight. Will Damon, the clever station-agent, at Manuelito, showed me a very beautiful set of table silver which Manuelito's brother had made for him. I would vastly prefer it to any American set that ever was fashioned. All these things are hammered out from American coin; the buttons from dimes, quarters and halves, and everything else from the silver dollars. Up at Houk's Tank, Thursday, I acquired a bracelet which simply captures the cake. Unlike the plain bands which snap over the wrist, this is a big plate, three inches square and curiously engraved, fixed upon a broad leather band which ties with buckskin thongs. It is one of the neatest things I ever saw.

If ever the masquerade fever catches me—as it isn't likely to—it will take only a wig and a little red paint to make a first-class big Injun of me, blanket, leggings and the whole queer toggery. The Navajos, as I have remarked, are awful hands to gamble. Monte is their game, and they are dead gone on it. That is the chief reason why their blankets and jewelry are obtainable at all. When a Navajo feels rich, you can't buy his property at any price; but the card-fever robs them of their most cherished treasures. Every trading post out along their reservation is a regular pawnshop, full of blankets, belts, guns, and jewelry "in soak" for the necessities of life or for money to gamble with. The ordinary dress of the tribe is a thin, bright-colored calico shirt—that is, once bright, but generally now dark with grease and dirt—a pair of long loose muslin drawers, smoke-tanned moccasins, and one of the coarse gray woolen blankets thrown about the shoulders. The women, in addition, have their legs cased in a sort of burlap leggin, worn above the moccasin and reaching from ankle to knee.

This is the every day rig; but on festal occasions such as dances, you will see a very different sight. The gay blankets are brought out and donned, the pounds after pounds of jewelry adjusted in every place where it can be hung, the plumed head-dresses put on and the ponderous silver belts buckled over the blankets. These belts are invariably made in the same style— oval discs (which pass current singly for $8 everywhere) strung upon a leather girdle. The engraving on these discs varies a little, but that is all. A Navajo has never got so far as to invent a square, round or diamond pattern.

Red, by the way, is *the* color among these Indians, though they use a good deal of the cheaper blue as a foil to the brighter hue. An amusing instance of this preference came to my notice at a trading post. The trader had a lot of soda, part in red papers and part in blue. If he handed out to an Indian one of the blue papers, it was no go; and not one of the blues could he sell until the reds were all gone—and then only under protest, as it were.

One thing about the Navajos that broke me up was the discovery that they couldn't sabe Mexicano. It was hard indeed to have rent so many undergarments in getting a tail-hold on the Spanish language, and then find it n.g. just where *I* most wanted to make myself understood.

The Navajo bucks are mostly tall, well-made warriors, but with faces to stop a clock. The squaws are rather tall for women, generally slender, have very small feet considering the amount of work they have to do, and faces a little less—but only a little less—ugly than those of the men.

One very noticeable fact is, that although the sale of firearms to the Indians is positively prohibited, two-thirds of the bucks wear six-shooters and belts of improved pattern, and many have Winchesters and other good rifles besides.

It is very fortunate that the kindred law forbidding the sale of liquor to the Navajos is better observed; for they are an ugly, treacherous, blood-thirsty set, with no love for the white man; and need only the alcoholic spark to kindle a flame that only blood could quench. However much some of the post-traders might like the big profits they could make by selling whiskey to the Navajos, they are restrained by a stronger motive than cupidity—the instinct of self-preservation. Nor do I think many of them sell firearms to the Indians, who procure most of their weapons from irresponsible travelers or Mexicans.

Among the many superstitions of the Navajos I find a curious fear of certain animals—as the bear, the coyote and the rattlesnake. These fellows, who are certainly not lacking in courage, will not touch nor eat bear meat, nor kill nor handle a coyote; and my snakeskin hat-band simply paralyzes them. It is bad medicine, and they keep a respectful distance from me, evidently deeming me a fighter from Bitter Creek.

The Navajo names are not particularly musical, and sound something like the utterances of a sprained accordion. Most of the chiefs are known by two names, one Mexican and the other Navajo. For instance, the Indian name of Maneulito is Tejano Badhani, which means "Texas Brother-in-Law." His squaw is Juanita, Assunni Manuelito—"Little Jane, the wife of little Manuel"—and this adding of the husband's name, as in civilized countries, prevails throughout the tribe. Another chief is named Klah, "the left handed." Klah is a brother of Manuelito, and the magnificent bronze Hercules I first met on Wednesday. Another is called in Mexican, "Ganadomuncho; With Many Herds;" and in Navajo "Tootsonahostene; Man of the Water Clan." The tribe, by the way, is divided up into many clans, varying greatly in size, and each under command of a chief. Juanito, or "Little John," is known at home as "Hostenoshkay, or Cross Man." Barbasueres, or Tagaslakeige, means the same in Spanish or Navajo—"White Moustache." My friend, Mr. Clarke, who is a Maine six-footer, is termed by the Indians, "Hostene Nase," or "Tall Man."

Well, as I could have prophesied a week ago, I am alone again barring Shadow, Brother Lockard's sand gave out at Manuelito, and there I left him, Thursday morning. After the pen picture I gave of him in a former letter, you may be sure I do not mourn deeply over the loss. A man of narrow ideas, no sense, and endless gall, I believe he was the most wearisome ass I ever had the misfortune to encounter; and I was just on the point of dissolving the copartnership violently when he providentially weakened. However, he had more nerve than any of his predecessors. Brother Phillips gave out in 38 miles, and Lockjaw— Lockard I mean—held out for 78. When I left him at Manuelito, he said he was afraid his shoes would give out before he got to the coast, so he guessed he'd better ride. I thanked him heartily for the resolution, to his great disgust, and came away light-footed.

From Manuelito I had some strikingly fine scenery and excruciatingly bad walking for the next 15 miles. Or rather, I had the fine scenery for 15 miles, and the infernal walking ever since. The little stream which the railroad follows from the summit of the Continental Divide—the Río Puerco of the West—runs almost continuously through a rough valley worn into the red sandstone. Some of the brilliant-colored mesas between Manuelito and Houk's Tank are scarcely less beautiful and wild than those which line the road from Bluewater to Wingate. But, oh, that walking! Four inches of snow on all the fields and over most of the track, and in the sun-made gaps, six inches of the Tom Nastiest, walking-stickiest mud I ever saw. The only possible way to get along was to walk the ties, and these were so slippery that I couldn't jump them, but had to take one at a time. And that, I can confidentially inform you, is hard work, when you keep it up for 10 or 11 hours. Soon after leaving Manuelito, my canteen went to leaking abominably, so I drank down its full contents and slung it away. Hereafter I shall trust to luck for something to soak my jaws with occasionally. It takes off a good deal off my load, too, for a gallon of water weighs considerable; and the change was duly appreciated since assuming the extra weight of my new blanket.

Well, Shadow and I poked along all day, Thursday, and late at night fetched up at Navajo Springs. I should have stopped there, but had lost considerable time already within the week, and my

Los Angeles date was staring me hard in the face; so as it was a better night than any in a long time I decided to press on. The wind and cold did a little to alleviate the mud, and we got along very cleverly in the clear starlight. There was nothing worthy of notice along the way, save the unusual number of trains—due to delays caused by a $10,000 wreck at Sanders, a few nights before. Along toward morning, I built a big fire in front of a hogan, and rolled up in my blanket for three hours' sleep. I had passed Billings, and the petrified forest which is 8 miles south of it, without stopping, for it was just beginning to dawn upon me with full force that to reach Los Angeles even by Feb. 7th, I must do some tall stepping, and furthermore I was in a hurry to get to Winslow for further mail. Just about daylight I awoke shivering, and crawled out. The day was cloudy and raw, threatening snow.

Not far down the track I spied the fresh tracks of a deer which could have crossed the road but little ahead of me, and off I went after him. It was the worst bargain yet. The tracks led up over a mesa, and I went around to the side, thinking to climb up and cut off Mr. Deer. Deer me! I got cut off myself. The rocks were ragged—a decomposing, shaly stuff, but I was bound to climb them, and at it I went. Half-way up the ledge, the rock upon which I was standing broke so suddenly that I had no time to catch on with my hands, and down I went 20 feet, nearly alighting upon Shadow, who was watching me worriedly. How he got out of the way I don't exactly know, but I do know I didn't fall on him—the cuts and bruises all over me are ample testimony to that. I sort of keeled over, I guess, for it hurt like fire, and when I got my head again my left arm was bent over between two sharp rocks and felt like a stocking-full of bumble bees.

I got to my feet like a man about 200 years old, crawled out to an open spot and sat down on my blanket to catch my breath. That arm felt so frumious that I began to get sour, and peeled off my two coats and rolled up my shirt-sleeves—every motion hurting like Bob Ingersoll's Nosuchaplace. Fun? Oh, certainly! The big bone of the arm was broken in a slant, and the lower sharp point I could feel through the skin. That was a rich mess for a man on such a trip as this and no notion of giving it up. But

I haven't been living all these years to learn to cry at my age, and I don't [know] what my cherished philosophy is good for unless just such cases.

I did curse the luck for a minute, but no more, and then got up to see what could be did. First I took the big canteen strap from my shoulder, wound it around my wrist and then a small cedar, and buckled it; then got up on a rock, shut my teeth and leaned back as hard as I could. That keeled me over again, for it hurt worse than the fracture itself, but it put the bone where it belonged, and that's what I was after. I don't think the little bone was broken, but cannot be sure. If it was, it is all right now. Then to keep the old thing in place I cut some sticks from a bush, held them in my teeth, whittled them smooth and curving to fit the arm, and then lashed them down with a pocketful of string. They make a pretty fair splint, too. Then I shouldered my traps and started back to the railroad.

I shall never forget that mile—its every step and stumble over the rough ground was like the tortures of the Inquisition. But at last the track was regained, and though walking was painful enough even there it was a red-lemonade picnic beside what had preceded. Two staves from an old keg beside the track made an immense improvement over my brush splints, and I made the change as fast as possible. Probably these details are dull enough to you, but they were powerful interestin' to me, and I mention them that you may understand how completely a man has to depend upon his own resources out here. So far as I can learn, there is not a doctor within 150 miles of that place. There is none even at Winslow, the biggest town in 400 miles.

Well, there I was hungry, faint, a little tired by the long walk, almost out of money and 52 miles to the nearest place where I could get any. It *was* tolerably hard times, but I felt mighty well content that things were no worse. Now if it had been my neck I should have felt justified in kicking like a gorgeous steer; and even had it been my right arm (which is also, of course, my write one) things would have been bilious. But only a left arm— pshaw! Who cares? I haven't any best girl out here to hug, so don't need two arms particularly. I shall be pretty apt to sleep with my clothes on for the next three or four weeks; but that won't bother me. Thank the Lord I've got some clothes to sleep in! But being thus knocked into a jug, with the handle all on one side, I have no particular use to tarry in this earthly paradise of mud, snow and rain any longer than the law requires; and you may put it on the ice as a bed-rock fact that I shall not. The necessity of getting somewhere at a gallop was particularly apparent when I struck the track after my misfortune, and I put on the spurs.

Of that 52 miles which followed, I have a very confused recollection. I remember widening valleys, decreasing hills, disappearing snow and undrying mud; now and then a lonely section-house, or the slow track workers who spoke to me curiously but kindly; the ceaseless barking of coyotes; the occasional roar of a passing train; a stop for a bread and butter lunch at one section house; the long, cold, drenching rain all day, and the chilling, comfortless night; and through all a chaos of aching legs, hollow stomach and throbbing head, with that arm dragging at my side, heavy as lead, and jumping like a hollow tooth.

That trip was undoubtedly the hardest job I ever undertook; and when at last, after more than 30 hours of continuous walking, I spied the big white station at Winslow, I was too nearly worn out to care much about it anyhow. When I staggered over to the post office at Winslow for my mail, I had traveled 113 miles in a trifle over 48 hours; nearly half of it with a broken arm, and all the way with a heavy load. There isn't gold enough in California to hire me to do it over again; but now it is all past and gone, I am glad it happened—one likes to know how much he can stand at a pinch, and I shall have one more lasting memory of the trip, pleasant in recollection if not in performance.

The accommodating postmaster stowed away about half a bushel of mail in my pockets, and I came over to the little "Arizona Central Hotel," a place which I shall remember with gratitude. A splendid dinner, a short nap and the perusal of my mail revived me, and by the middle of the afternoon I was

feeling as chipper as a game cock, though with one wing drooping. It was pretty good to find a lot of *Leader* awaiting me with
their Chillicothe news. I had had none for five or six weeks.
Then a lot of other papers, and a whole stack of letters from
valued friends, made me feel rich enough. *And* what do you
suppose? Why, a box of 35c. Havanas from the coast, and a big
bundle from thoughtful Phon Ireland containing a lot more of
the delicious weeds! Now that's what I call a royal finish of
good fortune. Who wouldn't be battered up, cold, wet, tired and
starved, for the sake of coming in and striking such fatness? I
would, every time. I'm like the boy who used to cut his finger
every now and then, "because it felt so good when it got well."
There can be no such thing as enjoyment unless we are able to
contrast it with pain; and I certainly got contrast enough at that
particular stage of my journey.

The only cloud upon my enjoyment was the presence of
Lockard, who turned up there again, more pig-headed, loud-
mouthed and disagreeable than ever. He had "beat" the train
from Manuelito, having imposed upon the conductor by some
pitiful tale or other, and felt proud of his "smartness." I hope the
Lord has private apartments in the future world for these obstreperous fools, where they can talk each other to death and
not paralyze anyone else. I should feel sorry to think that my old
friend, the devil, had to be bothered with them all. The devil my
friend? Why, certainly! One of the best I have. He lets me alone,
and I surely ought to be grateful for that. He can't do any harm
to white folks—it is to the wicked only that he is an enemy.

Winslow is a king town for this part of the country. It is about
the size of Hopetown, and is nothing but railroad, being the end
of the second division of the A. & P. It stands at the bottom of a
great basin between the Continental divide and the San Francisco Mountains, and has the lowest altitude of any point along
this route between Delhi, Col., and Peach Springs, Ar., a distance of 776 miles—excepting Isleta, which has the same
height, 4,808 feet. So, of course, it was quite summery, and the
snow which had waggled me for nearly 200 miles in a straight
line, had entirely disappeared there. Even the mud was pretty

well dried up, and despite some other drawbacks, that made me feel happy as a boy with his first long pants.

The failure of certain pecuniary mail to make connections with me there has kept me an impatient prisoner in Winslow, but the time wasn't wasted. Saturday afternoon I got off a three column letter, and Saturday night and Sunday morning two more besides numerous private epistles. Sunday noon, growing desperate at the non-arrival of my boodle, I telegraphed for some and sat down to take it easy. The pain in my arm has been enough to keep me from being very sleepy; but it is moderating now. With my perfect health and good blood the bone must knit very fast, and I shall be full-rigged again in a comparatively short time. Lockard left me again, Sunday night, going through to the coast in charge of a carload of other cattle. He doesn't owe me much, and I consider the money well spent, as it undoubtedly hastened his departure. I hope the Lord will watch over him— and not let him loose on me again.

I should have had a very good time in Winslow, but for the fact that I had to stay here when time was valuable. Everyone was very clever, and I made two or three real friends. Sunday, as I was writing away here at the Central House, a fat, jovial-looking young fellow picked up an old *Scioto Gazette* I had received, and remarked, "That's my town, or used to be." Whereupon we had a long and pleasant chat. My new acquaintance was George Martin, formerly of Chillicothe, Waverly and all around there. George drifted West in March, '77. He was on the A.T. & S.F.R.R. awhile, around Raton, and came down to twist wheels for the A. & P. the first of last December. He is now a freight brakeman running from Albuquerque to Winslow—296 miles—and looks round and contended as a ground hog. But he admits that in all his travels, nothing to equal the Scioto Valley has met his eye, and threatens to go back to the old home, sure, in the spring.

I am now past the Río Puerco, and on the Colorado Chiquito (Little Colorado). And speaking of this reminds me that I haven't seen a dam or any other such utilizations of water-power since I left Denver. It is doubtless because these measly little streams are not worth a dam. And for that matter, I have not seen or heard of a church—save among the Mexicans and Indians—since Albuquerque. I don't blame the Baptists much for staying away, but some of the other gospel-mills, that require less water, ought to be able to stand it.

This atmosphere, however, is not heavy with holiness being as light morally as barometrically, and perhaps the churches wouldn't thrive. All these little "towns" have more saloons than dwelling houses; and in many the juice-dispensatory is the only building beside the section-house. Here in Winslow the solid business men built and furnished a house and gave it to a prostitute; and are even now cursing the ungrateful thing because it burned down in 8 months and left them desolate. The leading merchant here is J. H. Breed, a gray-headed old fellow who hasn't yet wound up his business with the popular firm of World, Flesh & Devil. To give you a glimpse at him, and at the style prevalent hereabouts, I need only enclose the following certainly unique poster, which is to the point [see page 243]:

Well, I see by a *Leader* that you have been bothered about getting my letters in time, so I'll send this from here as it is about 60 miles to the next post-office. My long-awaited boodle came over the wires tonight, and I shall push on in the morning with all decent haste. My only important stop hereafter will be at the Grand Canyon of the Colorado. I shall leave the railroad at Daggett, Cal., and strike across the Mojave Desert to the coast. Shake hands with yourselves all around, and charge it up to my account. *Laben Sie viel.*

LUM

Peach Springs, Arizona
Tuesday, January 20th, 1885

Editors Leader:
   I die content. I have actually had two days of good walking through this month. Probably you won't believe it, but it's a fact. How the accident occurred, no mortal man can find out;

—STOP AND READ—

———

J.H. BREED

Having returned from Chicago with the

largest and

FINEST STOCK OF GOODS

Ever brought into Arizona, is prepared to

give the people of

—WINSLOW—

And surrounding country the

DAMNDEST BARGAINS

Ever heard of in this part of the World.

———

I Carry

A HELL OF A LARGE ASSORTMENT OF GOODS

Which space will not allow me to enumerate here,
but if you will hitch up, and call on the "OLD MAN,"
you can bet your shirt tail he will treat you right—
and sell you anything you may want in his line.

J. H. BREED*

Winslow, A.Z.

*During the 1870s, Justus K. Breed, sometimes called "Colonel" Breed,
established with a partner the Blanchard and Breed Trading Post, on the Little
Colorado River near Winslow. After the railroad was completed through Winslow in 1883, Breed erected several buildings in the town, made some money,
moved away and then returned to Winslow where he died in 1918. His obituary
identified his occupation as being a "capitalist." (Vada Carlson & Joe Rodriguez,
A Town is Born [Winslow, Arizona, 1981], pp. 13–14; Will C. Barnes, *Arizona
Place Names* [Tucson: University of Arizona, 1935]).

but I can guess. It's my private opinion that the Lord had to go out of town on business, and left the weather in charge of some unsalted cherub who didn't know any better than to make it pleasant. That is the only way I can account for it. It was evidently an error, and the boss rectified it as soon as he got home. I'll bet that cherub got a red-hot going over, too, for making such a break as to drop a chunk of summer down here. And still, I don't know as the Lord ought to blame him. His mistake shows that he is younger and didn't know any better. He'll get over it being clever, fast as he grows older—we all do. I'm going to take those two dates, when I get home with this trip, frame 'em and hang 'em up as curiosities. I shall also secure the affidavits of reputable parties along the road to the fact that those days *were* pleasant, and that the ground *was* dry. Without this precaution, I should be apt to think that my senses had deceived me, and that I had merely been fancying agreeable weather, while the snow was in reality sixteen feet deep.

As soon as I really knew that I need wait no longer in Winslow, a genuine affection for the measly place found lodgement in my breast. Still, Winslow is one of the things I am content to love and leave. I got acquainted with a lot of railroaders there— it is the end of a division—and several of them offered to carry me clear to the Needles in their respective engines or cabooses. But I gently said to them nay, and I undoubtedly acquired for myself thereby the reputation of a blooming crank. A man who would sooner walk than ride is looked upon with sinister suspicion. The people would think he preferred foot—locomotion is more convenient for robbing hen-roosts—if there were any such things as hens in this country, or any place for them to roost. I appreciated the friendliness of the offers, all the same, and will take them up some other trip.

I lit out of Winslow at 8:15, Tuesday morning, and hustled down the track in the cold, clear air. Far ahead of me towered the snowy range of the San Francisco Mountains, in whose recesses I knew I should meet trouble; but they were far off, and around me lay the fine valley, dry as a bone. The most noticeable peculiarity of the landscape right here, is that the whole

plane is red sand stone dust, broken in monotony by the insignificant mesas, and now and then a strange, conical knob, trun-
cated at the top. These knobs are not extinct volcanos, as one
would have first inferred, but merely water-worn remnants of
the former sand stone ledges. I have never seen just the same
formation elsewhere. Another thing that struck me as curious
was finding, on the hills for some miles from town, ledges of
something very much like white marble—a gypsum, I suppose.
Above this formation, and running through this loose soil—as
shown in the cuts—is a two inch vein of the beautiful "satin
spar." And on top, the hills are covered with grey flints.

It is enough to make a hen laugh to see how that railroad
wobbles straight up and down those hills for 25 miles beyond
Winslow. A profile of it would look something like the edge of a
saw. Each hill, however, is higher than those before it; and the
railroad is all the time gaining ground by those comical dents. It
[is] sort o' fun going over them, too, for you are better able to
gauge the distance than is usual in this deceptive country. We
skipped along in pretty lively fashion, to make up for that
aggravating delay, and now that it was no longer necessary to
walk on the ends of the ties in order to escape drowning, there
wasn't much work in knocking off the miles. I got a good
dinner—for a wonder—at Dennison, and then plugged away on
to Cañon Diablo, reaching that sulfurous-name station an hour
before sundown, after a pleasant, sunny trip of twenty-seven
miles. The section-houses—and that means the stations—on
this road, are now all about 13 miles apart; so by skipping one a
man gets a [day's] walk off just about the convenient and desirable length.

Unloading my traps at the station, I went on up to the canyon, half a mile beyond, and explored it until dark. It's truly a
remarkable freak. Right out in a plane as level as the streets of
Chillicothe, you come suddenly upon the brink of this great
abyss which is aptly christened "Devil's Canyon." Where the
fine iron bridge of the A. & P.—said to be the highest trestle in
the world—crosses it, the chasm is 225 feet deep and 520 wide.
It's walls are not perpendicular, but everywhere a series of rather

irregular terraces, rounded and scabbled by water. There is now
no stream at the bottom, which serves only as a channel for
semi-occasional storm-torrents, which flow through it to the
Little Colorado. The view from the bridge is a trifle disappoint-
ing, for it is impossible to credit the distance to the rocks
beneath; but climb down once to the bottom of that strange
gorge, as you may easily do, and look up. Then the effect is
remarkably impressive. You will find that the stone abutments,
which from above appear about the size of a carpenter's (horse),
are in reality 40 feet high in a proportionate base. The Canyon
runs its zig-zag course through the plain for many miles—I
don't know how many—and is everywhere about the same
unvarying, somber, lonely abyss. Within a mile beyond it, are
the beginnings of two other Cañon Diablos, one of which is
already over 100 feet deep. Give 'em time, and they'll both catch
up with "the old he one."

I had two good meals at the section-house—which is kept by
a very clever fellow with a notion for Indian curiosities—and
slept snugly in an easy chair beside the fire, finding this more
comfortable for my arm than a bed on the floor. Mr. McAlister,
the boss, furnished me with a handsome specimen of a remarkable Moqui basket work. If anybody can beat these strangest of
the Pueblos in making baskets from split fibers of the moli, or
soap-root, I should like to know it. That is all they do make,
however; and baskets are the distinctive stock and trade of the
Moquis, as blankets of the Navajos, and the fine pottery of the
Acomas and Zunis. Well, that was one of my good days, and it
was appreciated, you may be sure.

Next morning, however, dawned with snow in the air; and by
noon, when I had climbed well up the steep Cosnino Divide, I
was half-frozen and well-wet. I got badly fooled on dinner which I
expected to strike at the station alleged by that dod-gasted A. &
P. folder to be Angell. But when I got up there, having appeased
my stomach by liberal promises of an immediate filling, Angell
proved to consist of a five by ten coal shed and a side-track. I hope
that sort of Angell visits will indeed be few and far in between.
Over at Cosnino, however, I built a howling fire in a little shanty,

ate a big lunch, and felt more at peace. There are some relics of the strange cliff-dwellers near Cosnino, lying back in the mountains. I wanted the worst way to see them, but the snow was 2 feet thick through the pathless woods, and that settled it. I can't afford to catch cold just now. So I reluctantly turned my back on these interesting and unique homes of a forgotten race, and plodded on through the snow to funny [?] Flagstaff.

All this time, you must remember, I was getting up into the deep forest and wild recesses of the San Francisco Mountains. In crossing Arizona from east to west, you must pass over two great divides. The eastern one, and the least noticeable, is the continental, which I have already mentioned. It does not appear mountainous, but it is more like a gigantic ridge-pole. The western, or Arizona Divide, is formed by the San Francisco range, the noblest mountains in the territory. Some of their peaks are over 13,000 feet in height, and as wildly picturesque in contour as any of their northern brethren.

This is the only part of the country since the beginning of my trip which has looked familiar to me; but I could easily mistake a scene in the San Francisco Mountains for a little piece of Old Maine, save for one thing—the absence of the innumerable crystal brooks and lakes which beautify the Pine Tree state. There are the rocky slopes, the dark glades, the spar-like giant pines, the deep snow, and even the same game. All through the woods are countless tracks of every sort, from the rounded triangle of the Brer Rabbit to the great, trailing, barefoot prints of the lumbering bear. The hard beaten run-ways of the black-tailed deer; the alternate, dainty paw marks of the great mountain lion, and the smaller ones of the wild-cat; the dog-like trail of the coyote, and of the foxes little and big—all of these are there, and many more. I tell you, it does a hunter's heart and eyes good to see "those signs" in the snow among the tall, dark evergreens, even if he can't go out and rustle after the makers of the same. It wakes all the wild desire that has come down to us from the days when our forefathers lived by bow and arrow; when meat was the only food, and the passion for the chase was the essence and the guarantee of life.

I cut across the woods a little, going on up to Flagstaff, but without realizing anything for my great expectations. Flagstaff is the "swear by" of the A. & P. road, and is the busiest metropolis along the line. There must be 100 or 150 people right there, which is something heavy in this country. The little slab town lies far up among the pine forest, 6,935 feet in altitude, and is the coldest place around, unless it be Bellemont. The only industry in Flagstaff (aside from the saloons, which always flourish in this country) is lumber; and there are several pretty good-sized saw mills, which do a good business. I am told that the pines of the San Francisco forests make poor lumber, being too brittle. Flagstaff has one paper—a weekly—which some of us may envy. It is about the size of the "greaser," and has the gall to charge and the luck to get it, five dollars a year for itself.

Until I got up to the Cosnino Divide, I thought that straights must count on this road. For 100 miles the track streaks along in straight lines from 5 to 12 miles long, broken by obtuse angles. A straight road would be a good deal shorter, but you can't save any appreciable distance by cutting corners, the angles being so small and the straight stretches so long. But since Wednesday noon, all that has passed away, and the road goes winding through the mountains and down the sinuous valleys.

A dozen miles west of Flagstaff the road climbs to the summit of the Divide, balances there a moment 7,345 feet above the sea, and then pitches down rapidly toward Williams. The same scenery followed me all Thursday. Indeed it fringes the road for 50 miles. This time it did me more good, however. Despite the warning contained in the bandana sling around my neck, I couldn't keep out of those woods, but pranced about in them at every excuse. Wherever the railroad made a long bend—and it was pretty often—I would cut across over the hills, knee-deep in the snow, six-shooter in hand, with ears pricked up, and thinking of everything but my crippled condition. Perhaps a dozen of these trips were n. g. ["no good"], but at last I connected. I was toiling laboriously up a steep and thickly wooded slope, and coming over the sharp top, I almost stepped on a big deer! There were probably others about, but I didn't see anything but this noble buck not 20 feet away from me—even before he threw up his noble head and gathered his long body for a terrific leap. But he was too late. Before he had left the ground I had one bullet in him; and kept pumping the rest as fast as the old thing would work. He made a few desperate plunges, and then fell on his knees not 50 feet from where I first saw him.

I nearly broke my neck running down to him, and was greatly elated to find that of my six shots, five of them had taken effect. One ball—presumably the last—had passed clear through the head, from ear to eye, and another must have tickled the heart a little in its course. Talk about bull luck! What better would you want than to roll over such a beast as that 200 pounder, with no other weapon than a revolver? I might hunt a 100 years, and never again get near enough to a black tail for such work. It did gall me, though, to leave that splendid carcass out there in the wilderness for coyotes and ravens, but there was no help for it. The best I could do was to carve out three or four pounds of juicy steak, and wrap it in a piece of skin, which then went into my pocket.

Then I wanted the horns. That buck was no chicken, for the spikes on his antlers counted off seven years. I had tried to tote a handsome pair of five year old horns—given me by old Manuelito's brother—and had found them too much bone to carry, so I gave them away. But these were mine by conquest, not by gift, and that made a difference. Those antlers must hang in my sanctum upon the coast; but how to get them off was the next problem.

My efforts to hack them off with my hunting-knife were something like stabbing a turtle with a feather; and if the buck had been alive and had accidently found out that I was pecking at his skull, it would doubtless have irritated him. Invention, however, is the chicken of necessity, and it didn't take long to hit upon a successful scheme. I loaded up the six-shooter, got face to face with the head, and drove bullets into that skull until there was a circle of holes around the horns, and finally pulled them out with a chunk of bone uniting them. If you can find a handsomer pair of the same variety, I'll swallow these whole.

It was away late at night when I hobbled down the snow-bound track into Williams'; and everything was shut up so I kept on along the reascending grade towards Supai, and about two miles beyond Williams' found a hotel of [railroad] ties to suit me. The whole track is lined with piles of ties cut from the surrounding forest, and here and there the passing tramps have built them into little cubby-houses, some of which are tolerably snug. I struck one that was dry inside, rather tight and well-protected, and here raised my Ebenezer for the night. With the big hunting knife as an ax I slivered a lot of kindling, and soon was drying my feet and clothing at a roaring fire of ties, whose warmth filled my castle delightfully. Then three pounds or so of venison—roasted on the side of a tie near the fire—made a small supper, but a good one, though without salt or bread. I have a modest idea that I could have eaten the whole deer if he had been right on the spot.

As for Shadow, he was in no mood for eating. His usually invisible waist bulged out as if he swallowed a beer keg, and well it might. He had eaten enough of that deer to make a pretty sizable fawn, and for the first time since I have had the not unalloyed pleasure of his acquaintance had got to a point when he couldn't eat any more. The spirit, indeed, was willing, but the flesh was plum full. He went through the motions, chewed and chawed; but when he tried to swallow it, it was no go. He was loaded to the muzzle, and felt content the rest of the day to trot along at my heels, instead of sniffing over every rod of ground within a mile, as he usually does.

That was a mighty pleasant night up on the wintry side of Bill Williams' mountain, in the little tie pen, and I shall not forget it soon. The big supper settled with a 35 cent Escepcionale [cigar], the dozing revery beside the ruddy fire, and last of all the heavy Navajo blanket spread on a bed-stead of two dry ties, I tell you, it was "a way up." The snow lay two feet deep outside, the wind at this altitude of 7,000 feet whistled down the mountainside drearily, but none of it touched me. I was high, dry, full, warm and happy as a catfish in a mud hole.

It would have been money in the pocket of the A. & P. R. R., however, if the Lord had missed a day and never finished that piece of country from Williams' to twenty miles west of it. The profile of the road between those two points looks like the two sides of a house-roof. From Williams' to Supai the grade is about 90 feet; but going down the western slope it is 137 feet to the mile for ten miles. It takes two stout engines and a mammoth "pusher" to take a train of 18 cars eastward over that pitch.

Between Crookton and Chino the track winds down the rocky fastness of Johnson's Canyon, as wild a bit of scenery as you will often see, though on too small a scale to be really grand. The road runs along a narrow shelf cut in the rocks, with a quick-bed hundreds of feet below on the left, and rugged cliffs rising in equal distance to the right. Here, too, is the only tunnel on the whole road, and no great shakes of a tunnel, either. Wouldn't the Cincinnati Southern give it's boots to be in the same fix?

This Bill Williams' mountain, by the way, is a historic spot. It takes its name from the famous scout who met his death among its rocks, at the hands of the savage Apaches. Bill had his hiding place in a cave up on the mountain, and here the red skins beseiged and finally starved him out—but not until he had made 37 of their number bite the dust. The old man had good grit, anyhow, and died like a great wolf. There is a curious natural pillar of rock, 30 or 40 feet high, near the scene of his death-struggle, and this is known as "Bill Williams' Monument."

Johnson's Canyon furnished me further sport, and with time and two arms I fancy one might scare up pretty fat hunting here. Down below the tunnel I got a glimpse of two wildcats springing over the rocks, and of course had to get after them. I suppose nothing short of a broken neck will ever hold me down when there is game around. After following the bobtails half a mile over the rocks, I got one, but missed the other, though I had a far better show for him. Shadow, who has as little sense about such things as his master has, wanted to jump on those cats with both feet. I half wish I had let him, just for the fun of seeing him jump off. No dog on God's big gooseberry patch has any more business with a wildcat than I would have to buck a locomotive off the track bare-headed; and most dogs know it without a directory. Those that don't know it to start with, learn mighty soon, and the lesson leaves them looking like a heap of hash on four legs. But I want to take Shadow to the coast with me, and so called him back. He don't know, even yet, what a circus he missed.

Maybe it was a soft snap, though, to skin my game! Any expert will tell you that there is nothing harder to flay than any of the cat kind, even when you can put two hands to the job. This is partly because of the shape of the animals, and partly because the hide adheres much more firmly than in most brutes. Of course, I couldn't case the skin; and in fact it was only after a tremendous amount of grunting and perspiration that I got it off by splitting. Never could have done it, though, if I had worn false teeth! Well, the skin is a good one, and will pay me for my trouble when I get it lined with a piece of red army cloth and spread it on my floor.

From the canyon on westward, things improved rapidly. You are pitching down hill all the time at a pretty good grade; and the effect is of course the same as traveling southward. You can pass from the climate of Labrador to that of Alabama in two days of easy walking—and you may deliberately back it up with your last copper that I was mighty glad to strike Alabama. After passing Aubrey you will see no more snow, save on distant peaks; and I trust that there my feet packed the last snow that they will touch for many a year. Snow is good in its place, but I am no sleigh, and bare ground is good enough for me. The road now slides down narrow, smooth, pleasant valleys, whose sole drawback seems to be lack of water. And by the way there is less water out here than a flea could spit at a jump. The Lord didn't even leave enough for seed. Now from Challender, up on top of the San Francisco Mountains, down to the Truxton Canyon it is 112 miles, and there isn't a drop of water along the road except at Williams' and there it dries up, the first warm day.

All these little section-houses have barrels half-buried inside the track; and a freight train comes along every day and fills these from big tank-cars. Even at the lively town of Peach Springs, the end of the division, there is no water; and the supply has to be pumped from a spring back in the hills, 4½ miles away, and 990 feet lower than the town. Well, that makes one thing sure; you'll never hear of a suicide by drowning along here. And another curious little fact has struck me—I haven't seen any overhead bridge across the railroad since leaving Kansas City. So the brakemen out here don't get much exercise bowing to low bridges. Let one of them go back east, and I expect he would ram his head into about 40 bridges before he'd get acclimated.

But the lot of the railroader out here doesn't strike me as a peculiarly happy one. They get better pay, it is true, than on eastern roads; but they have to earn it. I was paralyzed to learn that they are now running (the freight brakemen) from Winslow to Peach Springs and back—360 miles—for a single trip! That takes them about 3 days; and in that time they get no sleep, and mighty oncartin [uncertain] rations. Passenger engineers are running from Winslow to The Needles and back—580 miles for one trip. Of course, all this is extra work, and brings extra pay; but pay or no pay, it's a dog's life and will break down an iron man in time—not a long time, either. I don't believe I'm afraid of work, but you can't sell me any such job as that. Sleep and grub aren't the only objects of life, but they do come in sort o' handy as often as once or twice a year.

This A. & P. road, by the way, has surprised me more than a little. I used to suppose that it was a tuppenny narrow-gauge; but it is, on the contrary, a fine standard—probably the best new road in the far West. It was built in 1881, reaches 575 miles (from Albuquerque, N.M., to The Needles, Cal.,) and is a good piece of work throughout. It has first class rolling stock, and some of the finest locomotives in the country. Since taking the Mojave branch of the Southern Pacific, last December, this road has been doing a tremendous freight business; and at the present tariff the sums realized must be enormous. There is a pretty heavy passenger business, too, almost entirely immigrants going out to locate in California—which seems to be at present the general Mecca.

For the first 400 miles the road has about the finest section-houses to be found anywhere; but west of Williams' the prosperity seems to have petered out. There are no more section-houses nor stations—save at Peach Springs—in the whole 197 miles to The Needles. What is there, you ask? Why, at each "town" there are 3 or 4 old box-cars, fixed up in more or less habitable style, as kitchen and bunk cars. That's where the boarding bosses, the section men, the agents and the operators live, move and have their being. I don't know why this state of things prevails at this late date. The road ought to carry a pound or two more freight, and devote the proceeds to putting up respectable buildings.

But if there are any files on this company when it comes to gilt-edged, brass knuckled, long-metre lines, just let me know by return mail. If old Ananias [Biblical figure struck dead for lying; Acts 5:1–5] could come back and read the A. & P. folder which I hold in my hand, he would blush till the blood ran out of his fingertips. Lie? Why, the prevaricating genius who gets up these circulars can lie faster than a dog can trot. In the first place, this road is willfully and feloniously asserted to be "the sunshine route—no snows, no burning sands, no simoons." Well, that's all right. Probably this two feet of stuff I have waded through for a couple hundred miles wasn't snow at all; I reckon it was condensed milk or vanilla ice cream. I am only sorry I didn't think to eat some while it lasted. Then that thrilling piece of fiction, (the folder), goes on to remark "the track is well built with heavy steel rails and rock ballast." Steel rail "goes," but the man that tells about the rock ballast of the A. & P. ought to tell just one more of the same brand and then die. There isn't ten miles of rock ballast on the whole road—the only place where it occurs at all being in the cuts where stone had to be used unless they went to the expense of hauling in dirt from outside. Everywhere else the ballast is earth—sometimes sand, sometimes gravel, sometimes unadulterated mud.

Next, this able-bodied twister of truth's tail takes his pen in hand to inform a gasping world that "the whole of the country traversed by this road is very picturesque and beautiful." So is the whole of a blind pig. There *are* beautiful and picturesque interesting places along the road, and a goodly number of them; but they are a few beads strung on the thinnest cord ever spun. Why, out in some of these long stretches, the devil himself wouldn't stay—he'd break for home at a full gallop, to get into something cheerful again.

Of the road's 575 miles, I figure that 300 is through a country besides which Gehenna would be a regular beer garden again. "The grazing areas in Arizona are supplied with good water." So they are, genial liar, so they are. That is to say, where there is good water there are grazing areas; but that is, as I have remarked, only about once in 50 or 100 miles. The poor miners on the spot would like to discover "the marvelous mines of Hackberry, where the ores are very rich." No one ever saw the richness except for this gimlet-eyed romancer of the A. & P., but this is a dangerous thing. I may want a free pass sometime, myself; and truth is just as safe, often times, under a bushel. All is, if anyone throws one of those folders at you, don't swallow it whole. The exuberance of its imagination might swell up in you and crowd your inner consciousness.

Aside from the pleasure of decent weather, I had no further experiences of note until Peach Springs, which ended Sunday's tramp. This is the nearest point to the Grand Canyon of the Colorado, and here of course I had to halt. I started out next morning over the hills to the north of the little saloon town, having a pocketful of provender, and no other luggage except the big blanket. A couple of miles out, the road jumps over a little hill and starts deeply down into a gigantic ravine—the Peach Springs Wash, and *not* the Diamond Wash, as that folder again perjures itself by asserting. Down, down, down, goes the rough and winding road, now cut into the sloping hillsides, and now following the dry bed of the supposititious creek.

We passed the little pumping house whence Peach Springs is watered, and a mile beyond were startled by seeing some "really and truly" springs in the valley. The sight of running water in this country is so unusual that a man is cautious about speaking of it—he doesn't know but what he has got 'em again. They are honestly there, however, for I sampled them pretty extensively. Thus far down the wash, the enclosing hills have been rapidly growing higher, but there is nothing unusual about their shape.

As you turn the corner of a small cliff beyond the last spring, however, there opens out before you a beautiful park, covering thousands of acres, and walled by an irregular and broken circle of strange mountain shapes. These great mesas—for such, really, are all the "mountains" you will see in that section—rise from the plain in smooth slopes at first. Then comes a perpendicular wall of rock; then perhaps a shorter and steeper slope, and another stone escarpment. So the foundation is really a vast combination of terraces, water-carved from the dull, brown sandstone—which is about the only rock you will see anywhere in the walls or washes of the Grand Canyon. The rocky bastions of these mesas hardly ever present a face square; most of them, in fact, are circling; and the general appearance of the walls in the first park is much like that of a giant block of houses with [false?] fronts. A long turn of the road around a giant promontory brings us at last to the second park, and here the scene again changes. The slopes at the foot of the cliffs are obliterated, and instead of one or two small terraces, the great cliffs tower 2,000 feet in an apparent perpendicularity. They are really terraced also; but you won't know that, unless you see them in profile.

For over 15 miles you travel down a nearly straight channel, though of course the road winds about a good deal, to accommodate itself to the rough ground. I believe one need not go farther than the middle of the Peach Springs Wash to find grander scenery than he could find anywhere outside of this section. It would seem to me at the time that in making the Grand Canyon of the Arkansaw the Lord had put in just about his best licks; but now I shall have to beg his pardon. This wash, which is merely the entrance to sublimer glories, discounts anything in

Colorado. It's wild, strange cliffs loom taller, statelier, more marvelous in configuration, at every step. Here stands a vast temple, whose towers and pinnacles break the blue sky 3,000 feet above your head. Yonder is a gothic castle, as tall and as imposing, and beyond it a palace of rich design and profuse ornamentation, within whose great walls a city might lie uncrowded. I could think of nothing else than that I stood in the streets of some great city of the gods—a capitol of all Olympus. Insensate water surely never carved this marvelous architecture, by undesigning chance. Man might go to work and in a thousand years build something with smoother and more regular walls, but he never could approach the grand but simple majesty of these giant piles.

Twelve miles of this ever-growing splendor, and you come to the banks of the little stream which ripples musically between the wondrous cliffs of the Diamond Wash. The canyon you have thus far been descending ends abruptly here, it's further progress blocked by a gigantic pyramidal dome of roseate rock. The Diamond Wash intersects it at right angles, and is it's outlet to the river. The sun was down behind the left-hand walls as I reached the little shanty "hotel" between the brook and began to stumble painfully down the latter's rocky bed; but the rock-hewn citadels and temples, domes and watch towers at my right were glorified by the ruddy western glow, which

> Lingered caressingly, as if God's hand,
> In radiant benediction rested there.

For another mile we toiled along, clambering over rocks, leaping the swift brook a score of times—and there are pleasanter things for me, just now, than a long, jarring jump—followed by the short, sharp angles of the Diamond Creek Canyon. We were less than 1,000 feet above sea level; and from the cold snows of two days before, had come into the tropics. All down along the wash, our way wound among the tall, graceful forms of the "woodstock cactus" or past the bristling rotundity of the large "barrel cactus." But now, on that last mile, the bushes were in full leaf, the spaces of sandy soil carpeted with soft green grass, here and there a tiny flower lifted its pink head. And at last, where the cliffs shrank wider apart, a vast rocky wall, 6,000 feet in the air, stood grimly facing us; and the shrill treble of the brook was drowned in a deep, horse baritone that swelled and swelled in volume as we climbed the barricade of loose boulders thrown up by the greater stream against the encroachments of the less. The red flush of sunset was on the sky and on the dizzy peaks as we strode out upon the high bank of fine white sand, and sank in silence beside the noble Río Colorado.

The river rolls out majestically from behind an angle in the eastern walls, pauses a moment to form a tiny lake in which the giant cliffs may see their deep reflection, and then goes soaring off again into deeper abysses over the debris swept in by the tributary stream. We sat there dumbly as the light faded from cliff and sky, and night came drifting down the soft, sweet air. Even the trifling pup was impressed and awed by that scene. He dared not leave my side, but crouched trembling and ill at ease with his head upon my arm. I did not start out to describe to you the Grand Canyon of the Colorado. Whatever may be your private opinion, I'm no fool, and there are some things which only a fool dares attempt. Why, the Lord himself couldn't describe that place. The best he could do was to put it there and let you see it for yourself—and that is what you must do if you would have any conception of it whatever.

Well, I dragged together a huge pile of driftwood and built a roaring fire on the soft sand. In half an hour I moved the fire, scooped a big hollow in the dry and heated sand, spread my blanket therein, whooped up the fire close by, rolled myself and Shadow in the blanket, and raked the sand in over us up to our necks. And there we slept, beside the turbid river whose hoarse growl filled the night; and under the grim shadow of the great cliffs whose flat tops were more than a mile above our heads. The night was warm and still, but it was hard to shut the eyes on such a scene.

Before daybreak, I was up, and climbing the rough sides of a cliff beside Diamond Creek; it was a slow, painful, dangerous job, that climb of 5,000 feet, but it's reward lay at the top. From the enormous lookout the eye ranged across a sweep of the world's most marvelous scenery. For probably 100 miles the glance takes in the great workshop of the Colorado—that indescribable wilderness of peaks broken by the windings of the greatest and the grandest of canyons. Far below, you catch the occasional glimpses of the river, a tiny ribbon of steel, and at a depth below your feet as great as the distance from Chillicothe's court house to Frey's corner. As far as choice goes, I should still be on that dizzy pinnacle of rock; but there are other things I have to consult just now. So we came down—and if the ascent was a terror, the descent was far more so. I expected every minute to break my blessed neck. But we "arriv" safely at the bottom, passed an hour in explorations of the wonderful Diamond Wash, and turned our faces up the steep road toward Peach Springs.*

At all events, there is no discount on the sublimity of the Grand Canyon, and if you want the biggest sensation in life, you should go and see it. They will charge you $10 to ride over there, and about $5 per day for all the time you are at the little hotel, but it is worth it. I made out on a dollar, however, and consider myself "way ahead of the game."

But this is an elegant sufficiency for the present. Time's precious to me now, or I'd talk you blind. Yes, the arm is doing very well, thank you. Still pretty painful, but improving fast, and will be tolerably hardy by the time I get it to the coast. Bye-Bye.

LUM

*Here Lummis claims to quote Charles Nordhoff, author of *California for Health, Pleasure, and Residence,* on the wonders of the Grand Canyon. He attributes the following description of the canyon to Nordhoff: "If you do not feel a greater sense of the awful and sublime than ever before in your life, then die!" No such comments appear in Nordhoff's book. This is an early instance of a problem which would become more pronounced in later years: Lummis' compulsion to distort, exaggerate, and even to lie in his printed works. The tendency eventually cost him dearly in respect among historians of the twentieth century, respect which he had desperately sought throughout his lifetime.

Mojave Desert near Daggett, California
Wednesday, January 28th, 1885

Editors Leader:
"The land of perpetual summer"—that's a poetical name for
this country I am in. A practical and accurate title would be,
"the land of general hell." Talk about bad lands, wildernesses,
and abomination of desolation! Why, I never would have supposed that if the Lord had taken a hair sieve and strained a
country to get out all the goodness, He could have left anything
so indecently and outlandishly worthless as this Mojave Desert.
It's a wonder to me that the very tarantulas don't commit suicide by hanging, sooner than stay in this hideous spot. But I
reckon a tarantula is just about devil enough to enjoy it.

Do you have any real idea what a desert means? I don't intend
to insinuate that you haven't read about deserts in your geogra-
phy, but that is not knowing what they are. Nor is it knowing, to
travel across on the cars—though then you begin to get a faint
idea. But take the dry gravel bank which allies Major Mason to
the City Council; catch that by the ends and stretch it out until
it is two hundred and fifty miles wide, and a thousand miles
long; take from it all water, grass and shade; send down a sun
heat of 100 to 130 degrees, until the sand is like molten lead;
send out winds that shall whirl that sand aloft by the thousand
tons and bury in it whatever lies in their path; people it with
naught but venomous creatures; and then you will have—no
idea at all about it. I can't tell you, either. If you want to know
what a desert is, come out and walk across this one. To try to
make anyone really comprehend the meaning of that simple
word of six letters, by any description, would be as senseless as
the way folks fix out the whole programme of what heaven is,
when none of them ever did see it, and most of them never will.
It is a subject on which language doesn't even graze the skin.

Let's see—I left you at Peach Springs, didn't I? Bad place to
leave you, too, for it is the chief stamping ground of the Huala-

pai (Walla-pie) Indians, the nastiest human beings I ever saw.
Ugly in form and feature, slovenly in dress and intolerably
filthy in person—I should hate to have any of my friends left
where they had to look at such disgusting creatures. It is provi-
dential that stock-raising hasn't as yet progressed very far in
that section. Any sober, steady-growing cow, of family intentions, would look at just one of those Hualapais and have a
miscarriage forthwith. These Indians are as worthless as a pair
of last year's linen pants. They don't make blankets, pottery, or
anything else, and their only industry seems to be prostitution.
The only hunting I ever knew them to do is upon one another's
head's, and the game captured there is esteemed by them the
greatest of delicacies. It always belongs, by the way, to the man
on whom it ranges, and his companions are obliging in helping
him in the chase. But I need not go farther with this ticklish
topic—enough has been said to give you an idea of the personal
attractions of a Hualapai.

By the way, you have heard, of course, of the wonderful expedition of Major Powell in boats through the Grand Canyon of
the Colorado. No journey was ever more be-written and be-
bragged. Well, I find out on the spot, people grin sardonically
when that trip is alluded to in their presence. There are lots of
men around Peach Springs who are keen to swear that Powell
took his boats from the river there, and never went down the
rest of the Canyon at all. If that is so—and it looks very plaus-
ible to me—there are several pretty highly-colored books which
will have to be re-written one of these days.

Well, starting out from Peach Springs, I entered upon an era of
good weather which I shall always remember gratefully. The air
was soft as summer, the ground hard and dry, and my feet just
seemed to skim along without touching. The road goes curving
down a wonderfully crooked valley among the lava-beds, making about twenty-five turns—and sharp ones—to the mile. That
sort of thing keeps up for seven or eight miles; and then the
valley opens out into a pleasant plain, in which there are several
ranches. These are a long way back from the railroad, however,
and did me no good.

It was not until Truxton that I found a place to fill an already aching void. Now perhaps you think Truxton is some Arizona metropolis, plumb full of saloons and sich-like. Well, it isn't. The city consists of two box-cars—in one of which the section-men sleep, while in the other they are fed by a German boss and his Mexican wife—a side-track and two water-barrels. It satisfied my purposes, however, for I got a filling dinner there. Thirteen miles more brought me to the town of Hackberry, where I tarried briefly to look over the mining section there. The camp is three years old, and the town one. There are three or four paying mines there, but nothing extravagant. The mineral is not high grade, and there isn't a great deal of it. The town, however, is a pretty good one for this country, has about a score of passable houses, stores, saloons, etc., and a dozen tents. There is water there—in wells—and some springs lie not far off, so of course there is considerable cattle and sheep ranching done in the vicinity. The place is on the banks of a dry creek called the Truxton Wash, which I had been following nearly all the way down from Peach Springs.

Back in a canyon 8 miles east of Hackberry, by the way, I saw the first running water beside the track since leaving the Río Puerco at Houk's Tank, 290 miles back. It was but a tiny stream, however, and ran only about a mile in sight, and then sank back into the sand. Along this same "wash," also, I had passed, that afternoon, a fine little farm some five miles east of Hackberry. Two eastern hustlers came out there a year ago, took up a homestead, fenced it in with brush, dug a well, put in a wind-pump, and now have about 20 acres of fine land cleared, irrigated and under cultivation, raising garden truck for the surrounding country. They were ploughing a new field as I came along, which seemed odd enough in the middle of January. A lot of their stuff was up, and looked finely—especially to one fresh from the deep snows and severe cold of the San Francisco mountains. Their little place looked as neat as one of your market gardens on the northern bank of Paint creek, and was the only oasis I have seen in 600 miles of practical desert.

The end of Wednesday's pleasant but thirsty thirty-six mile tramp brought me to Hualapai, another section-house on wheels. Three inhospitable dogs flew out and mounted Shadow with tooth and toe-nail, and I began to think this mightn't be a very rich place for the tramps. But you can't most always sometimes tell. I went into the kitchen car, and applied to the kind-faced Irishwoman there for supper and a chance to sleep beside the fire. (I had shipped my blanket, by the way, finding it too great a burden for one arm all through the long, hot day.) Mrs. Kelley—for that was the landlady's name—bustled around to get some fodder, while two bright boys proceeded to fill Shadow to the brim. As I sat down, she noticed my arm in its sling, and asked, "Phat's the matter wid yer hand?" I told her, and her big, Irish heart just reached out to me. "Och, the poor lad! The poor, brave lad! Out in this wicked country wid a broken arrum. Poor lad!" And she rushed off to get me some pie meant for the men's dinner, and other section-house delicacies, bound to sooth my stomach if she couldn't mend the arm—which I really believe pained her worse than it did me. I ate a generous meal, smoked a soothing pipe, and passed a long evening writing at the big table, or talking with my warm-hearted hostess, and her two boys. Then she dragged me in her own mattress from her lodging car, brought a big silk quilt, and made me as cozy a bed upon the floor as one could ask.

In the morning, after a good breakfast, I tried to pay her for my entertainment, but she would have none of it. In vain I told her that I had plenty of money, and didn't want anything without paying for it. She only said, "No, it's not myself that'll take the first cent from ye, ye poor lad. Ye'll need it if ever you get out of this sad place." Well, if I could hold on to a prayer with the two-hour grip of some people, I'd certainly give the Lord an earache in behalf of honest, kind-hearted Mrs. Kelley, of Huala-pai Siding. But this tobacco-burning has broken the edge of my wind, and furthermore, my Irish friend isn't one of the kind that need much praying for. If the Lord knows His business half as well as I reckon He does, He'll have the front rooms and the first

table in the heavenly hotel saved for just such folks. The only
trouble will be to get enough of them to make a fair party. Now,
in one way, her kindness was wasted, for I had the wherewithal
and the disposition to pay any bill she could have presented; but
in another way it was like an angel's visit. I have gone far past
the hospitable belt now; and to find out here among the sharks
and misers, whose sole life aim is to skin their fellows, this
little green oasis of kindly and spontaneous sympathy touched
my heart wonderfully. I know a lot of high-toned "ladies" who
will have to scrub that poor Irishwoman's floor in the next
world, if their little souls didn't get lost in slipping through the
key-hole of heaven.

Next morning I was off bright and early, streaking it up the
stiff grade toward Kingman in the cold crisp air. The nights and
mornings all through this country are cold enough to make a
fire indispensable, no matter how hot the days may be. I find it
so, even out here in this desert, where at midday, even in January, the heat is rather oppressive. It's a good scheme, too, and
away ahead of the Eastern style of summer nights, in which you
toss and sweat and fume and cuss the heat and mosquitoes, and
think you are going to die, and are afraid you won't. But, I can't
see quite the same perfection in these cold nights, now that I
have no longer a blanket.

I got over to Kingman in short meter and was agreeably
surprised in the little town, which is really about the most
prosperous-looking along the whole line of the A. & P. in Arizona. It has a row of excellent stores—one of which would size
up pretty well alongside of any grocery in Chillicothe. Kingman
is the depot for Mineral Park—the county seat—and the rather
prosperous surrounding mining region. I would have liked to
visit the mines there, but they were 18 miles off of my road, and
time is too valuable now to permit such sorties. I shall probably
take in Calico—just now the liveliest and most excited camp in
many hundred miles—as that is close to Daggett, where I turn
off to cut across to Los Angeles, but that will be the only stop I
can afford to make—and even for that a single day must suffice
to go out, inspect and return to the railroad.

Very much the same scenery met my eyes, the rest of that day, as on the foregoing—another long but insignificant volcanic canyon, followed by another open, sunny plain with its mountain fringe. Four miles below Kingman, I ran across my first Yucca palms—of which, however, I have been seeing an elegant sufficiency ever since. A curious, round, tree-like trunk, 4 to 6 feet high, and 6 to 12 inches in diameter, surrounded by a bristling tuft of sword-like leaves, thick and green—and there's your Yucca. They interested me then, but now I'd like to see something else.

How I did suffer with thirst that day! I had a bottle of water along, but it was only an aggravation, and my mouth and throat fairly crackled with drouth. Shadow felt it, too, and for the first time in our acquaintance paid no attention to the jacks and cotton-tails, but tagged along soberly and sadly at my heels, his parched tongue hanging far out. He got the biggest share of my water, but didn't seem to care much for it; and disdained the proffer of half my grub. He was evidently out of sorts, and I attributed it to his irresponsible habit of racing and rampaging about in the hot sun. Poor little fellow! I had no dream of the sad truth.

We got down to Yucca at night, after a severe trip of 39 miles, and fell among thieves who tried to shanghai us. The boarding-mistress of the section-house was a great, muscular virago, hard in face as in arm; and the food she set out for us was harder than either. She proposed to give us two meals for 70 cents: and when the meals had been eaten, tried to bulldoze a dollar from us. But I wouldn't have it so. My money goes pretty easy, but a cent looks as big as a cartwheel to me when anyone is trying to swindle me out of it. I couldn't get a bed or even a blanket for love or money, and things looked sort of frigid for me. I managed, however, to find a few gunny sacks, and spreading them upon the floor of the wind-pierced shanty, beside the little stove, gathered Shadow up to me and slept passably. The dog was restless, however, and rolled and groaned a good deal during the night.

In the morning after a seven o'clock breakfast, we sallied out.

Shadow had refused to eat anything, and I began to get worried. We got about four miles down the track, when he suddenly turned, and with his tail between his legs, dusted back to Yucca. This broke me in two, for it had always been impossible to keep him away from me at all. He seemed to be haunted by a fear that I would desert him; and if I were only in the next room he had to come too.

Marveling at his strange behavior, I tramped clear back to Yucca, where he came out to meet me, I put a strap around his neck, and led him off. He came along peaceably enough, and I had quite ceased to pay any further attention to him. But suddenly, as we were hurrying along, side by side, he gave a savage snarl and sprang up at my face. More instinct than anything else, I gave him a fling, with the strap and my foot, down the embankment; but he was upon his feet again in a second, and dashed at me with a growl that froze my blood. I saw his white teeth shining, while from his jaws dripped a thick froth, and as I looked I felt a dumb terror run through my whole body. *The dog was mad,* and there was I, so crippled as to be half helpless, my revolver carelessly swung far behind my back for convenience in walking, and those fangs, infinitely more terrible than a rattlesnake's, within six feet of me.

I have been in some tight places, and seen some tough experiences and close calls, but I would go through them again all in a lump, rather than feel as I did for a second or two there. My first reach, of course, was for the revolver, but it was slow work—too slow. I jumped to the edge of the embankment, caught the dog under the chin with my toe as he come up, and sent him rolling down again. Again he rallied and started for me, but this had given me time, and as he came up the bank within four feet of my hand, I threw down the heavy Colt and let her go. I flatter myself I am getting tolerably clever with that gun, but my hand wasn't very steady then. I was excited, and it had come to me that I was driving a bullet into a dear faithful friend. Poor dog! He rolled over, and then started like a bird for the brush. That steadied my nerve in a minute. My poor chum shouldn't go off to die by inches in the wilderness—and I caught him on the wing. And then I sat down and dropped a little salt beside the track, for I had lost such a friend as one don't find everyday.

There's many a human I'd shoot with a lighter heart than I did that little four-footed tramp of mine. Dear little Shadow— the comrade of more than a thousand dreary miles, the equal sharer of my scanty bed and scantier fare, the cheerer of the long and solitary days, the only true chum of the tramp—never quarrelsome, never obstinate, always ready with loving caress and with expressive wag of tail, as if to say "these other folks may be mean; these fellows that promise to chum it with us may peter out, but you and I stick together straight through, don't we, dear master?" I tell you I've seen a good many friends die—and pretty good ones, as friends go—and precious few of them left me as sore and sad as did that poor, loving dog. I don't know how the Lord got any notion that He was under obligations to whittle me out into a Job, jr. I haven't kicked on hunger, thirst, cold or heat, danger or broken bones, but when my dog has to go over the range, it strikes me it's rather crowding the mourners. Well, it's all over now, and I am getting used to playing a lone hand again, but it will be a long day before I forget my faithful little Shadow.

Sour and sore, and nearer to being lonely than ever I was before, I hurried down the hot track, now smoking an impatient pipe, and now cooling my parched lips at my priceless bottle. The country was fast growing more barren and more desolate. The reaches of hot sand grew wider and wider, and clouds of it came sweeping up the valley, stinging eyes and face like fire. The walking, too, grew no better fast. The last 30 miles of the road are poor enough, and hard alike on trains and on tramps. Five miles west of Yucca, the mileposts give out, and the track becomes abominably rough. Eight or ten miles of it has been moved from the old grade in the bed of the wash, and tacked up on the gravely hillsides.

The section-houses from Kingman west, are no longer even boxcars, but rough board shanties practically unprotected from either wind or rain, and would be poor samples of a New England hog pen. I got dinner at Powell, the last station upon the road in Arizona, and here I found the only person who has not been civil to me in a great while. The boarding boss' wife—a young and good-looking woman, too—tried to impress me with the idea that I was a yaller dog, and she the queen of trumps. When I politely asked her to help me fill my bottle, she nearly snapped my head off, and said I had the biggest cheek of anyone she ever saw.

But she is the exception. People out here want to make all the money they can out of you, but they have been wonderfully kind to me and have made my crippled condition much less of a terror, than I expected it to be. Pooh! I wouldn't be a two-handed man, anyhow—they're too common. If it were not for that busted arm I should have to cut up my own meat—no small job, sometimes, in this country—pull off my own coat, and do a lot of other things which I now escape. I don't know but it would be money in my pocket to keep the old thing broken right along.

There is a small camp of Mojave (Moha-vy) Indians at Powell, and a little distance beyond the station, where a long trestle crosses a pond of back water from the Río Colorado, I came upon an interesting group. Where the wagon-road crosses the pond on a little bridge, was a Mojave squaw doing up her week's wash. Standing upon a big timber nearly level with the water, she wet the clothing, laid it upon the timber, stood upon it with one foot, and with the other wobbled and mopped it about in the same fashion as that in which an American laundress manipulates the clothing upon her washboard. When the washing was completed, Madame Mojave put the articles into an enormous bundle of something, which must have weighed fully two hundred pounds. An enormously tall and powerful buck helped her to shoulder this, and to draw the strap over her forehead, and off she marched handily, with that great burden which the twain could barely lift to her back, and which was so large as to conceal her entirely, upheld by that band. Their necks must be muscled with steel. I'd like to gamble that there isn't a man in Chillicothe who could carry that load in that way.

Mojave Indian family near Needles, California, n.d. Photograph by
Charles Lummis. Courtesy of Southwest Museum: negative no. 4053.

But on the other side of the trestle, where the pond widens
out in a willow swamp, there was even more fun. A lot of ten-
foot bushes had been bent down until they lay in flat clumps in
the water, which was about three feet deep. Upon these brush-
piles were two stalwart Mojaves, almost in a state of nature, and
each armed with a short, stout pole, with which he kept bang-
ing and prodding the water and the bushes. Three other Indians
stood up to their waists in the water in front of the heaps. They
had each a long shallow basket, loosely woven from large willow twigs, and shaped something like a canoe, though rounder
at the ends. These were about ten feet long and three feet wide.
The Indians let these down in the water close to the brush-
heaps; and after the pole-handles had splurged around a minute
or two, would lift up the baskets, in which, each time, were
several score of small, smelt-like fish, three to six inches long.
The fishers had small deep baskets lashed upon their backs, and
into these they deftly tossed the fish, a handful at a time. They

appeared to be having a dandy time of it, too, and were shouting and laughing at a great rate.

From here on to the river the railroad makes a straight eight-mile shoot. Along the sandy grade I saw countless tracks of barefooted men and dogs—also of barefooted dogs and men—and some of them big enough to make me think the Cardiff Giant must have been taking a stroll that way. And presently I came to the interminable bridge which spans the sandy Colorado River—here a very different stream from that I had last seen in the Grand Canyon. The bridge is 1,000 feet long, and has a draw of 90 feet. I sat down at the middle of the river, with my heart in California and my liver in Arizona, and smoked a reflective pipe, and then jumped along the stringers until at last my feet pressed the sandy soil of the Golden State. A lot of Mojaves met me here, and kept up a perpetual jabber, most of them trying to dicker for a six-shooter. But I stood them off and pranced along up the now horribly crooked track for two miles and a half, and at last stood upon the platform of the big depot at The Needles.

I was very agreeably surprised in the little town, which looks more comfortable and substantial than anything I had seen since Albuquerque. There is a large, fine combination hotel and station, a row of handsome cottages for the railroaders, several really good stores, the usual saloons, and the numerous buildings which mark the end of a railroad division. A side-stretching supper, a lot of mail and a good smoke, set me up in good shape, and I put in the night till three o'clock writing in the hotel. The proprietor, Mr. J. A. Cole, is one of the cleverest men I have run across in a long time, and I am his debtor for many substantial courtesies. It looked odd enough to see a big, high-toned hotel out on the edge of his desert, surrounded by a country which has absolutely no redeeming feature or point of value.

A majority of the hangers on about the hotel were Mojave Indians, and I had a good chance to study these queer people at leisure. They are the best-built race I ever saw, especially the men. Tall, athletic, straight as a string, with good heads and intelligent features, they would command attention anywhere.

The squaws wear calico skirts tied around the waist and reaching to the knees; their legs and feet being bare. Some waist-like
arrangement covers their bodies loosely, and outside of all is a
scarlet government blanket. Their ornaments seem to be entirely of beads, generally alternate white and blue, which serve
for ear-rings, necklaces and bracelets.

The men's dress, what there is of it, is rather more unique. A
few wear civilized trousers and vests, but most disdain these
uncomfortable togs. Three out of four are content with a wardrobe that would make Alice Oates green with envy—an ordinary undershirt and a "G-string". Maybe you don't know what a
G-string is. Well, it's a piece of thin cloth, generally a bandana
handkerchief, folded into a triangle and put on in diaper fashion.
Some of the more toney bucks add a long scarf, whose ends float
gracefully upon the passing breeze. They never cut their hair,
and it falls in jetty masses often to their hips. After arriving at a
certain age, they braid it; and the braid lasts as long as the buck
does, for he never untwists it. In his ears he wears bead strings
three or four inches long; and at various points of his coiffure are
other still longer strings.

These Mojaves have some queer costumes [customs?], a few
of which I ran across. When one of them dies, the relatives build
a big pile of wood—generally ties stolen from the railroad—lay
the corpse thereon in its best rig and start her to going. The
mourners all stand around in a ring, as the fire proceeds, singing
dolefully; and when the blaze has turned to embers, they dump
into it all the earthly possessions of the deceased, followed by
the last rag of their own garments, and continue their song-and-
dance in woeful nudity. In case their friend died seized of a horse
[?], they have a grand barbecue, and gorge themselves over the
meat. That is why the Mojaves never get more than two doors
away from the poor-house, for no matter how much property
one may acquire, it is all cremated with him. There's one gain,
however, about this scheme—there are no contested wills
among the Mojaves, and I reckon lawyers wouldn't flourish in
one of their communities. One old woman lay dying, not long
since, and her son went up to Fort Mojave, paid $18 for blankets

to "keep her warm the last night," and burned them with her the next day. He was a good son, anyhow, if not a very prudent one.

The Mojaves live in little huts made of brush and earth, a good deal like the Navajo hogans. They are quite neat in dress and in person, and altogether a decidedly high-grade race of Indians. The Needles, by the way, gets its name from a jagged range of low mountains back south-east of Powell. The rocks are sharp and peculiar, but don't look any more like needles than does my jovial friend Nate McFadgen. Still "The Needles" goes; I have got over looking for consistency in names.

I got a late start from The Needles, and ploughed off westward through the desert, which grew less attractive at every step. For the first few miles the way is hemmed by apparently endless gravel-hills, cut out by the rain-rivulets on their way to the river. Then the track emerges upon a broad, desolate plain, made up of pebbles and sand, and dotted with disconsolate looking greasewood bushes, still in green leaf. The telephone poles are no longer poles, but joists, sawed into a sort of obelisk shape. I got up to Homer in good season, choking with thirst, and wet with sweat.

I had filled my pockets, before leaving The Needles, with chocolate and canned corned beef, so wasn't troubled by hunger. You may not know it, but chocolate contains more nourishment in the same bulk than almost anything else one can carry, and is a regular bonanza for the traveler in such a country as this. A fifty-cents cake of it made me four good meals, and helped me walk sixty miles.

At Homer I paused, the next station being nothing but a side track, and fell in with good company. The place is one of the five telegraph stations in 240 miles, and the operator proved very clever. Stopping with him temporarily, in hopes of a job, was John Minahan, whom many of your readers will remember as station agent at Coalton three years ago. I had a good time at Homer, did up a lot of writing, slept peacefully in an arm chair beside the stove—for the nights here are cold as a dog's nose—and got a good breakfast in the morning.

I went up to Fenner, Sunday morning, killing a couple of

queer lizards by the way, and scouring a few grasshoppers and beetles. Here I stopped a few moments to admire the city, which is the biggest place in the whole 100 miles between The Needles and Daggett. It has a fine large depot and freight house— being the station for the Providence mines, 25 miles north—a section house and a little shanty hotel, but no store. This was rough on me, for I wanted to lay in more provisions. As it was, I shall have to trust to luck and the kindness of track-walkers for the next 75 miles.

There at Fenner I fed my eyes on $6,500 worth of bullion from Providence, four heavy silver pigs, weighing in the aggregate 876 pounds. I also saw there a box-car which struck me as the most truthful thing in the country. On its ends were the initials "S. P. of A." which they told me stood for "Southern Pacific of Arizona." I know better, it means "Snidest Part of America," and it hits the bull's eye, too. This line from The Needles to Mojave was built by the Southern Pacific, and was recently bought by the A. & P. It was constructed by Chinese, and is a remarkably well-made road throughout—in track, tanks and buildings. The necessities of this torrid zone are illustrated in the latter. The tanks have a big house built over them, to keep the blistering sun from knocking them to pieces; and the section-houses have, about a foot above the roof, another roof on stilts.

I got abominably thirsty, that forenoon, having been so careless as to drink a cup of water before starting; and my one quart bottle lasted no longer, to use a western simile, than a snowball in h——l. You see, if a man begins the day by drinking, he has to keep it up or suffer a good deal. My habit is to touch no water before 1 o'clock, after which I can keep alive on one bottle. It is no picnic, however, I'll tell you. The blazing sun and almost equally blazing sand, along with the best of walking, beget an almost intolerable thirst, and a man would give a pretty handsome price for a good bucketful of wet along about the middle of the afternoon. But water is scarcer than gold. You can't get it— so water you going to do about it?

Passed Sunday night with the operator at Danby, sleeping in a chair beside the stove. Perhaps you think I don't miss my warm old blanket these nights of two inch ice! But carrying a blanket through these long, hot days is out of the question for me now, so I must grin and bear it. Have got up to Amboy now, without any experiences worthy of remark, save continual thirst, tolerably steady hunger, and poor show for sleep. It cannot last much longer, however. Wednesday, Feb. 4th, I shall, with good luck, march into Los Angeles with colors flying. So nine days will wind up the business. This will probably be the last communication I shall be able to get to you before my arrival upon the coast, for Friday morning I leave the railroad for good, and plunk it down across the howling desert 100 miles. Even this has to be dumped upon a passing train.

By the way, all my preconceived notions of this desert have been rather upset. Instead of being low and flat, it is high and mountainous. At Goffs I was 2,500 feet above the sea; and shall attain an almost equal altitude tomorrow. All around are sharp, low, rocky peaks, entirely devoid of vegetable life, breaking from the desolate plain. It is the same thing from end to end of this wretched stretch, and you almost come to fancy each morning that the Lord has picked up the very same ground you came over the day before, and set it down again in front of you. It is a good country to keep out of. But though I am having a rather tough time, the experience is good, and it will be all right ten days hence. Good-bye, then, until the coast.

LUM

Los Angeles, California
Sunday, February 8th, 1885

Editors Leader:
Whoop! Irk-a-doodle-doo! Hurrah for we'uns! Here I am at last, clothed and in my right mind, shaven, shorn, stuffed with provender, inserted into the coy, biled shirt and the rampant dude pantaloonacies once more, smoking one of Nate McFad-

gen's cigars—a relic of our parting—in place of the old corn-cob pipe; and in place of hammering from 75,000 to 100,000 ties a day, I am ringing in 14 hours out of the 24 hours at good solid work on the *Daily Times*. Truly, times change and we change with them; and that, by the way, is about the only change I have left. However, that's all right.

Well, it is pretty good to drop back into the breeching of civilization, the feeling of whose harness I had pretty well forgotten—though I still kick a little on the plug shirt.* After a man has been going it in the comfortable flannel for well-nigh five months, it's rather binding for him to return to that plank-like abomination of society. A little feeling of loneliness—a sort of Othello's-occupation's-gone sensation—did rub against my diaphragm as I looked down from a little bluff, Sunday midnight, and saw the electric lights of Los Angeles at my feet, and remembered that I wasn't to poke out into the sand again in the morning, nor lay my bones by night along the soft side of a plank floor; but I got over the feeling without the aid of a stomach pump. I was having a bang-up time out there in the desert; but being no hog can accommodate myself cheerfully to the present gilt-edged situation.

After slinging that *Leader* letter on board a passing train at Amboy, Monday afternoon, it struck me that a little let-up wouldn't be out of order, and then another break ahead, for Daggett seemed to me a pretty good place to get to. So I got at the section-house some much needed intestinal padding, which came just in time to keep my belt from dropping down over my feet; and then I began to cast about for a place to drop my eye-shutters for awhile. Mrs. Comstock, the landlady at the section-house, must be a new-comer in that section, for she hasn't caught the pecuniary epidemic yet. She actually didn't want anything for the lunch, and furthermore lent me two big quilts to keep me warm for a nap in the bunk-house. Maybe you think that's nothing remarkable, but you don't know that country.

---

*A stiff or starched shirt, perhaps even a dickey, which was very fashionable at the time.

You are quite as likely to kick up a ten-pound gold nugget in your back yard as to scare up anyone in that desert who is suffering from an overdose of kindness; and though I pay for what I get, it doesn't hurt my feelings a bit to meet some one now and then who tries to be clever. I went over to the bunk-house, rolled myself in Mrs. Comstock's quilts, and had a big snooze until 10 o'clock.

Upon awakening then, I found that the moon was shining brightly, and a soft, warm breeze stirring, and I decided to prance onward. It was a good deal pleasanter traveling then than in the blistering heat of the day, and I got along much faster, and with less friction. For about 60 miles the railroad does some big winding, and in that distance I saved about 15 miles by short cuts. One of these was a very long one, and took me through a little range of those peculiar desert hills, where I was at one time five or six miles from the railroad.

As I trudged along over the white, bare sand, or the areas of black, volcanic pebbles, the moonlight gleam on some peculiar object drew me over a few hundred feet to the right of my pathless course. As I came nearer and nearer, a thrill of awe ran through me, for the strange object slowly took shape to my eyes, a shape hideously suggestive in this desolate spot. As I knelt on the barren sands and lifted that bleached and flinty skull, or looked around at the bones which had once belonged to the same frame, now wide scattered by the snarling coyote, there came before my eye the tragedy of that Golgotha, vivid as day. I saw the summer glare of the merciless desert, the sun like fire overhead, the sand like molten lead below; the slow ox-teams of a little band of immigrants toiling in agony across that plain of death, where drivers, crazed by the fierce smiting of the sun, reeled stumblingly along, their cracked tongues unable even to curse; while the great, patient oxen, lifting their feet from the blistering soil, shook them and bawled piteously. I saw the gaunt faces as the blood-warm water in the kegs fell lower and lower, till one desperate man set out to seek for water among the nearest mountains. I saw him turn his back resolutely to the caravan and push bravely toward the desolate, rocky, treeless hills, while sun and sand grew yet more fearful in their white glow; and the strong breeze in his face brought no life, but was as the breath of a fiery furnace. I saw him plod on through the canyons drifted high with sand; over sharp, rocky spurs and down desolate declines where the feet of coyotes for thousands of years have worn deep path ways in the limestone floor; tearing up with trembling hands the sands of some mountain arroyo, only to find them still parched and burning, deep as his arm could reach. He struggled on for weary miles, gasping, burning, failing in strength and courage until nature could no more, and he sank exhausted upon the bare ground, half swooning and half delirious. But the demon of thrist soon dragged him to his feet again, and bade him return to the wagons; and he started back. But blinded eyes and shriveling brain were treacherous guides, and he wandered farther and farther from his only salvation, until at last the knowledge that he was lost seared itself upon his mind. That sobered him, and with desperate coolness he tried to get his bearings. But it was too late. His feet, heavy as lead, were big with enormous blisters; the sinews of his legs were warped and stiff and useless; and the hell of unquenchable thirst devoured him. The blood gushed from his nostrils; his eyes were like a clot of gore; strange whirring sounds filled his ears, and his tongue lolled out dry and rough as a file. And at last he fell unconscious upon the sands. The cool air of evening brought him to, and he tried to rise; but bone and muscle were past obedience, and he dropped back again. The sense of his situation came over him, and he screamed and cursed and prayed and raved in a husky throat whose half articulations could not have been heard a hundred yards away. Byeand-bye the voice—if voice it could be called—ceased. The coyotes among the hills barked louder, and the bloodshot eyes dimly traced one skulker outlined against the sky from the top of a hillock close by. The night wore away, and the sun leaped above the low horizon. The castaway had fallen upon his back, and the merciless rays smote full upon his face, but he was too weak to turn. Three or four big black ravens began to circle high overhead, and despite the daylight, the coyotes did not shrink back to their holes. The sun blistered his half-closed eyelids, and lizards flashed across his hands and face, but he knew it not. A deep, stentorious breathing was his only token that life remained, but it was enough to deter the sinister watchers. As the sun drew near the zenith, however, the crows swept lower, and some perched upon the rocky ledges hard by, with ominous croaking; while their four footed rivals sat upon their rumps, a few rods away, licking their chops expectantly. And last of all, as I sat in that hideous spot, and held that grinning relic in my hand, its hollow sockets staring me in the face, I saw the closing scene—a pack of wolves leaping and snarling and tearing at something prostrate, while a score of ravens hopped here and there with sickening strips hanging to their beaks.

That was the story of the skull, as a hunter could read it. It had been there long before the railroad came through, for it was bleached to ivory. It was a Caucasian skull, and a rather well-formed one. To those who know this desert and its history, this is enough to show that the owner of that skull met his death in very much the way my fancy painted it that night, and to those who don't know, I haven't time to explain.

On another short cut the next day, I came near being fooled to a similar end, myself. I was terribly in want of water, and did not dare reduce my half-empty bottle any further until I should come in sight of the next station. It was mid-afternoon, and the sun came down with frightful power. A plain that would have been beautiful but for its garb of desolation, stretched to the left, ending at last in a mountain-range probably at least 25 miles away. As I came up over a long hill and looked down upon this plain, I saw a large pond, very shallow, but at least six miles long, and apparently not two miles from where I stood. Lord, how it did make my mouth water, to look across to that lake! But I didn't start out for it, you may stake your life. It was a lake as plain as ever you saw one; but I knew there was no lake there, so my memory downed my eyes for once.

I turned my back—and it was a hard turn, too—on that alluring mirage, and hurried as fast as possible to the next station, ten miles ahead. I was afraid I might get crazy enough to let a mirage fool me, after all. This is a country of strange things; but there is none stranger, to my thinking, than the appearance of its mountains. They are the barest, barrenest, most inhospitable-looking peaks in the whole world; and they are as uncordial as they look. Many a good man has left his bones to bleach beside their cliffs or in their death-trap valleys. They are peculiar in the strange fashion in which they rise from the plain, and more so for their utter destitution of vegetable life in any form. But strangest of all is their color. The prevailing hue is a soft, dark, red brown, or occasionally a tender purple; but here and there upon this deep background are curious light patches where the fine sand of the desert whirled aloft and swept along by the mighty winds as common there, and rained down upon the mountain slopes where it forms deposits scores of feet in depth, and acres in extent.

The rock bases of the mountains are completely buried in gentle declivities of sand, while the cream or fawn-colored patches are often to be seen many hundreds of feet above the surrounding level. These mountains are not very high—none, I should judge, over 5,000 or 6,000 feet—but very vigorous in outline, and, at certain stages of the daylight, very beautiful in color. Nearly all, too, are rich in minerals, and will pay handsomely if the water problem is ever solved—as it is not over and above likely to be.

When I have said that, there is nothing left to be chronicled of my journey from Amboy to Daggett, save that I got some pretty scaly food at altitudinous prices, had to sleep cold and suffered a good deal during the day from heat and thirst. But a man doesn't look for grit in a country that is all sand, and to Daggett I finally got just before noon o' Wednesday. Daggett is a sizable town of several hundred people, but it is far more shantyish than The Needles. Its sole claim to existence is in its capacity as railroad setting-house, and as a station for Calico.

Now, perhaps you think Calico a sort of fool name; but it proves upon acquaintance to be a very appropriate one. Looking due north from Daggett, you will see a very curious-shaped and curious-colored mountain. It looks like a mammoth load of bread, covered with a faded red bandanna or with a piece of that old reddish brown calico your grandmother and mine used to wear, and perchance make into frock aprons for us. The ranges all around it for three or four miles are of similar color, but have not its remarkable shape. Right at its foot clusters a town of 600 people. From Daggett you look across a slight depression in the plain and see the houses of Calico, its quartz mills, mines, and the very people upon its streets, and you very likely start over there to explore the town; if you happen to have half an hour to spare. And before you get there, you'll wish you had never been born.

I thought I had these distances down tolerable fine, and am generally able to guess pretty near how far off an object is, even in the tricky atmosphere of the West—but I hope to turn Democrat if Calico didn't fool me just as badly as if I had been a tenderfoot. I'd have sworn it wasn't two miles away, and thereby should have become a straggler at the tail end of the procession of Truth. For it is seven good miles across that apparent stone's-throw. I had planned to visit Calico and write up the boom whose echoes are resounding through the whole West; but about ten minutes in Calico was enough to change my mind. I saw six or seven unoccupied buildings, a couple of hundred men loafing despondently about the streets instead of in the saloons, and that was as good as a poster to tell me that there was no boom at Calico that needed me. Booms don't run that way. A few interviews confirmed my impressions, and after getting my mail and dinner, I started away from civilization and began the trip across the desert toward San Bernardino, leaving the railroad—I trust, forever.

And by the way, since my safe arrival here, I have received a *Leader* containing some very lugubrious forecasts about my probable fate if I undertook that cut-off. Much obliged to Capt. Gilmore and the rest of you for getting your crepe ready; but please convey to the Captain, with my kindest regards, the suggestion that a hunter doesn't walk in circles. A dude might; and there are some I know who would be quite as useful swinging 'round a circle as anywhere else; and even a clever fellow without experience might; but I am not related to either.

I am a good deal more at home outdoors than in the house, and have been for years. I stayed at home and attended to business in Chillicothe, because there was nothing there that a native of the northern New England woods would condescend to pull trigger or line on, but you needn't think on that account that I am [as ignorant of] the lore of out-door life as those whose exploits have been confined to a stubble-field with a rail fence around it. If you want to learn any thing about it, ask Dr. McCrillis who it was that used to bring in more trout or pickerel in a day than all the other fishers around old Whiteface put together, and also whether it is the general opinion, in that country of hunters, that "Lum" needs a guardian anywhere out doors. Great king! How in the name of peppery perdition is a man going to walk in circles who can read in sun and moon and stars, in leaves and bark and winds, the points of the compass? And if he can't read nature's book—the only book the Lord ever condescended to write, and of which more people are brutally ignorant than any other, what business has the doddering idiot out in a wilderness? Pardon this digression. I have been aggravated for months by folks who thought me as dumb and helpless as them-selves, and it grows monotonous. The only thing I have to say, after their croaks, is that I am in Los Angeles. Let them put that in their pipe and smoke it.

Well, before dismissing Calico finally, I have a word to say of its boom. The mines are rich, especially the King, which is making $1,000 a week clear; but everything is overcrowded, and hundreds of men hang about, bare of money, unable to get work or to get out of the place without a desert tramp, such as few of them care to undertake—for you must know that it is 80 miles [8 miles] out of the desert from Daggett, the nearest way. Pneumonia is rampant, and over three percent of the entire population had died within a month when I was there. And still the *Calico Print*—their local sheet—keeps boosting the boom, and its trash is being republished and enlarged upon through half a dozen states and territories. So the deluded victims continue to pour in on every train, drop their last dollar for grub, and there they are. Work there is none, nor will there be until capital comes in and opens new mines.

I had hoped to give you a rest after this letter, but must disappoint you. Time is almost impossible for me to get at present, and I shall [be] obliged to escort you through the desert from Daggett to Los Angeles and give my impressions of the latter city in another letter. Just now I will merely say that I reached L.A. Sunday midnight, February 1st—having been spurred by impatience to get here after getting so near. I found the folks all well, all delighted with the glorious place, and all at least content to see the prodigal. I am like a bundle of steel wires, myself, and healthy as a quartz crusher. The arm is doing handsomely, and the Doctor says it can come out of the sling next week. She admits that it is about as well spliced as if put up by a professional. I had not intended to shin up the *Daily Times* staff for a week, so as to have time for unpacking and sight-seeing; but Col. Otis, the editor-in-chief, is "enjoying poor health" and one of the staff was dying to go to New Orleans with his Sunday girl, so I assumed the pressure within six hours after arrival. Since then I haven't had time to know which end I was standing on—up at 8 o'clock, for instance, yesterday morning, and not into bed again until 4:30 *this* morning. Therefore, fare-well. See you later.

LUM

Los Angeles, California
Sunday, February 15th, 1885

Editors Leader:
I don't believe prosperity just agrees with me. Indeed, for that matter, it doesn't agree with most people. Here I am in the country from which it is generally supposed the Lord got his

plans and specifications for heaven; basking in eternal summer while you poor creatures are building fires under the thermometer to keep it from freezing to death, and wading up to your knees in snow, eating four meals a day with Christian fortitude, not to count a super abundance of dried fruit; plugging away at work, which fits my intermittent intellect like a pair of dude pantaloons, and drawing a neat salary with the resignation of a martyr, and am fixed in just the swellest suite of rooms in the city, with all the furniture of domesticity—and still I am not happy. That is to say, I'm happy—I always am that, anywhere—but there's a sense of something lacking. It is too soon yet to forget my old exultant, careless life in the woods, called back so vividly by the experiences of the last five months, and the full, free blood and knotted muscles which grew from that life are not toned down enough yet to lie content between four walls. And so I sit and scratch away at the inoffensive paper as if I owed it a grudge while my thoughts go drifting out of the open window and across the purple mountains to—well, I call it *life*. The best that civilization can give is not much more than existence. However, by the time this Indian complexion fades out—as it is doing tolerably fast under the regimen of all-night work—I shall have gotten over the sharp edge of my hunger for the wilderness, probably.

Well, I never shall get out of the desert at this rate—so hook on here, and let's mosey along. It was a very large day when I started out from Daggett—at which I had arrived the same noon, you will remember—and got a divorce, with alimony, from the railroad. In fact, it was one of the most extensive days I ever saw, and there was more weather than there are scars on Johnny Kirchenschlaeger's dog.* (By the way, don't you suppose that dog's mangled condition is partly due to Johnny's having dropped the family name on him, sometime?) However, this is irrelevant. I filled my bottle with water, jammed into the pock-

---

*Presumably, "Kirchenschlaeger" was a name recognized by readers of the Chillicothe *Leader*.

ets of the big coat two pounds of chocolate, a pound of cheese, a pound of condensed meat, a loaf of bread and a half pound of tobaco [sic]. That was enough to keep life in a man for a week, and I knew whatever might chance I shouldn't starve.

Folks at Daggett advised me very strongly not to try the trip on foot and predicted all sorts of casualties—all of which, as in the case of a natural born mule, simply made me bound to go. They swore I'd lose the trail; would miss the water, roast to death, starve to death and everything cheerful. But just as I was starting out, a clever fellow I had seen in town came running after me, and said that if I was going across he'd go with me, for he wanted to get to San Bernardino too. You may be sure he was welcome to try it. So when I told him to come along, he ran back and got some provender and his blankets, and we were soon grunting up the rocky hills, side by side. Now maybe if you were to meet Albert Munier in the street you wouldn't care to associate with him; but it would be your loss quite as much as his. He proved incomparably the best traveling companion I had struck—that is, the best biped, for I won't put him ahead of poor Shadow, who beat them all—and lightened that trying march across the hideous desert, in a way I hardly expected. He had come in to Calico on the cars—like many another poor devil—with his employer. The latter turned out a rascal, gobbled Munier's little hoard, and turned him adrift; so within a week he was walking out penniless to seek employment in some less God-forsaken spot.

Lord! How hotly the sun blazed down that afternoon! How the half-molten sand blazed up in yet more blinding glare; and how the breeze, like a rush of flames made us gasp and choke! It was the hottest road I ever saw, and the sweat streamed from our every pores. Maybe you don't know what sweat is. It has become as unfashionable, I know, to sweat as to have legs, but when I get fashionable, may the Lord knock me on the head with a maul. Men, horses, and other things that the Lord made, sweat; but the dude, being the abortive offspring of a vacuum, "perspires"—and he doesn't do that when he can help it. And as for the people who have "limbs"—God pity them—what they need is a good hickory limb, about three inches through, laid over their barren skulls until there is a hole big enough to let some sense in. I took off my mental hat to a sweet modest thoroughbred lady in New Mexico, not many weeks ago, because when she meant legs she said legs, like a lady, and didn't frill up her mouth and say "limbs" as though she knew she had limbs, but wished the Lord had made her without the nasty, disgraceful, wicked appendages. Why, I wouldn't trust anybody that uses that prurient word, not so far as I could throw a bull by the tail. And if I had the bossing of things I'd hang every last soul that committed this hideous offense against good taste, common sense and decency. But to return to my own legs.

Mr. Roads had rustled around and found a man who had crossed the desert at this point, and from him got an estimate of distances which was a good deal more accurate than most such guesses, being only ten miles "out" in 130. He had also made out a table of watering places, with other information which came as handy as finding a *V* in last year's vest. According to this, it was 23 miles to the first water; so we had to push along in decidedly lively style, in order to get there before darkness came on. Nearly all the way the road is up hill, alternating with orthodox regularity between heavy sand, heaviest [heavier?] gravel, and heaviest dornicks.

I never really knew what the tortures of thirst are until that afternoon; but I think that I got then a pretty tolerable pointer; how Dives felt when he called up through the telephone to Lazarus—who had a front room in Abraham's bosom—to send him down just one drop of water by the bell-boy, for the love of God. He didn't ask for "the same," nor for soda with a stick in it, nor rootbeer, nor even ginger pop. He was no hog, and water was good enough for him. Lazarus has never regained my respect or confidence since he bluffed the poor fellow off and told him they didn't keep no water at that bar, 'n' he'd have to show the color of his money or he couldn't have a smell of a drink—or words to that effect. It was what I call a mighty low trick. Well, we didn't have any Lazarus to petition; but what was better, [we] did have my trusty bottle and Munier's small canteen.

We dared not drink much, for if anything went wrong the whole universe wouldn't be auction price for one drop of that water. So we chewed pebbles and expectorated cotton-battings until our mouths tasted like a shovelful of sand and thirst became unbearable. Then we built a hot little fire from the inflammable roots of the soap-wood and boiled a quart of chocolate in an old but clean tomato can we had brought along. That went a good deal further than the water it required would have done, and appeased our torments for awhile.

But I shall never forget that afternoon. If the Lord makes a mistake and sends me the wrong ticket one of these days—as folks think He ought to, who believe that trying to live square doesn't count unless a man is all the time playing the baby act, and whining for help to do what he ought to have sand enough to do by himself—I shall feel perfectly at home, after that experience in the Mojave desert. There isn't much exaggeration about the story that a man who died in the Mojave and went to hell, sent back in a few days for his blankets, and said he "never was much of a hand to stand cold weather, nohow." And if the Mojave is as bad in January as I found it, what must it be in August! It has made a blister in my brain, just thinking about it.

We kept a course two points west of due south, which I was convinced from maps and verbal information was about the proper line. Nothing short of fire could have turned me from that course, either—and I'd have waded a pretty sizable conflagration too, just to cool my feet from the sand—for the only way to get over such a country is to take some course and stick to it till hades freezes and then go on ice. There's many a time when you will think some other course would better; but if you try it, you're a goner. The trail on which we started from town soon faded out; but I wasn't going back, as we made a straight break for the direction in which I believed the Cajon (Kahone) Pass must lie.

About 6:30 PM, just as it grew dark, we spied the little station at Stoddard's Wells, on the slope of a hill opposite that over which we had just climbed. Water has been found there by boring into the hill, and is now piped out to a tank for the use of the caravans that cross the desert. There is a little shanty there, built of split shingles, and a stable of the same material. After filling ourselves so full of water that it near came spilling at the corners of our mouths, we went up to the house. Munier had an enormous ulster, so he didn't object to sleeping out; but I wasn't so well fixed. A fellow with a face like a lap dog came to the door, and to him I said, "Partner, I have a broken arm here, and don't dare to sleep out in the cold. Besides, I have had to ship my blanket, which was too hard for a cripple to carry, and I shall have to ask you for some sort of accommodation."

He looked at me in a sour-milk fashion and said, "You can sleep in the stable if you want to." I went down and opened the stable door. The cold wind of a 4,000-foot altitude shrilled through its lattice-like sides. There was no straw to sleep on, and the whole interior was as filthy as you might expect a man of his appearance to keep his stable! I returned to the house and said, pleasantly—though I was warm inside—"I'm afraid that isn't quite rich enough for my blood, partner. I'd like to get a bed and if you have none to spare, will pay you for letting me sleep in that chair." "Don't want to be kep' awake all night havin' you pokin' the fire," he snapped. "Well, never mind about the fire. I can manage to keep warm without it; so long as I'm in the house," I answered. But he wouldn't have it—said he didn't keep a hotel for tramps. "But I'm not a tramp. I've enough stuff in my pocket to buy out you and your whole mill-dam outfit. Do most of the tramps in this country carry gold watches, gold nuggets, six-shooters and a pocketful of coins?" and I showed him my credentials, which bulged a big pocketbook. But he waved them away, and said he couldn't read.

Well, he didn't look as if he could, but I happened to know he must. His name is Brown, and he lives in Los Angeles; but being far gone in consumption has moved out into the desert temporarily, hoping for help from the manager. I hope he will get well. He stood there a thin-chested, blood-spitting caricature of manhood, and insulted me until I left the house for fear I should disgrace a white man's conscience by hitting him. But it was hard work. On my honest word, I would have given both ears close to my head to have had him a man for a minute, no matter if he had been a giant. A smaller fellow than I am could thrash a hercules with such a heart as Brown's. And I am waiting for him. If the Lord wants to have him paid up in this world for his general meanness—for I find his treatment of me is only a sample—He'll let him get well and then let me at him. I have seen mean men before, but one that would duplicate his conduct, never!

Well, Munier and I went out into the night, while Brown, presuming upon his condition and the presence of his partner, stood in the door and reviled us as "lousy horse thieves." I asked the partner if he wouldn't fight, as Brown couldn't but he said Brown was boss, and he (the partner) hadn't anything to do about it. So we built a fire of soapwood under a bank, cooked a good supper and camped down for the night. Munier shared his ulster [long, heavy overcoat] with me, and this kept me from freezing. But I was too cold to sleep, and never closed my eyes the whole dreary, interminable might. I probably might have slept in a little but dared not for I should inevitably have taken cold; and that, ten to one, would have meant the loss of my arm. So I stayed awake and kept as warm as possible, which wasn't very warm. A bit of a nap would have come in pretty handy, too, after the day's hard trip of more than forty miles and with another day of hardship ahead.

At last, after what seemed a year, the night wore away, and

> "Jocund day
> Stood [stands] tip-toe on the misty mountain tops."
> [William Shakespeare, *Romeo and Juliet*]

We prepared and ate our breakfast of chocolate, salmon, cheese and bread, and filled a bottle and canteen for the start. I couldn't come away without saying good-bye to Brown, so we went to the house and I gave him my compliments in decent but energetic terms. I do fly off the handle of correct language, now and then, but never with a man like Brown—it seems too much like coming down to his level. But actions speak louder than words, and if the misbegotten shark ever gets well enough to call at the *Daily Times* editorial rooms, he can hear of something to his decided disadvantage.

Thursday's trip was shorter, but hardly less trying. The majority of the way was on a descending grade, so walking was easier, but we were also getting into a lower and more torrid country, and the heat grew more and more oppressive. In due season, however, we crossed our last ridge and looked down upon the glorious sight of a flowing stream—the Mojave River. A peculiar river you would call it in the East; but it merely follows the general rule in this country. Rising among the snowy mountains, it runs for a few miles through the desert— making a grassy oasis a quarter of a mile wide—and then suddenly disappearing in the sand. A few miles below it breaks out again, runs a little way, and again sinks. There are three or four such antics, and at last the stream drys up for good. It gets down to Daggett, finally, by a tremendous loop—that is, the bed does.

The water has been *non ent* ["nonentity" or nonexistant] for thirty miles. And yet, right out in the open plain between Daggett and Calico, a Chinaman was drowned last summer, and his body was never recovered. To look at the place now, you would as soon think of a man being drowned on top of Mount Logan. But in the rainy season this river—now at its best, some ninety feet wide and six inches deep—is a terrific howling torrent. It runs in great waves, heavy with sand; and what falls into it then is found no more, for the river buries its own victims. Of course the little valley, where the water runs above ground, is already taken up by farmers and rancheros. We stopped that night at Roger's Station, a comfortable place, owned by a gray-headed intelligent and pleasant farmer who is raising Angora goats extensively. I saw his bunch of 2,000 silk coated butters, in the morning, and made a hearty breakfast on their tender flesh.

We had now crossed forty miles of the desert since leaving Daggett, and had only twenty-five more between us and the fertile country beyond. Before us loomed the fine Sierra Madre range, the divide upon whose farther slopes lay the goal of our hopes; and it was with high hearts that we filled our water vessels at the river—icy cold in the morning but warm at noon—girded up our loins and sallied forth. It was another uphill stretch for twenty miles, but the sun wasn't quite as hot as on the preceding day though still fiery enough to cook eggs.

We plugged along as fast as possible—which wasn't very fast, for the sand was heavy, and Munier's feet were covered with blisters as big as a half dollar. So we halted every three or four miles, to take a breathing spell in the shade of the yucca palms— which barren, ugly growths, no longer short and stubby, but trees of thirty feet, were scattered here and there over the barren plain. You can't get sand—it can't be called soil—too mean for a yucca to enjoy it. Up, up, up we tramped, the Cajon peaks towering closer and closer; and at last, on a long, smooth, gentle upgrade, we came to the veritable jumping off place. Without any warning, we stood suddenly upon the brink of a vast gulf, two thousand feet deep, and big enough in area to have half of Ross county dumped into it flatwise. This was the Cajon Pass, and it took but a glance to show the fitness of the name, which means in English, the "Box Pass." In all my mountaineering I have never seen another defile of similar formation. Instead of being a winding cleft or long trough, with about equal slope at either end of the Cajon is shaped like a tad-pole, with the enormous excavation in the high tableland for a head; and for a winding tail the more normal passage in the south.

We paused a moment to look at the beautiful scene, and then plunged over the brink and down the steep hills into the "bottomless pit." After a mile of this we struck into the bed of a dry wash, and followed it down its rapid descent until the turning of a sudden corner disclosed the tanks and little house of Summit Station. At this point they strike water in the bed of the creek, a few feet below the surface, so the pass is becoming settled. It was about 6 o'clock when we reached this point, and here poor

Munier gave out. He had been mightily plucky through that awful trip, bearing his greater sufferings than mine with a stiff upper lip. And I had come to admire his sand. However, he was now on the outskirts of civilization, and could afford to drop. I gave him what provisions were left, whacked up my modest "boodle" with him and with a hearty full speed pushed on down the road.

Soon a little thread of water trickled over the wet sand at my feet, and it kept growing as we hurried side by side down the deepening canyon. Then I began to meet the surveyors and Chinese laborers of the railroad which will soon run through this wide defile. It is being built for the A. & P. and will make their road *the* great transcontinental route, in the course of time. Coming to the surveyor's camp, I had to make a stop for information desired by the *Times*, and then hurried on again in the deep twilight.

Mr. Roads had written me, "you will strike God's country at the Toll Gate," and verily he was right. I began to cross sparkling little brooks, dashing musically down from the walls of the pass to meet the central stream. The deep-green manzanito bushes, with their peduncles of tiny white blossoms, spread around me, and the soft night air that drifted up the notch seemed fraught with southern odors. I passed the Toll Gate, a beautiful little villa framed in orchards, and a trout pond in the front, and broke into song at seeing this fore-runner of the Eden I was entering. Four miles farther on, I strode between two fine orchards of peach, pear, apricot and English walnut—surrounded by the first fence I had seen in 500 miles—and drummed my knuckles against the door of a prosperous cottage, the home of Mr. Vincent. I shall never forget how good that civilized bed felt—this was the first time I had been able to undress fully and go to bed like a white man since breaking my arm—nor how the royal fare at the table tickled a much maltreated gullet.

Off early next morning, down the widening valley, at whose southern end I could see the broad plains, broken by snow-

capped mountains—ah, it was a pleasant walk. Four miles below Vincent's I turned to the right, and struck across the diminished walls of the pass, and was soon upon the fine table lands
which fringe the base of the Sierra Madre range. Hitherto my
course from Daggett had been nearly south but now it was
almost due west, paralleling the mountain wall. And once out
of the pass, I was in paradise. The air was that of June, warm and
balmy but not oppressive. Flowers nodded at me, and countless
butterflies danced past. Crystal brooks sang down from rugged
canyons, and upon their banks were houses and gardens, orchards and apiaries. The world was green with springing grass,
and full of the warble of a thousand birds. Do you know how
that looked to one fresh from the hideous desert, and into that
from Arizona snows. But that's a fool question—of course you
don't.

In the afternoon I was in Cucamonga, sampling the products
of its winery, and walking through its orange groves, heavy with
golden fruit. Then on past beautiful Ontario, and at last, late in
the evening, into thriving Pomona, whence I telegraphed to the
folks that I was gettin' thar. Up next morning with the sun, and
off through Arcadia, Puente and El Monte to San Gabriel, where
is the famous old mission. The whole country is one vast settlement, and there was never-cloying pleasure in the trip.

I got into San Gabriel in time for supper, and after a meta-
morphosing shave, sat down in the hotel to smoke a meditative
pipe. Then entered to me a portly military-looking man, took a
good look at the bandaged arm, and said, "Mr. Lummis." "Yours
truly," I replied, "but I can't reciprocate exactly." "Otis is my
name," said he—and so it was, Col. Harrison Otis of the *Times*.
He had sent a man out to Cucamonga to meet me whom I had
missed, and found me here himself after a long chase. Soon Mr.
Creighton—the Cucamonga man—came in. We had a long chat
and then all walked in the remaining ten miles to Los Angeles
in the brilliant moonlight. We struck the city at 11 o'clock—as
you see I did make it, after all, Feb. 1—had an oyster supper; and
in a few minutes more I was in the "buzzum of the family."

When I pulled off my shoes from blistered feet, that night, I had walked a tiny fraction over 3,507 miles (three thousand, five hundred and seven); which means 6,513,541 steps. I had been out 143 days, or nearly 5 months, and fully crossed 5 big states and territories. The total expense of the trip was under $175, which is cheap enough for 3,500 miles of travel and 5 months' board.

There is but one cloud on my content. When I left Amboy on that night trip, I carelessly forgot my dear old shoes, and didn't think of them again until I was 20 miles away. I wrote back from the first post office asking the section mistress to send them to me but upon arriving here found a letter from her saying my message came too late, the track-walker having burned them up. Wasn't that dirty? I wouldn't have taken a hundred-dollar bill for those ragged shoes. They had carried me 3,108 miles, and were good for 300 more. Peace to their ashes. I brought with me, or sent ahead, relics and curios worth four times the cost of the trip, so I consider myself ahead in every way. Later you shall hear something about Los Angeles; but at present time it must be *adios.*

LUM

Los Angeles, California
Sunday, March 1st, 1885 [Lummis' 26th birthday]

Editors Leader:

I'd sooner be taken out and kicked all over a ten-acre lot by George Washington's "old mar" than sit down to write again to-day. I just want to take gun or rod and scamper over the hills, in spite of Sunday. This weather pulls a fellow as if it had a ring in his nose; and if business didn't glue his feet down, I reckon he wouldn't do much but bum off in company with the careless wind. However, bein' as how I promised a letter, and as I've lost the breach-pin of my gun, I'll let the squirrels go, and hunt type.

Los Angeles is a brilliant sample of a tail that has come to wag the whole dog. In fact, it is hard to see the original dog at all, so completely does the tail overshadow him. A half-mile walk north from the present business center brings you to the queer precinct of Sonoratown, with its adobe houses, quiet streets and general Mexican air. I should judge it covered ten or fifteen acres. This is the original dog—a diminutive, lazy and ill-conditioned pup, something, over 100 years old. But such a tail! That tail is but a few years old, but as lively a wagger as ever you saw; while as for size, it is six miles square. It is as wide-awake and beautiful as the dog is neither, and makes more noise in a day than the dog does in a year. In less than another generation there will be no dog left at all, his whole personality being merged and lost in that greedy tail.

You may talk about your mongrel pups, but I doubt if you ever knew quite so polyglot a breed as this old dog comes of. He was born Sept. 4th, 1781, and his blood was a mixture from the veins of two Spaniards, four Indians, two negroes, two mulattoes, and two others too mixed to be classified—though one was called a Chino, which means a certain cross between Indian and negro. The females of the community were all mulattoes and Indians. Under contract with the native government, this colony of 46 souls—including 20 children—moved up from Mexico and settled here. They showed good taste, anyhow, in picking out their town site.

I don't know where they could have done better. In the picturesquely-broken plain at the foot of the beautiful Sierra Madre range, nestling between the round, grassy foothills and the sparkling river fresh from its canyon birthplace; blown across by the sweet, salt breath of the sea, in a climate never hot and never cold, these Mexican immigrants founded the gem city of the world. They probably didn't know what they were doing. It isn't characteristic of their race to look ahead more than one meal; and I suppose that after they had looked around remarked, "*Sta bueno; Sta muncho bueno,*" once or twice, they bothered their heads no more about it, but settled down to the usual routine of such hum-drum existence as they never discard. Thus they lived for half a century, scratching the ground tenderly with a pricked stick as if afraid of hurting it, and raising little crops of corn and chili, increasing their families and their herds with equal inattention to improvement of the stock. The Crown had given them a start—to each man a few cattle and one hoe. This list of agricultural implements would look rather slender to an American farmer, but it was full as much as a Mexican cared to handle.

By 1836, the town had grown to a population of 2,188, including 30 Americans and 10 Europeans. There were about 40,000 cattle, worth at an outside figure, $5 per head. The best saddle horse was worth $10 and no end of horses and mules were allowed to run wild in the mountains. From 1821 to 1833, the Mexican government made Los Angeles a city, and the capital of Upper California. Later, the citizens were so dumb as to let Sacramento carry off the plum. The place has witnessed a lot of gory Spanish insurrections and battles. In one, a couple of Mexicans carelessly ran against two stray bullets, and thereby killed themselves; in another, a gray mule was accidentally slain.

During the Mexican War, Los Angeles was taken and retaken several times, now by the Americans, now by the natives, but always without much blood shed. March 1, 1847, General P. W. Kearney became military governor of California, with headquarters in this city. The Mexican town council resumed biz at the old stand, and things began to move onward at the ordinary Mexican gait. The following month a mail route was established, running fortnightly from San Francisco, 490 miles north of here, to San Diego, 60 miles south. Americans dribbled in semi-occasionally, but there was no boom. It was not until seven years ago that the town really began to hump itself, but in that time it has proved itself no slouch of a humper.

In the last three years the population has doubled—growing from 15,000 to over 30,000. Today, the county contains twice the population of the city; and the city as big a population as the whole county had three years ago. In the last two years, 3,000 new buildings have been erected in Los Angeles. I don't believe any other city in the country can show such a proportion. And they are most good buildings, too. You see, Los Angeles is one of the most unique of cities. It is not a commercial emporium, not a political or railroad center. It is a great colony of prosperous and cultured seekers for a place of residence where the conditions of life shall be most favorable, where nature is most profuse in all her gifts—in fine, people who are not content to exist just anywhere, so that they do exist, but demand to live in the Garden of Eden.

Other western cities have been populated by the scum of the East, the better elements poking in later; but it was the flower of the country that has filled Los Angeles, and the bums are straggling in behind, attracted by the previous richness. It would astonish you to see the tide of immigration that is setting towards Southern California. This whole big county, 150 miles in length, is rapidly becoming one vast settlement. It's plains and hillsides are dotted everywhere with villas, farm-houses, orange, lemon, lime, nut and other groves, vineyards, apiaries, ranches, and so on without end. There is a chicken rancho, near the city, where enormous incubators are turning out future broilers by the thousand, and down near Anaheim is a big and profitable ostrich farm. You think you are doing pretty well in the Scioto Valley to sell land for $100 per acre, but any respectable acre out here would wiggle it's fingers on it's nose if you held out so paltry a sum to it. It will take $150 to $300 to touch it at all.

As should be expected from it's age, Los Angeles is not remarkably well laid out. The streets are often somewhat crooked, but most of them are wide and will be handsome. The sidewalks are shaded largely with the graceful pepper trees, whose drooping, willowy foliage keeps the same light green the year round. In front of the better houses are lawns, broken by the curious forms of a semi-tropical plant life—the century plant, fan palm and many more—while hedges of geraniums or callalilies divide the yards. There's only one thing at which I kick, and that is the prevalence of those arboricultural jim-jams, the clipped evergreens. They resemble nothing else in God's world but the trees in my boyhood Noah's Ark.

Around hundreds upon hundreds of houses are golden groves of the orange and lemon and you never know what makes a beautiful grove until you have seen one of these. There is no native grass, so the lawns are seeded; and for hay, barley is generally sown. The hills and fields are brilliant green throughout the winter—that being the rainy season—and dry and brown all summer. Just now the people are beginning to pray for rain, none of which has fallen for over six weeks. Don't you wish you had half of our disease? I sit in a fireless room in my shirt sleeves from 7 P.M. to 4 A.M., with open windows and doors. Next Sunday, I'm going to steal a while away and go down to Santa Monica for a swim in the soft Pacific surf. The bees are humming around, laying in honey for 10¢ a pound—and it is honey, too, not glue and brown sugar. Heliotrope and a hundred other flowers burden the city air with fragrance; while beyond the town, the fields sparkle with the lively gold of endless poppies.

I would just like to take an acre out of the heart of this county and send it back to Chillicothe, air and all, as a sample. In six months after its arrival there, there wouldn't be a soul left in Chillicothe, save those that couldn't raise the spondulics [money] to get out here, and a few folks who think that there can't be a better place than their defunct town, because the Lord never would have dared to make one without consulting them. And when they once get out here they would wonder how in the name of the holy jewsharp they ever managed to live at all in such a hole as Ohio. I wouldn't be found dead back East, even if you'd whack up on the coffin. The daisiest funeral that ever was would be no inducement at all.

The buildings of new Los Angeles are excellent throughout, counting many fine business blocks and beautiful residences. It is one of the best lighted cities in the country, the mast system of electric lamps being extensively and successfully used, not to mention no end of lights at an ordinary altitude. And stepping out for the first time into one of these nights you will realize that you never saw moonlight before; so incomparably more brilliant is the Southern California article than the cheap, adulterated Standard Oil brand you have in Ohio.

The city is full of metropolitan airs, which set not undignifiedly. On every block of the principal streets you will notice several real estate offices, and the sum total of them must reach far up in the hundreds. This means, of course, that there is some inflation of values; but it is neither excessive nor unhealthy. A house in an eligible location is hard to buy, and almost impossible to rent. Rents are about three times as high as in Chillicothe, and are invariably in advance. Coal is worth from $16 to $29 per ton, and wood is almost equally high. Fortunately there is hardly any need of either. Gas is $3.75 per M. Outside of these things and furniture and shoes, living is unusually cheap—and indeed it is cheap taken all in all; I wouldn't advise any professional men to come out here with the idea of going into business. The place is already overrun with doctors, lawyers and ministers. A large proportion of them have come out here for their own health, and hang out their shingles for the sake of partially defraying expenses.

But Southern California is above all every man's country. It is the rich man's, because here he can make the pleasantest residence in the world, and enjoy longer and happier life. It is the poor man's, because he cannot starve or be uncomfortable here, save by his own choice. On the contrary he may have, if he will, a comfortable home and a good living. Now, I have just had a letter from a very dear friend, asking if he would do well to come out here with his little nucleus of $3,000 and locate. And as I shall give him only the straightest goods, and as there may be many more among you in similar whack to his, I repeat here some of the advice I have given to him. I say to him, "You are over-worked and run down by suicidal business confinement. Your wife and lovely children are being murdered by the cutthroat climate in which you live. A long life and good health are the chiefest riches, they are first to be considered. Come out here, where you can and will live out of doors one half the time, the year around, and it will be the salvation of all of you. You oughtn't to be cooped up in an office even here; and there probably is no room for you in that line, even if you desired it. Take your small capital and invest it in a little rancho within half a day's drive of the city. You can get one already improved, with comfortable buildings, large orange and other fruit trees, mature vines and plenty of room.

From the day you move into that place you will have the pleasantest home you ever knew, and a comfortable living thrown in. Keep an old family horse so that you can come to town when you like, and have a cow or so. The fruit-growing business is not and cannot be overdone here. Raising poultry, turkeys, cattle or hogs is highly profitable. So is dairying. I don't know how much of a farmer you are, but you will have no trouble about getting along. Take a year or two of that, and you will again be in the physical condition a man ought to have. Your mind will feel clearer and your temper better. Your wife and children will be new creatures. Then, if you wish to return to the city and business life, you can do it, and still draw a revenue from the little rancho. But I doubt if you will wish to. The sweet, free independence of life under your own vine and fig tree there—with no man to say go or come, do this or do that, entirely your own master—will have taken hold upon you. I have places in my mind now, which I think would suit you. You will find health, happiness and a livelihood here. And two or three years from now, look me in the eye and say, "Lum, that advice has been the making of us. It opened to us the best and happiest period of our lives. God bless you—and hurrah for Southern California!"

Now, I must be back to work. I have yet to tell you of Chinatown, the beaches, wines, and many other interesting things which shall be taken up as time allows. Take care of yourselves as well as you can—and the best way to do it is to emigrate p.d.q.

By the way, I am sorry to see that I am misconstrued as giving my friend Capt. Gilmore and the *Leader* a "turning over" in regard to the desert. Such was not my intent. You don't know how I have been aggravated by dudes and croakers, until I'm not as tolerant as I should be of the misgivings of friends. Still, they can't be blamed, as they have had no particular chance to know heretofore. It will dawn upon them sometime that I am not a dude. I don't suppose anyone has much more stock in this concern than the Little Doctor [Lummis' wife, Dorothea], and I'll bet she never worried about me in her life—for she has discovered a tolerable ability to look out for herself. Well, if I turned you over, consider yourselves turned back. I am proud to kiss and make up.

LUM

CHARLES LUMMIS:
A BIBLIOGRAPHICAL ESSAY

CHARLES LUMMIS left a prodigious number of publications, none probably as inspired and well-executed as these letters to the Chillicothe *Leader*. In fact, the man probably will be remembered more for his role as a patron of other writers such as Mary Austin and Adolph Bandelier than for his own works. In 1977, the University of Arizona's Library and the university's Graduate Library School published *Charles F. Lummis: A Bibliography*, edited by Mary A. Sarber. The following essay somewhat reflects Sarber's comprehensive collection.

Volume I of *Birchbark Poems* appeared in 1879. Money from sales of the book helped Lummis pay his way through Harvard University. In Chillicothe, in 1883, Lummis published a second—and much less well-known—volume of these poems. During his years at Isleta Pueblo, 1888 to 1892, Lummis worked on all of the books for which he later would be known: *A New Mexico David* (1891), *Some Strange Corners of Our Country* (1892), *A Tramp Across the Continent* (1892), *The Land of Poco Tiempo* (1893), and *The Spanish Pioneers* (1893). His diaries show that Lummis worked feverishly to write these books, usually two or three at a time. True scholarly research characterized very few of Lummis' productions, and these books were no exception. Yet they are the publications which have endured as his most recognizable ones. After some earnest research together with much serious pruning and grafting, Lummis in 1925 re-published *Some Strange Corners of Our Country* as *Mesa, Cañon and Pueblo*, quite defensibly his most creditable publication. Some Southwest cultural devotees today perceive *The Land of Poco Tiempo* as an important part of the gospel of the region's mystique. As of 1988, only *A Tramp Across the Continent* was still in print.

In New Mexico and Peru Lummis collected native folk tales and published them in several volumes: *The Man Who Married the Moon* (1894), *The Gold Fish of Gran Chimu* (1896), *The Enchanted Burro* (1897), and *The King of the Broncos* (1897). In *The Awakening of a Nation* (1898), Lummis attempted to give a broad and substantial significance to his view of "the Mexico of To-day." But the publication lacked credibility and stature. His most significant book-writing period was over. Reprints of his collections of stories appeared in the early 1900s, and his new work tended toward "memorials" and other pamphlets such as *My Friend Will*, Lummis' account of his use of "will"-power to overcome his illnesses and other problems. In 1923, he co-authored a sheet music collection, *Spanish Songs of Old California.* Just before he died in 1928, Lummis hurried to anthologize many of his poems. The collection, *A Bronco Pegasus*, appeared that year. In 1929, Houghton, Mifflin and Co. posthumously published *Flowers of Our Lost Romance*, a maudlin and forgettable pastiche "history" of the Americas.

Between 1882 and 1928, Lummis authored numerous articles and essays. He wrote regular columns for the *Scioto Gazette, Land of Sunshine, Out West,* and the *Los Angeles Times.* His articles on anthropology, geology, natural history, folklore, and travel appeared frequently in a variety of publications, many of them aimed at a children's audience: *Inland Monthly, Journal of American Folklore, Kansas Magazine, Youth's Companion, Drake's Magazine, Cosmopolitan, St. Nicholas, Scribner's Magazine, Harper's Young People, Outlook, Harper's Monthly,* and many others.

A number of biographical articles about Lummis, published during his lifetime and since, have attempted to capture and integrate the man's numerous activities, multiple interests, eclectic appetite, diverse character traits, and flamboyant life-style. However, no compellingly definitive biography is extant. Three books do make an attempt: Edwin R. Bingham, *Charles F. Lummis: Editor of the Southwest;* Dudley Gordon, *Charles F. Lummis: Crusader in Corduroy;* and Turbese

Lummis Fiske and Keith Lummis, *Charles F. Lummis: The Man and His West*. Two recently published works affirm a renewed interest in Lummis: *Charles F. Lummis: The Centennial Exhibition*, edited by Daniela Moneta, and *Lummis in the Pueblos*, a collection of Lummis' pueblo photographs, edited by Patrick T. Houlihan and Betsy E. Houlihan.

The manuscript of Lummis' autobiography, "As I Remember," can be found with some of his other papers in the Special Collections of the University of Arizona Library, while the bulk of Lummis' collection of manuscripts, documents, clippings, and photographs (including a great number of glass negatives) are housed in the Southwest Museum archives in Highland Park, California. In addition, the Los Angeles Public Library and the Henry E. Huntington Library hold smaller Lummis document collections.

INDEX

ABOUT THE EDITOR

J AMES W. BYRKIT was born and raised in Jerome, Arizona, a copper mining community whose diverse social and multi-ethnic environment brought him in contact with miners, ranchers, New England metallurgical engineers, east- and south-European immigrants, Hispanics, and Yavapai Indians. With this background, he was interested to learn that New Englander Charles Lummis had probably done more than anyone else to record and publicize the conventional imagery of the Hispanic and Indian heritage of the Southwest. In 1973, he joined the faculty of Northern Arizona University, where he has taught courses in the American frontier, Arizona and the Southwest, and regional images. His first book, *Forging the Copper Collar: Arizona's Labor-Management War, 1901–1921*, was published by the University of Arizona in 1982.

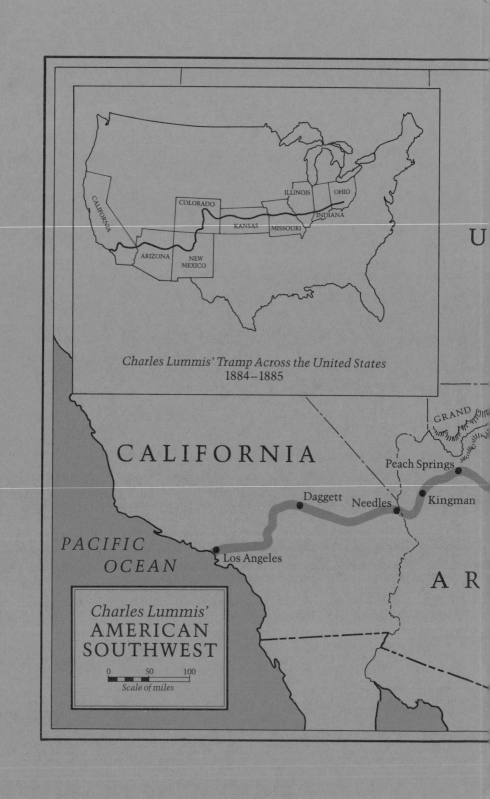

CALIFORNIA
COLORADO
ILLINOIS
OHIO
INDIANA
KANSAS
MISSOURI
ARIZONA
NEW
MEXICO

Charles Lummis' Tramp Across the United States
1884–1885

U

CALIFORNIA

GRAND

Peach Springs

Daggett   Needles   Kingman

PACIFIC
OCEAN   Los Angeles

A R

Charles Lummis'
AMERICAN
SOUTHWEST

0   50   100
Scale of miles